SQL
from the Ground Up

Mary Pyefinch

Osborne/**McGraw-Hill**

Berkeley   New York   St. Louis   San Francisco
Auckland   Bogotá   Hamburg   London   Madrid
Mexico City   Milan   Montreal   New Delhi   Panama City
Paris   São Paulo   Singapore   Sydney
Tokyo   Toronto

Osborne/**McGraw-Hill**
2600 Tenth Street
Berkeley, California 94710
U.S.A.

For information on translations or book distributors outside the U.S.A., or to arrange bulk purchase discounts for sales promotions, premiums, or fund-raisers, please contact Osborne/**McGraw-Hill** at the above address.

SQL from the Ground Up

234567890 AGM AGM   019876543210

ISBN 0-07-211974-8

Publisher
Brandon A. Nordin

**Associate Publisher and
Editor in Chief**
Scott Rogers

Acquisitions Editor
Wendy Rinaldi

Project Editor
Ron Hull

Editorial Assistant
Monika Faltiss

Technical Editor
Rima Regas

Copy Editor
Marcia Baker

Proofreader
Stefany Otis

Indexer
Irv Hershman

Computer Designers
Gary Corrigan
Mickey Galicia

Illustrators
Robert Hansen
Brian Wells
Beth Young

Series Design
Roberta Steele

To Mom, Bridget, Charlie and Louise, with love.

Contents

Acknowledgments

Writing a computer book is a very frenetic undertaking. You have many chapters to write and a short time to finish it, and add to this the demands of running a consulting business and you have a very demanding schedule. If it wasn't for a very loving and supporting family, I would be in psychotherapy by now.

The first people I would like to thank are my daughter, Bridget, who is a sharing and caring person and my nephew Charlie, who is my little buddy. Thank you, my loves, for allowing me to borrow time from you to write this book. I also want to thank my mother, Louise Sr., my best friend, who provided moral support and who is a great grandmother to Bridget and Charlie. Also, I want to thank my sister, Louise, who ran the household while I wrote this book. Two more family members I need to thank are my dogs, Heidi and Max, who stayed by my side while I wrote this book.

Since this is my first book, I want to thank Wendy Rinaldi, Acquisition Editor at Osborne, who provided guidance to a new writer. I've enjoyed working with you and thank you for believing in me. I also would like to thank,

Monika Faltiss, Editorial Assistant, who kept me on track and who has the patience of a saint. I couldn't have asked for a better technical editor than Rima Regas, who was always there with notes of encouragement and technical corrections. Also a special thanks to Ron Hull and his department for their hard work on copyediting this book. Grammar has a tendency to suffer when you are writing swiftly during the wee hours of the night.

There are two authors who contributed to this book that I would like to thank. Evangelos Petroutsos kindly lent his expertise to Chapters 16 and 17. Robert Mykland a programming dynamo, wrote Chapter 20. Thank you gentleman for helping me keep this book on schedule.

Finally, I would like to thank my agent, Chris van Buren of Waterside Productions, who took care of all the paperwork and was there to answer my questions and who introduced me to Wendy.

Introduction

Let's face it, computers are a part of our lives. Chances are that you probably work with computers on your job. No longer can we stereotype the computer professional as those "nerds with pocket protectors." We are all in varying degrees computer professionals.

If your job includes working with databases, then learning Structured Query Language (SQL) is a necessity. SQL is the programming language used in all relational databases. Therefore, whether you are a longtime programmer or a neophyte who needs to learn SQL in a hurry, you will find useful information in this book.

SQL from the Ground Up is divided into four parts, and each part builds on the next. Each chapter is a building block. When you have completed the book, you will have learned the structure of the SQL language and laid a good foundation for your programming career. The goal of this book is that, by the conclusion, the reader will be proficient in SQL and can go forth and program.

What This Book Covers

This book is a cornucopia of SQL coding instruction. Even the inside covers provide you with the most commonly used SQL code, at your fingertips. Between the covers there is much more. The following is a synopsis of what is covered in each chapter.

Part I, "SQL Basics—Easy as ABC" contains the following chapters:

◆ **Chapter 1, "What is SQL?"**   This chapter provides an introduction to and a brief history of SQL.

◆ **Chapter 2, "The Database—A Place for Everything and Everything in Its Place"**   This chapter covers databases models and, specifically, the relational database model.

◆ **Chapter 3, "Understanding SQL"**   This chapter introduces the SQL language, its commands, operators, and functions.

◆ **Chapter 4, "Building Tables and Views"**   This chapter teaches you how to build tables and views using Oracle8.

◆ **Chapter 5, "Transaction Management"**   This chapter introduces you to the concept of transaction management and its SQL commands and syntax.

◆ **Chapter 6, "Database Security"**   This chapter discusses how to secure your database using SQL. The SQL commands and syntax are introduced.

Part II of the book is titled "Queries—The Heart and Soul of SQL." This part deals with the main use for SQL: retreival of data from a database. Part II contains the following four chapters:

◆ **Chapter 7, "The Simple One-Table Query"**   This chapter explains the simple query through examples.

◆ **Chapter 8, "Complex Multitable Queries"**   This chapter builds upon the previous chapter and provides examples of complex queries.

◆ **Chapter 9, "The Subquery"**   This chapter introduces another type of complex query, the subquery. The uses of subqueries are discussed and examples provided.

◆ **Chapter 10, "Optimizing SQL"**   This chapter teaches you how to improve your queries. It also discusses the database optimizing tools vendors supply with their databases.

Part III is "Putting It All Together: SQL In Action," and it contains the following:

◆ **Chapter 11, "Building the Sample Database"**   In this chapter, we begin work for a fictional client. You learn how to conduct a needs analysis, create a data flow model, and draw an entity relationship diagram.

◆ **Chapter 12, "Building a Front End for the Database"**   In this chapter you get a brief introduction on how to build a front end, or graphical user interface (GUI). We discuss design and usability issues, as well as development tools that are available.

◆ **Chapter 13, "Creating Forms"**   This chapter teaches you how to build forms (screens) that your users will use for entering data into the database. A section on how to use Access is included. You will learn how to use bound and unbound forms and learn how to link the forms to the database tables.

◆ **Chapter 14, "Querying the Database"**   Here, you will use the Query Wizard provided in Access. In addition you will learn how to use SQL directly in Access and how to create complex queries.

◆ **Chapter 15, "Reporting"**   This chapter stresses how important it is to consider reporting as part of the development cycle of an application; reporting should not be an afterthought. The types of reporting tools are listed. In addition there is a discussion on how to choose the best reporting tool for you. You will get a chance to learn how to design reports using Access, Crystal Reports, and BusinessObjects.

In Part IV, "SQL Today and Tomorrow," you'll find the following chapters:

◆ **Chapter 16, "Transact SQL and Stored Procedures"**   This chapter introduces Transact SQL. It covers cursors and stored procedures.

◆ **Chapter 17, "Advanced Transact SQL"**   This chapter continues your lesson on T-SQL with more advanced constructs of Transact SQL.

◆ **Chapter 18, "SQL*Plus—The Interface to Oracle's Relational Database"**   This chapter teaches you how to use SQL*Plus as your interface to Oracle's database. You will learn commands, variables, functions, and how to print reports using this program.

◆ **Chapter 19, "Oracle's PL/SQL"**   This chapter introduces you to the complex procedural language that Oracle uses to program databases.

This chapter gives you a mini-course on everything you ever wanted to know about PL/SQL.

◆ **Chapter 20, "SQL and Other Programming Languages"**   Since SQL is not a true procedural programming language, other programming languages use SQL to build database applications. The languages discussed in this chapter are Visual C, Visual Basic, and Java.

◆ **Chapter 21, "Everyone Makes Mistakes"**   This chapter covers the top ten mistakes you can make while using SQL. Tips on how to avoid these mistakes are discussed.

◆ **Chapter 22, "The Future—SQL 3"**   This chapter discusses the proposed revisions and additions to the standard.

What You Need for This Book

There is a database available to download from www.osborne.com. The name of the database is HUSH.mdb. It is an Access 97 database, so you will need to have Access 97 in order to run this program.

If you wish to follow along with the Oracle8 examples used in this book, you can go to the Oracle Web site, www.oracle.com, and download a 30-day trial version of Personal Oracle8. If you plan on working with Oracle in your career, you should buy the product. You can purchase it from the Web site at the Oracle Store.

The other example database is from Microsoft SQL server 6.5 or 7. A trial CD-ROM of SQL Server 7 can be ordered from www.microsoft.com/backoffice/sql/70/trial.html. The CD-ROM is a 120-day evaluation copy.

PART I

SQL Basics—Easy as ABC

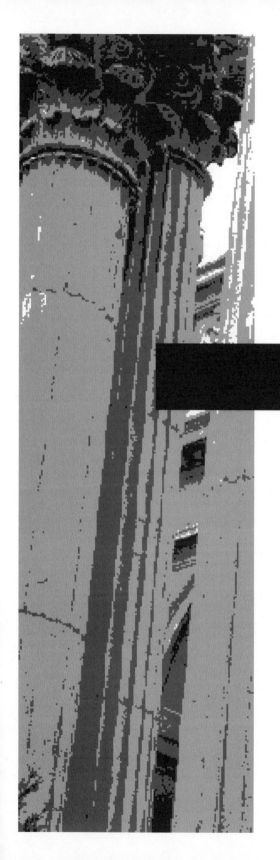

7-25. 1314

CHAPTER 1

What Is SQL?

The American National Standards Institute (ANSI) has endorsed SQL as the language of choice for manipulating databases. SQL is the most important relational database language used by most of the database management system (DBMS) products. Vendors of DBMSs like Oracle, IBM DB2, Sybase, and Ingres, use SQL as the programming language for their databases.

What Is SQL?

SQL is also sometimes pronounced see-kwul. Although both pronunciations are acceptable, the preferred pronunciation is ess-cue-el.

SQL (pronounced *ess-cue-el*) is a data sublanguage used to organize, manage, and retrieve data from a relational database, which is managed by a relational database management system (RDBMS). Before you can fully understand the importance of SQL, however, you must understand a bit about its history and the evolution of programming itself.

Evolution of Programming

A *programming language* is a set of rules used to tell a computer what operations to perform. Different levels of computer programming languages exist. These levels indicate an evolution in programming.

The terms "lower" and "higher" are used to describe how close the language is to the language the computer uses. For example, if a programming language uses 0's and 1's, it is called a "lower" level language because it resembles the language the computer uses, binary code. If a programming language is more English-like, it is considered a "higher" level language. The five levels or generations of programming languages are

◆ **Machine language**   This type of language represents data as 0's and 1's, binary digits that are the "on" and "off" electrical states of the computer.

◆ **Assembly language**   This language uses mnemonic codes such as *A* for Add and *C* for Compare.

◆ **High-level language**   Programs are written in an English-like way. This third generation language (3GL) evolved in the '60s and '70s. Responsible for the surge in data processing, 3GL was the beginning of the "computer revolution." You may be familiar with these languages: BASIC, FORTRAN, COBOL, PASCAL, and C, to name a few.

◆ **Very high-level language**   The fourth generation languages (4GL) are shorthand-programming languages. They are nonprocedural. SQL is a 4GL data sublanguage.

◆ **Natural language**   The fifth generation language (5GL) is the type of programming that resembles more closely the way English is spoken. These languages are used to interact with knowledge-based systems. 5GL is the basis of artificial language.

SQL is part of the fourth generation language and, as such, is English-like. SQL is a *nonprocedural language,* which defines only *what* you want the computer to do. You provide no details to the computer. On the other hand, a *procedural language* tells the computer *how* a task is to be performed.

The first three generations are all procedural. They provide programmers with language constructs such as GO, DO UNTIL, CASE, which are *how* functions. SQL does not have these constructs. If you were developing an application, therefore, a primary programming language would have to be used with SQL to perform these functions. This is the reason SQL is a data sublanguage as opposed to an application language.

History of SQL

The origin of SQL and the development of relational databases go hand-in-hand down the historical path. The relational database concept was developed by Dr. E. F. Codd, an IBM researcher. In June 1970, Dr. Codd published an article entitled, "A Relational Model of Data for Large Shared Data Banks," describing his mathematical theory of how data could be stored and manipulated in tables. SQL was conceived in an IBM San Jose research laboratory in the mid-1970s as a database language for the new relational database model.

SEQUEL (pronounced *see-kwul*) for Structured English Query Language was the name of this new language for the new relational database model. You may hear many people refer to the current SQL as Structured English Query, but this is a misnomer. It is not SEQUEL but, instead, SQL. SEQUEL development was part of a project called System R. IBM also developed a research database by the same name. SEQUEL was an Application Program Interface (API) to the System R database.

In the late '70s, IBM was ready to develop a relational database system, SQL/DS RDBMS. Upon the news of this development, other vendors rushed to develop their own RDBMS. A small company, Relational Software, Inc., beat IBM to the market with its own RDBMS. Relational Software, Inc. later became Oracle Corporation. The race was on!

By the late '80s and early '90s, many databases were on the market using their own version of SQL. Thus, SQL became a sort of standard for the relational database systems market. Each vendor used its own particular form of SQL, however, and compatibility across platforms was bad. Cries came from the masses to establish a standard to which all vendors would have to comply.

In 1986, ANSI released a standard called SQL-86. This standard was then updated in 1989 to SQL-89. Both standards were criticized as incomplete. The standards did not allow anyone to alter the database. You could not create tables or assign new users. In 1992, a third revision was written that enhanced the functionality of the SQL language. SQL-92 is the current standard and is the version you learn in this book.

SQL-92: What Does It Have That the Others Didn't?

This version includes improved diagnostic capabilities and error-handling facilities. Also it enables users to create, alter, and delete tables. In addition, a new feature called a "flagger" informs you when you are using nonstandard SQL.

SQL-92 has three levels:

◆ Entry SQL

◆ Intermediate SQL

◆ Full SQL

Entry SQL is almost identical to SQL-89. Entry SQL includes statements for defining schemas, data manipulation language, referential integrity, check constraints, and default clauses from ANSI-1989. It also includes options for module language and embedded SQL interfaces to seven different programming languages, as well as direct execution of data manipulation statements.

Entry SQL also includes features related to deprecated features from ANSI-1989. *Deprecated features* are those features included in SQL-92 so programs written in SQL-89 will continue to function. These features (commas and parentheses in parameter lists, SQLSTATE parameter, and renaming columns in the SELECT list) will probably be excluded from future revisions.

In addition, Entry SQL has features related to incompatibilities with SQL-89 (colons preceding parameter names, WITH CHECK option, constraint-limited identifiers) and aids for transitioning from ANSI X3.135-1989 to ANSI-1992. Finally, Entry SQL contains changes to correct defects found in ANSI-1989 (ANSI X3.135–192, p. 60).

Intermediate SQL covers almost half of the new features of SQL-92. It includes all features of Entry SQL plus major new facilities such as:

- Statements for changing schemas
- Dynamic SQL
- Isolation levels for SQL transactions
- Multiple-module support
- Cascade delete on referential actions
- Row and table expressions
- Union joins
- Character string operations
- Table intersection and difference operations
- Simple domains
- CASE expression
- Casting between data types
- Diagnostic management for data administration
- Comprehensive error analysis
- Multiple-character repertoires
- Interval and simplified datetime data types
- Variable-length character strings
- Flagger requirement to aid in writing portable applications

An *SQL flagger* is a facility able to identify SQL language extensions or other SQL processing alternatives, which may be provided by a conforming SQL implementation (RDBMS vendors). An SQL flagger aids programmers in producing SQL language that is portable and interoperable among different conforming SQL implementations.

Full SQL includes all Intermediate SQL features plus:

◆ Deferred constraint checking

◆ Named constraints

◆ User-defined datetime data types

◆ Self-referencing updates and deletes

◆ Cascade update on referential actions

◆ Subqueries in check constraints

◆ Scrolled cursors

◆ Character translations

◆ Bit string data type

◆ Temporary tables

◆ Additional referential constraints options

Vendor database compliance falls between Entry SQL and Intermediate SQL. It will take quite a few versions for vendor databases to be compliant at the Full SQL level.

The following are the new features as outlined in the ANSI SQL-92 document (ANSI X3.135–192, p. xii):

◆ Support for additional data types (date, time, timestamp, interval, bit string, variable-length character, and national character strings)

◆ Support for character sets beyond that required to express SQL language itself and support for additional collations

◆ Support for additional scalar operations, such as string operations for concatenate and substring, date and time operations, and a form for conditional expressions

◆ Increased generality and orthogonality in the use of scalar-valued and table-valued query expressions

◆ Additional set operators (for example, union join, natural join, set difference, and set intersection)

◆ Capability for domain definitions in the schema

- Support for schema manipulation capabilities (especially DROP and ALTER statements)

- Support for bindings (modules and embedded syntax) in the MUMPS language

- Additional privilege capabilities

- Additional referential integrity facilities, including referential actions, subqueries in CHECK constraints, separate assertions, and user-controlled deferral of constraints

- Definitions of an information schema

- Support for dynamic execution of SQL language

- Support for certain facilities required for remote database access (especially connection management statements and qualified schema names)

- Support for temporary tables

- Support for transaction consistency levels

- Support for data type conversions (CAST expressions among data types)

- Support for scrolled cursors

- Requirement for a flagging capability to aid in portability of application programs

This may seem like Greek to you now but the concepts will become clearer as you read this book. These are the new features in SQL-92. The complete ANSI SQL-92 standard document is 577 pages long.

TIP: Reading this book will get you programming in SQL much faster than reading the ANSI standard. The ANSI standard is a good reference tool, however, for anyone developing a relational database application system.

There are new "reserved words" in SQL-92. A *reserved word* is a word used as part of the programming language. It is best not to use these words in the naming of tables or fields. In case you must use one of the reserved words, however, SQL-92 enables you to put quotation marks around the reserved word you have chosen. For example, if you had a table named DAY, you would need to type "DAY" to keep the program from using the word as a reserved word.

Here are the reserved words:

ABSOLUTE	ACTION	ADD	ALL
ALLOCATE	ALTER	AND	ANY
ARE	AS	ASC	ASSERTION
AT	AUTHORIZATION	AVG	
BEGIN	BETWEEN	BIT	BIT_LENGTH
BOTH	BY	CASCADE	CASCADED
CASE	CAST	CATALOG	CHAR
CHARACTER	CHARACTER_LENGTH	CHAR_LENGTH	CHECK
CLOSE	COALESCE	COLLATE	COLLATION
COLUMN	COMMIT	CONNECT	CONNECTION
CONSTRAINT	CONSTRAINTS	CONTINUE	CONVERT
CORRESPONDING	COUNT	CREATE	CROSS
CURRENT	CURRENT_DATE	CURRENT_TIME	CURRENT_TIMESTAMP
CURRENT_USER	CURSOR	DATE	DAY
DEALLOCATE	DEC	DECIMAL	DECLARE
DEFAULT	DEFERRABLE	DEFERRED	DELETE
DESC	DESCRIBE	DESCRIPTOR	DIAGNOSTICS
DISCONNECT	DISTINCT	DOMAIN	DOUBLE
DROP	ELSE	END	END-EXEC
ESCAPE	EXCEPT	EXCEPTION	EXEC
EXECUTE	EXISTS	EXTERNAL	EXTRACT
FALSE	FETCH	FIRST	FLOAT
FOR	FOREIGN	FOUND	FROM
FULL	GET	GLOBAL	GO
GOTO	GRANT	GROUP	HAVING
HOUR	IDENTITY	IMMEDIATE	IN
INDICATOR	INITIALLY	INNER	INPUT
INSENSITIVE	INSERT	INT	INTEGER

INTERSECT	INTERVAL	INTO	IS
ISOLATION	JOIN	KEY	LANGUAGE
LAST	LEADING	LEFT	LEVEL
LIKE	LOCAL	LOWER	MATCH
MAX	MIN	MINUTE	MODULE
MONTH	NAMES	NATIONAL	NATURAL
NCHAR	NEXT	NO	NOT
NULL	NULLIF	NUMERIC	OCTET_LENGTH
OF	ON	ONLY	OPEN
OPTION	OR	ORDER	OUTER
OUTPUT	OVERLAPS	PAD	PARTIAL
POSITION	PRECISION	PREPARE	PRESERVE
PRIMARY	PRIOR	PRIVILEGES	PROCEDURE
PUBLIC	READ	REAL	REFERENCES
RELATIVE	RESTRICT	REVOKE	RIGHT
ROLLBACK	ROWS	SCHEMA	SCROLL
SECOND	SECTION	SELECT	SESSION
SESSION_USER	SET	SIZE	SMALLINT
SOME	SPACE	SQL	SQLCODE
SQLERROR	SQLSTATE	SUBSTRING	SUM
SYSTEM_USER	TABLE	TEMPORARY	THEN
TIME	TIMESTAMP	TIMEZONE_HOUR	TIMEZONE_MINUTE
TO	TRAILING	TRANSACTION	TRANSLATE
TRANSLATION	TRIM	TRUE	UNION
UNIQUE	UNKNOWN	UPDATE	UPPER
USAGE	USER	USING	VALUE
VALUES	VARCHAR	VARYING	VIEW
WHEN	WHENEVER	WHERE	WITH
WORK	WRITE	YEAR	ZONE

These are the reserved words for SQL-92. No guarantee exists that this list will remain the same for future revisions. More reserved words will probably be added in later versions.

SQL Is Divided into Three Parts

Like Caesar, who divided Gaul into three parts, SQL, too, can be divided into three parts:

◆ Data Definition Language (DDL)

◆ Data Manipulation Language (DML)

◆ Data Control Language (DCL)

SQL gives you everything you need to create, maintain, and control your database. Some users will never have to create a database and will be content with the querying processes in SQL found in the DML language. Others will not only need to create databases but will also have to maintain and administer databases. For these users, SQL provides DDL, DML, and DCL.

Data Definition Language (DDL)

With DDL you can create and delete tables, schemas, domains, indexes, and views. You can change them, too. Three SQL verbs can accomplish these tasks: CREATE, ALTER, and DROP. These changes to the database can be made while running the DBMS; the database structure is dynamic. Chapter 4 covers these SQL verbs in more detail.

A CREATE statement for a database table would identify the table name, the column names, the data type, and, usually, a constraint (restriction on the data). For example, you are creating a database for your CD collection. The table you create is the Compact Disc table.

```
CREATE TABLE CD (
CD_ID        INTEGER    NOT NULL,
CD_TITLE     CHARACTER (30),
CD_COMPANY   CHARACTER (30));
```

The following shows the result of this statement. Sample data has been added.

```
CD_ID   CD_TITLE          CD_COMPANY
100     Mozart's Hits     CBS Music
101     Beethoven's 5th   ABC Music
```

An ALTER statement changes the table. To ALTER your CD table, you would use the following statement:

```
ALTER TABLE CD
      ADD NO_DISCS INTEGER;
```

This adds another column called NO_DISCS to your table. The results are:

```
CD_ID     CD_TITLE          CD_COMPANY    CD_NO_DISCS
100       Mozart's Hits     CBS Music               2
101       Beethoven's 5th   ABC Music               1
```

If you decided you don't want the table, you can delete the table from your database by using the DROP verb. The DROP table command is simple:

```
DROP TABLE CD;
```

With this command, you delete your table's data and your table.

Data Manipulation Language (DML)

As the name states, DML is the part of SQL that manipulates the data in the database. The statements you can use in DML are SELECT, INSERT, UPDATE, and DELETE. DML statements can vary from simple to complex. The English-like attribute of 4GL languages is apparent in some SQL DML statements, but the complex DML statements may seem like a foreign language to you. Writing complex statements takes practice and to get to the complex you must begin with the simple statements. Several chapters of this book are dedicated to teaching you how to write SQL DML statements. In this chapter, the four main SQL verbs are discussed.

SELECT

The SELECT verb is the most used verb in SQL. You must begin your query process with a SELECT statement. The following is an example of a SELECT statement (as well as other DML expressions used in SQL):

```
SELECT *
FROM CD
WHERE CD_COMPANY = 'CBS MUSIC';
```

This statement returns the following table:

```
CD_ID      CD_TITLE         CD_COMPANY      NO_DISCS
100        Mozart's Hits    CBS Music              2
```

Here's another example:

```
SELECT CD_TITLE
FROM CD
WHERE CD_ID > 1;
```

It produces the following results:

```
CD_ID      CD_TITLE            CD_COMPANY
100        Mozart's Hits         CBS Music
101        Beethoven's 5th       ABC Music
```

And here's a third example:

```
SELECT COUNT (CD_ID)
FROM CD;
```

This query provides the count of the two CDs in the table.

All of the preceding examples illustrate the use of SELECT as the method to retrieve data from your database.

INSERT

The INSERT verb enables you to enter data directly into your table. Let's add a CD to your CD collection. The statement for this is

```
INSERT INTO CD (CD_ID, CD_TITLE, CD_COMPANY, CD_NO_DISCS)
    VALUES (202,'JAGGED LITTLE PILL','MAVERICK',1);
1 row inserted.
```

Your table now displays

```
CD_ID      CD_TITLE            CD_COMPANY      CD_NO_DISCS
100        Mozart's Hits         CBS Music                2
101        Beethoven's 5th       ABC Music                1
202        Jagged Little Pill    Maverick                 1
```

1

UPDATE

The UPDATE verb enables you to modify data already stored in a table in your database. If you make a mistake on the number of discs for a CD, you could update the information. For a single item, the statement is

```
UPDATE CD
  SET NO_DISCS = 2
WHERE CD_ID = 202
1 row updated.
```

The CD table is now updated and displays the changes:

CD_ID	CD_TITLE	CD_COMPANY	CD_NO_DISCS
100	Mozart's Hits	CBS Music	2
101	Beethoven's 5th	ABC Music	1
202	Jagged Little Pill	Maverick	2

You can also make many changes to your database. For example, if you want to increase the number of discs to three for each row, you may do so.

```
UPDATE CD
  SET NO_DISCS = 3
3 rows updated.
```

Your CD Table displays the changes:

CD_ID	CD_TITLE	CD_COMPANY	CD_NO_DISCS
100	Mozart's Hits	CBS Music	3
101	Beethoven's 5th	ABC Music	3
202	Jagged Little Pill	Maverick	3

DELETE

The final DML SQL verb is the DELETE verb. This statement removes selected rows of data from a single table. In the next example, you have decided CD_ID #202 does not fit in this CD collection. You can remove it by using the DELETE statement.

```
DELETE FROM CD
WHERE CD_ID = 202
1 row deleted.
```

Your table will display

```
CD_ID    CD_TITLE          CD_COMPANY    CD_NO_DISCS
100      Mozart's Hits     CBS Music               3
101      Beethoven's 5th   ABC Music               3
```

As with the INSERT statement, DELETE can be used to delete multiple rows. If you wanted to remove all your rows from the CD table, you could do it with the following statement:

```
DELETE * FROM CD
2 rows deleted.
```

Your table would now be empty and only the database structure would remain.

In the preceding examples you have created, updated, and dropped a database table. You have manipulated your data by inserting rows, updating columns, and deleting rows. You have also queried your table in the database and retrieved information about your data. One part remains to discuss: Data Control Language.

Data Control Language (DCL)

The DCL provides security for your database. You probably wouldn't mind if someone accessed your CD database. You may decide, however, that you don't want anyone to see what CDs you have available. This is where DCL comes in handy. The Data Control Language has four main commands: COMMIT, ROLLBACK, GRANT, and REVOKE. This chapter provides an overview of Security. See Chapter 5 for a more detailed discussion.

COMMIT

The COMMIT command pertains to any transactions you make to your database. It protects your database by restricting operations that make changes to your database. SQL makes temporary copies of your data. Only when you are finished with your transaction (create, insert, update, delete) and you make the COMMIT statement, are changes allowed to be made to the database.

```
INSERT INTO CD (CD_ID, CD_TITLE, CD_COMPANY, CD_NO_DISCS)
VALUES (202,'JAGGED LITTLE PILL','MAVERICK',1);

UPDATE CD
  SET NO_DISCS = 3
```

1

```
DELETE FROM CD
WHERE CD_ID = 202

COMMIT WORK
```

ROLLBACK

The ROLLBACK statement restores the system to its previous state prior to the changes you just made to the database. So, if in the preceding example you had erred (oh, how unlikely), you could use this ROLLBACK statement to correct the error and return the database to the prior state.

```
INSERT INTO CD (CD_ID, CD_TITLE, CD_COMPANY, CD_NO_DISCS)
VALUES (202,'JAGGED LITTLE PILL','MAVERICK',1);

UPDATE CD
  SET NO_DISCS = 3

DELETE FROM CD
WHERE CD_ID = 102

COMMIT WORK
```

Uh oh! You meant to type 202.

```
ROLLBACK WORK
```

You are saved and all is right with the world.

GRANT and REVOKE

These are the commands that deal with who has access to your database. The GRANT command enables you to grant privileges to users. You can grant privileges on seeing, adding, changing, deleting, referencing, and using.

If you want your cousin Harry to see the tables in your database, you would use the GRANT SELECT command. If you desire, you can allow him to insert or update your data in the tables. The commands you would use are GRANT INSERT or GRANT UPDATE.

Whatever you grant, however, you may also revoke. The REVOKE command enables you to take away privileges you previously granted. The commands you would use are REVOKE SELECT, REVOKE INSERT, or REVOKE UPDATE.

Let's give select privileges to your cousin Harry.

```
GRANT SELECT
    ON CD
    TO COUSIN_HARRY;
```

Your brother Vinny found out you gave Harry privileges and now Vinny wants his own privileges. He also wants to help you with your database. So you want to grant Vinny INSERT privileges.

```
GRANT INSERT
    ON CD
    TO BROTHER_VINNY;
```

You also need to give Vinny UPDATE privileges in case he makes a mistake.

```
GRANT UPDATE
    ON CD
    TO BROTHER_VINNY;
```

You are the only one who has DELETE privileges.

```
GRANT DELETE
    ON CD
    TO NUMERO_UNO;
```

If you want to take a privilege away, do the following:

```
REVOKE INSERT
    ON CD
    FROM BROTHER_VINNY;
```

Your brother Vinny no longer has the INSERT privilege to your CD table.

Now you have come full circle in your overview of database development using DDL, DML, and DCL. Congratulations! You have created a small, single-table database. You are now acquainted with the basics of SQL programming using SQL-92. Don't relax yet because you have only just begun to learn SQL.

DDL, DML, and DCL Commands in Review

Table 1-1 summarizes the SQL commands discussed in this chapter.

Command	Description
DDL	
CREATE TABLE	Creates the table in the database
ALTER TABLE	Changes the table in the database
DROP TABLE	Deletes the table from the database
DML	
SELECT	Selects data from the database
INSERT	Inserts rows of data into the database
UPDATE	Updates rows or columns in the database
DELETE	Removes rows of data from the database
DCL	
COMMIT	Restricts transactions from changing the database until the command is used
ROLLBACK	Restores the database to its original state
GRANT SELECT	Allows users the privilege of seeing the tables in the database
GRANT INSERT	Allows users the privilege of inserting data into tables
GRANT UPDATE	Allows users the privilege of updating data in the tables
REVOKE SELECT	Takes away the privilege of seeing the data
REVOKE INSERT	Takes away the privilege of inserting data into tables
REVOKE UPDATE	Takes away the privilege of updating data in tables

SQL
Command
Definitions
Table 1-1.

In this chapter, you learned SQL is a data sublanguage of the fourth generation language. You also learned SQL is the language endorsed by ANSI and is used in DBMS products such as Oracle, Sybase, and others. You are aware that the vendors' compliance is somewhere in between Entry SQL and Intermediate SQL standards, so you probably assume the same SQL is used by all vendor DBMSs.

Your assumption is wrong. Like snowflakes and fingerprints, no two vendors' SQL is exactly alike. It may be the same language, but many different dialects of SQL are in use today. The claims that applications using SQL are portable among different DBMSs are greatly exaggerated.

For instance, one application vendor whose program was written in SQLBASE exclaimed no problem would occur in operating their application in an Oracle environment. Two hundred grand later, an implementation team proved them wrong.

The differences between SQL dialects can be great. Never believe the move can be made without modification of the application. If you believe everything the vendor tells you, it could be a costly mistake.

PORTABILITY: Database Vendors and SQL

To illustrate the similarities and differences in SQL among database vendors, look at the CREATE, ALTER, and DROP commands.

In Sybase SQL Server 11, the commands are

CREATE command:

```
Create table CD_TABLE
(CD_ID      int not null,
CD_TITLE    char(30),
CD_COMPANY char(30))
go
```

ALTER command:

```
Alter table CD_table
add CD_DATE datetime null
go
```

DROP command:

```
Drop table cd_db.numero.uno.cd_table
go
```

In Oracle8, the commands are

CREATE command:

```
CREATE table CD
(CD_ID number,
CD_TITLE varchar2(30),
CD_COMPANY varchar2(30));
```

1

ALTER command:

```
ALTER table CD
add (CD_DATE date);
```

DROP command:

```
Drop table CD_TABLE;
```

In Microsoft SQL Server 7., the commands are

CREATE command:

```
Create table CD
(CD_ID numeric (10,0) identity,
CD_TITLE varchar (30) not null,
CD_COMPANY varchar (30) not null)
```

ALTER command:

```
ALTER TABLE CD
ADD CD_DATE date null
```

DROP command:

```
Drop table CD_TABLE
```

As you can clearly see with these three DDL commands, variations do exist among vendor DBMSs. Hence, variations in SQL code are presented throughout this book. The tables you create in Chapter 4 use Oracle SQL. The queries discussed in Part II are created using Access. In Part III, various DBMSs are discussed, as well as the SQL dialects the databases use.

This book presents SQL-92 in all its variations. If variety is the spice of life, then SQL is the spice of the 4GL programmer's life.

Now that you know a little SQL, we can delve further into the relational database model and learn database design.

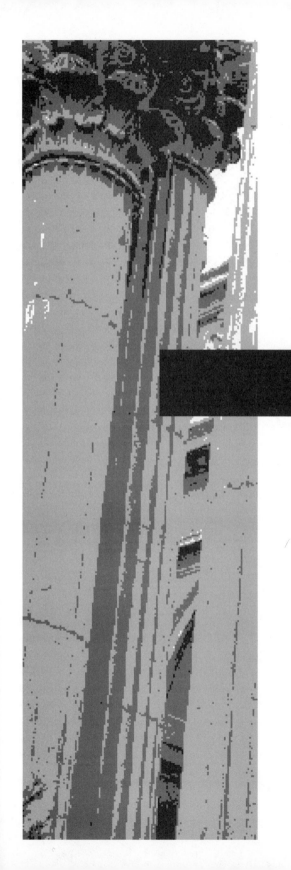

CHAPTER 2

The Database—A Place for Everything and Everything in Its Place

People are natural born collectors. Art collectors store their art in galleries or museums. Baseball card collectors store their collections in shoeboxes or glass cases. From the individual to the corporation, we are a nation of collectors and we all need a place to store our stuff.

The advent of the computer age enabled businesses to store volumes of data on computers. The introduction of the personal computer empowered individuals to take their valuable collections and store information about them on the computer. Whether you collect recipes, coins, cards, art, or beanie babies, you can keep track of them on your PC. So what is this grand storage place called? It is the *database*.

The database is much more than a collection of data. This collection needs to consist of interrelated files. A good database defines itself and does not tolerate redundancy. A database is based on the business needs of the user: How does the user want to organize his or her collection? What is the data and how will it be used? Once the purpose of the database is discussed and requirements are agreed upon, then the definition of the structure can begin. This definition of structure is called a *data dictionary* (some vendors refer to it as *metadata* or *systems catalog)*. To summarize, a database is a nonredundant, self-defining collection of interrelated files, designed according to the user's business requirements.

Study this definition and become one with it. In the following chapters, you will define user requirements and create tables, views, triggers, stored procedures, indexes, and populate the database through the use of forms. You will also deliver the data back to your user in the form of reports. This will enable the user to analyze the data and to make decisions, which is why he or she wanted a database in the first place.

The database and its DBMS organizes data in a way that is fast and easy to access. Database systems provide many benefits:

◆   Integrated files

◆   No redundancy

◆   Ease in updating

◆   Quick and efficient

◆   Enables users to share data

◆   Centralized security

Types of Databases

The way databases store files depends on the type or model of the database. The three types are

◆ **Hierarchical**　Some records are subordinate to others in a structure resembling a tree. The hierarchical structure accommodates a simple data structure. Retrieving data requires moving through records, up, down, and sideways, one record at a time. It resembles an organizational chart. IBM's Information Management System (IMS) developed in 1968 and running under MVS, is still the DBMS installed on many IBM mainframes today.

◆ **Network**　Subordinate records can be subordinate to more than one record child and a child record may have more than one parent. These records form a one-to-many and a many-to-many relationship. The network database allows for a more complex data structure and increases performance. Minicomputers such as Digital Equipment Corporation and Data General had network databases. The network may have been more flexible than the hierarchical structure, but it was still rigid. If you needed to make a change in the structure, you had to rebuild the whole database.

◆ **Relational**　The relational database organizes data in a table format consisting of related rows and columns. The hierarchical and network databases are more commonly used by mainframe and minicomputers. Relational databases can be run on the PC, as well as on the mainframe and minicomputers. SQL is based on the relational model.

What Is in a Database?

Figure 2-1 represents the hierarchy of the database objects.

A *cluster* is a group of catalogs you can access through the same database connection to the server.

A *catalog* contains multiple schemas and the information about each schema. All catalogs include a schema called INFORMATION_SCHEMA, which includes all the system tables. The name of catalogs must be unique within each cluster.

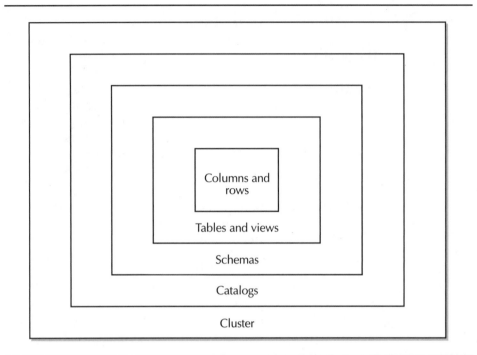

Database
object
hierarchy

Figure 2-1.

Schema

A *schema* is a collection of tables and views from a single database. The name of each schema must be unique within each catalog. A schema consists of

◆ The schema name

◆ The authorization identifier of the owner of the schema

◆ The character set name of the default character set for the schema

◆ The descriptor of every component of the schema

The SQL statement to create a schema is

```
CREATE SCHEMA schema_name AUTHORIZATION owner_user_id
```

Here is an example:

```
CREATE EMPLOYMENT AUTHORIZATION numero_uno
```

The full name of schema objects would consist of a catalog name, schema name, and table name. For example,

```
EMPLOYMENT.APPLICANTS.ADDRESS
```

2

The cluster, catalog, and schema are all implementation-defined, which means they are not defined in ANSI SQL-92.

Table

A *table* is a multiset of rows. A *row* is a nonempty sequence of values. Every row of the same table has the same cardinality and contains a value of every column of that table. The row is the smallest unit of data that can be inserted into a table or deleted from a table.

A table is a base table, a viewed table, or a derived table.

◆ A *base table* is a named table defined by a table definition that does not specify TEMPORARY.

◆ A *derived table* is a table derived directly or indirectly from one or more other tables by the evaluation of a query expression.

◆ A *viewed table* is a named derived table that is listed in the data dictionary of the database.

Every table descriptor includes the number of column descriptors and the column descriptor of each column in the table.

The following are types of base tables:

◆ *Base table* is a named table defined by a table definition that does not specify TEMPORARY.

◆ *Global temporary table* is a named table that specifies GLOBAL TEMPORARY.

◆ *Created local temporary table* is a named table that specifies LOCAL TEMPORARY.

◆ *Declared local temporary table* is a named table that is declared as a component in a module.

Global and created local temporary tables are effectively created only when referenced in an SQL-session. These instances cannot be shared between SQL-sessions or between modules of single SQL-sessions. The definition of a global and a created temporary table are stored in the schema.

Global temporary table contents are distinct within SQL sessions. Created local temporary tables are distinct within modules and embedded SQL programs within SQL sessions. Temporary tables do not exist past the end of the SQL session and they are empty at the start of an SQL session. The created local temporary tables are only available when procedures within the module are executed or as a SQL statement within an embedded SQL program.

All these tables are defined by the CREATE TABLE statement in SQL. In Chapter 1 you learned the CREATE TABLE statement. To refresh your memory, here is another example of CREATE TABLE:

```
CREATE TABLE ADDRESS
(address_appid int,
address_type char (1)
address_home varchar(35),
address_city varchar (30),
address_state char (2),
address_zip  char (5),
PRIMARY KEY (address_appid))
```

To create a view, your SQL statement would be

```
CREATE VIEW SALARY_HISTORY AS
    SELECT * FROM SALARY
        WHERE ACTION_DATE < "1998,01,01" AND SALARY_REVIEW = "Y";
```

Creating a temporary table is similar to creating a base table:

```
CREATE LOCAL TEMPORARY TABLE ADDRESS_TEMP
(address_appid int,
address_type char (1)
address_home varchar(35),
address_city varchar (30),
address_state char (2),
address_zip  char (5),
PRIMARY KEY (address_appid))
```

To create a global temporary table:

```
CREATE GLOBAL TEMPORARY TABLE ADDRESS_TEMP
(address_appid int,
address_type char (1)
address_home varchar(35),
```

```
address_city varchar (30),
address_state char (2),
address_zip  char (5),
PRIMARY KEY (address_appid))
```

When these definitions are executed, the data dictionary for these tables is put into your schema. The DBMS does not allocate space to hold the data. Only when you execute your first SQL statement does your table really exist. For instance,

```
SELECT * from ADDRESS_TEMP
  where address_temp.address_type = 'H';
```

At this time, the database system allocates space for the data requested. Once you end the SQL session, the database deallocates the space. The table is empty once again.

Domains

A *domain* is a set of permissible values. A domain is defined in a schema and is identified by a domain name. The purpose of the domain is to constrain the set of valid values. It includes a default clause that specifies the values to be used in the absence of an explicitly specified value or column default.

Suppose you want to create a domain on the address_type and include a default. The SQL statement would be

```
CREATE DOMAIN Address_Type char (1)
DEFAULT 'H'
CHECK (UPPER(VALUE) = 'H' or UPPER(VALUE) = 'S' or
       UPPER(VALUE) = 'O')
```

With this statement, you have created a domain with a default of 'H' for home. The CHECK clause means only to accept a capital *H, S,* or *O*. VALUE is the data being checked.

Column

A *column* is a multiset of values that may vary over time. All values of the same column are of the same data type or domain and are values in the same table. Every column has a column name. A value of a column is the smallest unit of data that can be selected from a table and the smallest unit of data that can be updated. Columns can be specified to take on various properties such as data types, default values, nullability, collation, and character sets.

Data Types

A *data type* is a set of representable values. The logical representation of a value is a literal (non-null value). A value is a null value or a non-null value. There is no literal for a null value. The keyword NULL is used by many DBMSs, however, to indicate that a null value is acceptable. SQL defines distinct data types named by the keywords described in the following paragraphs.

CHARACTER and CHARACTER VARYING are referred to as *character string types*. For example, "How Green Is My Valley" and "12 Angry Men" are examples of character string types. A character string type falls into three categories: Those defined by national or international standards (NATIONAL CHARACTER and NATIONAL CHARACTER VARYING), those provided by implementation, and those defined by applications. All character strings contain the <space> character. Character sets defined by standards or by implementation reside in the INFORMATION_SCHEMA in each catalog.

BIT and BIT VARYING are bit string types like B'01111110' or B'0111111100000111', respectively. A *bit string* is a sequence of bits, each having a value of 0 or 1. A bit string length is 0 or a positive integer.

All these data types are called *string types* and the values of string types are called *strings*.

Two kinds of numeric types exist: exact and approximate. Here are examples of both types:

- Exact numeric type
  - NUMERIC – 5.98
  - DECIMAL – 2.99
  - INTEGER – 321239
  - SMALLINT – 99
- Approximate numeric type
  - FLOAT – 3.04E-2
  - REAL – 2.23E-4
  - DOUBLE-PRECISION – 5.1628384932E00

Values of numeric types are called *numbers*.

An exact numeric value has a precision and a scale. The *precision* is a positive integer that determines the number of significant digits in a particular binary or decimal. *Scale* is the number of digits in the fractional part of a numeric data time.

Approximate numeric value consists of a signed numeric value and a signed integer that specifies the magnitude of the signed numeric value. It has a precision. The precision is a positive integer that specifies the number of significant binary digits in the signed numeric value.

Values of datetime types are called *datetimes*. These are the main datetimes:

2

◆   DATE – DATE '1999-10-31'

◆   TIME – TIME '09:00:15.05'

◆   TIMESTAMP – TIMESTAMP '1999-10-31 23:00:00.00'

Other datetime data types are

◆   YEAR

◆   MONTH – month within the year

◆   DAY – day within the year

◆   HOUR – hour within the day

◆   MINUTE – minute within the hour

◆   SECOND – second, and possibly fraction of a second, within a minute

◆   TIMEZONE_HOUR – hour value of time zone displacement

◆   TIMEZONE_MINUTE – minute value of time zone displacement

The order of significance for datetime fields are YEAR, MONTH, DAY, HOUR, MINUTE, and SECOND.

Another date type is called an interval type:

◆   INTERVAL – INTERVAL '12:00' MINUTE TO SECOND

Two classes of intervals exist. One class, called *year-month intervals*, has an express or implied datetime precision that includes no fields other than YEAR and MONTH, though both are not required. The other class, called *day-time intervals,* has an express or implied interval precision that can include any fields other than YEAR or MONTH. The valid values for fields in INTERVAL items are

◆   YEAR – unconstrained except by interval leading field precision

◆   MONTH – months (within years) (0-11)

◆   DAY – unconstrained except by interval leading field precision

◆ MINUTE – minutes (within hours) (0-59)

◆ SECOND – seconds (within minutes) (0-59.999…)

NOTE: Each host language has its own data types. These are separate and distinct from SQL data types, even though similar names may be used to describe the data types. Not every SQL data type has a corresponding data type in every host language.

Data Dictionary (Catalog, Metadata)

The *data dictionary* is the definition of the structure of the database. The data dictionary contains the INFORMATION_SCHEMA that includes all the system tables. The dictionary stores all the definitions of columns in each table, integrity constraints on tables, security information (authorization), and other structural element definitions, such as views and domains.

Codd's Rule 12 stresses that the only way a user can get to the database is through the path of the data dictionary. The relational DBMS is ruled by the data dictionary.

Figures 2-2 and 2-3 are examples of the System table and System Column table from Oracle8.

```
Oracle8 Navigator - [DBA_TABLES]                                    _ □ ×
  File  Edit  View  Window  Help                                   _ ᵉ ×
```

	OWNER	TABLE_NAME	TABLESPACE_NAME	CLUSTER_NAME	IOT_N
1	SYS	IND$	SYSTEM	C_OBJ#	
2	SYS	FILE$	SYSTEM		
3	SYS	UNDO$	SYSTEM		
4	SYS	CLU$	SYSTEM	C_OBJ#	
5	SYS	BOOTSTRAP$	SYSTEM		
6	SYS	ICOL$	SYSTEM	C_OBJ#	
7	SYS	FET$	SYSTEM	C_TS#	
8	SYS	CDEF$	SYSTEM	C_COBJ#	
9	SYS	CON$	SYSTEM		
10	SYS	UET$	SYSTEM	C_FILE#_BLOCK#	
11	SYS	TAB$	SYSTEM	C_OBJ#	
12	SYS	OBJ$	SYSTEM		
13	SYS	COL$	SYSTEM	C_OBJ#	
14	SYS	USER$	SYSTEM	C_USER#	
15	SYS	TS$	SYSTEM	C_TS#	
16	SYS	CCOL$	SYSTEM	C_COBJ#	
17	SYS	SEG$	SYSTEM	C_FILE#_BLOCK#	
18	SYS	UGROUP$	SYSTEM		
19	SYS	TSQ$	SYSTEM	C_USER#	
20	SYS	SYN$	SYSTEM		
21	SYS	VIEW$	SYSTEM		
22	SYS	TYPED_VIEW$	SYSTEM		
23	SYS	SEQ$	SYSTEM		

```
For Help, press F1                                   Contents of 'Synonym'
```

Oracle8
System table
Figure 2-2.

2

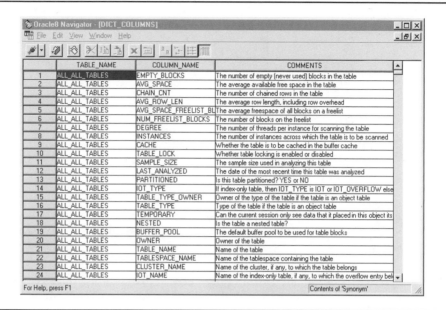

	TABLE_NAME	COLUMN_NAME	COMMENTS
1	ALL_ALL_TABLES	EMPTY_BLOCKS	The number of empty (never used) blocks in the table
2	ALL_ALL_TABLES	AVG_SPACE	The average available free space in the table
3	ALL_ALL_TABLES	CHAIN_CNT	The number of chained rows in the table
4	ALL_ALL_TABLES	AVG_ROW_LEN	The average row length, including row overhead
5	ALL_ALL_TABLES	AVG_SPACE_FREELIST_BL	The average freespace of all blocks on a freelist
6	ALL_ALL_TABLES	NUM_FREELIST_BLOCKS	The number of blocks on the freelist
7	ALL_ALL_TABLES	DEGREE	The number of threads per instance for scanning the table
8	ALL_ALL_TABLES	INSTANCES	The number of instances across which the table is to be scanned
9	ALL_ALL_TABLES	CACHE	Whether the table is to be cached in the buffer cache
10	ALL_ALL_TABLES	TABLE_LOCK	Whether table locking is enabled or disabled
11	ALL_ALL_TABLES	SAMPLE_SIZE	The sample size used in analyzing this table
12	ALL_ALL_TABLES	LAST_ANALYZED	The date of the most recent time this table was analyzed
13	ALL_ALL_TABLES	PARTITIONED	Is this table partitioned? YES or NO
14	ALL_ALL_TABLES	IOT_TYPE	If index-only table, then IOT_TYPE is IOT or IOT_OVERFLOW else
15	ALL_ALL_TABLES	TABLE_TYPE_OWNER	Owner of the type of the table if the table is an object table
16	ALL_ALL_TABLES	TABLE_TYPE	Type of the table if the table is an object table
17	ALL_ALL_TABLES	TEMPORARY	Can the current session only see data that it placed in this object its
18	ALL_ALL_TABLES	NESTED	Is the table a nested table?
19	ALL_ALL_TABLES	BUFFER_POOL	The default buffer pool to be used for table blocks
20	ALL_ALL_TABLES	OWNER	Owner of the table
21	ALL_ALL_TABLES	TABLE_NAME	Name of the table
22	ALL_ALL_TABLES	TABLESPACE_NAME	Name of the tablespace containing the table
23	ALL_ALL_TABLES	CLUSTER_NAME	Name of the cluster, if any, to which the table belongs
24	ALL_ALL_TABLES	IOT_NAME	Name of the index-only table, if any, to which the overflow entry bel

Oracle8
System
Column table
Figure 2-3.

In Figure 2-2, the System table describes the tables in the database, including the data dictionary tables.

In Figure 2-3, the System Column table describes the columns for all tables in the database.

You will become more familiar with these data types in the following chapters when you create your tables. You have learned about the major components in the relational database. In the next section, you learn about the relational database model and how SQL is used within this model.

The Relational Model

In 1970, Dr. Edgar (E. F.) Codd wrote a brilliant paper, "A Relational Model of Data for Large Shared Data Banks," *Communications of the ACM*, Vol. 13, No. 6, June 1970. Reprints of the article are available from ACM for a small fee. A partial reprint, which is a must-read for database designers, is available on the Web at: http://www.acm.org/turing/classics/nov95. This book deals with the concepts outlined in this paper.

Dr. Codd created the relational data model. He believed the existing data models of the 60s were not conducive to representing the relationships in a database. Dr. Codd based this model on the mathematical set theory and the

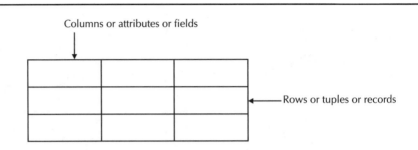

Columns or attributes or fields

Rows or tuples or records

Table layout
Figure 2-4.

concept of relation. A *relation* is a table. The *attributes* are columns (fields) and the *tuples* are rows (records) as shown in Figure 2-4. From this mathematical set theory evolved the idea of a relational database model.

Codd's 12 Rules

In 1985, Codd outlined the 12 rules to which a database must adhere if it was to be considered a relational database. ("Is Your Database Really Relational?," *Computerworld,* October 14, 1985: ID1-ID9.) The rules are as follows:

1. *The information rule.* All information in a relational database is represented explicitly at the logical level and in exactly one way—by values in tables.

2. *Guaranteed access rule.* Each and every datum (atomic value) in a relational database is guaranteed to be logically accessible by resorting to a combination of table name, primary key value, and column name.

3. *Systematic treatment of null values.* Null values (distinct from the empty character string or a string of blank characters and distinct from zero or other numbers) are supported in fully relational DBMS for representing missing information and inapplicable information in a systematic way, independent of data type.

4. *Dynamic online catalog based on the relational model.* The database description is represented at the logical level in the same way as ordinary data, so that authorized users can apply the same relational language to its interrogation as they apply to the regular data.

5. *Comprehensive data sublanguage rule.* A relational system may support several languages and various modes of terminal use (for example, the fill-in-the-blanks mode). However, there must be at least one language whose statements are expressible, per some well-defined syntax, as

2

character strings, and that is comprehensive in supporting all of the following items:

- ◆ Data Definition
- ◆ View Definition
- ◆ Data manipulation (interactive and by program)
- ◆ Integrity constraints
- ◆ Authorization
- ◆ Transaction boundaries (begin, commit, and rollback)

6. *View updating rule.* All views that are theoretically updateable are also updateable by the system.

7. *High-level insert, update, and delete.* The capability of handling a base relation or a derived relation as a single operand applies not only to the retrieval of data but also to the insertion, update, and deletion of data.

8. *Physical data independence.* Application programs and terminal activities remain logically unimpaired whenever any changes are made in either storage representations or access methods.

9. *Logical data independence.* Application programs and terminal activities remain logically unimpaired when information-preserving changes of any kind that theoretically permit unimpairment are made to the base tables.

10. *Integrity independence.* Integrity constraints specific to a particular relational database must be definable in the relational data sublanguage and storable in the catalog, not in the application programs.

11. *Distribution independence.* A relational DBMS has distribution independence.

12. *Nonsubversion rule.* If a relational system has a low-level (single record at a time) language, that low level cannot be used to subvert or bypass the integrity rules and constraints expressed in the higher-level relational language (multiple records at a time).

NOTE: Just as no DBMS conforms completely to SQL-92, no available relational DBMS meets all 12 of Codd's rules.

Rule 1 dictates tables (relations) be the only data structure used in the relational database.

Rule 2 states you need only know the table name, column name, and primary key to locate your data in the database.

Rule 3 maintains the database provide for missing data through null values.

Rule 4 requires your database be self-describing and your data dictionary have the same structure as your data tables. This means the database must contain system tables that describe the structure of the database.

Rule 5 describes the components of the data sublanguage: Creating a database, retrieving and entering data, implementing security, and transactions, to name a few. SQL-92 complies to this rule.

Rule 6 states views that are updateable must be updateable by the DBMS and must be able not only to update the views, but the base tables as well.

Rule 7 mandates the system must be able to insert, update, and delete both single and multiple rows of data.

Rules 8 and 9 allow for the capability to move or change the database without affecting the end user working in the database.

Rule 10 deals with the integrity of the database. This is an important rule because without referential integrity your data could be corrupted and prove unreliable. Some DBMS ignore this rule because checking for integrity rules in the data dictionary decreases the performance of the database.

Rule 11 involves the distributed database. A *distributed database* is a database where the data is located on multiple computer systems. In this rule, where the data is stored should not be a concern to the user. It should look like a centralized database. This is a challenge for all DBMS vendors.

Rule 12 does not allow for other ways to access the data and, therefore, bypass the referential integrity rules stored in the data dictionary.

Now that you have reviewed the rules of the relational database model, let's discuss relationships.

It's All Relative

As you learned previously in this chapter, a relation is a table with columns (attributes) and rows (tuples).

The name of a column must be unique within the table, however, you can have the columns named the same when they exist in different tables. For instance, in our address_temp table, we could have two tables with the column name of address_appid. What differentiates them is the name of the table, for example, **address_temp.address_appid** and **address.address_appid**. In addition, the values in a column come from only one domain. Every column has its own domain.

2

A row in a relational database has only one value and that value can be found where the column and the row intersect. In addition, each row must be unique. No duplicate rows can exist.

As you learned earlier in this chapter, most DBMSs do not have validation checks for relational integrity. One way to achieve the uniqueness of the rows is through the use of a primary key.

Keys

A *primary key* is the column or set of columns that makes every row in the table unique. This primary key ensures you will receive all the data you put into your database. A primary key cannot contain a null value.

Choosing a primary key can be tricky. Most people want to assign a primary key an easy-to-remember number or a meaningful character. The best practice is to create an arbitrary, meaningless number that has no chance of being duplicated or becoming null. In Microsoft Access, you can allow Access to assign an arbitrary number. Most database vendors allow for this automatic numbering for a primary key.

Sometimes you may not want to use an automatically assigned number. You may also have a table where no single nonduplicate column exists. In this case, you may take two or more columns and combine them to form a primary key for the table. The rule is to combine the least amount of columns necessary to create a primary key.

Another key you should know is the foreign key. The *foreign key* is a column that is a key in one or more tables, other than the one in which it appears. For example, Figure 2-5 represents three tables in the Applicant schema. The primary key is underlined and the foreign key is italicized.

The Address table has one primary key as does the Applicants table. The Track table has a foreign key (App_ID) and the primary key is a combination of the Requisition ID and the App_ID. You see, the Requisition ID on the Track table can be duplicated if more than one Applicant_ID has been matched to the requisition. Here you would use the Primary Key

Applicants Table

APP_ID	LAST NAME	FIRST NAME	MIDDLE	SS#
234	Smith	Penelope	Ann	234-12-5678
235	Jones	George	Frederick	123-24-6890
236	Appleby	James	Christopher	456-90-2333

Address Table

APP_ID	ADDRESS	CITY	STATE	ZIP
234	123 Pilgrim	Milton	MA	02111
235	234 Inverleith	Oakland	CA	94532
236	456 Mariposa	Los Angeles	CA	93002

Track Table

REQUISITION ID	*APP_ID*	ACTION CODE	STATUS CODE	ACTION DATE
YR9801	234	A1	S3	07/01/99
YR9803	235	A9	S10	08/10/99
YR9803	236	A10	S1	08/11/99

Three tables and their keys

Figure 2-5.

Requisition_ID and the Foreign Key Applicant_ID to get a unique row of data. For instance,

```
SELECT * FROM TRACK
    where REQUISITION_ID = 'YR9803';
```

This query would return

```
YR9803    235    A9    S10    08/10/99
YR9803    236    A10   S1     08/11/99
```

To get a unique row, you would need to query

```
SELECT * FROM TRACK
  where REQUISITION_ID = 'YR9803' and APP_ID = 235;
```

This would return one row:

```
YR9803    235    A9    S10    08/10/99
```

As you can see, foreign keys may be a part of a combined primary key. If they are not part of a combined primary key, they may be null.

2

The Relationship Between Tables

A relationship is created when a pair of tables is joined through a Primary key and a Foreign key or is joined together through a third table, called a *linking table*. These relationships help maintain data integrity because they ensure no duplicate data.

Three possible types of relationships exist among tables (cardinality), as follows:

- ◆ One-to-one relationship exists between a pair of tables if a single record in the first table is related to only one record in the second table and the single record in the second table is related to only one record in the first table.

- ◆ One-to-many relationship exists between a pair of tables if a single record in the first table can be related to *one* or *more* records in the second table, but a single record in the second table can be related to only one record in the first table.

- ◆ Many-to-many relationship exists between a pair of tables in a single record if the first table can be related to *one* or *more* records in the second table and a single record in the second table can be related to one or more records in the first table.

Look at the tables in Figure 2-6 and evaluate their relationship type.

The one-to-one relationship exists between the Applicants and Address tables. The applicant can only have one address and only one address can belong to an applicant.

An example of a linking table is seen among the Applicants, Track, and Requisition tables.

An example of a one-to-many relationship exists between the Applicants and Telephone Numbers table. Here the applicant can have more than one telephone number, but a telephone number can belong to only one applicant.

Applicants

APP_ID	LAST NAME	FIRST NAME	MIDDLE	SS#
234	Smith	Penelope	Ann	234-12-5678
235	Jones	George	Frederick	123-24-6890
236	Appleby	James	Christopher	456-90-2333

One-to-many *1:N*

Telephone Numbers

APP_ID	TYPE	AREA CODE	TELEPHONE NUMBER
234	Home	(916)	555-0222
234	Work	(415)	555-0333

One-to-one *1:1*

One-to-one *1:1*

Address

APP_ID	ADDRESS	CITY	STATE	ZIP
234	123 Pilgrim	Milton	MA	02111
235	234 Inverleith	Oakland	CA	94532
236	456 Mariposa	Los Angeles	CA	93002

Track

REQUISITION ID	APP_ID	ACTION CODE	STATUS CODE	ACTION DATE
YR9801	234	A1	S3	07/01/99
YR9803	235	A9	S10	08/10/99
YR9803	236	A10	S1	08/11/99
YR9803	234	A2	S9	07/10/99

One-to-one *1:1*

Requisition

REQUISITION ID	STATUS	RECRUITER ID	POSITIONS AVAILABLE	DATE OPENED
YR9801	Open	Tamo	3	10/01/99
YR9802	Closed	Miro	1	12/30/99
YR9803	Open	Amis	2	07/01/99

The relationships between five tables

Figure 2-6.

The final example is of a many-to-many relationship. In this example, a simple database, consisting of the Spa Members and Class tables, is used to illustrate.

Spa Members

SPA MEMBER ID	MEM F_NAME	MEM L_NAME
100	John	James
200	Sarah	Conrad
300	James	Quigley
400	Tina	Harris

Classes

COURSE NO	SPA MEMBER ID	TITLE
303	300	Aerobics
500	400	Feel the Burn
550	300	No Pain No Gain

As you can see, Spa Members may attend many classes and a class may have many students. This example is of a many-to-many relationship. Anytime you have a many-to-many relationship, you may get redundant data, which may cause a problem with updating or deleting the data. At this point, the table needs to be normalized. This brings you to your next topic, normalization.

Normalization

Normalization is the ability to create a database with relational tables, which have no redundant data and can be consistently and correctly modified. Theoretical rules that a relation must meet are called *normal forms*. The higher the normal form, the better the design of the database. Five normal forms, designed by E. F. Codd, exist. You may think of these forms as a sort of bulls-eye, meaning they are nested within one another, as shown in Figure 2-7.

Only the first three normal forms are discussed because forms four and five are not within the scope of this book.

First Normal Form

The first normal form (1NF) must have data stored in a two-dimensional table with no repeating groups. A *repeating group* is a column with more than one value in each row.

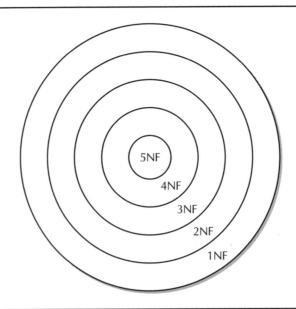

The five
normal forms

Figure 2-7.

For example, suppose the Applicants table included the telephone numbers
of the applicant in the same column. Remember, an applicant can have more
than one telephone number. A repeating group would look like this:

Applicants

APP_ID	L_NAME	F_NAME	M_NAME	TELEPHONE#	SS#
234	Smith	Penelope	Ann	312 555-1000, 312 555-1001	234-12-5678
235	Jones	George	Frederick	415 555-1002, 415 555-1003	123-24-6890
236	Appleby	James	Christopher	925 555-1004	456-90-2333

As you can see, more than one telephone number is entered into this
column. No way exists to know which telephone number is the home or
business number. If you want to find only home numbers for these
applicants, how could you determine this? The solution is to eliminate this
repeating group column. What is needed is a new table. This way, searching
for a home number will be easier.

Telephone Numbers

APP_ID	TYPE	AREA CODE	TELEPHONE NUMBER
234	Home	(312)	555-1000
234	Work	(312)	555-1001
235	Home	(415)	555-1002
235	Other	(415)	555-1003
236	Home	(925)	555-1004

Problems exist with 1NF tables beyond the repeating group error. First, normal form tables contain redundant data. Redundancy causes update anomalies. For example, if you had included recruiter information on the Requisition table, you would have a problem.

Requisition

ID	STATUS	RECRUITER ID	RECRUITER LOCATION	POSITIONS AVAILABLE	DATE OPENED
YR9801	Open	Tamo	Detroit	3	10/01/98
YR9802	Closed	Tamo	Detroit	1	12/30/98
YR9803	Open	Amis	New York	2	07/01/98

Update anomalies occur when you try to update, insert, or delete. For example, if you delete a row, the information about the recruiter and recruiter location is lost. If you go to update (change) the location for the recruiter, you must change it at least twice. If you insert a requisition, you would have no information about the recruiter until you insert the requisition with the new recruiter information.

Second Normal Form

The *second normal form* includes only tables that do not have composite primary keys. In other words, a table is in first normal form and all the non-key columns are functionally dependent on the entire primary key.

Functional dependency means all other columns are dependent on the primary column. In your Requisition table, the Status, Recruiter ID, Recruiter Location, Positions Available, and Date Opened are all dependent upon the Requisition ID. The reverse is not true, however, Requisition ID does not depend on all the other columns.

Requisition ID → Status, Recruiter ID, Recruiter Location, Positions Available, Date Opened

Our Requisition table meets the requirements for a 2NF table. Yet, does it meet the requirements of a 3NF?

Third Normal Form

A *third normal form* table requires that the table is already a 2NF table and every non-key column is nontransitively dependent upon its primary key. A *transitive dependency* occurs when a non-key column, which is a determinant of the primary key, is the determiner of other columns.

> Requisition ID → Recruiter ID
> Recruiter ID → Recruiter Location

Is there a transitive dependency here? Yes. To make this a third normal form table, you need to create another table. This table would be named the Recruiter table. You would move the determiner columns from this Requisition table and put it into the Recruiter table. Then, you would delete the columns from the Requisition table that you put into the Recruiter table. At this point, you could also expand the Recruiter table and provide more information regarding the recruiter.

The following tables illustrate the progression of the Requisition table from a 2NF table to a 3NF table. Note that another table, Recruiter table, is created and it too is a 3NF table.

Requisition (2NF)

REQUISITION ID	STATUS	RECRUITER ID	RECRUITER LOCATION	POSITIONS AVAILABLE	DATE OPENED
YR9801	Open	Tamo	Detroit	3	10/01/98
YR9802	Closed	Tamo	Detroit	1	12/30/98
YR9803	Open	Amis	New York	2	07/01/98

Requisition (3NF)

REQUISITION ID	STATUS	POSITIONS AVAILABLE	DATE OPENED
YR9801	Open	3	10/01/98
YR9802	Closed	1	12/30/98
YR9803	Open	2	07/01/98

Recruiter (3NF)

RECRUITER ID	RECRUITER LOCATION
Tamo	Detroit
Tamo	Detroit
Amis	New York

NOTE: The key to normalization is to keep creating new tables until you reach the third normal form.

2

At the third normal form, you have created a table free of redundant data, which has no update anomalies, plus it saves you space in your database. Most database designers think the third normal form gives you a good database design. Exceptions exist to most rules, and the fourth and fifth normal form deals with these. Appendix B provides references for additional reading material on normalization.

In this chapter, you have learned about the types and components of databases. Now you learn about the architecture in which a database operates: client/server architecture.

Client/Server Architecture

Client/server is a relationship between several computers that work together over a network. The server runs services and the client requests those services. The server's duties include determining the access of clients to the shared services. A server can be the same computer as the client or it can be another computer or group of computers.

Four different types of client/server exist. First are *file servers,* in which the client requests files from the server. This is great when you need to share documents over a network, such as a repository of project documentation.

Second, is the *database server,* in which the client passes SQL requests to the server. The server uses its own power to process the request. For instance, suppose you send the following SQL statement:

```
Select * from Requisition
   where Requisition_ID > 2000;
```

In this example, the database server would search the database for the records that match the criteria and would only return the records that match the criteria. In other words, if the database table contained 10,000 records, the request would return approximately 8,000 records back to the client.

Third, is the transaction server. The *transaction server* client calls remote procedures that are on the SQL database engine. These remote procedures run a group of SQL statements. These grouped SQL statements are called *transactions*. You create the client/server application by writing the code for both. These applications are called *online transaction processing* (OLTP) applications. You will learn more about transactions in Chapter 4.

The fourth and last server of importance is the W*eb server*. The World Wide Web is the largest client/server to date. In a Web server, you have a thin client that communicates to a fat server. A *thin client* is one in which little of the application code is run on the client. A *fat server,* then, is one in which most of the application code resides and processes on the server. These are easier to manage because most of the code runs on the server. The thin client interacts with the server through remote procedure calls.

Another way to explain this concept is by using the term *multitier architecture* or *2-tier/3-tier*. In a 2-tier system, the application code is either on the client or server or both. In a 3-tier system, you have the client tier, the application tier (middle tier), and the server tier. The application code resides in the application tier. This streamlines the process and makes the system flexible, scalable, and powerful.

The art of achieving an elegant client/server application is determined by many things. For instance, how you split up the duties between the client and the server and the middleware you choose can affect the quality of your application. *Middleware* is the software that enables the client to request data from the server. For instance, for a database server, middleware such as ODBC, OLE DB, ADO, EDA/SQL, and Oracle Glue are integral to various applications. You have many choices, so pick the one that best serves your needs. The next section explains ODBC connections to the various RDBMSs that exist.

Open Database Connectivity (ODBC)

Open Database Connectivity (ODBC) is a standard developed by the Microsoft Corporation. This standard enables many different types of data to be accessed by a single application. ODBC is a widely accepted application programming interface (API) for database access, based on the Call-Level Interface (CLI) specifications from X/Open and ISO/IEC standards for database APIs. It uses SQL as its database access language. ODBC is a mutation of SAG (SQL Access Group) CLI from X/Open.

ODBC 3.0 is the current version. Most vendors now support the ODBC 3.0 API in addition to their own native SQL APIs. A *driver* is translation code. In this case, the ODBC driver is one that accepts a CLI call and translates it into the native database server's access language.

Usually RDBMS vendors or front-end applications supply the ODBC drivers. Or, they may be purchased from middleware vendors. Intersolv Suite software provides many ODBC drivers for over 35 database servers.

The future of ODBC is uncertain with the upcoming changes by Microsoft, however. This will become a whole new playing field for data access.

2

OLE DB and ADO—Universal Data Access

Microsoft recently introduced OLE DB and ADO. OLE DB does not replace ODBC, but is an extension of ODBC. It enables data access to a much broader set of data providers, such as nonrelational database systems and e-mail systems, to name a few.

ADO (Access Data Objects) is a high-level interface to OLE DB, optimized for access over the Internet and intranet. In the future, Microsoft's ADO will eventually replace the company's current data-access models, thereby providing a model for universal data access for all. SQL will still be the data access language. The future looks bright for users of databases.

With this introduction to relational databases, you now have the rudimentary knowledge to continue on to the SQL basics.

CHAPTER 3

Understanding the SQL Language

In the last chapter, you learned about relational databases. In this chapter, you learn about the language that will enable you to build your database and to retrieve data from that database.

The first section covers the SELECT statement and its clauses. Then you learn about expressions, conditions, operators, and functions. When you finish with this chapter, you will have the building blocks to build your own database.

The SELECT Statement and Its Clauses

The *SELECT statement* is used to query the database and also to create views from your tables. The SELECT statement in its simplest form consists of two clauses: the SELECT clause and the FROM clause.

The SELECT and FROM Clause

The syntax for the SELECT and FROM clause is

```
SELECT <Column 1>, <Column 2>, <Column 3>
FROM <Table Name>
```

This SELECT statement chooses specific column names from a table. For example, in the Employee table, there are multiple columns. Suppose you only need to see three columns from this table. Your SELECT statement might be

```
SELECT LNAME, FNAME, MINIT
FROM Employee;
```

Your SELECT statement returns

```
LNAME       FNAME       MINIT
-----       -----       -----
Abbott      Catherine   L.
Baker       Ramsey      J.
Conway      Ken         H.
Dempsey     Mary        C.
```

To select all columns from this table, the syntax is

```
SELECT *
FROM <TABLE>
```

The asterisk means *all columns*.

Here is an example using the Employee table:

```
SELECT *
FROM Employee;
```

This statement would return

3

LNAME	FNAME	MINIT	STATUS	GENDER	BIRTHDATE
Abbott	Catherine	L.	Regular	F	11/01/58
Baker	Ramsey	J.	Summer	M	01/23/55
Conway	Ken	H.	Regular	M	08/04/62
Dempsey	Mary	C.	Regular	F	10/10/72

When you use SELECT you must use it with FROM. The SELECT and FROM clauses provide you with either some columns and all rows or all columns and all rows. If you want only certain rows, however, you need to add another clause, the WHERE clause.

The WHERE Clause

The *WHERE clause* creates a more definitive SELECT statement. It searches for a condition and narrows your selection of data. For instance, the Employee table has 2,000 rows of employee data. If you don't have a WHERE clause, you will get all 2,000 rows. If you add a WHERE clause to your SELECT statement,

```
SELECT LNAME, FNAME, MINIT
FROM Employee
WHERE LNAME = 'Conway';
```

The following row would be returned:

```
Conway    Ken    H.
```

Another example of the WHERE clause:

```
SELECT *
FROM Employee
WHERE Status = 'Regular';
```

Here are the results:

LNAME	FNAME	MINIT	STATUS	GENDER	BIRTHDATE
Abbott	Catherine	L.	Regular	F	11/01/58
Conway	Ken	H.	Regular	M	08/04/62
Dempsey	Mary	C.	Regular	F	10/10/72

The GROUP BY Clause

Another helpful clause is the GROUP BY clause. A *GROUP BY clause* arranges your data rows into a group according to the columns you specify. In the next example, you group your Employee table by Status.

```
SELECT *
FROM Employee
GROUP BY Status;
```

LNAME	FNAME	MINIT	**STATUS**	GENDER	BIRTHDATE
Abbott	Catherine	L.	**Regular**	F	11/01/58
Conway	Ken	H.	**Regular**	M	08/04/62
Dempsey	Mary	C.	**Regular**	F	10/10/72
Baker	Ramsey	J.	**Summer**	M	01/23/55

If you want to group by more than one column, all you must do is add another column name:

```
SELECT *
FROM Employee
GROUP BY Status, Gender;
```

This result is a little different from your last GROUP BY:

LNAME	FNAME	MINIT	**STATUS**	*GENDER*	BIRTHDATE
Abbott	Catherine	L.	**Regular**	*F*	11/01/58
Dempsey	Mary	C.	**Regular**	*F*	10/10/72
Conway	Ken	H.	**Regular**	*M*	08/04/62
Baker	Ramsey	J.	**Summer**	*M*	01/23/55

The first GROUP BY is Status and the second GROUP BY is Gender.

NOTE: Remember, grouping is important when you use functions such as SUM and AVG in your SELECT statement. Functions are covered in the next section.

The ORDER BY Clause

The ORDER BY clause is similar to the GROUP BY clause in that you arrange your data in a specific way. The *ORDER BY clause* enables you to sort your data in either ascending or descending order. In most databases, new rows are inserted at the bottom of the table. Earlier databases sometimes made use of space differently, however. They may have inserted new rows in rows from which data was deleted. As a rule, a good practice is to use ORDER BY to guarantee you get rows sorted your way.

In the following example, you sort your data by LNAME.

```
SELECT *
FROM Employee
ORDER BY LNAME asc;
```

The results are

LNAME	FNAME	MINIT	STATUS	GENDER	BIRTHDATE
Abbott	Catherine	L.	Regular	F	11/01/58
Baker	Ramsey	J.	Summer	M	01/23/55
Conway	Ken	H.	Regular	M	08/04/62
Dempsey	Mary	C.	Regular	F	10/10/72

Again you may use multiple columns to GROUP BY:

```
SELECT *
FROM Employee
ORDER BY LNAME asc, FNAME asc;
```

Here are your results:

LNAME	FNAME	MINIT	STATUS	GENDER	BIRTHDATE
Abbott	Catherine	L.	Regular	F	11/01/58
Baker	George	O.	Regular	M	06/24/60

```
Baker         Ramsey         J.         Summer      M          01/23/55
Conway        Ken            H.         Regular     M          08/04/62
Dempsey       Mary           C.         Regular     F          10/10/72
```

The HAVING Clause

Your next clause, the HAVING clause, is similar to the WHERE clause. The *HAVING clause* does for aggregate data what the WHERE clause does for individual rows. The HAVING clause is another search condition. In this case, however, the search is based on each group of the grouped table. The difference between a WHERE clause and a HAVING clause is in the way the query is processed. In a WHERE clause, the search condition on the rows is performed before rows are grouped. In a HAVING clause, the groups are formed first and the search condition is applied to the group. An example of a HAVING clause is

```
SELECT LNAME, FNAME, Status, Gender
FROM Employee
GROUP BY Status, Gender
HAVING Gender = "F";
```

This statement returns

```
LNAME         FNAME          STATUS      GENDER
-----         -----          ------      ------
Abbott        Catherine      Regular     F
Dempsey       Mary           Regular     F
```

You can use a WHERE and a HAVING clause together. For instance, how many female employees have birthdays later than July 1, 1960? The statement would be

```
SELECT *
FROM Employee
WHERE Birth_date > '1960,07,01'
GROUP BY Status, Gender
HAVING Gender = 'F';
```

Your result would be

```
LNAME         FNAME      STATUS      GENDER      BIRTHDATE
-----         -----      ------      ------      ---------
Dempsey       Mary       Regular     F             10/10/72
```

NOTE: Only the columns used in the GROUP BY statement may be used for the HAVING clause. The search condition is placed on the group as a whole.

The STARTING WITH Clause

The *STARTING WITH clause* works in conjunction with the WHERE clause and is used by many DBMS vendors. It is similar to the LIKE expression, which is covered in the next section. Here is the statement using STARTING WITH:

```
SELECT LNAME, FNAME, Birth_date
FROM Employee
WHERE LNAME STARTING WITH ('D%');
```

The *percent sign (%)* is a wildcard that represents more than one character. An *underscore (_)* is a wildcard that represents only one character. This statement returns the following:

```
LNAME        FNAME      BIRTHDATE
-----        -----      ---------
Dempsey      Mary       10/10/72
```

Expressions, Conditions, and Operators, Oh My!

The expression in SQL returns a value, conditions are found in the WHERE clause, and operators are used in an expression to explain how you want the conditions to get the data. Got that? Let's explore each in more detail.

Expressions

In the previous section, you learned about the SELECT statement and its clauses. Well, an *expression* is everything that comes after SELECT and FROM. For example, in

```
SELECT LNAME, FNAME, MINIT, STATUS
from Employee;
```

LNAME, FNAME, MINIT, and STATUS are all expressions.

Conditions

Conditions are found in the WHERE clause. A *condition* has a variable, a comparison operator, and a constant. Note the condition after WHERE:

```
WHERE Birth_date > '1960,07,01'
```

Let's break this WHERE clause down into the parts of a condition:

```
    Birth_date = Variable
             > = Comparison operator
  '1960,07,01' = Constant
```

Conditions can also be found in a HAVING clause, as follows:

```
HAVING Gender = "F"
```

The conditions are

```
    Gender = Variable
         = = Comparison operator
       "F" = Constant
```

Operators

Operators help you set your conditions to retrieve data. The most familiar type of operators are the mathematical operators: plus, minus, multiply, and divide.

Plus (+)

You can use the *plus operator* in a number of ways. First, you can use the plus operator to add columns together like:

```
SELECT Product_ID, Cost, Cost + 1.00
FROM Product;
```

In this SELECT statement, you are adding $1.00 to the cost of each product as the results show in the following:

```
PRODUCT_ID              COST      COST + 1.00
----------              -----     -----------
Blue Womens Sweater     15.00          16.00
Red Argyle Sweater      50.00          51.00
Wool Trousers           40.00          41.00
Silk Scarf              20.00          21.00
Half-Slip, White        15.00          16.00
Slippers, Leather       45.00          46.00
```

If you want to rename the Cost + 1.00 column to Merchant_Cost, all you need to do is

```
SELECT Product_ID, Cost, (Cost + 1.00) Merchant_Cost
FROM Product;
```

You create a new column based on adding one dollar to the Cost column.

```
PRODUCT_ID              COST      MERCHANT_COST
----------              -----     -------------
Blue Womens Sweater     15.00          16.00
Red Argyle Sweater      50.00          51.00
Wool Trousers           40.00          41.00
Silk Scarf              20.00          21.00
Half-Slip, White        15.00          16.00
Slippers, Leather       45.00          46.00
```

PORTABILITY: Depending on your DBMS SQL, you may also see the following used to indicate an alias for the new column:

```
SELECT Product_ID, Cost, Cost + 1.00 = Merchant_Cost FROM Product;
```

The plus operator, as you can see, can be used to add columns and to create an alias for a column. Later in this chapter, you learn the other uses for the plus operator.

Minus (-)

The *minus operator* has two uses: the first is to change the sign of a number and the second is to subtract. You cannot use the minus operator with a character field. To illustrate the minus operator, the ProfLoss table will be used. In this example, you select the Profit_Loss column, an integer data type:

```
SELECT Region, Month, Profit_Loss
FROM ProfLoss;
```

Notice the Profit_Loss column contains both positive and negative numbers:

```
REGION    MONTH        PROFIT_LOSS
------    -----        -----------
North     February        -2,000
South     February         1,000
West      February          -500
East      February         5,000
```

Apply the minus operator to the statement:

```
SELECT Region, Month, - Profit_Loss
FROM ProfLoss;
```

Look at what happens:

```
REGION    MONTH      PROFIT_LOSS
------    -----      -----------
North     February        2,000
South     February       -1,000
West      February          500
East      February       -5,000
```

The positive numbers are negative and the negative numbers are positive. The previous statement results gave the company a better profit for February.

The second use of the minus operator is to subtract:

```
SELECT Product_ID, Cost, Merchant_Cost, (Merchant_Cost - Cost) Profit
FROM Products;
```

You create a new column, Profit, to represent the (Merchant_Cost – Cost) column:

```
PRODUCT_ID              COST      MERCHANT_COST     PROFIT
----------             -----      -------------     ------
Blue Womens Sweater    15.00             16.00       1.00
Red Argyle Sweater     50.00             51.00       1.00
Wool Trousers          40.00             41.00       1.00
Silk Scarf             20.00             21.00       1.00
Half-Slip, White       15.00             16.00       1.00
Slippers, Leather      45.00             46.00       1.00
```

3

Divide (/)

The *division operator* only divides. The Product table is used to illustrate:

```
SELECT Product_ID, Cost, (Profit/4) Sale_Discount
FROM Product;
```

Again, a new column is created in place of the Profit/4 column:

```
PRODUCT_ID              COST      MERCHANT_COST     PROFIT    SALE_DISCOUNT
----------             -----      -------------     ------    -------------
Blue Womens Sweater    15.00             16.00       1.00              .25
Red Argyle Sweater     50.00             51.00       1.00              .25
Wool Trousers          40.00             41.00       1.00              .25
Silk Scarf             20.00             21.00       1.00              .25
Half-Slip, White       15.00             16.00       1.00              .25
Slippers, Leather      45.00             46.00       1.00              .25
```

Multiply (*)

The *multiply operator* is a single-use operator. The Product table is used to illustrate this simple operator and we added another column, New_Merchant_Cost:

```
SELECT Product_ID, Cost, New_Merchant_Cost, (New_Merchant_Cost * .10) Profit
FROM Product;
```

Here are your results with the new Profit column:

```
PRODUCT_ID              COST      NEW_MERCHANT_COST     PROFIT
----------             -----      -----------------     ------
Blue Women Sweater     15.00                 16.50       1.50
Red Argyle Sweater     50.00                 55.00       5.00
```

```
Wool Trousers         40.00           44.00      4.00
Silk Scarf            20.00           22.00      2.00
Half-Slip, White      15.00           16.50      1.50
Slippers, Leather     45.00           44.50      4.50
```

Now you know all your mathematical operators. Are you ready for more operators?

NULL

The following example searches for a NULL value for Gender:

```
SELECT *
FROM Employees
WHERE Gender IS NULL;
```

```
0 rows returned.
```

IN DEPTH

What Is Null?

Null is that database value of UNKNOWN. It is not an empty column. The database stores a value that represents null so it can be distinguished from a character string with a blank space in it. As you learned in the last chapter, a primary key field cannot be NULL.

IS NULL is an operator that can be used to select NULL fields from your query. Null values are used to eliminate blanks, 0 or –1, to indicate the unknown or missing data. A Null cannot be compared to another Null. Any mathematical operation with a Null will return a Null.

A Null isn't a zero or a blank string. If you add a zero to another zero you get a zero. If you add a Null to another field, that field becomes Null. Nulls produce Nulls.

You can also search for NOT NULL:

```
SELECT *
FROM Employees
WHERE Gender IS NOT NULL;
```

Your results are quite different:

LNAME	FNAME	MINIT	STATUS	GENDER	BIRTHDATE
Abbott	Catherine	L.	Regular	F	11/01/58
Baker	George	O.	Regular	M	06/24/60
Baker	Ramsey	J.	Summer	M	01/23/55
Conway	Ken	H.	Regular	M	08/04/62
Dempsey	Mary	C.	Regular	F	10/10/72

3

You learn more about NULL as you progress through this book.

When you write queries, you often need to do comparisons. Hence, the need for Comparison operators, which compare expressions and return TRUE, FALSE, or UNKNOWN. UNKNOWN means none of the choices you provided in your SELECT statement have been found.

Equal (=)

This handy operator is used a great deal with the WHERE clause. As you saw earlier, the equal operator can also be used to express an alias in conjunction with the plus operator. The equal operator is straightforward.

```
SELECT * from Employees
WHERE LNAME = 'Abbott';
```

The following is the result:

LNAME	FNAME	STATUS	GENDER
Abbott	Catherine	Regular	F

NOTE: When using the equal operator, you must be aware of the case-sensitivity of the data. If you requested WHERE LNAME = "ABBOTT" you would get

```
No rows selected.
```

Greater Than (>) and Greater Than or Equal To (>=)

Suppose you want to know about the profits you made for February. You are only interested in profits and not losses. The ProfLoss table is used for this example:

```
SELECT * FROM ProfLoss
WHERE Profit_Loss > 0;
```

Or, in this example, you could use **>=** to get the same results:

```
SELECT * FROM ProfLoss
WHERE Profit_Loss >= 0;
```

```
REGION     MONTH      PROFIT_LOSS
------     -----      -----------
South      February        1,000
East       February        5,000
```

Remember, you had losses for the North and the West Regions.

Less Than (<) and Less Than or Equal To (<=)

Less Than is the opposite of the Greater Than operator.

```
SELECT * FROM ProfLoss
WHERE Profit_Loss < 0;
```

Or, in this example, you could use **<=** to get the same results. (In most cases, however, these two operators would produce different results.)

```
SELECT * FROM ProfLoss
WHERE Profit_Loss <= 0;
```

Note that your results are different from the **>=** operator:

```
REGION     MONTH      PROFIT_LOSS
------     -----      -----------
North      February       -2,000
West       February         -500
```

NOTE: You can use either of these two comparison operators with character fields.

3

The Employee table appears next to illustrate how these operators can be used with character fields:

```
SELECT * FROM Employee
WHERE LNAME >= 'A%' and LNAME <= 'Sm%';
```

LNAME	FNAME	MINIT	STATUS	GENDER	BIRTHDATE
Abbott	Catherine	L.	Regular	F	11/01/58
Baker	George	O.	Regular	M	06/24/60
Baker	Ramsey	J.	Summer	M	01/23/55
Conway	Ken	H.	Regular	M	08/04/62
Dempsey	Mary	C.	Regular	F	10/10/72

As you can see, the complete table is here because all of the character fields in the LNAME column are less than "Sm%".

Inequalities (<> or !=)
Inequalities is a handy operator when you want to find something that is not equal to a specific field or fields. For example:

```
SELECT * FROM Employees
WHERE FNAME <> 'C%';
```

The following is the result:

LNAME	FNAME	MINIT	STATUS	GENDER	BIRTHDATE
Baker	George	O.	Regular	M	06/24/60
Baker	Ramsey	J.	Summer	M	01/23/55
Conway	Ken	H.	Regular	M	08/04/62
Dempsey	Mary	C.	Regular	F	10/10/72

As you can see, Catherine Abbott is missing from the results.

Next you learn about changing your character strings through the use of character operators. You learn about LIKE, concatenation (||), and the underscore (_).

LIKE

How can LIKE help you? If you want to find a pattern of data, but you don't know what matches, you can use LIKE to solve this problem. LIKE is similar to the STARTING WITH clause you learned about earlier.

```
SELECT * FROM Employee
WHERE FNAME LIKE '%a%';
```

Here, the results are those with a first name that contains the letter *a*:

LNAME	FNAME	MINIT	STATUS	GENDER	BIRTHDATE
Abbott	Catherine	L.	Regular	F	11/01/58
Baker	Ramsey	J.	Summer	M	01/23/55
Dempsey	Mary	C.	Regular	F	10/10/72

Underscore (_)

Suppose you have a situation where you know all parts of the pattern except for one character. What would you do? You would use the *underscore operator*.

```
SELECT * FROM Employees
WHERE LNAME LIKE '_mith';
```

The result returns no rows for this statement.

Concatenation (| |)

The *concatenation operator* brings two or more character strings together. For example, the FNAME and LNAME columns from the Employees table would look much nicer if they were concatenated and a new column, Name, was created:

```
SELECT LNAME ||   || FNAME NAME
FROM Employees;
```

Here's the resulting column:

```
NAME
--------------------------
Abbott          Catherine
Baker           George
Baker           Ramsey
Conway          Ken
Dempsey         Mary
```

Do you notice the extra spaces between the LNAME and the FNAME? This is the actual field size of LNAME. Certain data types have right padding. You learn how to fix this later in this chapter.

PORTABILITY: Some DBMS vendors use the plus operator to represent concatenation. This is yet another use for the plus operator.

Other Operators (AND, OR, NOT, IN, BETWEEN)

When you need to use more than one condition, you can do so by using either AND or OR. Of course, the *AND operator* joins more than one condition in your SELECT statement. The *OR operator* says give me this condition or that condition. The following illustrates how they are used in SQL:

AND   This example illustrates the use of the AND operator:

```
SELECT LNAME from Employees
WHERE Birth_Date >= '1960,01,01'
AND
Birth_Date <= '1980,12,31';
```

This statement returns the following:

```
LNAME      FNAME      MINIT     STATUS     GENDER     BIRTHDATE
-----      -----      -----     ------     ------     ---------
Baker      George     O.        Regular    M          06/24/60
Conway     Ken        H.        Regular    M          08/04/62
Dempsey    Mary       C.        Regular    F          10/10/72
```

OR   The following example illustrates the OR operator at work:

```
SELECT * FROM Employees
WHERE Birth_Date > '1959,01,01'
OR
FNAME LIKE '%y%';
```

Here is the result:

LNAME	FNAME	MINIT	STATUS	GENDER	BIRTHDATE
Baker	George	O.	Regular	M	06/24/60
Baker	Ramsey	J.	Summer	M	01/23/55
Conway	Ken	H.	Regular	M	08/04/62
Dempsey	Mary	C.	Regular	F	10/10/72

Look what happens. Three employees have a birth date later than January 1, 1960 and one employee has a birthday on January 23, 1955. Does Ramsey Baker belong in this result? Not if you selected only birth date. However, you also selected LNAME containing a *y*. Mary Dempsey meets both conditions. Yet the others only meet one of the conditions, which is sufficient for an OR operator.

NOT   The *NOT operator* means the condition must not be true. For example:

```
SELECT * FROM Employees
WHERE Status NOT LIKE 'R%';
```

Here are the results:

LNAME	FNAME	MINIT	STATUS	GENDER	BIRTHDATE
Baker	Ramsey	J.	Summer	M	01/23/55

Set Operators
Set operators produce sets of data. The set operators are: UNION, UNION ALL, and INTERSECT.

3

UNION   The *UNION operator* returns the results of two or more queries minus the duplicate rows.

```
SELECT * FROM MC_SPA;

NAME
----
Andrew
Cary
Charlie
David
Larry
```

The following results include all rows from the Mc_Spa and the W_Spa tables:

```
SELECT * FROM W_SPA;

NAME
----
Betty
Cary
DiDi
Janet
Charlie
```

Do you have people who attend two spas?

```
SELECT Name FROM MC_SPA
UNION
SELECT Name FROM W_SPA;
```

The results are

```
NAME
----
Andrew
Cary
Charlie
David
Larry
Betty
DiDi
Janet
```

The UNION operator only returns eight names from the statement. No duplicates are listed. What if you wanted to see all members? Here is what you would do:

```
SELECT Name FROM MC_SPA
UNION ALL
SELECT Name FROM W_SPA;
```

Here you have everyone represented, duplicates and all:

```
NAME
----
Andrew
Cary
Charlie
David
Larry
Betty
Cary
DiDi
Janet
Charlie
```

NOTE: In the UNION and UNION ALL operators, you must have the same number of columns and the same data types in each table selected. If you do not, you will receive an error message. For example, if you requested

```
SELECT Name, SPA_ID FROM MC_Spa UNION SELECT Name FROM W_Spa;
```

You would receive an error message stating you did not have the proper number of columns.

The next operator is vital if you need to know who are members of both spas. For this answer, you need the INTERSECT operator.

INTERSECT   The *INTERSECT operator* returns only the rows found by both SELECT statements.

```
SELECT * from MC_Spa
INTERSECT
SELECT * from W_Spa;
```

```
NAME
----
Cary
Charlie
```

You can ask one last question about these two tables: "Who is in the Mc_Spa table and not in the W_Spa table?" The operator that provides the answer is MINUS.

```
SELECT * FROM Mc_Spa
MINUS
SELECT * FROM W_SPA;
```

Your answer is

```
NAME
----
Andrew
David
Larry
```

The final set of operators to be covered here are IN and BETWEEN.

IN   The IN operator is used in the same way as the OR operator, but it is easier to type. If you want to find out about profits in your regions:

```
SELECT * FROM ProfLoss
WHERE
Region IN ('North','South','West');
```

Here is your result using the IN operator:

```
REGION    MONTH      PROFIT_LOSS
------    -----      -----------
North     February         2,000
South     February        -1,000
West      February           500
```

You could achieve the same result by using the OR operator:

```
SELECT * FROM ProfLoss
WHERE
Region = 'North"'
```

```
OR
Region = 'South'
OR
Region = 'West';
```

As you can see, you need to type more to get the same results.

BETWEEN   The use of the BETWEEN operator is another way to reduce the amount of typing you need to do:

```
SELECT * FROM Employees
WHERE
Birth_Date BETWEEN '1960,01,01' AND '1962,12,31';
```

Or you could use

```
SELECT * FROM Employees
WHERE
Birth_Date >='1960,01,01'
AND
Birth_Date <= '1962,12,31';
```

The results are the same:

LNAME	FNAME	MINIT	STATUS	GENDER	BIRTHDATE
Baker	George	O.	Regular	M	06/24/60
Conway	Ken	H.	Regular	M	08/04/62

The BETWEEN operator is useful when you need a specific range of data. Remember, the range is inclusive.

NOTE: The NOT operator can be used with the following operators you have learned: NULL, LIKE, BETWEEN, IN.

TIP: Bookmark this chapter. It will be useful when you learn how to write queries.

Functions

Functions help you manipulate your data in various ways. This is the final section and also the most useful. What you learned in the first section on clauses will help you with the following grouping functions. The GROUP BY clause does not necessarily have to be present when these functions are used. The reason is grouping is assumed.

Grouping Functions

3

The five grouping functions are: COUNT, SUM, AVG, MAX, and MIN. These functions are represented in most DBMS SQL implementations.

The following table will be used to illustrate these five functions:

```
SELECT * FROM Antiques;

NAME            ACQ_DATE   PURCH_PRICE   CUR_VAL   SELL_PRICE   PREV_OWN
----            --------   -----------   -------   ----------   --------
Pers Rug         2/14/95         2,000    10,000       15,000          2
Vict Diam ring  12/23/95        15,000    20,000       30,000          6
Ming Vase        3/2/95         35,000    40,000       60,000          7
Pre-Col Figure   2/24/95         8,000    20,000       35,000         15
Walking Stick    7/4/96          1,000    10,000       25,000          7
Barbie Doll      3/5/97            400       500        2,000          1
1st Ed Dickens   9/9/96          3,000    20,000       35,000         12
```

COUNT

The *COUNT function* returns the number of rows that result from the condition in the WHERE clause. In this example, you want to know how many of the antiques are worth $5,000 or more in Current Value.

```
SELECT Count(*) Cur_Val_Over_5000 FROM Antiques
WHERE Cur_Value > 5000;
```

Your result:

```
CUR_VAL_OVER_5000
-----------------
                6
```

The WHERE clause creates the count of 6. If no WHERE clause existed, the field count would be 7.

SUM

The *SUM function* returns the sum of all values in a column. If you ask the question, "How much was originally spent to purchase this collection?" the SELECT statement would be

```
SELECT SUM(Pur_Price) TOTAL_EXPENSE, SUM(CUR_VALUE) TOTAL_VALUE
FROM Antiques;
```

Your totals would be

```
TOTAL_EXPENSE        TOTAL_VALUE
-------------        -----------
       64,004            120,500
```

This represents a pretty good investment. In fact, what is your profit?

```
SELECT (TOTAL_VALUE - TOTAL_EXPENSE) PROFIT
FROM Antiques;
```

The resulting profits are fantastic:

```
PROFIT
------
56,496
```

Who wants to go antique hunting?

NOTE: The SUM function works only with numbers.

AVG

The *AVG function* is the average of a column. Using the Antiques table, find the average for the Pur_Price column.

```
SELECT AVG(Pur_Price) Avg_Pur_Price
FROM Antiques;
```

The average is

```
AVG_PUR_PRICE
-------------
        9,143
```

Now suppose you want to know what the average profit is? You need to do the following:

```
SELECT AVG(Cur_Value)-AVG(Pur_Price) Avg_Profit
FROM Antiques;
```

The average profit is

```
AVG_PROFIT
----------
     8,071
```

NOTE: The AVG function only works with numbers.

MAX

As the name infers, the *MAX function* finds the largest value in the column chosen. If you want to know the largest/highest amount of an item purchased, the SELECT statement would be

```
SELECT MAX(Pur_Price)
FROM Antiques;
```

This might seem easy and trivial because you could always eyeball the Antiques table to get the answer. However, most tables in a database are larger than several rows, so this is quite useful.

Here is the maximum purchase price:

```
MAX(PUR_PRICE)
--------------
        35,000
```

3

NOTE: Have you noticed a clause missing in the last few illustrations? If you answered the WHERE clause is missing, you are correct. Do you know why the WHERE clause is missing? It is because the WHERE clause does not work with grouping clauses or functions.

MIN

The *MIN function* works like the MAX function, except it gives you the lowest value of the column. Thus, if you need to know the antique with the lowest number of prior owners, you would

```
SELECT MIN(Prev_Owner), Name
FROM Antiques;

MIN(PREV_OWNER)       NAME
---------------       ----
              1       Barbie Doll
```

NOTE: Both MIN and MAX functions can be used with either numbers or characters.

Date and Time Functions

You can still use the Antiques table to illustrate the date and time functions.

NEXT_DAY

The *NEXT_DAY function* finds the first day of the week that is equal to or later than the date defined. For example, you have to provide a report on Mondays:

```
SELECT ACQ_DATE, NEXT_DAY(ACQ_DATE, 'Monday')
FROM Antiques;
```

The following provides the next day for the Acq_Date:

```
ACQ_DATE      NEXT DAY
--------      --------
 2/14/95       2/20/95
12/23/95      12/25/95
  3/2/95        3/6/95
```

```
2/24/95      2/27/95
 7/4/96       7/8/96
 3/5/97      3/10/96
 9/9/96      9/16/96
```

ADD_MONTHS

The *ADD_MONTHS function* is self-explanatory; it adds months to your date type column. For instance, you want to add three months to your Acq_Date. Why? To provide an example of this function from the Antiques table.

3

```
SELECT Name, Acq_Date, ADD_MONTHS(Acq_Date,3) New_Acq_Date
FROM Antiques;
```

The results are

```
ACQ_DATE     NEW_ACQ_DATE
--------     ------------
 2/14/95        5/14/95
12/23/95        3/23/96
 3/2/95         6/2/95
 2/24/95        5/24/95
 7/4/96        10/4/96
 3/5/97         6/5/96
 9/9/96        12/9/96
```

MONTHS_BETWEEN

The *MONTHS_BETWEEN function* provides the months between *x* date and *y* date. You will use these columns to provide the two dates: Acq_Date and New_Acq_Date. You already know the outcome.

```
SELECT Name, Acq_Date, New_Acq_Date,
MONTHS_BETWEEN(New_Acq_Date,Acq_Date) Difference
FROM Antiques;
```

NAME	DIFFERENCE	ACQ_DATE	NEW_ACQ_DATE
Pers Rug	3	2/14/95	5/14/95
Vict Diam ring	3	12/23/95	3/23/96
Ming Vase	3	3/2/95	6/2/95
Pre-Col Figure	3	2/24/95	5/24/95
Walking Stick	3	7/4/96	10/4/96
Barbie Doll	3	3/5/97	6/5/96
1st Ed Dickens	3	9/9/96	12/9/96

LAST_DAY

This is the final date function covered in this chapter. The *LAST_DAY function* returns the last day of the month. If you want to know the last day of the month for Acq_Date, you would

```
SELECT Name, Acq_Date, LAST_DAY(Acq_Date)
FROM Antiques;
```

NAME	ACQ_DATE	LAST_DAY(ACQ_DATE)
Pers Rug	2/14/95	2/28/95
Vict Diam ring	12/23/95	12/31/96
Ming Vase	3/2/95	3/31/95
Pre-Col Figure	2/24/95	2/28/95
Walking Stick	7/4/96	7/31/96
Barbie Doll	3/5/97	3/31/97
1st Ed Dickens	9/9/96	9/30/96

Mathematical Functions

Most of the data you deal with in databases are numbers, so learning these mathematical functions will help in your daily tasks. For these examples, the JustNumbers table is used.

```
SELECT *
FROM JustNumbers;
```

POS_NUMBERS	NEG_NUMBERS	DEC_NUMBERS
10	-20	10.34
20	-40	20.115
30	-60	30.01
40	-80	40.3
50	-50	50.555

ABS

The *ABS function* provides the absolute value of the number. To illustrate:

```
SELECT ABS(Neg_Numbers) Absolute
FROM JustNumbers;
```

The results are

```
ABSOLUTE
--------
      20
      40
      60
      80
     100
```

As you can see, it returned positive numbers for all the negative numbers.

CEIL and FLOOR

The *CEIL function* gives you the smallest integer greater or equal to the argument. The *FLOOR function* is the opposite, giving you the largest integer equal or less than the argument. Here's an example of the CEIL function at work:

```
SELECT Dec_Numbers, CEIL(Dec_Numbers) Ceiling
FROM JustNumbers;

DEC_NUMBERS    CEILING
-----------    -------
      10.34         11
      20.115        21
      30.01         31
      40.3          41
      50.555        51
```

And here's an example of FLOOR:

```
SELECT Dec_Numbers, FLOOR(Dec_Numbers) FLOOR
FROM JustNumbers;

DEC_NUMBERS    FLOOR
-----------    -----
      10.34       10
      20.115      20
      30.01       30
      40.3        40
      50.555      50
```

EXP

The *EXP function* enables you to raise *e* (mathematical constant) to a power. The following example takes Pos_Number to the EXP:

```
SELECT Pos_Number, EXP(Pos_Number) EXP
FROM JustNumbers;

DEC_NUMBERS                       EXP
-----------      ----------------------
      10.34             22026.46579
     20.115            485165195.40979
     30.01           10686474581524.5
     40.3        235385266837020000.0
     50.555   5184705528587070000000.0
```

MOD

The *MOD function* enables you to show the remainder of *A* divided by *B*. Here you use

```
SELECT Pos_Number, Dec_Number, Mod(Dec_Number,Pos_Number)
FROM JustNumbers;

POS_NUMBERS      DEC_NUMBERS       MOD
-----------      -----------     ------
         10            10.34      0.34
         20           20.115      0.115
         30            30.01      0.01
         40            40.3       0.3
         50           50.555      0.555
```

POWER

The *POWER function* raises one number to the power of another. In this example, Pos_Number is raised to the power of the Neg_Number:

```
SELECT Pos_Number, Neg_Number, POWER(Pos_Number,Neg_Number)
FROM JustNumbers;

Pos_Numbers  Neg_Numbers                                            Power
-----------  -----------  -------------------------------------------------
         10          -20                             10240000000000
         20          -40               1099511627776000000000000000000000
         30          -60    2210739197207330000000000000000000000000000000
                           0000000000000000
         40          -80    1329227995784920000000000000000000000000000000
```

```
                             000000000000000000000000000000000
    50              -50   88817841970012500000000000000000000000000000
                             000000000000000000000000000000000000000000
```

SIGN

The *SIGN function* returns –1 if the argument is less than 0, 0 if its arguments is equal to 0, and 1 if the argument is greater than 0, for example:

```
SELECT Dec_Number, SIGN(Dec_Number)
FROM JustNumbers;

DEC_NUMBERS     SIGN
-----------     ----
     10.34        1
     20.115       1
     30.01        1
     40.3         1
     50.555       1
```

SQRT

The *SQRT function* gives you the square root of an argument. To illustrate, we'll use the Pos_Number column:

```
SELECT Pos_Number, SQRT(Pos_Number)
FROM JustNumbers;

Pos_Numbers      SQRT(Pos_Number)
-----------      ----------------
     10               3.16227766
     20               4.472135955
     30               5.477225575
     40               6.32455532
     50               7.071067812
```

NOTE: This function cannot work with negative numbers.

LN and LOG

You think of logarithms when you use these two functions. The *LN function* returns the natural logarithm of its argument. On the other hand, the *LOG function* takes two arguments and returns the first argument in the base of the second. Are you ready for examples?

The LN function example uses only one argument:

```
SELECT Pos_Number, LN(Pos_Number)
FROM JustNumbers;

Pos_Numbers     LN(Pos_Number)
-----------     --------------
        10        2.302585093
        20        2.995732274
        30        3.401197382
        40        3.688879454
        50        3.912023005
```

NOTE: LN requires the numbers to be positive.

The LOG function example requires two arguments:

```
SELECT Pos_Numbers, LOG(Pos_Numbers, 10)
FROM JustNumbers;

Pos_Numbers     LOG(Pos_Number)
-----------     --------------
        10                    1
        20          1.301029996
        30          1.477121255
        40          1.602059991
        50          1.698970004
```

Character Functions

Aren't you glad you are finished with mathematical functions? Now, here are some fun ways to manipulate your characters and strings of characters.

CONCAT

If this looks familiar, it should! You learned about the concatenation operator in the previous section. CONCAT is a function that joins two or more strings together. Here is the example:

```
SELECT CONCAT(LNAME,FNAME) 'NAME'
FROM Employees;
```

Here is what the CONCAT function does to these two strings:

```
NAME
---------------------------------
Abbott                   Catherine
Baker                    George
Baker                    Ramsey
Conway                   Ken
Dempsey                    Mary
```

The LNAME field is 25 characters long and the FNAME field is 12 characters long. One way to eliminate this padding is to use either of the next two functions, RTRIM and LTRIM.

LTRIM and RTRIM

Trimming the excess padding from your fields is simple:

```
SELECT RTRIM(LNAME)
FROM Employees;
```

Here, the padding is removed from the right of LNAME:

```
RTRIM(LNAME)
------------
Abbott
Baker
Baker
Conway
Dempsey
```

Now use LTRIM on LNAME:

```
SELECT LTRIM(LNAME)
FROM Employees;
```

The *LTRIM* works exactly like *RTRIM* except the padding is removed from the left side. Now go back to LNAME and concatenate and trim to provide a sleek-looking column, Name:

```
SELECT CONCAT(RTRIM(LNAME)(LTRIM(FNAME)) 'NAME'
FROM Employees;
```

In this example, the padding is removed from the right of the LNAME and left of the FNAME:

```
NAME
----
AbbottCatherine
BakerGeorge
BakerRamsey
ConwayKen
DempseyMary
```

All spaces from both columns are removed.

PORTABILITY: Be sure to check your DBMS vendor documentation for proper use of these functions. For example, in Oracle8, the syntax is as follows:

```
LTRIM(char[,set] or RTRIM(char[,]
```

Also, || is the preferred method for concatenation in Oracle8. When using the concatenation function in Oracle8, the padding is eliminated. For example:

```
SELECT Concat(concat(LNAME, ' ,'),FNAME) "NAME"
from Employees;
```

In this example, a comma is added to the CONCAT function:

```
NAME
----
Abbott, Catherine
Baker, George
Baker, Ramsey
Conway, Ken
Dempsey, Mary
```

Lower and Upper

The *LOWER function* changes all the characters in a column to lowercase. The *UPPER function* changes all the characters in a column to uppercase. Such as:

```
SELECT UPPER(LNAME), LOWER(FNAME)
FROM Employees;
```

In this example, the LNAME is all uppercase and the FNAME is all lowercase:

```
LNAME     FNAME
-----     -----
BAKER     george
BAKER     ramsey
CONWAY    ken
DEMPSEY   mary
```

Substring

The *substring function* (SUBSTR) takes one or many characters out of your string. You can substring the FNAME:

```
SELECT SUBSTR(FNAME,1,1)
FROM Employees;

SUBSTR(FNAME)
-------------
G
R
K
M
```

What has happened is the first argument tells you the column, the second argument tells you what is the first output character, and the third argument tells you how many characters to show. Let's try another one:

```
SELECT LNAME, SUBSTR(LNAME,2,2)
FROM Employees;
```

Note the use of the substring function in these results:

```
LNAME     SUBSTR(LNAME)
-----     -------------
Baker     Ke
Baker     Ke
Conway    Nw
Dempsey   Mp
```

Replace

The *REPLACE function* has three arguments: The first is the string to be searched, the second is the search key, and the third is the replacement string. The last argument is optional and if it is NULL or not used, the search key on the string to be searched is removed and not replaced with anything.

```
SELECT LNAME, REPLACE(LNAME, 'n') REPLACED
FROM Employees;
```

As you can see, the *n* was in Conway and the search string found it and left it out because no replacement argument was given:

```
LNAME      REPLACED
-----      --------
Baker      Baker
Baker      Baker
Conway     Coway
Dempsey    Dempsey
```

Length

The *LENGTH function* tells you how long the column is in the argument. For instance:

```
SELECT LNAME, LENGTH(LNAME)
FROM Employees;
```

Look at these results; does something look strange to you?

```
LNAME      LENGTH(LNAME)
-----      -------------
Baker                 25
Baker                 25
Conway                25
Dempsey               25
```

Well, it does. Yet it gave you exactly what you requested. To get a true measure of the length of the LNAME, you must:

```
SELECT LNAME, LENGTH(RTRIM(LNAME))
FROM Employees;
```

These results are much better, aren't they?

```
LNAME       LENGTH(LNAME)
-----       -------------
Baker                   5
Baker                   5
Conway                  6
Dempsey                 7
```

In the first SELECT statement, you requested the length of the column, which is 25—the full length, including spaces. You need to use a RTRIM function to get the actual length of the LNAME values without spaces.

Conversion Functions

The two conversion functions TO_CHAR and TO_NUMBER change numbers to characters and characters to numbers.

TO_CHAR

The *TO_CHAR function* converts numbers to characters. This is a useful function when you create queries and reports. Here's an example. First, let's see what the TESTGRP looks like before you change it:

```
SELECT * FROM TESTGRP;

NUMBER_STRING    TESTNUM
-------------    -------
           30         40
           20         60
```

The next SELECT statement converts a number to a character field and then performs the substring function.

```
SELECT TESTNUM, SUBSTR(TO_CHAR(TESTNUM),1,1)
FROM TESTGRP;
```

You can see that the TO_CHAR function worked. If it didn't you would not have been able to perform a substring function on a number field.

```
TESTNUM    SUBSTR(TO_CHAR(TESTNUM),1,1)
-------    ----------------------------
     40                               4
     61                               6
```

Remember, SUBSTR can only be used on a character or character string.

TO_NUMBER

The TO_NUMBER function converts characters to numbers. Look at this example:

```
SELECT TESTNUM, SUM(TO_NUMBER(NUMBER_STRING)) 'SUM'
FROM TESTGRP;
```

The results provide a summed number:

```
SUM
---
100
```

Again, this function worked successfully. Otherwise, you wouldn't have been able to SUM a character.

What's Next?

This chapter has instructed you in the basics of the SQL language. You studied clauses, conditions, expressions, operators, and functions. These are the building blocks of the SQL language. You now have the tools to build queries and manipulate the data stored in databases.

You will use what you have learned here throughout the rest of this book. The next chapter provides you with practical experience in the creating of tables and views using Oracle. The project in Part III provides additional experience creating tables and views in Access and SQL Server 7.0.

CHAPTER 4

Building Tables and Views

This chapter takes you through building tables and views using Oracle8 Personal Edition. Although the Personal Edition is not a server, you can design and develop database objects, such as tables, views, indexes, and synonyms. Oracle8 Personal Edition is the perfect tool for this chapter's lessons. To download a 30-day trial version of this product, go to www.oracle.com/products/trial/html/trial.html.

Overview of Oracle8

Oracle Corporation has come a long way since it beat IBM to the market with the first vendor DBMS. The company name was Relational Software Inc. back then, and it hasn't lost its fervor to be the first vendor out with the latest technology.

Today, Oracle is dedicated to the Network Computing Architecture (NCA), which provides a cross-platform environment for developing and deploying network-centered applications. Oracle offers the developer a large tool chest for developing databases.

Oracle8 delivers easy-to-use features for distributed work-group computing. It is a universal data server that is the foundation of the NCA. Oracle8 focuses on online transaction processing (OLTP) and data warehouse requirements. Oracle8 can scale to support over 10,000 users and support a database of over 100 terabytes (a terabyte is 1,048,576,000,000 bytes) in size. This is a *very large database* (VLDB) indeed.

The following are the tools and utilities in Oracle8:

◆ The SQL database language enables you to store and retrieve data in Oracle databases. *SQL*Plus* is the primary ad hoc access tool to Oracle8. It supports the SQL syntax for creating object tables using the newly defined object types, as well as all the new DML syntax to access the object tables. *PL/SQL* enables you to link several SQL commands through procedural logic. Chapter 18 covers SQL*Plus and Chapter 19 covers PL/SQL in more detail.

◆ *Oracle8 Enterprise Manager* (OEM) is Oracle8's framework for managing the Oracle environment. OEM supports the new features, such as partitioning, queuing, password management, and server managed backup and recovery. The OEM provides graphical user interface for all OEM functions. The Backup Manager is speedier and more secure.

◆ *Designer/2000* is the business application modeling tool that can generate complete applications from these models. Designer/2000 generates and reverse engineers Oracle database objects, Developer/2000 client/server and Web applications, Visual basic applications, and C++ mappings for database objects.

◆ *Object Database Designer* aids in the design, creation and access of object relational database management systems (ORDBMSs).

◆ *Developer/2000* is a client/server and Web development tool for building scalable database applications. The common programming language used is PL/SQL. These applications can be used in two-tier or multitier architectures in a client/server or Web environment.

4

◆ *Sedona* is the development environment for building component-based applications. This toolpack from Oracle makes Oracle8 a powerful database, which explains why Oracle has a large share of the database market.

◆ In Personal Oracle8, *Oracle Navigator* is a GUI application that can perform most database administration tasks. You use this application to create tables and views.

Building Tables with Oracle8

Your assignment is to create three tables. You create the first table using SQL*Plus. You create the second table using the Oracle Navigator Table Wizard. You create the third table manually, using the Navigator.

Before you delve into this assignment, a review of tables is warranted.

What Is a Table?

A *table* is a multiset of rows. It is a two-dimensional array of rows and columns. A table is a base table, defined by a table definition, a derived table, derived from one or more tables by the evaluation of a query, or a viewed table (view), a named derived table listed in the data dictionary of the database.

A table is usually independent of other tables in the database. Most tables include a primary or foreign key. The *primary key* ensures every row in your table is unique and a primary key cannot contain a null value. A *foreign key* is a column that is a key in one or more tables other than the one where it appears. Most tables should be of the third normal form. A *third normal form table* is a table free of redundant data.

Before you begin building tables, you need to analyze the business needs of your client. Why do you need to build the tables? What is the data to be contained in these tables? How will this data be used? Needs assessment is covered in more depth in a later chapter. For now, use the following information to build your tables.

Needs Assessment

Your client is Joe Snoop, owner of Hush Detective Agency. This agency is a small firm that requires a database to track clients, cases, and suspects. Mr. Snoop requests a simple database that enables his detectives to enter their own clients and cases. The client information required is personal information, such as name, address, and telephone number. The case information needed is case ID, case name, client ID, type of case (murder, missing person, divorce, corporate espionage, or employee background check), date case opened, date case closed, and case description. The suspect information is suspect ID, suspect name, case ID, prior criminal record, on parole, parole officer, suspect address, and evidence.

Of course, security is an issue, so Mr. Snoop would like access to all records. His other detectives should have the same access. They also want to have reports based on all open and closed cases, client lists, the suspect list for each case, and so on.

Are you ready to begin?

Create Tables

The first table is the Client table. Here you will use SQL*Plus to create the table. The first step is to start SQL*Plus and get connected to the database as shown in Figure 4-1.

Once connected, you begin by typing the following:

```
Create table Client
(client_id number(10)not null,
last_name varchar2(30),
first_name varchar2(15),
m_init varchar2(1),
address_1 varchar2(30),
address_2 varchar2(30),
city varchar2(15),
state varchar2(2),
zip_code number(5),
area_code varchar2(5),
phone_number varchar2(8));
```

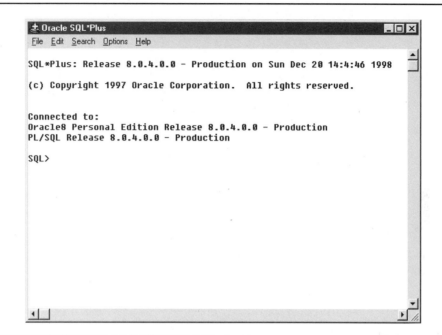

**SQL*Plus
connection
window**

Figure 4-1.

To run the statement, you may use a semicolon (;) or a slash (/). The SQL*Plus statement is shown in Figure 4-2.

If you want to check your table, you can type:

```
Desc Client;
```

SQL*Plus then describes your table as you can see in Figure 4-3:

You have just created one table. The "create table" statement gives the table and each of its columns a name and determines the data type of each column. The following is a list of a few of the data types available in Oracle:

◆ **Char**   Stores fixed length character data, maximum size is 2,000

◆ **Varchar2**   Stores variable-length character data, maximum size is 4,000

◆ **Varchar**   Same as Char

◆ **Date**   Stores dates from January 1, 4712 B.C. to December 31, 4712 A.D.

◆ **Long**   Stores variable-length character data up to 2 gigabytes

```
± Oracle SQL*Plus                                          _ □ ×
 File  Edit  Search  Options  Help
ERROR at line 12:
ORA-00922: missing or invalid option


SQL>
Wrote file afiedt.buf

  1   create table client
  2   (client_id number(10) not null,
  3   last_name  varchar2(30),
  4   first_name varchar2(15),
  5   m_init varchar2(1),
  6   address_1 varchar2(30),
  7   address_2 varchar2(30),
  8   city varchar2(15),
  9   state varchar2(2),
 10   zip_code number(5),
 11   area_code varchar2(5),
 12*  phone_number varchar2(8))
SQL> /

Table created.

SQL>
```

Creating a
table in
SQL*Plus

Figure 4-2.

```
± Oracle SQL*Plus                                          _ □ ×
 File  Edit  Search  Options  Help
  9   state varchar2(2),
 10   zip_code number(5),
 11   area_code varchar2(5),
 12*  phone_number varchar2(8))
SQL> /

Table created.

SQL> desc client;
 Name                            Null?     Type
 ------------------------------- --------  ----
 CLIENT_ID                       NOT NULL  NUMBER(10)
 LAST_NAME                                 VARCHAR2(30)
 FIRST_NAME                                VARCHAR2(15)
 M_INIT                                    VARCHAR2(1)
 ADDRESS_1                                 VARCHAR2(30)
 ADDRESS_2                                 VARCHAR2(30)
 CITY                                      VARCHAR2(15)
 STATE                                     VARCHAR2(2)
 ZIP_CODE                                  NUMBER(5)
 AREA_CODE                                 VARCHAR2(5)
 PHONE_NUMBER                              VARCHAR2(8)

SQL> |
```

Client table
description

Figure 4-3.

◆ **Raw**   Raw binary data with a maximum length of 2,000 bytes

◆ **Blob**   A binary large object, maximum size is 4 gigabytes

◆ **Number(l,d)**   Stores numeric data, *l* stands for length and *d* stands for the number of decimal digits

Your second table is the Case table. You will use the Oracle Navigator Table Wizard to produce this table. Open the Oracle Navigator, and then follow these steps:

1. Double-click the Personal Oracle Database folder. The tree will expand.
2. Choose Table and double-click to expand the tree.
3. Click New Object Icon on Toolbar.
4. The New Table dialog box will appear, as shown here:

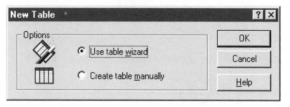

The default is for wizard. Click OK.

5. In Table Wizard - Page 1 of 7, enter the table name and owner of the table, as shown here:

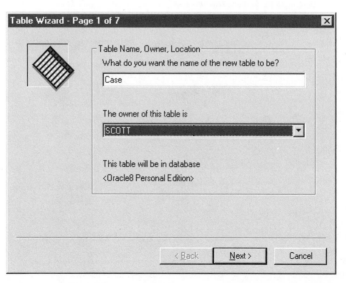

6. The next page of the wizard, shown here, begins the column descriptions. Type Column Name, use the drop-down list for Column Type, and enter a Size for the column. To create a new column, click the New button. When you finish entering each column, click the Next button.

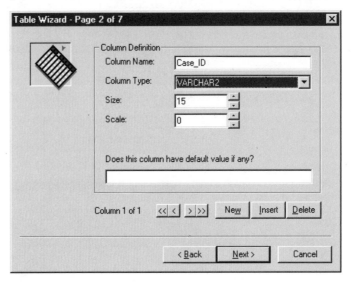

7. On Page 3 of the Table Wizard, shown next, choose whether your columns shall be null values or unique. You must answer the questions for each column. Notice the directional arrows next to Column 1 of 1. Use these arrows to move through the columns. Click the Next button to go to the next page.

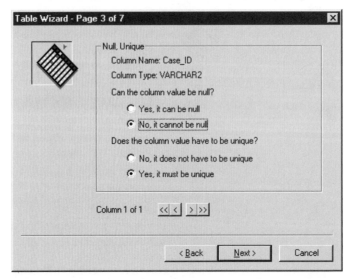

8. Page 4 requests information about foreign keys and the check condition for the column. You may assign a foreign key for your other columns by using the directional arrows next to Column 1 of 1. Click the Next button to go to the next page.

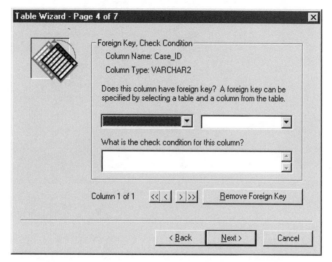

9. Page 5, shown here, asks if you would like to assign a primary key to this table. You only need to complete this page once. If you have more than one primary key, you may click the primary key field of each column to designate the position of the column in the primary key.

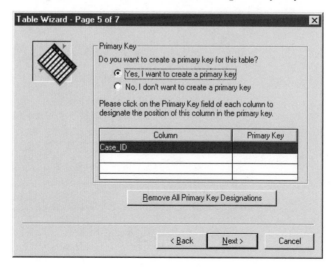

10. Page 6 shows you the columns you have created and enables you to order your columns by selecting a column and moving it up or down.

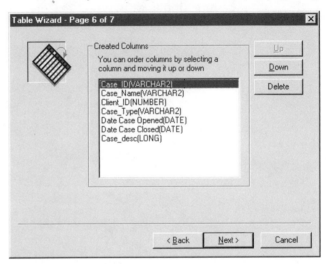

11. Page 7 is the end of the table creation. You have a choice of adding the data now or waiting until later. The default is to add the data. Choose No and click the Finish button.

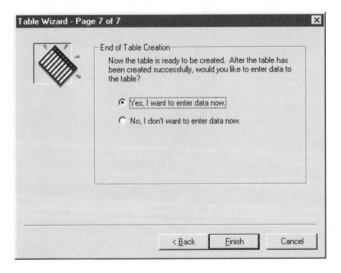

Now you have finished the Case table.

If you go to the Oracle Navigator window and double-click the Table folder, the tree will expand and you will see your new table, Case. Select Case, right-click, and choose Properties. Click the Design tab and you will see the table design of Case, as shown in Figure 4-4.

The SQL*Plus code would be

```
Create table Case
(Case_ID varchar2(15) unique not null,
Case_Name varchar2(30),
Client_ID Number(10) not null,
Case_Type varchar2(20),
Date_Case_Opened Date,
Date_Case_Closed Date,
Detective_ID Number,
Case_Desc Long);
```

4

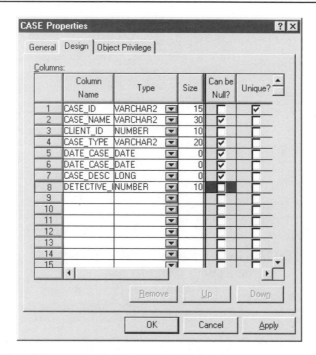

Properties of
the Case table

Figure 4-4.

The next table you need to create is the Suspect table. Here you manually create the table using Oracle8 Navigator. The procedure is quite simple.

1. Double-click the Personal Oracle Database folder. The tree will expand.
2. Choose Table and double-click to expand the tree.
3. Click New Object icon on the toolbar.
4. The New Table window will appear. The default is for wizard. Select Create Table Manually.
5. In the New Table Properties window, enter **Suspect** for Name and enter **SCOTT** for Owner, as shown here. When you finish entering the information, click the Design tab.

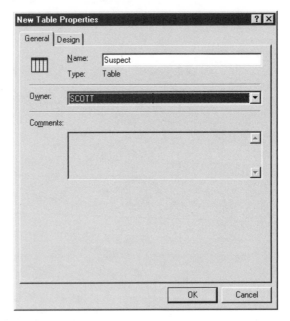

6. This Design area is where you enter all your column information for the Suspect table, as shown next.

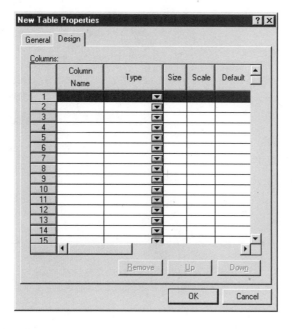

The completed Suspect table's properties are shown in Figure 4-5.

The SQL*Plus code for this table is

```
Create table Suspect
(Suspect_ID Number(10) not null,
Case_ID Varchar2(15) not null,
Suspect_LNAME Varchar2(25),
Suspect_FNAME Varchar2(15),
Prior_Crim_Rec char(1),
On_Parole char(1),
Parole_Officer varchar2(25),
Sus_addr_1 varchar2(30),
Sus_addr_2 varchar2(30),
Sus_City varchar2(20),
Sus_state char(2),
Sus_zip number(5),
Sus_area_Cde varchar2(5),
Sus_Phone_No varchar2(8)
Evidence Long);
```

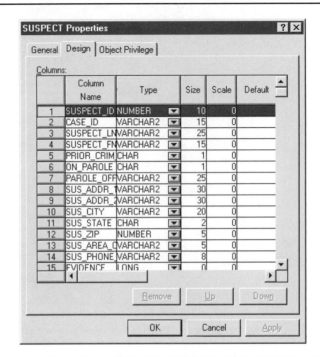

Properties
of the
Suspect table
Figure 4-5.

As the preceding steps have shown, Oracle gives you three ways to create
tables. Choose the one that fits your needs. In addition, you can populate
tables in two different ways. You can use the INSERT command, which is part
of SQL's DML, or you can use the Design tab of the Properties window to
insert your rows of data. For example, to use the INSERT command in
SQL*Plus, you enter:

```
Insert into Client values
(4,'McDonald','Bridget','M','123 Pinter St','NA','Boston','MA',02126,'(605)','555-1098');
Commit;
```

Figure 4-6 shows the results of this INSERT command.

▥ CLIENT						_ ▢ ✕
	CLIENT_ID	LAST_NAME	FIRST_NAME	M_INIT	ADDRESS_1	AD
1	1	Purdue	Clara	S	234 First Ave	
2	2	Stratton	Norman	W	450 Longacre Way	Apt B
3	3	Fullmer	Stanton	E	9 Stratton Place	Suite 200
4	4	McDonald	Bridget	M	123 Pinter St	NA

Client table
with new row
added

Figure 4-6.

4

Another way to insert into the table is to use the Properties Design feature in Oracle8 Navigator:

1. Open the Client table and click the right mouse button. Select Insert After to enter a new row, as shown here.

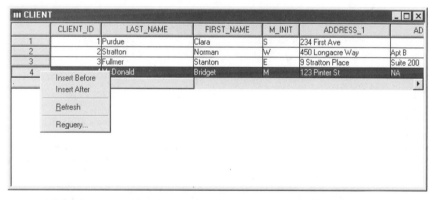

2. Enter the new row of information and then close the table. To close the table, click the × in the upper right corner of the window. This will commit the row.

3. Reopen the table and you see the new row has been added, as shown next.

	CLIENT_ID	LAST_NAME	FIRST_NAME	M_INIT	ADDRESS_1	
1	1	Purdue	Clara	S	234 First Ave	
2	2	Stratton	Norman	W	450 Longacre Way	A
3	3	Fullmer	Stanton	E	9 Stratton Place	S
4	4	McDonald	Bridget	M	123 Pinter St	N
5	5	Strazinski	Igor	V	77 Claremont Drive	

Now that you have created these tables, you need to assign security. You will assign Joe Snoop access to select any table. This gives Joe the privilege to look at all three tables and all the data. You can achieve this through the SQL GRANT command.

```
GRANT SELECT,UPDATE
ON SCOTT.CLIENT
TO SNOOP;

GRANT SELECT,UPDATE
ON SCOTT.CASE
TO SNOOP;

GRANT SELECT,UPDATE
ON SCOTT.SUSPECT
TO SNOOP;
```

Granting the DELETE option to a user is unwise. This should be reserved for the DBA, for the sake of maintaining referential integrity.

Views—Virtual Tables

You will create a few views to provide an environment for report generation. A *view* also adds security because you can choose which columns the user can view. For instance, if you create a view for the detectives, you may not want the detectives to know each other's cases. In this case, you could restrict access based on the Case.Detective_ID column. You will create views named Detective_View_One and Detective_View_Two, which will allow detectives to see their own clients and suspects.

Here is the SQL for Detective_View_One:

```
Create View Detective_View_One as
Select Client.Client_ID, Client.Last_Name, Client.First_Name, Client.M_Init,
Case.Case_ID, Case.Case_Name, Case.Date_Case_Opened, Case.Date_Case_Closed,
Case.Case_Desc, Suspect.Suspect_LNAME, Suspect.Suspect_FNAME, Suspect.Evidence
FROM Scott.CLIENT Client, Scott.CASE Case, Scott.SUSPECT Suspect
'Scott is the owner of the tables
WHERE Client.Client_ID = Case.Client_ID and
Case.Case_ID = Suspect.Case_ID (+) and
Detective_ID = 20;
```

4

This view includes a left outer join for Case.Case_ID and Suspect.Case_ID.
This query requests all rows from the Case table and from the Suspect table.
Only the rows where the Case ID is the same as the Case.Case_ID will appear.
As you can see here, only one match occurs from this query:

The SQL for Detective_View_Two is almost the same, except the
Detective_ID is 30:

```
Create View Detective_View_Two as
Select Client.Client_ID, Client.Last_Name, Client.First_Name, Client.M_Init,
Case.Case_ID, Case.Case_Name, Case.Date_Case_Opened, Case.Date_Case_Closed,
Case.Case_Desc, Suspect.Suspect_LNAME, Suspect.Suspect_FNAME, Suspect.Evidence
FROM Scott.CLIENT Client, Scott.CASE Case, Scott.SUSPECT Suspect
WHERE Client.Client_ID = Case.Client_ID and
Case.Case_ID = Suspect.Case_ID (+) and
Detective_ID = 30;
```

Here are the results obtained by the Detective_View_Two:

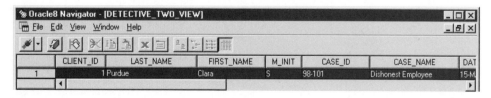

NOTE: Remember, as useful as views can be, some drawbacks also exist. You cannot update records in your views and you cannot use the DELETE statement on multiple table views.

You can also create views using the Oracle Navigator, as explained in the following steps.

1. To begin, double-click the View folder to expand the tree. Click the New Object icon, located at the far left of the toolbar, as shown here:

New Object button

You now have the New View Properties window open.

2. Enter **SNOOP** in the Name field and **SCOTT** in the Owner field, as shown here. Click the Design tab.

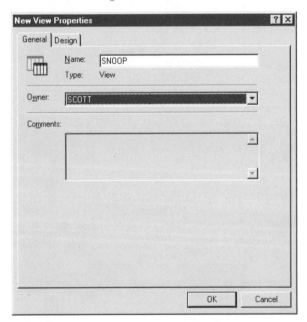

3. You will be prompted for a password. Enter **Tiger** and click OK.

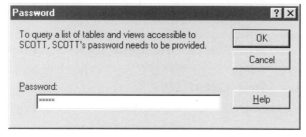

4. On the Design tab, choose <Oracle8 Personal Edition> for your database.

5. For Source Tables and Columns, double-click SCOTT to expand the tree.

6. Double-click CASE. This reveals the columns (see Figure 4-7).

7. Double-click Case_ID, Case_Name, Case_Type, Date_Case_Opened, Date_Case_Closed, Case_Desc, Detective_ID, and Client_ID. As you double-click, the columns are entered into the Selected Columns area.

8. Double-click Client. This reveals the columns.

4

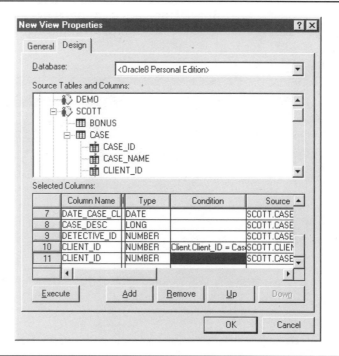

Design tab of the New View Properties window

Figure 4-7.

9. Double-click Last_Name, First_Name, M_Init, and Client_ID.

10. Under Selected Columns, go to Client.Case_ID and in the Condition field enter **Client.Client_ID = Case.Client_ID**.

11. Select Client_ID for Case. In the New Name Column, enter **Case_Client_ID**.

12. Click the Execute button.

The view results and SQL statement are shown in Figure 4-8.

The SQL*Plus code is

```
Create view SNOOP as
SELECT SCOTT.CLIENT.LAST_NAME, SCOTT.CLIENT.FIRST_NAME, SCOTT.CLIENT.M_INIT,
SCOTT.CASE.CASE_NAME, SCOTT.CASE.CASE_TYPE, SCOTT.CASE.DATE_CASE_OPENED,
SCOTT.CASE.DATE_CASE_CLOSED, SCOTT.CASE.CASE_DESC, SCOTT.CASE.DETECTIVE_ID,
SCOTT.CLIENT.CLIENT_ID, SCOTT.CASE.CLIENT_ID FROM SCOTT.CLIENT, SCOTT.CASE WHERE
Client.Client_ID = Case.Client_ID;
```

Oracle8 Personal Edition provides the tools you need to create your tables and views. Yet, even though Oracle8 was released about one year ago, Oracle is on the forefront of emerging technology with the release of Oracle8i. *Oracle8i* is the database for Internet computing.

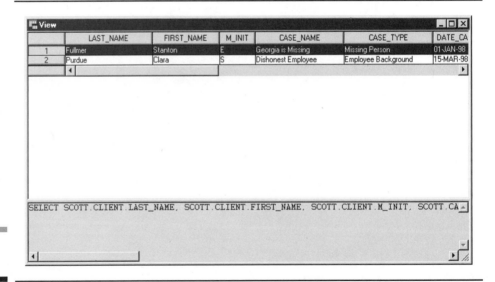

View results

Figure 4-8.

Oracle8i is a database server, a Web server, a file server, and an application server. Oracle8i could be the best relational database yet. Oracle has added the following to the Oracle8 core:

◆ **An HTTP engine** You can process HTTP requests and server Web pages.

◆ **An Internet File Server (iFS)** Users can store files: Web pages, documents, spreadsheets, and images. Files in the database can also be accessed over the Internet using a standard URL. All of these files get the same security, recovery, and transaction services that come with the standard Oracle8.

◆ **Multimedia Content Management** Oracle interMedia services can manage and interpret multimedia content for storage in Oracle8i.

◆ **A Java Virtual Machine** You can write stored procedures using Java or PL/SQL. Oracle is an Enterprise JavaBeans (EJB)-compliant Java application server. *JavaBeans* is a component model that enables application developers to develop applications and package them as components. These can be assembled with components created by other developers to build complete applications.

4

What this means to the business world is an infrastructure platform exists that meets the performance, scalability, and availability requirements of the Internet. Keep an eye on Oracle. This company will continue to lead you into the future.

You have learned how to create tables and views using both SQL*Plus and Oracle8 Navigator. In following chapters, you learn to create a database and all its tables and views using Access.

CHAPTER 5

Transaction
Management

In Chapter 1, you got a glimpse of what transactions could do. Remember the ROLLBACK and COMMIT commands? If you don't remember them, you will by the end of this chapter. Transaction management falls under the auspices of the Data Control Language (DCL) of SQL. *Transaction management* protects your database from potential errors.

A *transaction* is a unit of work saved to the database. For example, you add a new employee to your Employee table. This is a transaction. You update another employee's home address in the Address table. This is another transaction. You go to the store and buy a quart of milk. The clerk charges you $2.50 and rings the sale on the register. This is a transaction. The inventory of the store is debited one quart of milk. This is another transaction. The store manager orders another quart from the supplier. This is yet another transaction.

Any type of work can produce hundreds or thousands of transactions in the course of a day. If a computer is involved, double that amount. If Murphy's Law exists, and you know it does, imagine what can go wrong in the course of a day. Chaos would reign supreme if you did not have transaction management.

Transaction management is important when you have many users or applications using the database. The transactions each user or application performs in the database are running concurrently, so the possibility of database corruption always exists. Transaction management keeps the database clean when you have concurrent users access the database or if the systems fail. There are four important properties transactions should have. A mnemonic device used to remember these properties is *ACID*:

◆ **Atomic**   The transaction completes in the entirety or aborts.

◆ **Consistent**   The transaction leaves the database in a consistent state after it completes or fails.

◆ **Isolated**   The transaction does not interact or conflict with another transaction.

◆ **Durable**   The completed transaction lasts even in the event of a power failure or database crash.

The SET TRANSACTION Statement

A transaction is implied whenever you produce a SELECT statement, an UPDATE statement, or a CREATE table statement (part of the DML). The database transaction is a sequence of SQL statements performed in a logical order. The SET TRANSACTION statement is

```
SET TRANSACTION
Mode [,mode]...
```

The *transaction mode* consists of:

◆ Isolation level
◆ Transaction access mode
◆ Diagnostic size

Isolation Level

5

An *isolation level* is concerned with concurrency control and with what happens when two or more transactions are made to the database. The isolation level specifies the degree of access a transaction has to read data modified by another, uncommitted transaction. Four isolation levels exist:

◆ **Serializable**   A transaction with this isolation level is fully isolated from other transactions. Here, Transaction A is completed before Transaction B has begun, or Transaction B is completed before Transaction A. Can you understand why you should have transactions that are atomic? If your isolation level is serializable and you have large transactions, the performance of the database is compromised.

◆ **Repeatable Read**   This transaction can read the same data more than once, retrieving rows that satisfy a WHERE clause. For example, if Transaction B has inserted and committed rows before Transaction A reads, the repeated read of the data may return different rows than the first.

◆ **Read Committed**   This transaction can also read the same data more than once, but the read returns the same rows.

◆ **Read Uncommitted**   This transaction can read the same data more than once and read updates made to the data by other uncommitted transactions. This transaction enables minimal isolation from concurrent transactions.

Transaction Access Mode

The access mode is either Read Only or Read Write. If you specify Read Only, then you cannot execute any statement that will change the database, that is, UPDATE, INSERT, and DELETE. Basically, all you can do is query the database. In Read Write, you can query and also update the database.

Diagnostic Area

The *diagnostic size* is an integer that indicates the size of the diagnostic area. This integer indicates the number of conditions the area can store for each SQL statement you execute.

Examples of the SET TRANSACTION statements are

```
SET TRANSACTION
    READ ONLY,
    ISOLATION LEVEL READ UNCOMMITTED,
    DIAGNOSTIC SIZE 3
```

or

```
SET TRANSACTION
    READ WRITE,
    ISOLATION LEVEL SERIALIZABLE,
    DIAGNOSTIC SIZE 12
```

or

```
SET TRANSACTION
    READ WRITE,
    ISOLATION LEVEL REPEATABLE READ,
    DIAGNOSTIC SIZE 9
```

If you don't write a SET TRANSACTION statement, SQL produces a default transaction.

```
SET TRANSACTION
    READ WRITE,
    ISOLATION LEVEL SERIALIZABLE,
    DIAGNOSTIC SIZE (determined by DBMS)
```

If you want to be a good programmer, though, you should always write your applications using a SET TRANSACTION statement. This way, months from now when you look at your code, you will know what you were doing. Also, if another programmer has to update the code, this provides good documentation.

Now that you have learned the syntax of the SET TRANSACTION statement, you may be wondering what all this means.

A transaction begins with a SELECT, UPDATE, or CREATE statement. A *COMMIT statement* indicates the successful end of the transaction. A *ROLLBACK statement* indicates the unsuccessful end of the transaction. A transaction is an all-or-nothing deal. If one SQL statement fails, they all fail, and a ROLLBACK statement is needed. If all the SQL statements work, then a COMMIT statement is needed.

5

The database keeps track of these transactions by creating a transaction log. If you update the database, the database writes a record in the log showing two copies of each of the rows affected by the update. The first is the *before update* copy, and the second is the *after update* copy. If you COMMIT your work, the ending of the transaction is logged. If, however, you initiate a rollback, the database goes to the log and looks for the *before update* copy of each row. The database uses the copies to restore the rows to their original condition. If your systems crashes, your database administrator (DBA) can run a recovery utility that rolls back any of the incomplete transactions. This is how transactions are handled in a perfect world.

In the real world, things can be quite different. For instance, the next section discusses the four major problems that can occur when you have a multiuser database and concurrent transactions.

The Four Transaction Problems

There are four known problems that occur when certain isolation levels are used: lost update, uncommitted data, inconsistent data and the phantom insert. The following explains when and how these problems occur.

The Lost Update Problem

Welcome to the Mega Books Company, an Internet bookstore. In this scenario, you have two users ordering the same title, *Great Expectations*. Annette starts entering her order for this book. At the same time, Bill starts his order. Each order begins a query to the database to check the inventory.

Annette sees one book is left and she orders it. Bill, too, sees only one book is left and he orders it. Both orders are accepted, but only one book is available. It looks like Annette's update has been lost. When she purchased one book, the inventory should have been reduced to zero and a notice should have been sent to Bill notifying him he would have to wait two weeks to receive the book. This shows the problem that occurs when two programs read the same data and use this data to make a calculation.

The Uncommitted Data Problem

In this scenario, Annette orders her book. This time, she queries the inventory table, discovers only one book remains, and the table is updated with the order so zero quantity is available. Annette then continues to browse other selections. Bill orders his selection only to find out no books are left to order. Bill cancels his order. Now a zero balance exists in inventory and a note is sent to the manager to order more books. Meanwhile, Annette decides she really doesn't want the book, cancels her order, and the program performs a rollback to abort the transaction.

Bill, however, saw the uncommitted update of Annette's purchase and decided not to buy the book because he didn't want to wait two weeks to get it. In this problem, Bill saw the uncommitted update and he canceled his order, thus, an error was produced.

The Inconsistent Data Problem

In this scenario, Annette and Bill are still trying to order *Great Expectations*. Annette initiates the order process for the book. A little later, Bill starts thinking about ordering this book and his program does a single-row query to find out how many copies are available. This time, Bill is also thinking about another book, *Moby Dick,* as his second choice and he does another single-row query on that row. Annette finishes her order for *Great Expectations* and performs a COMMIT (that is, she presses the Buy button) to finalize the order. Bill makes a decision to order the same book and does a new single-row query only to find the book is now sold out.

This example is a little different than the previous two. The database status is accurate; no books are left. You do not have a problem letting Bill see the uncommitted data from Annette. Yet, from Bill's point of view, the database did not remain consistent during his transaction. At the beginning of the transaction, the row contained certain data and later in the same transaction, the data was different. This can cause problems if the program is totaling or calculating statistics; you cannot be sure you are getting a consistent view of the data.

The Phantom Insert Problem

In this scenario, suppose you are a sales manager trying to see how well your sales force is doing. You print a report from your Sales Rep Revenue table. You are requesting data on your top performer, Alex Coffin. After you run the report, Alex makes a large sale (for $10,000). This transaction is entered into the database table and is committed. You are having a bad day and spill coffee all over your report, so you need to run the report again. This time, you notice Alex's sales total has increased by $10,000.

As in the previous example, you are getting inconsistent data. The database integrity is intact, but the same query reports different results. In the last example, the problem was caused by an UPDATE statement. In this example, the problem is caused by an INSERT statement. The additional row did not exist in the first query. Now it shows up as a phantom row in the second query. Again, this can cause errors in your calculations.

Table 5-1 illustrates the isolation levels and at what level these problems are found to exist.

Notice the highest isolation level is Serializable. At this level, each transaction is processed like no other transactions are happening. This is the default isolation level. This is the ideal level for a SQL database.

The Repeatable Read level is the second highest level. The problem at this level is, if you want to make a multirow query during a single transaction and another transaction makes a multirow query, the other transaction may become visible during your transaction. A phantom insert can happen here.

5

Isolation Level	Lost Update	Uncommitted Data	Inconsistent Data	Phantom Insert
Serializable	Prevented by DBMS	Prevented by DBMS	Prevented by DBMS	Prevented by DBMS
Repeatable Read	Prevented by DBMS	Prevented by DBMS	Prevented by DBMS	Can happen
Read Committed	Prevented by DBMS	Prevented by DBMS	Can happen	Can happen
Read Uncommitted	Prevented by DBMS	Can happen	Can happen	Can happen

Multiuser Concurrent Transaction Problems

Table 5-1.

The Read Committed level is the third highest level. Your transaction is not allowed to see uncommitted updates from other transactions. However, updates that are committed by other concurrent transactions may be visible during the course of your transaction.

The lowest level is the Read Uncommitted; here users could see the uncommitted transaction of the other. Multiple problems could occur with this level. This is usually called a *dirty read*. Your transaction can be affected by committed or uncommitted updates from other transactions.

Application designers and developers should choose an isolation level based on the application performance and consistency needs, as well as application coding requirements. For environments with many concurrent users rapidly submitting transactions, designers must assess transaction performance requirements in terms of the expected transaction arrival rate and response time demands. For high-performance environments, the choice of isolation levels involves a trade-off between consistency and concurrency (transaction throughput).

According to SQL-92, a few rules must be observed when setting your transactions. For instance, if you indicate a Read Write access mode, the level of isolation cannot be Read Uncommitted. If an access mode is not specified and the level of isolation is Read Uncommitted, then Read Only is implicit. Otherwise, Read Write is implicit.

Locking

How does the DBMS handle these concurrent transactions? Most DBMSs use locking techniques to handle these concurrent SQL transactions. For example, Transaction A accesses the database; the DBMS locks each piece of the database the transactions retrieves or modifies. Transaction B, at the same time, tries to access the same part of the database that is now locked. The DBMS blocks Transaction B, causing it to wait for the data to be unlocked. The database unlocks the part only when a Commit or Rollback operation is performed. The DBMS then allows Transaction B to continue.

Locking gives the transaction exclusive access to a part of the database temporarily. Locking prevents lost updates, uncommitted data, and inconsistent data from corrupting the database. Locking could also cause its own problem, however. A transaction may have to wait a long time to get to the piece of the database it needs.

Locking Levels

You can imagine what sort of performance issues you would have if you allowed the DBMS to lock the entire database for each transaction. This is why locking levels were created.

◆ *Table-level locking* is where the DBMS locks only the tables accessed by a transaction. This allows other transactions to proceed as long as they are using different tables. If you have many transactions using the same tables, however, performance will once again suffer.

◆ *Page-level locking* is where the DBMS locks individual blocks of data from the disk (pages) as they are accessed by the transaction. Page sizes generally range from 2K to 16K. A large table could involve over a hundred or sometimes even a thousand pages. In this way, two transactions could access the table as long as they were accessing different pages.

◆ *Row-level locking* is where two concurrent transactions access different rows of a table. These two rows might exist on the same page. This facilitates concurrent transactions, but the tradeoff is that the DBMS must keep track of all the locks for rows. Any DBMS that uses online transaction processing (OLTP) today uses this level.

5

Shared and Exclusive Locks

A *shared lock* is used when a transaction wants to read data from the database. Another transaction can also get a shared lock on the same data, allowing this transaction to read the data also. An *exclusive lock* is used when a transaction wants to update data in the database. When a transaction has this type of lock, no other transaction can get any type of lock on the data. A transaction can get an exclusive lock only if no other transaction has a shared or an exclusive lock on the data. Various DBMSs can also have more than just these two types of locks. The whole purpose of these locks is to allow the greatest possible concurrent access to the database.

Deadlocks

A *deadlock* is when two transactions each request—at the same time—a piece of the table to which the other has access. For example, Transaction A is using the Sales Rep table, thereby locking a piece of it. Then Transaction B is using the Commission table, thereby locking a piece of it. Transaction A tries to update the Commission table and Transaction B now tries to update the Sales Rep table. If no monitoring is done, the two transactions could be in deadlock limbo.

DBMS logic, however, periodically checks the locks held by transactions. When it finds this deadlock limbo, the DBMS picks a transaction as the loser and rolls back the transaction. The loser receives an error that a deadlock has occurred and it has lost. You can reduce deadlocks by planning database updates carefully. This is where the advanced locking features come into play. The isolation levels discussed previously are examples of an advanced locking technique.

Advanced Locking Techniques

The advanced locking techniques are

◆ **Explicit locking**   A program can lock an entire table or part of the table if it is used repeatedly by the program. A bulk update program, which goes through each row of the table, locks the entire table as it proceeds. Explicit locking is ideal for this situation. This eliminates the possibility that other transactions will lock part of the table, causing the bulk update to wait, thus eliminating a deadlock. You can have an Exclusive lock or a Shared lock on the table.

◆ **Isolation levels**   This technique tells the DBMS that a specific program will not allow any transaction to impact the data visible during the course of your transaction.

◆ **Locking parameters**   This technique allows the DBA to manually adjust the size of the "lockable pieces" of the database. The DBA can also use parameters to fine-tune the database performance. Some parameters used by DBMS' vendors are

  ◆ *Lock size*   This could be table-level, page-level, or row level, or other lock sizes.

  ◆ *Number of locks*   A DBMS has some limits to the number of locks.

  ◆ *Lock escalation*   The DBMS replaces small locks with a single larger lock (replacing many row locks with one page lock).

  ◆ *Lock timeout*   A timeout feature, where a SQL statement fails if it cannot obtain the locks needed within a certain period of time. The DBA can usually set the timeout period.

These locks vary from one DBMS to another. A rule to remember is, the more locks you have, the more time it takes to process transactions.

Transactions in Action

The previous sections have shown you the syntax of the SET TRANSACTION statement, and explained both what a transaction is and why you need transaction management. This section demonstrates the SET TRANSACTION statement in action. Oracle8 and SQL Server 7 transactions are used to illustrate.

SQL Server 7 Transactions

In SQL Server 7, a transaction begins with BEGIN TRAN and ends with COMMIT TRAN or ROLLBACK TRAN. For example:

5

```
BEGIN TRAN
    INSERT EMPLOYEE
    VALUES (300,'SMITH','LAURA','JANE','REGULAR')
    SELECT * FROM EMPLOYEE
COMMIT TRAN
```

You can abbreviate TRANSACTION to TRAN.

This is called an *explicit transaction.* In this explicit transaction, you use keywords such as BEGIN TRANSACTION, COMMIT TRANSACTION, COMMIT WORK, ROLLBACK TRANSACTION, ROLLBACK WORK, and SAVE TRANSACTION.

Implicit transactions are enabled in the session by typing the following statement:

```
SET IMPLICIT_TRANSACTION ON
```

The following statements would need to have an explicit COMMIT or ROLLBACK to end the statement:

◆ ALTER TABLE	◆ GRANT	◆ REVOKE
◆ CREATE	◆ DROP	◆ DELETE
◆ SELECT	◆ INSERT	◆ UPDATE
◆ TRUNCATE TABLE	◆ FETCH	◆ OPEN

The BEGIN TRAN statement is not needed, however.

To disable implicit transactions, type

```
SET IMPLICIT_TRANSACTION OFF
```

You must also be able to cancel transactions. You can do this by using ROLLBACK TRANSACTION. Here's an example:

```
BEGIN TRAN
DELETE EMPLOYEE WHERE EMP_ID = 300
IF @@ERROR >0
    ROLLBACK TRAN
ELSE
    COMMIT TRAN
```

If you want to semicommit your transaction halfway through the statement, however, you can use *savepoints,* as demonstrated in the following example:

```
BEGIN TRAN
    INSERT EMPLOYEE VALUES(302,'TANG','SIMON','LEE','SUMMER')
    SAVE TRAN EMPADD
    INSERT EMPLOYEE VALUES (303,'CARROLL','HAROLD','JOHN','REGULAR')
    IF @@ERROR > 0
        ROLLBACK TRAN EMPADD
    IF @@ERROR > 0
        ROLLBACK TRAN
ELSE
    COMMIT TRAN
```

Oracle8

In Oracle8, a commit looks like this:

```
SET TRANSACTION
    INSERT INTO EMPLOYEES VALUES
    (350, "Collins", "John", "David", "Regular")
COMMIT;
SELECT * FROM EMPLOYEES;
```

While the transaction is processing, error-checking also takes place, to make sure it is running successfully. To cancel a transaction, Oracle8 also uses ROLLBACK:

```
SET TRANSACTION
    INSERT INTO EMPLOYEES VALUES
    (500, "Larabee", "Lionel", "James", "Summer");
ROLLBACK;
SELECT * FROM EMPLOYEES;
```

In this example, the Larabee file would not be inserted into the Employee table because a rollback was performed.

Oracle also allows savepoints to be added to statements, as you can see here:

```
SET TRANSACTION
    INSERT INTO EMPLOYEES VALUES
    (550,"Jones", "Sally", "Lou", "Regular");
    SAVEPOINT EMPADD
    DELETE FROM EMPLOYEE WHERE EMP_ID = 525
ROLLBACK TO SAVEPOINT EMPADD;
COMMIT;
    SELECT * FROM EMPLOYEES;
```

In this example, the rollback would go back to the first part of the transaction. The delete would be removed. However, if you put ROLLBACK immediately after the ROLLBACK TO SAVEPOINT EMPADD, the entire transaction would have been rolled back.

The transaction log in Oracle8 is called the *Redo Log*. Oracle records all changes or transactions that happen to the database in the Redo Log. A copy of all transactions is recorded to the online Redo Logs. The final copy of the changes is recorded back to the physical datafile. The database can always recover from the Redo Logs. Oracle requires the database to have two online Redo Logs. The Oracle database runs in two modes: ARCHIVELOG mode, which saves all transaction logs, and NOARCHIVELOG mode, which discards all old Redo Logs. The best practice is to run in the ARCHIVELOG mode for obvious reasons.

What's Next?

You have learned the SET TRANSACTION statement, worked with COMMIT, ROLLBACK, and savepoints. You studied the inner workings of the transaction management from the DBMS side. When working with a DBMS system, reviewing documentation on transactions and locking is best. Each is unique in its own way of handling concurrent transactions. All abide by the minimal ANSI SQL-92 standard, however, which states no transaction should affect another concurrent transaction. The ACID properties apply as the minimal properties of a transaction as far as SQL-92 standards.

Of course, each DBMS vendor competes in the marketplace and each does its utmost to outperform the other. Most database applications now use online transaction processing and, therefore, must support row-level locking (or better). Transaction management can either hinder or ensure the success of an application and the database. The one who can handle the most transactions at the fastest speed wins the accolades and gets the biggest slice of the business.

In Chapter 6, you learn about security and database management.

CHAPTER 6

Database Security

Security in SQL databases is important because of the nature of SQL databases—they are interactive. When you have multiple users accessing your database, you need to ask yourself the following questions:

◆ Who needs access to the database tables?

◆ What type of access do they need?

In Chapter 1, you learned a few commands that provide privileges to your users: INSERT, UPDATE, SELECT, and DELETE. These commands are part of the Data Control Language (DCL) of SQL and they are covered in more detail in this chapter.

Since enforcing security restrictions is the responsibility of the DBMS software, you learn how DBMS vendors handle security and how it varies from vendor to vendor. In addition, you learn the role the *database administrator* (DBA) plays in the life of your database. Then you delve into the philosophical question database developers and end users ask themselves often: How much security is too much security?

What Does a DBA Do?

A database may be quite large and have many users, so someone is needed to manage the database. It's a dirty job, but someone must do it. Every large database must have at least one DBA. A database administrator's main functions are

◆ Installing and upgrading the server and the application tools

◆ Allocating system storage and planning future storage requirements for the database system

◆ Creating primary objects (tables, views, indexes) once developers have designed an application

◆ Modifying the database structure from information given by developers

◆ Enrolling users and maintaining system security

◆ Ensuring compliance with the licensing agreement of the vendor

◆ Controlling and monitoring user access to the database

◆ Monitoring and optimizing the performance of the database

◆ Planning for backup and recovery of database information

♦ Maintaining archived data on tape

♦ Backing up and restoring the database

♦ Contacting the vendor for technical support

Sometimes the functions may be overwhelming for just one DBA. If the database is very large, you may divide the functions between two or more DBAs.

How SQL Handles Security

The Data Control Language statements protect the database from unauthorized users, concurrent multiuser transactions, power failures, and equipment glitches.

The security is based on users, database objects, and privileges. Users are given user IDs and passwords. Access to database objects (tables, views, forms, programs, and databases) is controlled by the DBA. Privileges are granted to users to enable them to access these database objects.

6

SQL-92 enables controlled access to six database management functions:

♦ **INSERT**   The INSERT privilege enables you to insert new rows into a table or a view.

♦ **SELECT**   The SELECT privilege enables you to retrieve data from a table or a view.

♦ **UPDATE**   The UPDATE privilege enables you to change rows of data in a table or view.

♦ **DELETE**   The DELETE privilege enables you to delete rows of data in a table or a view.

♦ **REFERENCES**   This privilege enables you to reference the table as a foreign key in a new table you create.

♦ **ALL PRIVILEGES**   This privilege enables you to have all the preceding rights to the table or view.

As you learned in Chapter 2, all rights to tables and views are stored in the data dictionary. Anytime a user requests to manipulate the table in any way, the DBMS checks the data dictionary to see if the user has the privilege to do so.

Before you can grant privileges on tables and views, you must first create users in the database. *Users* are the people who access the database. What exactly do these individuals need in order to access the database? Don't forget you are generally protecting your data from the users. You assign security to protect sensitive data and you also protect the data from potential user errors.

Creating a User

For each person who needs access to the database, you need to create a user and a password. The user name must be unique to the database. Once you assign the user name and password, you must provide the user with privileges.

The following example demonstrates the SQL syntax for CREATE USER in Oracle8.

```
CREATE USER OPS$$dsmith
    IDENTIFIED EXTERNALLY
    DEFAULT TABLESPACE data_ts
    TEMPORARY TABLESPACE temp_ts
    QUOTA 100M ON test_ts
    QUOTA 500K ON data_ts
    PROFILE operator;
```

In this example, the user will be able to use the operating system's login and password as the login and password for the database (the user is "IDENTIFIED EXTERNALLY"). This is an efficient use of time and resources.

The *tablespace* is a collection of one or more datafiles. All database objects are stored in tablespaces. For the most part, however, tablespaces usually hold tables. In this statement, you are identifying the user and the password, but you are also giving the user space for any tables or views the user may create. The *quota* provides users with privileges to create certain types of objects that can use the specified tablespace. Oracle limits the amount of space that can be allocated for storage of a user's objects within the tablespace by setting the quota.

The *profile* limits the resources a user can consume. The types of resources a user might consume include connect time, idle time, and concurrent sessions, to name a few. In this example, the profile this user has is Operator. An Operator profile consists of the following:

```
CREATE PROFILE Operator LIMIT
    SESSIONS_PER_USER 1
    IDLE_TIME 30
    CONNECT_TIME 600;
```

In the Operator profile, the user is limited to one session per user, the system cannot be inactive for more than 30 minutes, and the connect time cannot exceed 600 minutes per session.

If you want to have the *database* assign the user ID and password (instead of using the operating system or network service ID and password), you would use the syntax demonstrated in the following example:

```
CREATE USER msmith
    IDENTIFIED BY scooter
    DEFAULT TABLESPACE users
    TEMPORARY TABLESPACE temp_ts
    QUOTA 500K ON users
    PROFILE operator;
```

After IDENTIFIED BY, assign a password for the database instead of using EXTERNAL to indicate an external password.

6

In SQL Server 7, you would run the following Transact-SQL command:

```
EXEC sp_grantdbaccess 'msmith\scooter'
```

SQL Server 7 and Sybase Server 11 uses stored procedures (sp) for many of the administrative tasks. It also provides a default GUEST user for each database.

In Sybase Server 11, you can add a user to your database as shown in the following example:

```
sp_adduser msmith
go
```

The password is not listed in the command because when the user login was created, so was the password. The password is already assumed from the login. The login code is

```
sp_addlogin msmith,scooter,pubs
```

Here you have the user name, password, and name of the database.

 NOTE: All parameters in the command sp_addlogin are case-sensitive.

You can also change a user with ALTER in Oracle8:

```
ALTER USER msmith
IDENTIFIED BY schooner;
```

With this statement you have changed the password of the user. You can also change the tablespace, quota, profile, and the role of the user. ALTER USER is used by Oracle8. Both SQL Server 7 and Sybase Server 11 have other ways of changing the password for a user.

Create a Role

So far you have learned how to assign individuals access to the database. In addition, you can assign roles to a group of users. A *role* is a privilege or set of privileges. Remember, you will never win an Oscar for the role you play in the database, but you can win access to certain privileges that can help you do your job.

Roles are created to ease the administration of an end-user system and schema object privileges. Assigning roles is more efficient than granting the same set of privileges to several users individually. If you grant the privileges to a group of users, then only the role needs to be granted to each member of the group. This way, if the privileges of the group change, you only need to change the privileges of the role and not each user. The data dictionary keeps track of all roles.

A database role can optionally require authorization when a user attempts to enable the role. Passwords can be used by the database, operating system, or network service to provide the necessary authorization.

To provide you with a useful example of how role creation is done, you will create a role HRASSIST and then assign the role to Karen Della Cruz and Connie Martin.

In Oracle8, you would use the following:

```
CREATE ROLE HRASSIST IDENTIFIED BY ihelpu;
    'Assign the users:

Grant HRASSIST to kdcruz;
Grant HRASSIST to cmartin;
```

```
    'Assign the privileges:

Grant Insert on Employee to HRASSIST;
Grant Insert on Department to HRASSIST;
Grant Insert on Salary to HRASSIST;
Grant Select on Employee to HRASSIST;
Grant Select on Department to HRASSIST;
Grant Select on Salary to HRASSIST;
```

In SQL Server 7, the syntax is as follows:

```
Create Role HRASSIST IDENTIFIED BY ihelpu

    'Assign the users:

sp_addrole 'HRASSIST','kdcruz'
sp_addrole 'HRASSIST','cmartin'

    'Assign the privileges:

Grant Insert on Employee to HRASSIST;
Grant Insert on Department to HRASSIST;
Grant Insert on Salary to HRASSIST;
Grant Select on Employee to HRASSIST;
Grant Select on Department to HRASSIST;
Grant Select on Salary to HRASSIST;
```

6

In Sybase Server 11, it looks like this:

```
Create role HRASSIST identified by ihelpu
'Assign the users:

sp_role "grant",HRASSIST,kdcruz
sp_role "grant",HRASSIST,cmartin
go
    'Assign the privileges:

grant insert on employee to HRASSIST
grant insert on department to HRASSIST
grant insert on salary to HRASSIST
grant select on employee to HRASSIST
grant select on department to HRASSIST
grant select on salary to HRASSIST
go
```

One more thing about roles should be mentioned. If you grant a role to a user and add WITH ADMIN OPTION, you allow that user to grant roles to other users. The syntax for this is:

```
Grant role To user WITH ADMIN OPTION
```

PORTABILITY: In Oracle8, a set of predefined roles are automatically defined for the database. These roles are provided for backward compatibility to earlier versions of Oracle. You can grant and revoke privileges and roles to these predefined roles much the way you do with any role. SQL Server 7 also has a set of predefined roles, as does Sybase Server 11.

Table 6-1 is a list of the predefined roles in Oracle8:

Role Name	Privileges Granted To Role
CONNECT	Alter Session, Create Cluster, Create Database Link, Create Sequence, Create Session, Create Synonym, Create Table, Create View
CREATE TYPE	Create Type, Execute, Execute Any Type, Admin Option, Grant Option
RESOURCE	Create Cluster, Create Procedure, Create Sequence, Create Table, Create Trigger
DBA	All system privileges, WITH ADMIN OPTION
EXP_FULL_DATABASE	Select Any Table, Backup Any Table, Insert, Delete and Update on the Tables: Sys.Incvid, Sys.Incfil, and Sys.Incexp
IMP_FULL_DATABASE	Become User
DELETE_CATALOG_ROLE	Delete privileges on all dictionary packages for this role
EXECUTE_CATALOG_ROLE	Execute privilege on all dictionary packages for this role
SELECT_CATALOG_ROLE	Select privilege on all catalog tables and views for the role

Oracle8
Predefined
Roles
Table 6-1.

Public Role

In Oracle8 and SQL Server 7, a role is provided by the server as a default role. The PUBLIC role exists in each database and cannot be removed. Privileges and roles can also be granted to and revoked from the PUBLIC role. PUBLIC is accessible to every database user. All privileges and roles granted to PUBLIC are accessible to every database user.

Assigning Privileges

Once you have created your user, you now may give them permission (privileges) to the database.

GRANT Command

To do this, you issue a GRANT command:

```
GRANT privilege-list
    ON object
    TO user-list [WITH GRANT OPTION]
```

6

To illustrate how this is done, you will be granting security to Charles and Dwight, who work in the Human Resources Department. They need access to the Human Resource Information System (HRIS) database. They need the following:

Charles Delancy (the manager in charge of HRIS) needs access to all three tables: Employees, Salary, and Department. He can update, insert, delete, and select from these tables.

In Oracle8, you would use the following GRANT commands:

```
GRANT Select, Insert,Delete, Update
    ON Employees
    TO cdelancy;

GRANT Select, Insert,Delete, Update
    ON Salary
    TO cdelancy;

GRANT Select, Insert,Delete, Update
    ON Department
    TO cdelancy;
```

In SQL Server 7, the GRANT command is used as follows:

```
GRANT Select, Insert, Delete, Update
    ON Employees
    To cdelancy;

GRANT Select, Insert, Delete, Update
    ON Salary
    TO cdelancy;

Grant Select, Insert, Delete, Update
    ON Department
    TO cdelancy;
```

In Sybase Server 11, you grant the privileges like this:

```
grant select, insert, delete, update
    on employees
    to cdelancy

grant select, insert, delete, update
    on salary
    to cdelancy

grant select, insert, delete, update
    on department
    to cdelancy
go
```

Dwight Shelton (a data entry clerk) needs access to Employees and Department. He can select, insert, and update these tables.

In Oracle8, the privileges are granted as follows:

```
GRANT SELECT, INSERT, UPDATE
    ON Employees
    TO dshelton;

GRANT SELECT, INSERT, UPDATE
    ON Department
    TO dshelton;
```

In SQL Server 7, the GRANT command is used like this:

```
GRANT SELECT, INSERT, UPDATE
    ON Employees
    TO dshelton

GRANT SELECT, INSERT, UPDATE
    ON Department
    TO dshelton
```

In Sybase Server 11, you use the following syntax:

```
grant select, insert, update
    on employees
    to dshelton

grant select, insert, update
    on department
    to dshelton
 go
```

In these examples, the person who receives the privileges cannot pass them along to any other users. For either Charles or Dwight to be able to pass these privileges on to other users, you would need to add WITH GRANT OPTION to the GRANT statement:

In Oracle8:

```
GRANT SELECT, INSERT, UPDATE
    ON Department
    TO dshelton WITH GRANT OPTION;
```

In SQL Server 7:

```
Grant Select, Insert, Update
    On Department
    To dshelton With Grant Option
```

In Sybase Server 11:

```
Grant select, insert, update
    on department
    to dshelton with grant option
go
```

The WITH GRANT OPTION allows this user to grant the privileges he has to other users. For example, Dwight wants to give the SELECT privilege on the Department table to his colleague, Jim Frey. Notice, Dwight is only giving SELECT privileges, but he could also give Jim INSERT and UPDATE. Dwight could not grant Jim DELETE privileges, however, because Dwight does not have the DELETE privilege.

You don't need to grant privileges to a whole table. For example, Jeff Cannon, an HRIS clerk, needs to see the salary_grade and the inc_date columns from the Salary table.

In Oracle8:

```
Grant Select (sal_grade, inc_date)
    On Salary
    To jcannon;
```

In SQL Server 7:

```
Grant Select (sal_grade, inc_date)
    On Salary
    To jcannon
```

In Sybase Server 11:

```
grant select (sal_grade, inc_date)
    on salary
    to jcannon
go
```

Two remaining privileges need to be explained: REFERENCES and ALL PRIVILEGES. REFERENCES privilege enables you to reference the table as a foreign key in a new table you create. For example:

```
GRANT REFERENCES (sal_review_date)
    ON Salary
    TO jcannon;
```

The sal_review_date is from the Sal_History table and you defined a foreign key on the sal_review_date column of Sal_History to point to the Salary table. To control access by other users who have the foreign key to your table, you issue the GRANT REFERENCE statement to allow only authorized users that privilege.

ALL PRIVILEGES grants every privilege on an object on which the user executing the GRANT has a grantable privilege. For example, Charles Delancy provided privileges to John Jameson:

```
GRANT ALL PRIVILEGES
    ON Employees to jjameson;
```

What exactly has this done for John? John now has the following privileges: SELECT, INSERT, DELETE, and UPDATE on the Employees table.

Revoke Command

What you can grant, you can also revoke. The next command you learn is REVOKE. If the previous employees left the Human Resources Department, standard protocol would be to revoke their privileges if their duties no longer require them to use this database. The REVOKE statement is similar to the GRANT statement:

```
REVOKE privilege-list
    On object
    From user-list [Restrict|Cascade]
```

What RESTRICT does is to have the system check to see if the privilege previously granted was passed on to others. In other words, was WITH GRANT OPTION used? If it was, you will receive an error message and the privilege will not be revoked. If it wasn't used, the privilege will be revoked. If WITH GRANT OPTION was used, then you can use the CASCADE keyword to revoke any dependent privileges granted as a result of the original WITH GRANT OPTION. You will now revoke some privileges from Charles and Dwight.

The syntax is as follows in Oracle8:

```
REVOKE Delete
    ON Employees
    FROM cdelancy;

REVOKE Delete
    On Department
    FROM cdelancy;

REVOKE Delete
    On Salary
    FROM cdelancy;
```

In SQL Server 7 the syntax is the same.

In Sybase Server 11, the REVOKE statement looks like this:

```
Revoke delete
    on employees
    from cdelancy
go

revoke delete
    on department
    from cdelancy
go

revoke delete
    on salary
    from cdelancy
go
```

Now it is Dwight's turn to have some privileges revoked. If you remember, you gave him WITH GRANT OPTION on the Department table. You will now revoke it:

```
REVOKE Insert, Update
    On Department
    From dshelton CASCADE;
```

In SQL Server 7 the syntax is the same.

In Sybase Server 11, it looks like this:

```
Revoke insert,update
    on Department
    from dshelton cascade
go
```

If you need to revoke the REFERENCES privilege, you would use the following statement:

```
REVOKE REFERENCES On Salary from jcannon Cascade Constraints;
```

Any foreign key currently defined that uses the revoked REFERENCES privilege is dropped when the CASCADE CONSTRAINTS option is specified.

A warning about the REVOKE statement: The REVOKE statement is not necessarily a simple process of revoking privileges and you're done. As you may have guessed by the example of the RESTRICT keyword, dependencies can exist on privileges. This is true when WITH GRANT OPTION is given to a user.

Take our HRIS database as an example. Suppose Dwight gave INSERT and UPDATE privileges to two other users. Next, Dwight created a view using the Department table. If you were to revoke these privileges from him, you would also revoke the privilege from the two other users and any grants they gave. In addition, the view Dwight created using the Department table would have the privilege revoked. You have prompted a series of errors to take place throughout your database. The lesson to learn is to take care when you revoke privileges. Check for objects that have dependencies on the privilege you revoke.

Table 6-2 is a partial list of system privileges. These privileges are granted by the DBA. You should only entrust these privileges to trusted users of the database. In the wrong hands, these privileges could cause trouble for both the database and the DBA.

6

System Privilege	Operations Permitted
Database	
ALTER	Alter the database; add files to the operating system via Oracle.
DATABASE	Ignore operating system privileges.
Privilege	
GRANT ANY PRIVILEGE	Grant any system privilege (not object privileges).
Procedure	
CREATE PROCEDURE	Create stored procedures, functions, and packages in own schema.
CREATE ANY PROCEDURE	Create stored procedures, functions, and packages in any schema.
ALTER ANY PROCEDURE	Compile any stored procedure, function, or package in any schema.

Oracle8
System
Privileges
Table 6-2.

System Privilege	Operations Permitted
DROP ANY PROCEDURE	Drop any stored procedure, function, or package in any schema.
EXECUTE ANY PROCEDURE	Execute any procedures or functions, or reference any public package variable in any schema.
Role	
CREATE ROLE	Create roles.
ALTER ANY ROLE	Alter any role in the database.
DROP ANY ROLE	Drop any role in the database.
GRANT ANY ROLE	Grant any role in the database.
Table	
CREATE TABLE	Create tables in own schema. Also enables grantee to create indexes on table in own schema. (The grantee must have a quota for the tablespace or the UNLIMITED TABLESPACE privilege.)
CREATE ANY TABLE	Create tables in any schema.
ALTER ANY TABLE	Alter any table in any schema and compile any view in any schema.
BACK UP ANY TABLE	Perform an incremental export using the Export utility of tables in schema.
DROP ANY TABLE	Drop or truncate any table in any schema.
LOCK ANY TABLE	Lock any table or view in any schema.
COMMENT ANY TABLE	Comment on any table, view, or column in a schema.
SELECT ANY TABLE	Query any table, view, or snapshot in any schema.
INSERT ANY TABLE	Insert rows into any table or view in any schema.
UPDATE ANY TABLE	Update rows in any table or view in any schema.

Oracle8
System
Privileges
(continued)
Table 6-2.

System Privilege	Operations Permitted
DELETE ANY TABLE	Delete rows from any table or view in any schema.
Tablespace	
CREATE TABLESPACE	Create tablespaces; add files to the operating system via Oracle, regardless of the user's operating system privileges.
ALTER TABLESPACE	Alter tablespaces; add files to the operating system via Oracle, regardless of the user's operating system privileges.
MANAGE TABLESPACES	Take any tablespace offline, bring any tablespace online, and begin and end backups of any tablespace.
DROP TABLESPACE	Drop tablespaces.
UNLIMITED TABLESPACE	Use an unlimited amount of any tablespace. This privilege overrides any specific quotas assigned.
User	
CREATE ANY USER	Create users; assign quotas on any tablespace, set default and temporary tablespaces, and assign a profile as part of a CREATE USER statement.
BECOME ANY USER	Become another user.
ALTER USER	Alter other users, change any user's password or authentication method, assign tablespace quotas, set default and temporary tablespaces, assign profiles and default roles, in an ALTER USER statement.
DROP USER	Drop another user.
View	
CREATE VIEW	Create a view in own schema.
CREATE ANY	Create a view in any schema.
DROP ANY VIEW	Drop any view in any schema.

6

Oracle8
System
Privileges
(continued)

Table 6-2.

> *IN DEPTH*
>
> # The View as Security
>
> A *view* is a virtual table. If you carefully define a view and give the user permission to use the view, but not the source tables, you can restrict access to only selected columns and rows.
>
> In our HRIS database example, we provided access to Charles and Dwight. However, you need to assign Kate Driscoll and Harry Ford access to the Employee, Department, and Salary tables. They should only have SELECT privilege and they should only be able to see the information for everyone outside their department.
>
> Here is what you would do:
>
> ```
> Create View Payroll_View
> as Select * from Employee, Department, Salary
> where Employee.EMP_ID = Department.EMP_ID and
> Employee.Emp_ID = Salary.Emp_ID and
> Dept.Dept_ID <> 301;
>
> Grant Select on payroll_view to kdriscoll, hford;
> ```
>
> Now they have access to the view and can see all data from the Employee, Department, and Salary tables, except those that pertain to their department—301.
>
> Ready for another example? Penny Sharp is an executive assistant for the CEO and needs to run a report based on executive salaries. You need to create a view for her that allows her access to the Employee table, the Department table, and the Sal_grade, Salary_Annual, and Bonus from the Salary table.
>
> Here's how:
>
> ```
> Create view ExecSal_View
> as Select Employee.Lname, Employee.Fname, Dept.Dept_Name,
> Salary.Sal_grade, Salary.Salary_Annual, Salary.Bonus
> From HR.Employee Employee, HR.Department Department, HR.Salary Salary
> ```

```
WHERE Employee.Emp_ID = Salary.Emp_ID and
Employee.Dept_ID = Dept.Dept_ID and
Salary_Grade >= 20 and Salary_Annual >= 100000;

Grant Select on ExecSal_View to psharp;
```

If you make an error creating a view, you can use the ALTER VIEW command to make the correction. The code works like this:

```
ALTER VIEW ExecSal_View
as Select Employee.Lname, Employee.Fname, Dept.Dept_Name,
Salary.Sal_grade, Salary.Salary_Annual, Salary.Bonus, Salary.Inc_Date
From HR.Employee Employee, HR.Department Department, HR.Salary Salary
WHERE Employee.Emp_ID = Salary.Emp_ID and
Employee.Dept_ID = Dept.Dept_ID and
Salary_Grade >= 20 and Salary_Annual >= 100000;
```

6

You have added Salary.Inc_Date to the view. This is a timesaver when you are developing views. If you change your mind and don't want the view, you would use the following command:

```
DROP VIEW ExecSal_View;
```

As you have seen, through a view, the users can query and modify only the data to which they have access. The rest of the table or tables in the database are neither visible nor accessible. The privileges can be granted or revoked, regardless of the permissions in force on the underlying tables.

Views can be another way for you to limit access to your database. As you know, you cannot update a view. You can only use the SELECT privilege with Read-Only views to limit data retrieval. In addition, because the DBMS translates every access to a view into access to its source tables, views can add to the overhead of database operations. However, it is still the best way to limit users to certain rows and columns of tables.

How Much Security Is Too Much?

There is a saying: "You can never be too thin or too rich." Well, in the realm of IT, you can never have enough security. Hackers are always waiting in the wings to threaten your sense of security.

What steps can you take to ensure you will have a tamper-proof system? Besides carrying a rabbit's foot you can

◆ **Plan for security** It is never too early in the development of a database to start planning for your security system. Take a good look at your data. What is considered sensitive data? Who should see sensitive data? By asking these questions, you will begin the process of security planning and setting up standard operating procedures for your database. You should also consider the security that is already in place on your network and servers. Can you use it to your advantage?

◆ **Manage your plan** Once you have a plan and standard operating procedures, do not deviate from the course. If changes need to be made, implement and document. Also plan on how to add new software applications and networks that are going to be used in your company. How does this affect your database security?

◆ **Test, test, test** Try to breach security. Try to break your system. Test your plan, your standard operating procedures, and test the security. Can your database be accessed through other applications, reporting tools, or firewalls if you have your applications and database on the intranet or Internet? If your database is very large and the data very sensitive, hire experts to test your security. If you can, budget for it.

Again, security is an issue that should be discussed at all levels of your company. You must set the limits for your database. Remember to secure the data, but only from those who don't need it. You must provide your users enough access to complete the business processes of the company and allow users to do their jobs.

What's Next?

You have finished the administrative and SQL building blocks portion of the book. The next part of the book covers queries—the heart and soul of SQL. In Chapter 7, you learn how to create simple one-table queries. In Chapter 8, you learn how to join tables and to create more difficult queries. In Chapter 9, you learn all about subqueries. In Chapter 10, you learn how to optimize your queries and, ultimately, your database performance.

PART II

Queries—The Heart and Soul of SQL

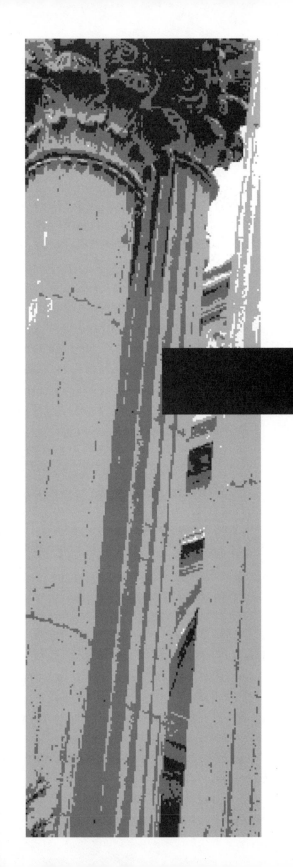

CHAPTER 7

The Simple
One-Table Query

This chapter is where you put all you have learned so far to the test. You begin by learning how to write simple queries and, in the next chapter, progress to the more complex queries. You revisit the SELECT statement and the clauses covered in Chapter 3.

Do you remember diagramming sentences in grammar school? If you do, this chapter will bring back some fond, or not so fond, memories for you. Learning how to query is similar to learning how to write a sentence. The SELECT statement is a sentence with a specific syntax. You work with four tables in both this chapter and in Chapter 8. You may want to review the definitions in Chapter 3 as you follow along with the examples.

So, without further ado, let's query!

The SELECT Statement

Figure 7-1 shows the full SELECT statement that consists of six clauses:

◆   SELECT

◆   FROM

◆   WHERE

◆   GROUP BY

◆   HAVING

◆   ORDER BY

NOTE: Not all clauses must be used in a query. The minimum you need for a SELECT statement is SELECT and FROM.

A *regular query* consists of

◆   SELECT

◆   FROM

◆   WHERE

◆   ORDER BY

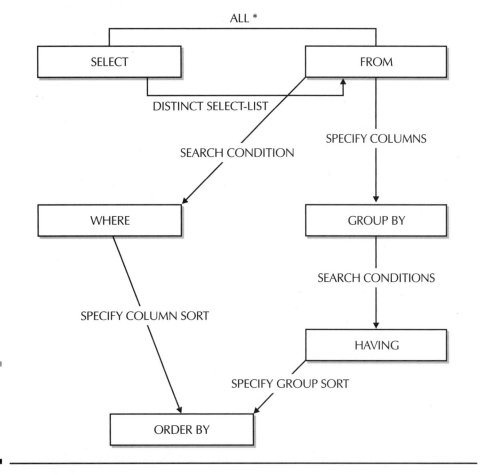

Syntactical
diagram of
the SELECT
statement
Figure 7-1.

A *summary (grouping) query* consists of

◆ SELECT
◆ FROM
◆ GROUP BY
◆ HAVING
◆ ORDER BY

Figures 7-2 through 7-6 show the properties of Oracle8 tables that are used in the query examples in this chapter.

In this chapter, you do not join the tables. You use each table separately when writing the SELECT statement. You'll also practice creating a view using the single-table query.

NOTE: Due to the row length of query results, a modified query result is shown in all examples.

Clauses Revisited

The SELECT clause specifies the data to be retrieved from the query. The SELECT list usually consists of column names, a constant that tells you the same value should appear in every row of the query, or an SQL expression (which means SQL must calculate the value to be placed in the query).

The FROM clause lists the tables containing the data you want to use in your query.

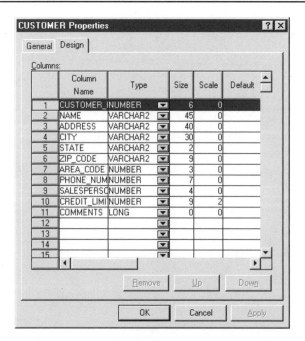

Properties of the Customer table

Figure 7-2.

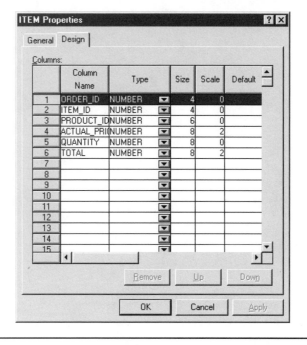

Properties of
the Item table

Figure 7-3.

7

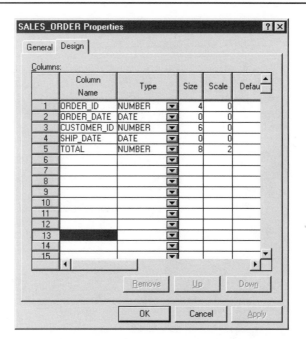

Properties of
the Sales
Order table

Figure 7-4.

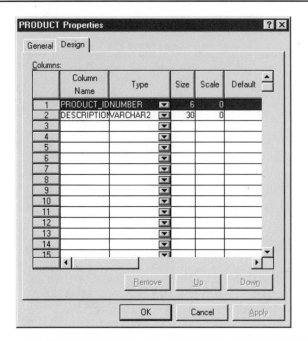

Properties of
the Product
table

Figure 7-5.

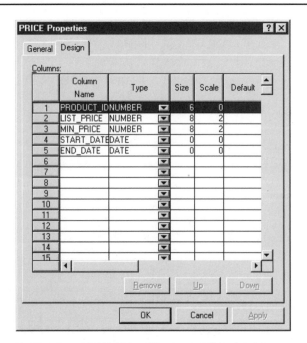

Properties of
the Price table

Figure 7-6.

The following example is a simple SELECT statement requesting four columns from the Sales_Order table.

```
SELECT Order_ID, Order_date, Customer_ID, Total
FROM Sales_Order;
```

```
ORDER_ID      ORDER_DATE     CUSTOMER_ID       TOTAL
--------      ----------     -----------       -----
     610      07-JAN-91              101       101.4
     611      11-JAN-91              102          45
     612      15-JAN-91              104        5860
     601      01-MAY-90              106        60.8
     602      05-JUN-90              102          56
     600      01-MAY-90              103          42
     604      15-JUN-90              106         642
     605      14-JUL-90              106        8374
     606      14-JUL-90              100         3.4
     .
     .
     .
100 rows selected.
```

7

This next example uses an asterisk (*), which denotes the query should display all the columns of the table. This comes in handy when you are working with a new database and want to get a sense of what the table data is like.

```
SELECT * FROM Product;
```

```
PRODUCT_ID    DESCRIPTION
----------    ---------------------------
    100860    ACE TENNIS RACKET I
    100861    ACE TENNIS RACKET II
    100870    ACE TENNIS BALLS-3 PACK
    100871    ACE TENNIS BALLS-6 PACK
    100890    ACE TENNIS NET
    101860    SP TENNIS RACKET
    101863    SP JUNIOR RACKET
    102130    RH: "GUIDE TO TENNIS"
    200376    SB ENERGY BAR-6 PACK
    200380    SB VITA SNACK-6 PACK
    103120    WIFF SOFTBALL BAT I
    103121    WIFF SOFTBALL BAT II
     .
     .
     .
31 rows selected.
```

Thus far, you have practiced two ways to retrieve columns from the table. The first is by using a select list and the second is through the use of '*' asterisk (all columns). You cannot use both in the same SELECT clause.

CAUTION: Stay away from the ALL COLUMNS (*) query when you use programmatic SQL (embedded) because this could cause problems. For instance, if the columns of the table decrease or increase, your program will look for the same number of columns as when the clause was written—and will very likely bomb.

This next example uses a calculation and an alias in the query.

```
SELECT product_id, actual_price, quantity,(actual_price * quantity)
    Subtotal
FROM Item;
```

PRODUCT_ID	ACTUAL_PRICE	QUANTITY	SUBTOTAL
100861	42	1	42
100890	58	1	58
100861	45	1	45
100860	30	100	3000
200376	2.4	12	28.8
100860	32	1	32
100870	2.8	20	56
100890	58	3	174
100861	42	2	84
100860	32	12	384
100860	32	7	224
100860	35	1	35
100870	2.8	3	8.4
200376	2.2	200	440
100860	35	444	15540
100870	2.8	1000	2800
100861	40.5	20	810
101863	10	150	1500
100860	35	10	350
200376	2.4	1000	2400
102130	3.4	500	1700

.
.
.

271 rows selected.

How SQL processes this query is by generating one row of query results for each row of the Item table. The first three columns of query results are directly from the columns, the fourth column is calculated—row by row—using the data values from the Actual_Price and Quantity columns.

For an example of a constant, look at the following SELECT statement:

```
SELECT Customer_ID, 'Has A Credit Limit Of', Credit_limit
FROM Customer
WHERE credit_limit in (1000,2000,3000,4000,5000)
ORDER BY Credit_Limit;
```

```
CUSTOMER_ID    'HASACREDITLIMITOF'     CREDIT_LIMIT
-----------    --------------------    ------------
        103    Has A Credit Limit Of           3000
        205    Has A Credit Limit Of           3000
        208    Has A Credit Limit Of           4000
        226    Has A Credit Limit Of           4000
        228    Has A Credit Limit Of           4000
        222    Has A Credit Limit Of           4000
        218    Has A Credit Limit Of           4000
        100    Has A Credit Limit Of           5000
        227    Has A Credit Limit Of           5000
        223    Has A Credit Limit Of           5000
        216    Has A Credit Limit Of           5000
        213    Has A Credit Limit Of           5000
        105    Has A Credit Limit Of           5000
        202    Has A Credit Limit Of           5000

14 rows selected.
```

You created a sentence-like feeling in your query. Only two columns from the table are used, however. You may also notice you have an IN expression, as well as an ORDER BY in this query.

The next example uses the DISTINCT keyword. You prevent duplicate rows when you use DISTINCT. Duplicate rows occur when the primary key of a table is left out of the query statement. In the Sales_Order table, Order_ID is the primary key. As you can see, it does not appear in the following query.

```
SELECT distinct customer_id from sales_order;

CUSTOMER_ID
-----------
        100
        101
```

```
102
103
104
105
106
107
108
201
202
203
204
205
206
207
  .
  .
  .
25 rows selected.
```

The WHERE clause lets SQL know to include only certain rows of data. The WHERE clause is the search condition you give SQL when you select your data. You learn more uses of WHERE when you get to subqueries in Chapter 9.

In the following example, you limit your data selection by restricting the rows returned to Customer ID 202.

```
SELECT customer_id, order_id, order_date, total
FROM sales_order
WHERE customer_id = 202;

CUSTOMER_ID   ORDER_ID    ORDER_DATE        TOTAL
-----------   -------     ----------       -------
        202       544     11-SEP-90          2358
        202       524     22-FEB-90          1979
        202       502     10-FEB-89           500
        202       539     26-JUN-90          1300
        202       511     17-AUG-89           647
        202       547     16-OCT-90         984.4
        202       540     15-JUL-90         861.2
        202       567     05-JUL-91           200
        202       570     17-JUL-91         663.6
        202       571     02-AUG-91        1095.6

10 rows selected.
```

In the next example, you see the use of a comparison test being done against the TOTAL column. You are restricting your data rows to return all rows that have a TOTAL of 1,000 or less.

```
SELECT customer_id, order_id, order_date, total
FROM sales_order
WHERE total < 1000;

CUSTOMER_ID   ORDER_ID    ORDER_DATE      TOTAL
-----------  ----------   ----------     -------
        101         610   07-JAN-91       101.4
        102         611   11-JAN-91          45
        106         601   01-MAY-90        60.8
        102         602   05-JUN-90          56
        103         600   01-MAY-90          42
        106         604   15-JUN-90         642
        100         606   14-JUL-90         3.4
        100         609   01-AUG-90       102.5
        104         607   18-JUL-90         5.6
        104         608   25-JUL-90        35.2
        .
        .
        .
44 rows selected.
```

7

Overall, when you conduct a search condition, you can get one of three results:

◆ If the search condition is true, the rows are included in the query results.

◆ If the search condition is false, the rows are not included in the query results.

◆ If the search condition has a NULL (unknown) value, the row is excluded from the query results.

The following two examples use the IS NULL and NOT IS NULL tests. Null values provide a three-valued logic in SQL. In this example, you want to know what products have a null end_date.

```
SELECT Product_Id, List_price, start_date, end_date
FROM price
WHERE (end_date) is null;
```

```
PRODUCT_ID  LIST_PRICE   START_DAT   END_DATE
----------  ----------   ---------   --------
    100890          58   01-JAN-89
    100860          35   01-JUN-90
    100861          45   01-JUN-90
    100870         2.8   01-JAN-90
    100871         5.6   01-JAN-90
    101860          24   15-FEB-89
    101863        12.5   15-FEB-89
    102130         3.4   18-AUG-89
    200376         2.4   15-NOV-90
.
.
.
31 rows selected.
```

In the following example, you want to find the products that actually have end_dates.

```
SELECT product_id, list_price, start_date, end_date
FROM Price
WHERE not (end_date) is null;
```

```
PRODUCT_ID  LIST_PRICE   START_DAT    END_DATE
----------  ----------   ---------    ---------
    100871         4.8   01-JAN-89    01-DEC-89
    100890          54   01-JUN-88    31-DEC-88
    100860          32   01-JAN-90    31-MAY-90
    100860          30   01-JAN-89    31-DEC-89
    100861          42   01-JAN-90    31-MAY-90
    100861          39   01-JAN-89    31-DEC-89
    100870         2.4   01-JAN-89    01-DEC-89
    103120        23.2   01-JAN-89    31-DEC-89
    103120          24   01-JAN-90    31-MAY-90
    103121        27.8   01-JAN-89    31-DEC-89
    103121        28.8   01-JAN-90    31-MAY-90
    103130           4   01-JAN-89    31-DEC-89
    103131         4.2   01-JAN-89    31-DEC-89
    104350          40   01-JAN-89    31-DEC-89
.
.
.
27 rows selected.
```

In the following example, you use one of the functions provided by SQL DBMS. The format different vendors use varies, however. In this example, you use Oracle8 to convert the start_date column to a more congenial date format by using the TO_CHAR function.

```
SELECT product_id, list_price, TO_CHAR(start_date,'fmMonth DD, YY),
TO_CHAR(end_date, 'fmMonth dd, yyyy')
FROM Price;
```

PRODUCT_ID	LIST_PRICE	TO_CHAR(START_DATE	TO_CHAR(END_DATE, 'fmMonth dd,yyyy')
100871	4.8	January 1, 1989	December 1, 1989
100890	58	January 1, 1989	
100890	54	June 1, 1988	December 31, 1988
100860	35	June 1, 1990	
100860	32	January 1, 1990	May 31, 1990
100860	30	January 1, 1989	December 31, 1989
100861	45	June 1, 1990	
100861	42	January 1, 1990	May 31, 1990
100861	39	January 1, 1989	December 31, 1989
100870	2.8	January 1, 1990	
100870	2.4	January 1, 1989	December 1, 1989
100871	5.6	January 1, 1990	
101860	24	February 15, 1989	
101863	12.5	February 15, 1989	
102130	3.4	August 18, 1989	
200376	2.4	November 15, 1990	
200380	4	November 15, 1990	
103120	23.2	January 1, 1989	December 31, 1989
103120	24	January 1, 1990	May 31, 1990
103120	25	June 1, 1990	
103121	27.8	January 1, 1989	December 31, 1989

.
.
.

58 rows selected.

In the following query, you conduct a "range test" using BETWEEN. In a *range test,* you check whether a data value lies between two values. The first expression indicates the column to be tested, and the second and third expressions define the low and high end of the range to be checked. The data types must be comparable for this to work successfully.

```
SELECT product_id, list_price,start_date, end_date
FROM price
WHERE start_date between '01-Jan-89' and '31-Dec-89';
```

PRODUCT_ID	LIST_PRICE	START_DAT	END_DATE
100871	4.8	01-JAN-89	01-DEC-89
100890	58	01-JAN-89	
100860	30	01-JAN-89	31-DEC-89
100861	39	01-JAN-89	31-DEC-89

.
.
.

```
    27 rows selected.
```

Here you use the ORDER BY clause. This clause provides the sorting for your query. You can sort from high to low—descending or from low to high—ascending. The default sort is ascending.

```
SELECT customer_id, Name, city, state, zip_code
FROM customer
WHERE state = 'CA'
ORDER BY State
```

CUSTOMER_ID	NAME	CITY	STATE	ZIP_CODE
100	JOCKSPORTS	BELMONT	CA	96711
101	TKB SPORT SHOP	REDWOOD CITY	CA	94061
102	VOLLYRITE	BURLINGAME	CA	95133
103	JUST TENNIS	BURLINGAME	CA	97544
104	EVERY MOUNTAIN	CUPERTINO	CA	93301

```
5 rows selected.
```

Here you ORDER BY multiple columns:

```
SELECT name, city, state
FROM customer
WHERE state in ('CA', 'WA')
ORDER BY state, city
```

```
NAME                    CITY                ST
---------------         ---------------     ----
JOCKSPORTS              BELMONT             CA
VOLLYRITE               BURLINGAME          CA
JUST TENNIS             BURLINGAME          CA
EVERY MOUNTAIN          CUPERTINO           CA
SHAPE UP                PALO ALTO           CA
TKB SPORT SHOP          REDWOOD CITY        CA
K + T SPORTS            SANTA CLARA         CA
WOMENS SPORTS           SUNNYVALE           CA

8 rows selected.
```

In the following examples, you learn about UNION and UNION ALL.

This is the first part of the UNION query. Note the rows returned for each query. You need these to see the difference in each of the queries.

```
'This is the first part of the query, you have 56 rows returned.

SELECT Order_Id, Total
FROM Sales_Order
WHERE Total > 1000;

  ORDER_ID       TOTAL
  ---------      -----
       612        5860
       605        8374
       620        4450
       613        6400
       614       23940
       619        1260
       617       46370
       618        3083
       509        1174
       523        1165
       549        1620
       516        1815
       553        4400
       526        7700
       543        8400
       555        8540
       528        3770
```

7

```
        531        1400
        558        1700
        565        4900
  .
  .
  .
56 rows selected.
```

Here is the second part:

```
'This is the second part of the UNION query, it has 157 rows returned.

Select Order_Id, Total
FROM Item
WHERE Quantity < 50;

ORDER_ID      TOTAL
--------- ---------
      600         42
      610         58
      611         45
      601       28.8
      601         32
      602         56
      604        174
      604         84
      604        384
      603        224
      610         35
      610        8.4
      612        810
      620        350
      616        450
      616        116
      616         34
      616         24
      615        180
      607        5.6
  .
  .
  .
157 rows selected.
```

This is the UNION query:

```
Select order_id, total
FROM sales_order
WHERE total > 1000
   UNION
Select Order_id, total
FROM Item
WHERE quantity < 50;
```

```
ORDER_ID      TOTAL
--------- ---------
      502        500
      503        236
      503        500
      503       1140
      503       1876
      504        250
      504        400
      504      784.7
      504     1434.7
      505        300
      506        300
      506     2600.4
      507        180
      507        706
      508        720
      508       1080
      509         34
      509         90
      509       1050
      509       1174
      .
      .
      .
211 rows selected.
```

The two separate queries had a combined total of 213 rows returned. A UNION combines the results of two or more queries into a single table of query results. What this indicates is duplicate rows exist in each single query. In your UNION query, you omit the duplicate rows. If you run a UNION ALL

7

query, you get a total of 213 rows returned because UNION ALL gives you the same results as if you ran each query separately and then added them together.

```
SELECT order_id, total
FROM sales_order
WHERE total > 1000
UNION ALL
SELECT order_id, total
FROM Item
WHERE quantity < 50;

ORDER_ID      TOTAL
--------   ---------
     612       5860
     605       8374
     620       4450
     613       6400
     614      23940
     619       1260
     617      46370
     618       3083
     509       1174
     523       1165
     549       1620
     516       1815
     553       4400
 .
 .
 .
213 rows returned.
```

The restrictions on UNION are as follows:

◆　The data type of each column must be the same.

◆　Neither of the two tables can be sorted with the ORDER BY clause. After you combine the two queries, however, you may insert an ORDER BY, as shown next.

```
SELECT order_id, total
FROM sales_order
WHERE total > 1000
UNION ALL
SELECT order_id, total
FROM Item
```

```
WHERE quantity < 50
ORDER BY Order_ID;

ORDER_ID     TOTAL
--------  ---------
     502       500
     503       236
     503       500
     503      1140
     503      1876
     504       250
     504       400
     504     784.7
     504    1434.7
     505       300
     506       300
     506    2600.4
     507       180
     507       706
   .
   .
   .
213 rows returned.
```

7

The Single-Table View

In this next example, you create a view you use in the next chapter. This
view is the Cust_View. In this example, you use the CREATE VIEW command
and the '‖' concatenation function.

```
CREATE VIEW cust_view as
SELECT Name, Address, City, State, zip_code, '('‖area_code‖')'‖
phone_number phone, credit_limit
FROM CUSTOMER
WHERE credit_limit >= 1000
```

NAME	ADDRESS	CITY	STATE	ZIP	PHONE	CREDIT LIMIT
JOCKSPORTS	345 VIEWRIDGE	BELMONT	CA	96711	(415)5986609	5000
TKB SPORT	490 BOLI RD.	REDWOOD CITY	CA	94061	(415)3681223	10000
VOLLYRITE	9722 HAMILTON	BURLINGAME	CA	95133	(415)6443341	7000
JUST TENNIS	HILLVIEW MALL	BURLINGAME	CA	97544	(415)6779312	3000
EVERY	574 SURRY RD.	CUPERTINO	CA	93301	(408)9962323	10000
K + T SPORTS	3476 EL PASEO	SANTA CLARA	CA	91003	(408)3769966	5000

```
SHAPE UP       908 SEQUOIA    PALO ALTO   CA  94301  (415)3649777   6000
WOMENS         VALCO VILLAGE  SUNNYVALE   CA  93301  (408)9674398  10000
NORTH WOODS    98 LONE PINE   HIBBING     MN  55649  (612)5669123   8000
STADIUM        47 IRVING PL.  NEW YORK    NY  10003  (212)5555335  10000
HOOPS          2345 ADAMS     LEICESTER   MA  01524  (508)5557542   5000
REBOUND        2 E. 14TH ST.  NEW YORK    NY  10009  (212)5555989  10000
THE POWER      1 KNOTS LNDG   DALLAS      TX  75248  (214)5550505  12000
POINT GUARD    20 THURSTON ST YONKERS     NY  10956  (914)5554766   3000
COLISEUM       5678 WILBUR PL SCARSDALE   NY  10583  (914)5550217   6000
FAST BREAK     1000 HERBERT   CONCORD     MA  01742  (508)5551298   7000
AL AND BOB'S   260 YORKTOWN   AUSTIN      TX  78731  (512)5557631   4000
AT BAT         234 BEACHEM    BROOKLINE   MA  02146  (617)5557385   8000
ALL SPORT      1000 38TH ST.  BROOKLYN    NY  11210  (718)5551739   6000
GOOD SPORT     400 46TH ST.   SUNNYSIDE   NY  11104  (718)5553771   5000
AL'S PRO       45 SPRUCE ST.  SPRING      TX  77388  (713)5555172   8000
BOB'S FAMILY   400 E. 23RD    HOUSTON     TX  77026  (713)5558015   8000
THE ALL AMER   547 PRENTICE   CHELSEA     MA  02150  (617)5553047   5000
HIT, THROW     333 WOOD COURT GRAPEVINE   TX  76051  (817)5552352   6000
THE OUTFIELD   346 GARDEN     FLUSHING    NY  11355  (718)5552131   4000
WHEELS AND     2 MEMORIAL     HOUSTON     TX  77007  (713)5554139  10000
JUST BIKES     4000 PARKRIDGE DALLAS      TX  75205  (214)5558735   4000
VELO SPORTS    23 WHITE ST.   MALDEN      MA  02148  (617)5554983   5000
JOE'S BIKE     4500 FOX COURT GRAND PRARIE TX 75051  (214)5559834   6000
BOB'S SWIM     300 HORSECREEK IRVING      TX  75039  (214)5558388   7000
CENTURY SHOP   8 DAGMAR DR.   HUNTINGTON  NY  11743  (516)5553006   4000
THE TOUR       2500 GARDNER   SOMERVILLE  MA  02144  (617)5556673   5000
FITNESS FIRST  5000 85TH ST.  JACKSON HGTS NY 11372  (718)5558710   4000
```

You have created a horizontal view, which means you have restricted the number of rows returned. This restricts the user's access to the underlying CUSTOMER table. Isn't this exciting? You have the power!

Naturally, you also have *vertical views*. These views restrict the access to only certain columns of a table.

```
CREATE VIEW RESPRICE AS
 SELECT Product_ID, List_Price
 FROM PRICE;

PRICE_ID  LIST_PRICE
--------  ----------
100871          4.8
100890           58
100890           54
100860           35
```

```
100860          32
100860          30
100861          45
100861          42
100861          39
100870         2.8
100870         2.4
100871         5.6
101860          24
101863        12.5
102130         3.4
200376         2.4
200380           4
103120        23.2
103120          24
103120          25
103121        27.8
103121        28.8
103121          30
103130           4
103130         4.2
103131         4.2
103131         4.5
103140          20
103141          20
   .
   .
   .
```

7

Finally, you can create a view that does both a horizontal and a vertical slice of the table. The horizontal and vertical views are not in the SQL language. This is used purely for explanation only.

```
CREATE VIEW ITEMS_View as
SELECT Order_ID, Item_ID, Product_ID, Total
FROM ITEM
WHERE Item_ID BETWEEN 1 and 3;

ORDER_ID    ITEM_ID    PRODUCT_ID    TOTAL
--------    -------    ----------    -----
600              1        100861       42
610              3        100890       58
611              1        100861       45
612              1        100860     3000
```

601	1	200376	28.8
601	2	100860	32
602	1	100870	56
604	1	100890	174
604	2	100861	84
604	3	100860	384
603	1	100860	224
610	1	100860	35
610	2	100870	8.4
614	1	100860	15540
614	2	100870	2800
612	2	100861	810
612	3	101863	1500
620	1	100860	350
620	2	200376	2400
620	3	102130	1700
613	1	100871	560
613	2	101860	4800
613	3	200380	600
619	3	102130	340
617	1	100860	1750
617	2	100861	4500
614	3	100871	5600
616	1	100861	450
616	2	100870	140
616	3	100890	116
619	1	200380	400
619	2	200376	240
615	1	100861	180
607	1	100871	5.6
615	2	100870	280
617	3	100870	1400
609	2	100870	12.5
609	3	100890	50
618	1	100860	805
618	2	100861	2250

.
.
.

The examples in this chapter represent what is possible to accomplish with a single-table query. You can create views and limit data access and you can complete mathematical functions with ease.

What's Next?

In the next chapter, you build upon what you have tried out here. You learn about joining tables, querying data from multiple tables, creating views from multiple tables, creating summary queries using the GROUP BY clause, and providing search conditions using the HAVING clause. The multiple table query is the most powerful query available in SQL.

7

CHAPTER 8

Complex
Multitable Queries

In this chapter, you have the opportunity to learn how to develop powerful queries by joining two or more tables together. Understanding the joins and how they impact what data you retrieve from your query is important. You also gain experience in using the various operators and functions available in SQL.

If you need to review the SELECT statement syntax that was introduced in the previous chapter, you should do so. Understanding the order of the clauses is important because you will be writing many SELECT statements.

The Ins and Outs of Joins

If you have more than one table in a query, joining the tables together is imperative. If you do not join tables, you will get a Cartesian (cross) product:

Cross Join

The following SELECT statement (query) gives you a Cartesian product.

```
SELECT *
FROM Item, Sales Order;
```

This gives you all possible pairs of rows from the two tables. So, if you had ten items and ten orders, you would have a row return result of (10*10) or 100 rows.

If you ran this query against a production database, many people would be angry with you because it would take a long time to run. Chances are, your DBA would probably kill the query and have a long chat with you in the process. The warning for this chapter is *always use a WHERE clause in a multitable join* unless you really need to use this type of query.

The WHERE clause forms pairs of rows by lining up the rows that match from each table, according to the type of join indicated in the WHERE clause.

Equi-Join

This is an *equi-join* (or *simple join*):

```
SELECT Sales_Order.Order_ID, Item.Order_ID, Item.Item_ID,
Item.Product_ID,Sales_Order.Total
FROM Item, Sales_Order
WHERE Sales_Order.Order_ID = Item.Order_ID;
```

An *equi-join* is a join based on an exact match between the ORDER_ID columns in both tables. The WHERE clause provides the search conditions that specifies the match of the columns between the tables.

This query is asking the database to provide all columns from both the Items and Sales_Order tables where the Order_ID columns match in both tables. So the rows to be returned are only the ones where an Item.Order_ID exists that matches exactly with the Sales_Order.Order_ID.

The relationship between the two tables is important when you decide on joining the tables. One relationship is the "parent/child." In a *parent/child* relationship, the primary key and foreign keys in the tables create the relationship. The table with the foreign key is the *child* in the relationship, and the table with the primary key is the *parent*. This type of join is considered to have a one-to-many relationship.

Other joins can also generate one-to-many relationships. For example, you have a one-to-many relationship when the matching column in at least one of the tables has a unique value for all rows of the table or if you join on arbitrary matching columns like two date datatype columns.

Non-Equi-Joins

An equi-join uses an equal sign (=) to indicate the type of join it is. A *non-equi-join* uses comparison operators that don't include an equal sign; for example, >, <, and <>.

8

```
SELECT Sales_Order.Order_ID, Item.Order_ID, Item.Item_ID,
Item.Product_ID,Sales_Order.Total
FROM Sales_Order, Item
WHERE Sales_Order.Order_ID >  Item.Order_ID;
```

In this query, each row of the query comes from a pair of rows, Sales Order, and Item, where the Sales_Order_ID is greater than the Item.Order_ID.

Equi-joins are more commonly used. Non-equi-joins can serve a practical use for decision support queries, however, when there's a need to compare and contrast data.

Column Names in Multitable Queries

In the previous example, you may have noticed two columns have the same column name: Order_ID. So the names are not confused by SQL, you must indicate a distinction in the names of the columns. This is accomplished by using the name of the table with the column name, Sales_Order, and Order_ID. If you do not include the table name, you receive an error stating you have an ambiguous column name.

You can write the distinct column names in two ways: The first is by using the name of the table and the column name. The second is by providing an alias for the table. In the current example, you can take the first letter of each table and use it as an alias.

```
SELECT S.Order_ID, I.Order_ID, I.Item_ID, I.Product_ID, S.Total
FROM Sales_Order S, Item I
WHERE S.Order_ID >  I.Order_ID;
```

This saves you time when you have long table names and long queries to write.

Self-Join

Sometimes you have a multiple-table query that has a relationship with itself. A bit narcissistic, but it happens. The only way you can accomplish this is by doing a *self-join* for the table in question.

For example, there is a Supervisor column in the Employee table. The only way you can identify the Supervisor *Name* from the Supervisor ID code column is to relate it back to the Employee ID in the same table. You see the Supervisor is an employee, and the Supervisor ID code is the Employee ID code. This is how you would accomplish this:

```
SELECT Name, Supervisor.Name
FROM Employer, Supervisor
WHERE Employer.Emp_ID = Supervisor.Supv_ID;
```

What you have done here is create a *table alias*. The FROM clause assigns the alias to the copy of the Employer table. The Supervisor Name is assigned to the one copy of the Employer table. Here are the results:

Name	Supervisor Name
Tom Arnold	Harry Schwartz
Harry Schwartz	Melanie Cage
Don Sharp	Harry Schwartz
Melanie Cage	Sam Cardinal

Inner Join

An *inner join* is where the rows of the tables are combined with each other and produce new rows equal to the product of the number of rows in each table. The inner join uses the rows to determine the result of the Where clause. If you haven't noticed, equi-joins and non-equi-joins are all inner joins. Here is the syntax:

```
SELECT *
FROM Table1 INNER JOIN Table2
USING (Column1, Column2)
```

Here is an example of an inner join:

```
SELECT *
FROM Sales_Order INNER JOIN Item
Using (Sales_Order.ORDER_ID, Item.Order_ID);
```

NOTE: This syntax is in most SQL products. Although it isn't recognized in Oracle8, it is recognized in SQL Server 7 and Sybase 11. Oracle8 does not recognize the new syntax. The SELECT statement for an inner join would be

8

```
SELECT *
FROM Sales_Order
WHERE Sales_Order.Order_ID = Item.Order_ID;
```

Outer Joins

An *outer join* preserves unmatched rows from one or both tables, so it returns the rows that are matched and unmatched from one or both tables. A *left outer join* returns matched and unmatched rows from the left table and only the matched rows from the right table. A *right outer join* returns matched and unmatched rows from the right table and only the matched rows from the left table. A *full outer join* is a combination of left and right outer joins; it returns unmatched rows from both tables.

The syntax presented may not be represented in the SQL products as outlined here. However, you learn how to accomplish these joins through the syntax used in Oracle8. You should check with your RDBMS documentation to see what is acceptable.

Here is an example of a left outer join using Oracle8:

```
SELECT Item.Product_ID, Item.Total, Sales_Order.Order_ID,
Sales_Order.Order_Date
FROM Item, Sales_Order
WHERE Item.Order_ID = + Sales_Order.Order_ID;
```

PRODUCT_ID	TOTAL	ORDER_ID	ORDER_DATE
100860	35	610	07-JAN-91
100870	8.4	610	07-JAN-91
100890	58	610	07-JAN-91
100861	45	611	11-JAN-91
100860	3000	612	15-JAN-91
100861	810	612	15-JAN-91
101863	1500	612	15-JAN-91
100871	550	612	15-JAN-91
200376	28.8	601	01-MAY-90
100860	32	601	01-MAY-90
100870	56	602	05-JUN-90
100861	42	600	01-MAY-90
100890	174	604	15-JUN-90
100861	84	604	15-JUN-90
100860	384	604	15-JUN-90
100861	4500	605	14-JUL-90
100870	1400	605	14-JUL-90
100890	290	605	14-JUL-90
101860	1200	605	14-JUL-90
101863	950	605	14-JUL-90
102130	34	605	14-JUL-90

Now here's an example of a right outer join using Oracle8:

```
SELECT Item.Product_ID, Item.Total, Sales_Order.Order_ID,
Sales_Order.Order_Date
FROM Item, Sales_Order
WHERE Item.Order_ID (+) = Sales_Order.Order_ID;
```

PRODUCT_ID	TOTAL	ORDER_ID	ORDER_DATE
100860	35	610	07-JAN-91
100870	8.4	610	07-JAN-91
100890	58	610	07-JAN-91
100861	45	611	11-JAN-91

100860	3000	612	15-JAN-91
100861	810	612	15-JAN-91
101863	1500	612	15-JAN-91
100871	550	612	15-JAN-91
200376	28.8	601	01-MAY-90
100860	32	601	01-MAY-90
100870	56	602	05-JUN-90
100861	42	600	01-MAY-90
100890	174	604	15-JUN-90
100861	84	604	15-JUN-90
100860	384	604	15-JUN-90
100861	4500	605	14-JUL-90
100870	1400	605	14-JUL-90
100890	290	605	14-JUL-90
101860	1200	605	14-JUL-90
101863	950	605	14-JUL-90
102130	34	605	14-JUL-90

Here is an example of a full outer join:

```
SELECT Item.Product_ID, Item.Total, Sales_Order.Order_ID,
Sales_Order.Order_Date
FROM Item, Sales_Order
WHERE Item.Order_ID (+) = + Sales_Order.Order_ID;
```

PRODUCT_ID	TOTAL	ORDER_ID	ORDER_DATE
100860	35	610	07-JAN-91
100870	8.4	610	07-JAN-91
100890	58	610	07-JAN-91
100861	45	611	11-JAN-91
100860	3000	612	15-JAN-91
100861	810	612	15-JAN-91
101863	1500	612	15-JAN-91
100871	550	612	15-JAN-91
200376	28.8	601	01-MAY-90
100860	32	601	01-MAY-90
100870	56	602	05-JUN-90
100861	42	600	01-MAY-90
100890	174	604	15-JUN-90
100861	84	604	15-JUN-90
100860	384	604	15-JUN-90
100861	4500	605	14-JUL-90
100870	1400	605	14-JUL-90
100890	290	605	14-JUL-90
101860	1200	605	14-JUL-90
101863	950	605	14-JUL-90
102130	34	605	14-JUL-90

8

The Oracle8 syntax for the outer joins is as follows:

◆ **Left outer join**   Column = + Column

◆ **Right outer join**   Column (+) = Column

◆ **Full join**   Column (+) = + Column

The new ANSI syntax is represented in SQL Server 7. For these examples, you need the SQL Server tables from the database PUBS, which is included with the SQL Server product. You use four tables: Authors, TitleAuthors, Titles, and RoySched. Figures 8-1 through 8-4 show the Properties windows of SQL Server 7 database for these tables.

Notice a picture of a key is located next to the primary key of the table. This is a nice addition to the Query Analyzer in SQL Server 7.

The following are examples of an equi-join, left outer join, and right outer join.

Here's an equi-join:

```
SELECT Titles.Title_ID, Titles.Title, Titles.Price, Titleauthor.Au_ID,
Titleauthor.Royaltyper FROM Titles, Titleauthor
WHERE Titles.Title_ID = Titleauthor.Title_ID
```

TITLE ID	TITLE	PRICE	AUTHOR ID	ROY
PS3333	Prolonged Data Deprivation	19.99	172-32-1176	100
BU1032	Busy Executive's Database Guide	19.99	213-46-8915	40
BU2075	You Can Combat Computer Stress!	2.99	213-46-8915	100
PC1035	But Is It User Friendly?	22.95	238-95-7766	100
BU1111	Cooking with Computers	11.95	267-41-2394	40
TC7777	Sushi	14.99	267-41-2394	30
BU7832	Straight Talk About Computers	19.99	274-80-9391	100
BU1032	Busy Executive's Database Guide	19.99	409-56-7008	60
PC8888	Secrets of Silicon Valley	20.00	427-17-2319	50
TC7777	Sushi	14.99	472-27-2349	30
PC9999	Net Etiquette		486-29-1786	100
PS7777	Emotional Security	7.99	486-29-1786	100
TC4203	Buckingham Palace Kitchens	11.95	648-92-1872	100
TC7777	Sushi	14.99	672-71-3249	40
MC2222	Silicon Valley Gastronomic	19.99	712-45-1867	100
MC3021	The Gourmet Microwave	2.99	722-51-5454	75
BU1111	Cooking with Computers	11.95	724-80-9391	60
PS1372	Computer Phobic AND Non-Phobic	21.59	724-80-9391	25
PS1372	Computer Phobic AND Non-Phobic	21.59	756-30-7391	75
TC3218	Onions, Leeks, and Garlic	20.95	807-91-6654	100
PC8888	Secrets of Silicon Valley	20.00	846-92-7186	50
MC3021	The Gourmet Microwave	2.99	899-46-2035	25
PS2091	Is Anger the Enemy?	10.95	899-46-2035	50
PS2091	Is Anger the Enemy?	10.95	998-72-3567	50
PS2106	Life Without Fear	7.00	998-72-3567	100

25 records selected.

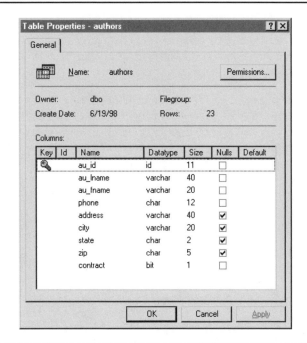

Properties of
Authors table
Figure 8-1.

8

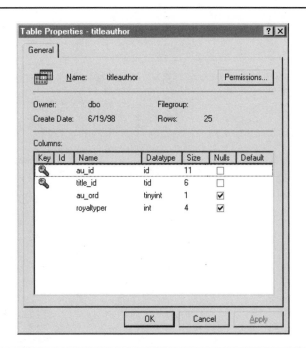

Properties of
TitleAuthor
table
Figure 8-2.

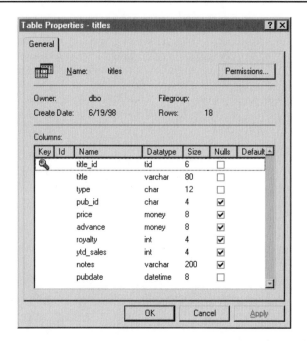

Properties of
Titles table

Figure 8-3.

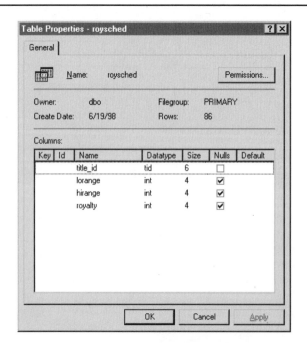

Properties of
RoySched
table

Figure 8-4.

For the left outer join example, you use the TitleAuthor and Titles tables. What you need to find is a list of all titles and the authors who wrote them. What this query does is to give you a list of all titles (left table) and only the authors that match from the Titles table.

Here's the left outer join example:

```
SELECT titles.Title_ID,titles.Title, Titles.Price,
Titleauthor.au_id,Titleauthor.royaltyper FROM Titles left outer join
Titleauthor on
Titles.Title_ID=Titleauthor.Title_ID
```

TITLE ID	TITLE	PRICE	AUTHOR ID	ROY
BU1032	Busy Executive's Database Guide	19.99	213-46-8915	40
BU1032	Busy Executive's Database Guide	19.99	409-56-7008	60
BU1111	Cooking with Computers	11.95	267-41-2394	40
BU1111	Cooking with Computers	11.95	724-80-9391	60
BU2075	You Can Combat Computer Stress!	2.99	213-46-8915	100
BU7832	Straight Talk About Computers	19.99	274-80-9391	100
MC2222	Silicon Valley Gastronomic	19.99	712-45-1867	100
MC3021	The Gourmet Microwave	2.99	722-51-5454	75
MC3021	The Gourmet Microwave	2.99	899-46-2035	25
MC3026	The Psychology of Computer Cooking			
PC1035	But Is It User Friendly?	22.95	238-95-7766	100
PC8888	Secrets of Silicon Valley	20.00	427-17-2319	50
PC8888	Secrets of Silicon Valley	20.00	846-92-7186	50
PC9999	Net Etiquette		486-29-1786	100
PS1372	Computer Phobic AND Non-Phobic	21.59	724-80-9391	25
PS1372	Computer Phobic AND Non-Phobic	21.59	756-30-7391	75
PS2091	Is Anger the Enemy?	10.95	899-46-2035	50
PS2091	Is Anger the Enemy?	10.95	998-72-3567	50
PS2106	Life Without Fear	7.00	998-72-3567	100
PS3333	Prolonged Data Deprivation	19.99	172-32-1176	100
PS7777	Emotional Security	7.99	486-29-1786	100
TC3218	Onions, Leeks and Garlic	20.95	807-91-6654	100
TC4203	Buckingham Palace Kitchens	11.95	648-92-1872	100
TC7777	Sushi Anyone	14.99	267-41-2394	30
TC7777	Sushi Anyone	14.99	472-27-2349	30
TC7777	Sushi Anyone	14.99	672-71-3249	40

27 records selected.

8

The right outer join example provides unmatched rows for the right table (TitleAuthor) and only those rows that match for the left table (Titles).

Here is the right outer join example:

```
SELECT Titles.Title_ID, Titles.Title, Titles.Price, Titleauthor.Au_ID,
Titleauthor.Royaltyper
FROM Titles right outer join Titleauthor on
Titles.Title_ID = Titleauthor.Title_ID
```

TITLE ID	TITLE	PRICE	AUTHOR ID	ROY
PS3333	Prolonged Data Deprivation	19.99	172-32-1176	100
BU1032	Busy Executive's Database Guide	19.99	213-46-8915	40
BU2075	You Can Combat Computer Stress!	2.99	213-46-8915	100
PC1035	But Is It User Friendly?	22.95	238-95-7766	100
BU1111	Cooking with Computers	11.95	267-41-2394	40
TC7777	Sushi	14.99	267-41-2394	30
BU7832	Straight Talk About Computers	19.99	274-80-9391	100
BU1032	Busy Executive's Database Guide	19.99	409-56-7008	60
PC8888	Secrets of Silicon Valley	20.00	427-17-2319	50
TC7777	Sushi Anyone	14.99	472-27-2349	30
PC9999	Net Etiquette		486-29-1786	100
PS7777	Emotional Security	7.99	486-29-1786	100
TC4203	Buckingham Palace Kitchens	11.95	648-92-1872	100
TC7777	Sushi Anyone	14.99	672-71-3249	40
MC2222	Silicon Valley Gastronomic	19.99	712-45-1867	100
MC3021	The Gourmet Microwave	2.99	722-51-5454	75
BU1111	Cooking with Computers	11.95	724-80-9391	60
PS1372	Computer Phobic AND Non-Phobic	21.59	724-80-9391	25
PS1372	Computer Phobic AND Non-Phobic	21.59	756-30-7391	75
TC3218	Onions, Leeks, and Garlic	20.95	807-91-6654	100
PC8888	Secrets of Silicon Valley	20.00	846-92-7186	50
MC3021	The Gourmet Microwave	2.99	899-46-2035	25
PS2091	Is Anger the Enemy?	10.95	899-46-2035	50
PS2091	Is Anger the Enemy?	10.95	998-72-3567	50
PS2106	Life Without Fear	7.00	998-72-3567	100

25 rows selected.

So what does the new ANSI syntax for inner and outer joins do? It puts the search conditions in the FROM clause instead of in the WHERE clause, thereby enabling faster processing.

The next example illustrates what to do when you have two tables you cannot join and you must add a third table to join the two tables together. The third table is called the *linking table*.

Two tables are in the PUBS database that you need to join to get the columns you need. They are the Authors table and the Titles table. Look at Figures 8-1 and 8-3. There are no columns that we can use to join these two tables.

However, if you look at Figure 8-2, TitleAuthor table, you see the Au_ID and the Title_ID are both in this table. We can join the tables now by using the TitleAuthor table as the linking table.

You need to get an author name and telephone number, title and royalty percent for a project. The query would be

```
SELECT authors.au_lname, authors.au_fname,authors.phone,titles.Title,
titleauthor.royaltyper
FROM authors, titleauthor, titles
WHERE authors.au_id = titleauthor.au_id and
titleauthor.title_id = titles.title_id
ORDER BY authors.au_lname
```

LNAME	FNAME	PHONE	TITLE	ROY
Bennet	Abraham	415 555-9932	Busy Executive's Database Guide	60
Blotchet-Hal	Reginald	503 555-6402	Buckingham Palace Kitchens	100
Carson	Cheryl	415 555-7723	But Is It User Friendly?	100
DeFrance	Michel	219 555-9982	The Gourmet Microwave	75
del Castillo	Innes	615 555-8275	Silicon Valley Gastronomic	100
Dull	Ann	415 555-7128	Secrets of Silicon Valley	50
Green	Marjorie	415 555-7020	Busy Executive's Database Guide	40
Green	Marjorie	415 555-7020	You Can Combat Computer Stress	100
Gringlesby	Burt	707 555-6445	Sushi	30
Hunter	Sheryl	415 555-7128	Secrets of Silicon Valley	50
Karsen	Livia	415 555-9219	Computer Phobic AND Non-Phobic	75
Locksley	Charlene	415 555-4620	Net Etiquette	100
Locksley	Charlene	415 555-4620	Emotional Security	100
MacFeather	Stearns	415 555-7128	Cooking with Computers	60
MacFeather	Stearns	415 555-7128	Computer Phobic AND Non-Phobic	25
O'Leary	Michael	408 555-2428	Cooking with Computers	40
O'Leary	Michael	408 555-2428	Sushi	30
Panteley	Sylvia	301 555-8853	Onions	100
Ringer	Albert	801 555-0752	Is Anger the Enemy?	50
Ringer	Albert	801 555-0752	Life Without Fear	100
Ringer	Anne	801 555-0752	The Gourmet Microwave	25
Ringer	Anne	801 555-0752	Is Anger the Enemy?	50
Straight	Dean	415 555-2919	Straight Talk About Computers	100
White	Johnson	408 555-7223	Prolonged Data Deprivation	100
Yokomoto	Akiko	415 555-4228	Sushi	40

8

Summary Queries

In *summary queries,* you use the GROUP BY clause. In a Group query, the groups of data from your tables produce a single summary row for each row group. The columns you specify in your GROUP BY are your "grouping columns." *Grouping columns* determine how the rows are divided into groups.

To see the difference the group column has on a query, look at the following examples:

```
SELECT AVG(Actual_Price)
FROM Item

AVG(ACTUAL_PRICE)
-----------------
        19.029926
```

This first query gives you the average actual price of all items. The next query gives you the average actual price by order.

```
SELECT Item.Order_ID, Avg(Actual_Price)
FROM ITEM
GROUP BY Order_ID;

ORDER_ID AVG(ACTUAL_PRICE)
--------- -----------------
      501               3.6
      502                50
      503              37.2
      504         37.473333
      505             11.75
      506         14.793333
      507             22.15
      508             20.25
      509              15.8
      510            12.535
      511              10.5
      512              19.7
      513         22.616667
      514                38
      515             21.94
      516               4.7
      517              26.7
      518             21.05
      519             11.25
      520             3.885
      521            21.615
```

The first query is a simple summary query. The second query is a grouping query.

SQL computes the average for each group (Order_ID) for all the rows in the group and returns a single summary row (Order_ID and Average Actual Price) of query results.

When you have a group query based on two or more columns, SQL provides only a single level of grouping.

```
SELECT Item.Order_ID, Item.Item_ID, Avg(Item.Actual_Price)
FROM Item
GROUP BY Item.Order_ID, Item.Item_ID;
```

ORDER_ID	ITEM_ID	AVG(ITEM.ACTUAL_PRICE)
501	1	3.6
502	1	50
503	1	38
503	2	23.6
503	3	50
504	1	40
504	2	22.42
504	3	50
505	1	3.5
505	2	20
506	1	20.88
506	2	3.5
506	3	20
507	1	35.3
507	2	9
508	1	36
508	2	4.5
509	1	35
509	2	9
509	3	3.4
510	1	20.88

8

This query returns a summary row for each Order_ID/Item_ID pair.

There are some restrictions to grouped queries. For instance, the grouping columns need to be actual columns of the tables named in the FROM clause.

You cannot group rows based on the value of a calculated expression. In addition, the items that appear on the SELECT-list of a grouped query must have single value for each of the grouped rows. So what can be in a group query? The following items:

◆ A constant

◆ A column function that produces a single value summarizing the rows in the group

◆ A grouping column

◆ An expression involving combinations of these items

When you create the group query, a common error is omitting a column from your SELECT-list. Look at what happens when you do:

```
SELECT Item.Order_Id, Item.Item_ID Item.Total
FROM Item
GROUP BY Product_Id;

SELECT Item.Order_Id, Item.Item_ID Item.Total
                                         *
ERROR at line 1:

ORA-00923: FROM keyword not found where expected
```

In this error message, you are told you should have Item_Product_ID in your SELECT-list. If you fix the problem, you will have a happy result:

```
SELECT Item.Product_ID, Item.Order_Id, Item.Item_ID, Item.Total
FROM Item
GROUP BY Product_Id

SELECT Item.Product_ID, Item.Order_Id, Item.Item_ID, Item.Total

                        *

ERROR at line 1:

ORA-00979: not a GROUP BY expression
```

What went wrong here? You put in the Product_ID, right? Well, you need to list all SELECT-list items in the GROUP BY clause:

```
SELECT Item.Product_ID, Item.Order_Id, Item.Item_ID, Item.Total
FROM Item
GROUP BY Product_Id, Item.Order_Id, Item.Item_ID, Item.Total;
```

PRODUCT_ID	ORDER_ID	ITEM_ID	TOTAL
100860	601	2	32
100860	603	1	224
100860	604	3	384
100860	610	1	35
100860	612	1	3000
100860	614	1	15540
100860	617	1	1750
100860	618	1	805
100860	620	1	350
100861	600	1	42
100861	604	2	84
100861	605	1	4500
100861	609	1	40
100861	611	1	45
100861	612	2	810
100861	615	1	180

8

Eliminate Duplicate Rows with Distinct
In the last chapter, you learned about the DISTINCT keyword, but you need to know something else. You can eliminate rows from your query before you apply a column function to it. This example illustrates how this is done:

```
SELECT Count(Distinct Order_ID)
FROM Item

COUNT(DISTINCTORDER_ID)
-----------------------
                    100
```

The standard allows the DISTINCT keyword for SUM( ), AVG( ), and COUNT( ). Some vendors also provide DISTINCT MIN( ), MAX( ). Remember, you cannot use DISTINCT for Count(*)(all columns); it must be used for DISTINCT (column).

Nulls in Group Column

What happens when the value of the group column is unknown? Into which group should it be placed? The ANSI standard considers two NULL values are equal in the GROUP BY clause. This, of course, is contrary to the rule that if two nulls are compared, the result is NULL. The two nulls are not equal.

So what does this mean to the grouping? If two rows have nulls in the same group column and have identical values in all their non-NULL group columns, they are grouped together in the same row group. Note, this ANSI standard is not implemented by all SQL DBMSs. The following is an example of a NULL present in a GROUP BY clause and how Oracle8 deals with the situation:

```
SELECT Date_Case_Closed, case.Case_ID, Case.Case_Name, Client_ID
FROM Scott.Case
GROUP BY
Date_Case_Closed, case.Case_ID, Case.Case_Name, Client_ID;

DATE_CASE CASE_ID         CASE_NAME                           CLIENT_ID
--------- --------------- ----------------------------------- ---------
31-MAR-98 98-101          Dishonest Employee                          1
          98-100          Georgia is Missing                          3
```

It still shows the NULL and accepts it.

IN DEPTH

The HAVING Clause

Group search conditions are handled by the HAVING clause and not the WHERE clause. The HAVING clause is used to select and reject row groups. The format of the HAVING clause is similar to the WHERE clause, consisting of the keyword HAVING and the search conditions. The HAVING clause enables you to use aggregate functions in the same way the WHERE clause does for individual rows.

What the HAVING clause does is evaluate each group and reject an individual row that did not meet the search conditions. You can have more than one condition in a HAVING clause and you can use an aggregate function that is not in the SELECT statement.

The HAVING clause is illustrated in the following examples.

This example uses two search conditions, as well as having a group column (Credit_Limit), which is not in the SELECT-list.

```
SELECT Customer.Customer_ID, Customer.Name, Customer.City,
Customer.State
FROM CUSTOMER
GROUP BY Customer.State, Customer.Customer_ID, Customer.Name,
Customer.City, Customer.Cred
HAVING Customer.State = 'CA' and Credit_Limit > 1000;
```

```
CUSTOMER_ID   NAME                                      CITY           ST
-----------   ------------------------------------      -------------  --
100           JOCKSPORTS                                BELMONT        CA
101           TKB SPORT SHOP                            REDWOOD CITY   CA
102           VOLLYRITE                                 BURLINGAME     CA
103           JUST TENNIS                               BURLINGAME     CA
104           EVERY MOUNTAIN                            CUPERTINO      CA
105           K + T SPORTS                              SANTA CLARA    CA
106           SHAPE                                     PALO ALTO      CA
107           WOMENS SPORTS                             SUNNYVALE      CA

8 rows selected.
```

Here is another example of a HAVING clause:

```
SELECT Item.Order_ID, Item.Item_ID, Item.Product_ID, Item.Quantity
FROM Item
GROUP BY Item.Order_ID, Item.Item_ID, Item.Product_ID, Item.Quantity
HAVING AVG(Quantity) > 300;
```

```
ORDER_ID   ITEM_ID   PRODUCT_ID   QUANTITY
--------   --------   ----------   --------
     526          2       105124        500
     543          2       105124        500
     553          1       105127        500
     553          2       200376        800
     555          2       105124        500
     605          2       100870        500
```

8

```
614          1        100860          444
614          2        100870         1000
614          3        100871         1000
617          3        100870          500
617          4        100871          500
617          5        100890          500
620          2        200376         1000
620          3        102130          500
```

14 rows selected.

Now here's an example of a HAVING clause with OR:

```
SELECT Item.Order_ID, Item.Product_ID, Item.Actual_Price, Item.Quantity
FROM Item
GROUP BY item.Product_ID, Item.Order_ID, Item.Actual_Price,
Item.Quantity
HAVING SUM(ITEM.Actual_Price) > 2000
OR
MIN (Quantity) > 20;
```

ORDER_ID	PRODUCT_ID	ACTUAL_PRICE	QUANTITY
601	100860	32	1
603	100860	32	7
604	100860	32	12
610	100860	35	1
612	100860	30	100
614	100860	35	444
617	100860	35	50
618	100860	35	23
620	100860	35	10
600	100861	42	1
604	100861	42	2
605	100861	45	100
609	100861	40	1
611	100861	45	1
612	100861	40.5	20
615	100861	45	4

IN DEPTH

CONTINUED

616	100861	45	10
617	100861	45	100
618	100861	45	50
621	100861	45	10
605	100870	2.8	500

As in the WHERE clause, the HAVING clause search condition can present one of three results: If the search condition is true, the row group is retained. If the search condition is false, the row group is not included. And if the search condition is NULL, the row group is not included.

Putting It All Together—the Whole Enchilada!

The following are queries based on an applicant tracking system. The reports that were needed were complex. Additional views were needed because the business requirements were at odds with the database design.

8

This first query solved a problem that existed due to the user requirement to include all untracked applicants. The linking table, Track, linked the Requisition table to the Resume table. The only applicants that resided on the Track table were those applicants who were tracked.

Variables were created: untracked, tracked and candidate_type. The first SELECT statement identified all the fields needed for the view. Then a UNION join was created and the second SELECT statement selected untracked applicants only.

Because the untracked applicants did not have corresponding requisition information, one was created with this:

```
0 as SYS_REQ_ID, ' ' as USER_REQ_ID, ' ' as Dept_ID, ' ' as Job_ID,
' ' as Recruiter_ID, ' ' as Class, 0 as Total_Openings, 0 as Total_Hired.
```

The 0's were used for number fields and ' ' was used for string fields. This tricked the system into placing untracked applicants onto the Track table.

The following WHERE clause

```
Resume_MST.Resume_ID = (+) Track.Resume_ID and (Track.Resume_ID) is null
```

indicated a left outer join and where the Track Resume ID was null (the 0 field added). It worked beautifully. You see, sometimes you have to be a little inventive to get what you need out of a database.

UNION Join

Here is the SQL used for the UNION join query:

```
SELECT 'Tracked' as Candidate_Type, Resume_MST.Source_ID,
Resume_Mst.Date_Received, Resume_Mst.Middle_Name,
Resume_MST.Last_Name, Resume_MST.First_Name, Resume_MST.Resume_ID,
Requistn.Sys_Req_ID, Requistn.User_Req_ID, Requistn.Dept_ID,
Requistn.Job_ID, Requistn.Recruiter_ID, Requistn.Class,
Requistn.Total_Openings, Requistn.Total_Hired, Resume_MST.EEO_Sex,
Resume_MST.EEO_Minority
    FROM Resume_MST Track, Requistn
    WHERE Resume_MST.Resume_ID = Track.Resume_ID and
    Requistn.Sys_req_ID=Track.Sys_Req_Id

UNION

SELECT 'Untracked' as Candidate_Type, Resume_MST.Source_ID,
Resume_Mst.Date_Received,Resume_Mst.Middle_Name,Resume_MST.Last_Name, Re-
sume_MST.First_Name, Resume_MST.Resume_ID,
0 as SYS_REQ_ID, ' ' as USER_REQ_ID, ' ' as Dept_ID, ' ' as Job_ID, ' ' as Re-
cruiter_ID, ' ' as Class, 0 as Total_Openings, 0 as Total_Hired,
Resume_MST.EEO_Sex, Resume_MST.EEO_Minority

    FROM Resume_MST Resume_MST, Track
    WHERE Resume_MST.Resume_ID = (+)Track.Resume_ID and
    (Track.Resume_ID) is null
```

The next case involves the same applicant database, but a different sort of problem. Based on the business requirements, the user only needs to see the highest degree an individual attained. In addition, a new table was created by the DBA, which was used as a lookup table for the Res_Edu.School Code. No description column was provided by the database. A school description was a necessity.

Also a query was used to get the correct population. The query was used in the FROM clause and grouped the applicants by Resume_ID, thus creating a result set. In the WHERE clause, this result set is joined to the Res_Edu table degree description column.

Finally, a RTRIM is used to trim the code so it can be joined to the new School table.

Multitable Join with Different Functions
Here is the multitable join:

```
SELECT max_degree.DEGREE_DESC AS MaxOfDEGREE_DESC,
RES_EDU.DEGREE_CODE, RESUME_MST.RESUME_ID,
RESUME_MST.FIRST_NAME, RESUME_MST.LAST_NAME,
RES_EDU.MAJOR_CODE, RES_EDU.MAJOR_DESC,
RES_EDU.SCHOOL_CODE, RES_EDU.SCHOOL_DESC,RES_EDU.SCHOOL_RAW,
RES_EDU.GPA,
RES_EDU.END_YEAR,Schools.name

    FROM  (select RESUME_ID,max(degree_desc) degree_desc from
    resumix.res_edu group by resume_id) max_degree,
    RESUMIX.RESUME_MST RESUME_MST,
    RESUMIX.RES_EDU RES_EDU,RESUMIX.Schools

    WHERE
    RESUME_MST.RESUME_ID = (+) RES_EDU.RESUME_ID and
    res_edu.resume_id = max_degree.resume_id and
    res_edu.degree_desc = max_degree.degree_desc and
    RTRIM(Res_Edu.School_Code)=Schools.Code
```

As you can see, understanding SQL is only the beginning of working with data in your queries. You need to understand your user's needs and your database, and you need to have a creative mind to problem-solve. Try not to "think in the box" all the time. Do not get wrapped up in the literal nature of programming. Sometimes you need to be a little devious and use your variables and your wit.

What's Next?
The next chapter takes you deeper into querying. You learn subqueries and nested subqueries and their uses. In addition, you look at how Crystal Reports handles subqueries.

8

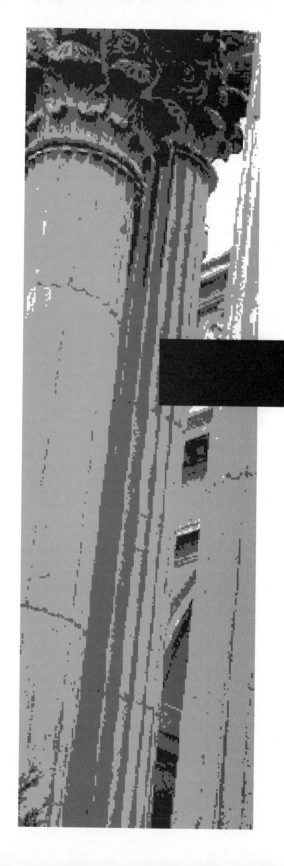

CHAPTER 9

The Subquery

Did you know the subquery is the most natural way to express a query because it parallels the English-language description of the query? It is because of the ability to query within a query that the word "structured" appears in the name Structured Query Language. So what is a subquery? Inquiring minds need to know!

The Subquery Revealed

A *subquery* is a query that is in a WHERE or HAVING clause. A subquery is always enclosed in parentheses, but it has the familiar form of a SELECT statement. Some differences exist between an ordinary query and a subquery, however:

◆ The subquery must produce a single column of data as its query results. A subquery always has a single item in its SELECT clause.

◆ No ORDER BY is used in a subquery.

◆ A subquery cannot be the union of several single SELECT statements.

The following subquery would not work if you did not include a group function, such as SUM.

```
SELECT City
    FROM Customer
    WHERE Credit_Limit > (SELECT SUM(TOTAL)
                          FROM Sales_Order
                          WHERE Customer.Customer_ID =
                          Sales_Order.Customer_ID)


CITY
------------------------------
REDWOOD CITY
BURLINGAME
CUPERTINO
SUNNYVALE
HIBBING
NEW YORK
CONCORD
DALLAS
MALDEN
IRVING
HUNTINGTON
SOMERVILLE

12 rows selected.
```

The query wouldn't work because the subquery would have returned more than a single row.

The main query in the preceding example takes its data from the Customer table and the WHERE clause selects which cities will be included in the query result. SQL goes through row by row and applies the test stated in the WHERE clause. Now, to test the Credit_Limit value, SQL carries out the subquery, finding the sum of the totals for customers in the Sales_Order table and compares it against the credit-limit in the Customer table.

Outer References

An *outer reference* is a column name that does not refer to any of the tables named in the FROM clause of the main query. The value of the column in an outer reference is taken from the row being tested by the main query. In the following example, the outer reference is the Product_ID.

```
SELECT Order_ID, Product_ID
FROM ITEM
    WHERE Actual_Price >= (SELECT AVG(LIST_PRICE)
                           FROM PRICE
                             WHERE Item.Product_ID = Price.Product_ID)


 ORDER_ID PRODUCT_ID
--------- ----------
      600     100861
      610     100890
      611     100861
      601     200376
      602     100870
      604     100890
      604     100861
 .
 .
 .
120 rows selected
```

9

Search Conditions

Because a subquery is in the WHERE or HAVING clause, it has search conditions. The search conditions are

◆ **Subquery comparison test**   This compares the value of an expression to a single value of a subquery.

- **Subquery set membership test**   This checks if the value of an expression matches one of the set of values produced by the subquery.

- **Existence test**   This checks to see if a subquery produces any rows of query results.

- **Quantified comparison test**   This compares the value of an expression to each of the set of values produced by a subquery.

Subquery Comparison Test

This test compares the value of an expression to the value produced by a subquery and returns TRUE results if the comparison is true. Remember, these are the comparison operators:

- Equal comparison =

- Not Equal comparison <>

- Less Than <

- Greater Than >

- Less Than or Equal <=

- Greater Than or Equal >=

You use this test to compare a value from the row being tested to a single value produced by a subquery.

```
SELECT Order_ID, Product_ID
FROM ITEM
    WHERE Actual_Price >= (SELECT AVG(LIST_PRICE)
                           FROM PRICE
                           WHERE Item.Order_ID >= 610)


ORDER_ID PRODUCT_ID
--------- ----------
      610     100890
      611     100861
      612     100860
      610     100860
      614     100860
      612     100861
      620     100860
      613     101860
      617     100860
      617     100861
```

```
616      100861
616      100890
615      100861
617      100890
617      101860
618      100860
618      100861
621      100861
```

18 rows selected.

NOTE: If the subquery produces multiple rows, the comparison does not compute and SQL reports an error condition.

Following is another example of the comparison test:

```
SELECT Order_ID, Item_ID, Product_ID
 FROM Item
 WHERE Quantity < (SELECT Min(List_PRICE)
  FROM Price WHERE Item.Product_ID = Price.Product_ID)
```

```
ORDER_ID   ITEM_ID PRODUCT_ID
---------  --------- ----------
     600         1    100861
     610         3    100890
     611         1    100861
     601         2    100860
     604         1    100890
     604         2    100861
     604         3    100860
     603         1    100860
     610         1    100860
     612         2    100861
     620         1    100860
     616         1    100861
     616         3    100890
     615         1    100861
     607         1    100871
     609         3    100890
     618         1    100860
     621         1    100861
```

95 rows returned

9

Here's another example:

```
SELECT Order_ID, Item_ID, Product_ID
FROM Item
WHERE Quantity < (SELECT Min(List_PRICE)
FROM Price WHERE Item.Product_ID <> Price.Product_ID);
```

ORDER_ID	ITEM_ID	PRODUCT_ID
600	1	100861
610	3	100890
611	1	100861
601	2	100860
610	1	100860
607	1	100871
609	3	100890
608	1	101860
609	1	100861
606	1	102130
552	3	102136
552	4	200376

```
12 rows selected.
```

The Set Membership Test

The *set membership test* takes a single data value and compares it to the column of data values produced by the subquery. If the data value matches one of the values in the column, it returns a TRUE result. This is similar to the use of IN for your regular query.

The following are examples where set membership is tested:

What cities are my customers located in who have orders totaling $5,000 or more?

```
SELECT customer.city, customer.state
FROM customer
WHERE customer.customer_ID in (SELECT customer_ID
FROM sales_order WHERE sales_order.total > 5000);
```

CITY	ST
BURLINGAME	CA
CUPERTINO	CA

```
SANTA CLARA                CA
PALO ALTO                  CA
HIBBING                    MN
HOUSTON                    TX
```

6 rows selected.

With this query, you can find out where your biggest orders are coming from.

In this next query, you need to see a list of the customers who do not live in California and whose orders total more than $5,000.

```
SELECT customer.name, customer.city, customer.state
FROM customer
WHERE customer.state <> 'CA' and customer.customer_id not in(SELECT
sales_order.customer_id FROM Sales_Order WHERE total >= 5000)
ORDER BY customer.state, customer.city;
```

NAME	CITY	ST
AT BAT	BROOKLINE	MA
THE ALL AMERICAN	CHELSEA	MA
FAST BREAK	CONCORD	MA
HOOPS	LEICESTER	MA
VELO SPORTS	MALDEN	MA
THE TOUR	SOMERVILLE	MA
ALL SPORT	BROOKLYN	NY
THE OUTFIELD	FLUSHING	NY
CENTURY SHOP	HUNTINGTON	NY
FITNESS FIRST	JACKSON HEIGHTS	NY
STADIUM SPORTS	NEW YORK	NY
REBOUND SPORTS	NEW YORK	NY
THE COLISEUM	SCARSDALE	NY
GOOD SPORT	SUNNYSIDE	NY
POINT GUARD	YONKERS	NY
AL AND BOB'S SPORTS	AUSTIN	TX
THE POWER FORWARD	DALLAS	TX
JUST BIKES	DALLAS	TX
JOE'S BIKE SHOP	GRAND PRARIE	TX
HIT, THROW, AND RUN	GRAPEVINE	TX
BOB'S FAMILY SPORTS	HOUSTON	TX
BOB'S SWIM, CYCLE, AND RUN	IRVING	TX
AL'S PRO SHOP	SPRING	TX

23 rows selected.

9

Did you notice an ORDER BY is used in this query? It is all right to have the ORDER BY in a query, as long as it is not in the subquery (between the parentheses).

In these examples, the subquery delivers a column of data values and the WHERE clause of the main query checks to see if a value from a row of the main query matches the one value in the column.

The Existence Test

In this test, you want to check if a subquery gives you any rows of query results. This test is used only with subqueries.

You can take the previous example and rephrase the question: Do any customers exist with an order of $5,000 or more?

```
SELECT customer.customer_ID, customer.name,customer.city, customer.state
FROM customer
WHERE customer.state <> 'CA' and exists (SELECT customer_ID
FROM sales_order
WHERE sales_order.total >= 5000)
ORDER BY customer.state, customer.city;
```

CUSTOMER_ID	NAME	CITY	ST
211	AT BAT	BROOKLINE	MA
216	THE ALL AMERICAN	CHELSEA	MA
207	FAST BREAK	CONCORD	MA
202	HOOPS	LEICESTER	MA
223	VELO SPORTS	MALDEN	MA
227	THE TOUR	SOMERVILLE	MA
108	NORTH WOODS HEALTH AND FITNESS SUPPLY CENTER	HIBBING	MN
212	ALL SPORT	BROOKLYN	NY
218	THE OUTFIELD	FLUSHING	NY
226	CENTURY SHOP	HUNTINGTON	NY
228	FITNESS FIRST	JACKSON HEIGHTS	NY
201	STADIUM SPORTS	NEW YORK	NY
203	REBOUND SPORTS	NEW YORK	NY
206	THE COLISEUM	SCARSDALE	NY
213	GOOD SPORT	SUNNYSIDE	NY
205	POINT GUARD	YONKERS	NY
208	AL AND BOB'S SPORTS	AUSTIN	TX
204	THE POWER FORWARD	DALLAS	TX
222	JUST BIKES	DALLAS	TX

```
224        JOE'S BIKE SHOP                    GRAND PRARIE       TX
217        HIT, THROW, AND RUN                GRAPEVINE          TX
215        BOB'S FAMILY SPORTS                HOUSTON            TX
221        WHEELS AND DEALS                   HOUSTON            TX
225        BOB'S SWIM, CYCLE, AND RUN         IRVING             TX
214        AL'S PRO SHOP                      SPRING             TX

25 rows selected.
```

What happens here is SQL processes this query by going through the Customer table and performing the subquery for each customer. If any such customers exist with totals over $5,000, the test is TRUE. You can also use the reverse of this and use NOT EXISTS. In this case, if the customers do have orders over $5,000, the NOT EXISTS is false.

Do you see another way of writing this subquery? The EXIST search conditions aren't using the results of the subquery at all. Instead, it is just checking to see if the results exist. You could have just as easily written:

```
SELECT customer.customer_ID, customer.name,customer.city, customer.state
FROM customer
WHERE customer.state <> 'CA' and EXISTS (SELECT * FROM sales_order
WHERE sales_order.total >= 5000)
ORDER BY customer.state, customer.city;
```

Here is another example using EXISTS:

9

```
SELECT customer.name,customer.city, customer.state
FROM customer WHERE customer.customer_ID = (SELECT
sales_order.customer_ID FROM Sales_order
WHERE customer_ID > 204)
and NOT EXISTS (SELECT * from item
WHERE item.quantity > 10);
```

```
No rows returned.
```

And here's another example:

```
SELECT Customer.name
FROM Customer
WHERE EXISTS (SELECT * FROM Sales_Order WHERE
Customer.Customer_id = Sales_Order.Customer_ID
and Sales_Order.total < 1000);
```

```
NAME
---------------------------------------------
JOCKSPORTS
TKB SPORT SHOP
VOLLYRITE
JUST TENNIS
EVERY MOUNTAIN
SHAPE UP
WOMENS SPORTS
STADIUM SPORTS
HOOPS
REBOUND SPORTS
THE POWER FORWARD
POINT GUARD
THE COLISEUM
FAST BREAK
AL AND BOB'S SPORTS
JUST BIKES
VELO SPORTS
BOB'S SWIM, CYCLE, AND RUN
FITNESS FIRST

19 rows selected.
```

The subquery in an EXISTS test always contains an outer reference that joins the subquery to the row being tested by the main query.

The Quantified Tests

Quantified tests make use of ANY and ALL. Both of these compare a data value to the column of data values produced by a subquery.

The ANY Test   The *ANY test* is used with the comparison operators discussed earlier in this chapter. You take your test expression and add one comparison operator with ALL and your subquery. The syntax is

```
Test Expression [=,>,<,>=,<=,<>] ANY Subquery
```

SQL uses the comparison operator to compare the test value to each data value in the column. If any of the comparisons produce a True result, then the ANY test returns a true result.

Here's an example. Suppose you want to list the customers whose credit limit is less than their total for an order. You would use the following ANY test:

```
SELECT Customer.Name
FROM Customer
WHERE customer.Credit_limit < ANY (SELECT total
FROM Sales_order WHERE customer.customer_id = sales_order.customer_ID)

NAME
----------------------
VOLLYRITE
K + T SPORTS
SHAPE UP
FITNESS FIRST
```

Four customers seem to have exceeded their credit limit with an order.

This query tests each row of the Customer table, row by row. The WHERE clause of the main query uses the credit_limit as a test value, comparing it to every order produced by the subquery.

NOTE: If an ANY test produces no rows of query results, or if the query results include NULL values, the operation of the ANY test may vary from vendor to vendor.

9

The SQL-92 rules for this test are as follows:

◆   The subquery produces an empty column of query results, the ANY test returns FALSE.

◆   When the test is true for at least one of the data values, the ANY search condition returns TRUE.

◆   When the test is false for every data value in the column, then the ANY search condition returns FALSE.

◆   When the test is not TRUE for any data value in the column, but is NULL for one or more of the data values, then the ANY search condition returns NULL.

Another way to think about ANY, is to consider what you are asking the query to do. When you say give me any rows of a column, you are really asking please give me some. You don't care what the "some" is, as long as it returns something that matches the test comparison.

So how would you ask for NOT ANY? In this next example, you want to find a list of customers and their sales reps who haven't placed a sales order. What you are getting at is what customer is not in the Sales_Order table. The correct query statement is

```
SELECT customer.name, customer.salesperson_ID
FROM customer
WHERE not (customer_ID = ANY (SELECT customer_ID
FROM sales_Order));
```

NAME	SALESPERSON_ID
AT BAT	7820
ALL SPORT	7600
GOOD SPORT	7600
AL'S PRO SHOP	7564
BOB'S FAMILY SPORTS	7654
THE ALL AMERICAN	7820
HIT, THROW, AND RUN	7564
THE OUTFIELD	7820

8 rows selected.

You could ask the same question using the EXIST test:

```
SELECT customer.name, customer.salesperson_ID
FROM customer
WHERE NOT EXISTS (SELECT *
FROM sales_Order
WHERE customer.customer_ID = sales_order.customer_ID);
```

You get the same row results.

The ALL Test   This is similar to the ANY test because it, too, uses the six SQL comparison operators. It, too, compares the single test value to a column of data values produced by a subquery. If *all* the comparisons are true, the ALL test returns a TRUE result.

Here is a great example of this test:

```
SELECT customer.name, customer.city
FROM  Customer
WHERE credit_limit > ALL (SELECT sales_order.total
FROM Sales_Order
WHERE customer.customer_id = sales_order.customer_ID);
```

```
NAME                                              CITY
------------------------------------------------- ---------------
JOCKSPORTS                                         BELMONT
TKB SPORT SHOP                                     REDWOOD CITY
JUST TENNIS                                        BURLINGAME
EVERY MOUNTAIN                                     CUPERTINO
WOMENS SPORTS                                      SUNNYVALE
NORTH WOODS HEALTH AND FITNESS SUPPLY CENTER       HIBBING
STADIUM SPORTS                                     NEW YORK
HOOPS                                              LEICESTER
REBOUND SPORTS                                     NEW YORK
THE POWER FORWARD                                  DALLAS
POINT GUARD                                        YONKERS
THE COLISEUM                                       SCARSDALE
FAST BREAK                                         CONCORD
AL AND BOB'S SPORTS                                AUSTIN
AT BAT                                             BROOKLINE
ALL SPORT                                          BROOKLYN
GOOD SPORT                                         SUNNYSIDE
AL'S PRO SHOP                                      SPRING
BOB'S FAMILY SPORTS                                HOUSTON
THE ALL AMERICAN                                   CHELSEA
HIT, THROW, AND RUN                                GRAPEVINE
THE OUTFIELD                                       FLUSHING
WHEELS AND DEALS                                   HOUSTON
JUST BIKES                                         DALLAS
VELO SPORTS                                        MALDEN
JOE'S BIKE SHOP                                    GRAND PRARIE
BOB'S SWIM, CYCLE, AND RUN                         IRVING
CENTURY SHOP                                       HUNTINGTON
THE TOUR                                           SOMERVILLE

29 rows selected.
```

9

In this query, the main query tests each row of the customer table one-by-one. The subquery finds all customers whose credit-limit is greater than the total sales order. If all the credit-limits are greater than the sales orders, then the ALL test is true and query results are returned.

Here are the SQL-92 rules for the ALL test:

◆ When the subquery produces an empty column of query results, the ALL test is TRUE.

◆ When the comparison test is true for every data value in the column, then the ALL search is TRUE.

◆ When the comparison test is false for any data value in the column, then the ALL test is FALSE.

◆ When the comparison test is not false for any data value in the column, it is NULL for one or more of the data values, then the ALL search condition returns NULL. You can't say one way or another that a value is produced by the subquery for which the test does not hold true.

You can also substitute EXISTS and get the same query results as you did with the ANY test.

Subqueries and Joins

Did you notice you could also write these subqueries as multitable joins? In most cases, SQL enables you to write these queries either way. It is flexible. Here's an example:

```
SELECT Price.Product_ID, Price.List_Price
FROM Price
WHERE Price.Product_Id in (SELECT Item_ID
FROM Item
WHERE Item.Quantity = 50);
```

As a join, the query would be

```
SELECT Price.Product_ID, Price.List_Price
FROM Price,Item
WHERE Price.Product_ID = Item.Product_ID
AND Item.Quantity = 50
```

In some situations, the subquery will not work and a multiple-table join is your only answer. Then again, sometimes a subquery is your only solution:

```
SELECT Item.ID, Item.Quantity
FROM Item
WHERE Quantity > (SELECT AVG(Quantity) FROM Item);
```

```
CUSTOMER_ID     TOTAL
-----------   ---------
        101     101.4
        102        45
        104      5860
        106      60.8
        102        56
        103        42
        106       642
        106      8374
        100       3.4
        100     102.5
        104       5.6
        104      35.2
        102       224
        100      4450
        102     23940
        103       764
        104      1260
```

You couldn't join these queries because one is an inner query and the other is an outer query. You cannot put them in a single join.

Nested Subqueries

In this section, you experience something a little different. In the previous section, you always had a main query and a subquery. Here you have a subquery inside a main query, hence, the name *nested subquery*. You can also make life interesting and have a subquery within another subquery. You can stack them high and deep.

The best way to understand these queries is to begin with the inner query, which ultimately provides the column for your next outer layer query, and so on.

9

The following is representative of a 3-layer query:

```
Query….WHERE clause
              … (query..WHERE clause
                               ..(query..WHERE clause ))
```

Let's begin with the innermost subquery:

```
(SELECT customer.city FROM Customer WHERE customer.city = 'Concord'))
```

This produces a column containing the customers from the city of Concord.

Your next subquery:

```
(SELECT Customer_ID
FROM Sales_Order WHERE Customer_ID In
```

This provides a column containing the specific customers who are in the city of Concord.

The outermost subquery:

```
SELECT Item.Quantity
FROM Item
WHERE Order_ID In
```

This provides the quantity of items for the chosen customers.

Have you figured out what we're looking for? We want the quantity of items ordered from customers in Concord.

Here is the full subquery:

```
SELECT Item.Quantity
FROM Item
WHERE Order_ID in
   (SELECT Customer_ID FROM Sales_Order WHERE Customer_ID In
                               (SELECT customer.city
                                FROM Customer
                                WHERE Customer.city = 'Concord'));
```

SQL-92 does not set a limit on nested levels for this type of subquery. As you can see, however, it is time-consuming and more difficult to read and write the more levels you have. Although SQL-92 does not restrict the levels, your database vendor usually does. As a standard practice, check the documentation from your vendor.

Correlated Subqueries

A *correlated subquery* is one in which SQL performs a subquery and produces the same results for every row or row group. Or, you can think of a correlated subquery as a subquery that contains an outer reference. A subquery can contain an outer reference to a table in the FROM clause of any query that contains the subquery, even four or more nested layers deep. So things don't become confusing, SQL interprets a column reference in a subquery using the closest FROM clause available.

In this subquery, both the main query and subquery use the same table. To have an outer reference, you need to use a table alias to force the outer reference. Proditem.total is the outer reference.

```
SELECT order_id, product_id, Actual_Price
FROM Item proditem
WHERE Actual_price > 25 and proditem.product_ID in
            (SELECT orditem.product_ID FROM Item Orditem
             WHERE orditem.total > proditem.total);
```

ORDER_ID	PRODUCT_ID	ACTUAL_PRICE
600	100861	42
610	100890	58
611	100861	45
612	100860	30
601	100860	32
604	100890	58
604	100861	42
604	100860	32
603	100860	32
610	100860	35
612	100861	40.5
620	100860	35
617	100860	35
616	100861	45
616	100890	58
615	100861	45
609	100890	50
618	100860	35
618	100861	45
621	100861	45
609	100861	40

9

The HAVING Clause with Subqueries

The subquery in the HAVING clause works as part of the row group selection in the HAVING clause. The following example shows how this works:

List the customers who have a credit limit of $5,000 and see if their average total is greater than the average total of the entire customer base.

```
SELECT Name, Avg(Total)
FROM Customer,Sales_Order
WHERE Customer.Customer_ID = Sales_Rep.Customer_ID
  AND customer.credit_limit = 5000
GROUP BY Name
HAVING Avg(Total) > (SELECT AVG(total) FROM Sales_Rep);


NAME                                             AVG(TOTAL)
------------------------------------------------ ----------
K + T SPORTS                                          46370
THE TOUR                                              4900
```

The subquery calculates the overall average of the total. The main query groups the customers by name and provides the customers with credit-limits equal to $5,000. The HAVING clause checks each row group to see if the average total for the customers is larger than the average total for the whole customer base. The SELECT clause shows you the name and the average total of these customers.

A HAVING clause can also use a correlated subquery. In this subquery, the subquery is evaluated once for each row group. All outer references in the correlated subquery must be single-valued for each row group. If you make a slight adjustment to the previous example, you have a HAVING clause with a correlated subquery:

```
SELECT Name, Avg(Total)
FROM Customer,Sales_Order
WHERE Customer.Customer_ID = Sales_Order.Customer_ID
    AND customer.credit_limit = 5000
GROUP BY Name, Customer.Customer_ID
  HAVING AVG(Total) >= (SELECT AVG(total) FROM Sales_Order WHERE
    customer.customer_ID = sales_order.customer_ID);
```

```
NAME                                               AVG(TOTAL)
---------------------------------------------      ----------
HOOPS                                                 1058.88
JOCKSPORTS                                           1321.475
K + T SPORTS                                            46370
THE TOUR                                                 4900
VELO SPORTS                                              237.6
```

As you can see, the subquery must produce the overall average total for each customer whose row group is currently being tested by the HAVING clause.

When you use a subquery in a WHERE clause, the results of the subquery are used to select the individual rows that provide data to the results. When you use a subquery in a HAVING clause, the results of the subquery are used to select the row groups that produce data to the results.

Queries—A Review

This is the last chapter on queries so let's review what makes a query one more time.

♦ The SELECT clause dictates what data values appear as columns in the final query result.

♦ The FROM clause lists the source tables you need for your query results. These columns must not be ambiguous.

♦ The WHERE clause selects the rows from the source table that you need for your query results. This is where your search conditions are placed. Subqueries are placed in this clause and are evaluated for each individual row.

♦ The GROUP BY clause groups the individual rows selected by the WHERE clause into row groups.

♦ The HAVING clause chooses row groups to participate in the query results. Subqueries in this clause are evaluated for each row group.

♦ The DISTINCT keyword eliminates duplicate rows from query results.

♦ The UNION operator merges the query results produced by separate SELECT statements into a single set of query results.

♦ The ORDER BY sorts the final query based on one or more columns.

9

Remember, you do not need all of these clauses to produce a query. The minimal you need is SELECT and FROM if you use a single-table query, and SELECT, FROM, and WHERE if you have a multiple-table query.

The following query is an example of the types of queries you may be requested to write. This query was written to provide a report from a training database. The user designed the training database. The user requested the tables be designed in a specific way, much to the chagrin of the developer. The following query would have been unnecessary if the developer was allowed to design tables to the 3NF.

```
SELECT tabLTCW_Meetings.CourseID,
tabLTCW_Meetings.Meeting_act_St_Date,
tabLTCW_Meetings.MEETING_DATE,
tabLTCW_Meetings.Meeting_Part1,
(SELECT (Name_last & ', ' & name_first) from tabLTCW_student
   WHERE stempid=meeting_part1) AS partname1,
'[...same code is used through partname10]
tabLTCW_Meetings.Meeting_type,
tabLTCW_Meetings.Meeting_Sch_ST_DATE,
tabLTCW_Meetings.Meeting_End_Date,
tabLTCW_Meetings.Int_Facil1_CAI,
tabLTCW_Meetings.Int_facil2_CAI,
tabLTCW_Meetings.Ext_Consl_Name,
tabLTCW_Meetings.Bus_Issue_Wk_Sh,
tabLTCW_Course.Course_Sh,
tabLTCW_Course.Course_Lg
FROM tabLTCW_Meetings INNER JOIN tabLTCW_Courses
ON tabLTCW_Meetings.CourseID = tabLTCW_Course.CourseID
WHERE (((tabLTCW_Meetings.MEETING_Part1)>' "))
ORDER BY tabLTCW_Meetings.CourseID, tabLTCW_Meetings.Meeting_Act_St_Date;
```

Again, knowing the syntax of a query is just the beginning. You need to understand the user needs and also to be prepared to work with databases that may not be the best design.

IN DEPTH

Report Writers and SQL

Report writers are tools that use a graphical user interface to handle SQL queries and purports to make life easier for the user. Sometimes in its quest to make life easier for you, your SQL options may be limited. This is the case for subqueries. Unless the reporting tool has a query designer included, you are likely to find you are limited in the use of subqueries. Some report writers limit the amount of nested subqueries you may use, while others don't allow them at all.

In earlier versions of Crystal Reports, you were not allowed to use subqueries. Since Version 4.5, Crystal has provided a Query Designer with its tool that does allow you to make use of subqueries. If you try to write a subquery in the Report Designer, however, you will find you cannot do it. The Report Designer circumvents this limitation by allowing you to create "subreports," which you may link to your main report. You can write these subreports and include the subquery you would have used in your regular subquery.

So if you are looking for a reporting tool, be sure you can make use of most of the SQL language with the tool.

9

What's Next?

In this chapter, you learned about subqueries. Chapter 10 is about how to optimize your queries and tune your application and database for maximum performance. Then, in Part III, you design and build your own database.

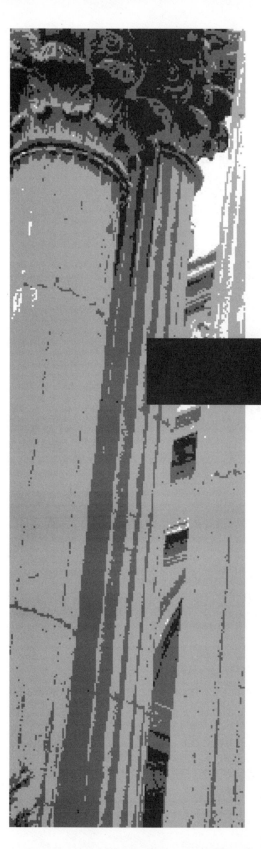

CHAPTER 10

Optimizing SQL

Now that you have learned about SQL and queries, the next step is to learn how you can streamline your queries and optimize your database. For the most part, optimizing applications and databases fall under the auspices of the DBA. You do play an important part in the application, however, whether you design the application, design tables, or write the queries. So understanding the concepts involved in database tuning is important. Understanding how the database engine processes the SQL statements you write helps you to think about the best way to write your queries.

In addition, the DBMS vendors usually include tuning tools with their products. Some third-party vendors also specialize in tuning tools for your database. You take a brief look at the tuning tools Oracle provides with Oracle8.

Just when you think you have learned it all, you find there is more to learn. There is always more. Don't worry, this is useful information. You see, by optimizing your SQL you save time, money, and reduce the stress in your life.

How the Database Engine Processes SQL

Within a database engine, there is an optimizer. Think of the optimizer as the commander in charge of your database. This commander has authority over all of your selects, joins, and SET operations. The commander's job is to determine what sequence of the selects and joins will answer the request to the database most efficiently, and with the fewest casualties (time and resources). The optimizer has an SQL compiler, which produces an executable program. This executable program produces an execution plan. The commander uses the plan for strategizing. The plan is the optimizer's description of how the query will run against the database.

The optimizer looks at table statistics and indexes to help find the best way to handle the request. The plan can change if indexes are added or dropped or if table size changes. In fact, the plan changes whenever changes are made to the SQL statement that produced the execution plan.

Oracle SQL Statement Processing

Oracle SQL statements are processed in three phases: parse, execute, and fetch.

Parse
With *parsing,* Oracle examines the code from the bottom to the top. It looks at the different kinds of words on the statement, such as its own words and jargon, words that refer to your tables and columns, and all other

miscellaneous words. Then it tries to find out what objects and columns are in the statement. Next, it checks for the syntax: parentheses, commas, and location of reserved words. The final step in the parse phase is when the execution plan is determined after the optimizer evaluates the available excess paths. The optimizer makes choices based on the tables accessed in the SQL statement and the way the statements are worded.

Execute

Execute is when the reads and writes required to process the statement are performed.

Fetch

The final phase is the *fetch* phase. All the rows that meet the SQL statement qualifications are fetched. The results are formatted and displayed according to the query's instructions.

TIP: Reusing your parsed statement in the Shared Pool moves you one step closer to tuning the application.

IN DEPTH

Oracle8's Shared SQL Pool

10

The *Shared SQL Pool* is your program cache. All your programs are stored here. The cache contains all parsed SQL statements that are ready to run. This pool resides in the *System Global Area* (SGA), which is a place in memory where the Oracle database stores information about itself.

The SGA is divided into major areas: the data cache, the Redo Log cache, the dictionary cache, and the shared SQL cache. The *data cache* stores the most recently used blocks of database data and is available for a user process to see. The *dictionary cache* contains rows from the data dictionary. Remember, the data dictionary contains information Oracle uses to manage itself, what users have access to the database, what objects users can access, what objects users own, and where the objects are located. The *Redo Log Buffer* is the transaction log. So, before the transaction log can reside in the online redo logs, it must first reside in this buffer.

Indexing

When a query has no WHERE clause, the database performs a *full-table scan,* which means reading every block from the table. The database locates the first record of the table and then reads sequentially through all other records in the table. A full-table scan is also done with updates and deletes. Imagine if you have a large table, this could be quite time-consuming.

When you query specific rows, the database uses an index to speed the retrieval of the desired rows. An *index* maps logical values in a table to their ROWIDs, which, in turn, map them to a specific physical location. Using indexes is the preferred method of processing a query.

Each row of data in a database has a ROWID. Here's an example:

```
00000038.0000.0004
```

Columns 1-8	The block ID
Columns 10-13	The sequence number of the row within that block (row 0000 is the first)
Columns 15-18	The file ID

The ROWID points to a specific physical location within a datafile. You can compare the file ID portion of the ROWID to the FILE_ID column of the DBA_DATA_FILES view (see Figure 10-1) to determine which file is used.

Because Oracle is a relational database, the physical location of the data is not as important as the logical place in the application. The key to tuning SQL lies in the search for the data. The shortest search path is usually the best.

An index provides a fast access path to data in a database. Indexes point directly to the location of the rows containing specified data. Indexes may be unique—in which case no more than one occurrence exists for each value—or they are nonunique. You can also index several columns together. This is called a *concatenated* or *composite index.*

Another type of index that can be used is a clustered index. In a *clustered index,* the table is sorted in a particular order. This allows for planning sequential searches and joins based on knowing the order of the rows. Due to the way the index is ordered, you can only have one clustered index per table. Be forewarned, though, a clustered index takes a lot of space, at least 120 percent of the size of the table.

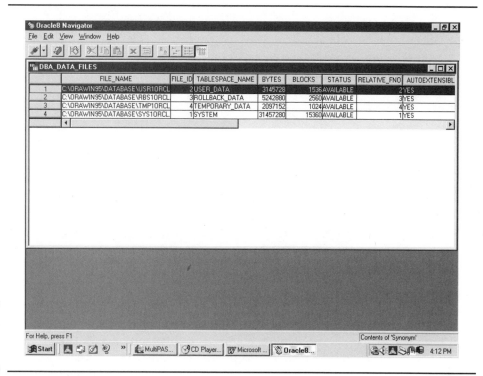

DBA_DATA_
FILES view
Figure 10-1.

Before you create an index, do your table and columns meet these criteria?

◆ You should index columns that are in the WHERE or AND sections
of an SQL statement.

◆ You should index columns with a range of distinct values. If a value
in a table is present in 20 percent or less, then index it.

Remember, this usually is the responsibility of the DBA. The DBA will know
the global effects that adding an index will have on the database. The syntax
for creating an index is

```
CREATE [UNIQUE] INDEX <index name>
    ON <table name> (<column name> (ASC|DESC),…)
```

```
FOR ORACLE8:
```

```
CREATE INDEX city
    ON Customer (city);
```

10

If you wanted a concatenated or composite index, you would use the following code:

```
CREATE INDEX order_item_ndx
   ON Sales_Order (Order_ID, Item_ID)
```

The syntax in SQL Server 7 is a little different:

```
CREATE [UNIQUE] {CLUSTERED | NONCLUSTERED] INDEX index_name
  On [owner,]table_name (column_name[,column_name...n])
[WITH
  [Pad_Index] [,] FILLFACTOR = x]
  [[,] Ignore_dup_key] 'duplicate rows are discarded when running a
         multiple update against a table with a unique clustered index
  [[,] Drop_Existing] 'existing index should be dropped and recreated
  [[,] Statistics_Norecompute]] 'recomputes statistics on indexes as
                                    needed
[On filegroup]

Create index cityindex on customer (customer_city)
```

The *fillfactor option* specifies how full each page in the leaf level of an index should be. A *leaf level* is the lowest level in the binary tree. The pad_index applies the fillfactor to the nonleaf pages, as well. Figure 10-2 represents the typical index outlined in the *binary tree* or *B+ tree*.

To navigate the tree, you start at the root page. The *root page* contains index entries, as well as pointers to each page below the root page. Each index may have more than one intermediate level, which has an index value and a pointer to the page below. On the leaf page, what you find is an entry for every row in the table being indexed, as well as a pointer to the data page and row number that has the actual data row.

This is the process the index uses to find the logical location. Once an index is created, however, you can look at the index via the Oracle8 Navigator. Figure 10-3 shows the index created for the Oracle8 Sales_Order table.

Indexing can provide order to the table and enables fast searching of the table. What happens when two tables are frequently queried together?

If two tables are queried together, you may notice increased performance if you use clusters. *Clusters* store rows from multiple tables in the same physical data blocks, based on their logical values (cluster key). A new type of cluster, a hash cluster, is in Oracle 7 and 8. This cluster stores a row in a specific

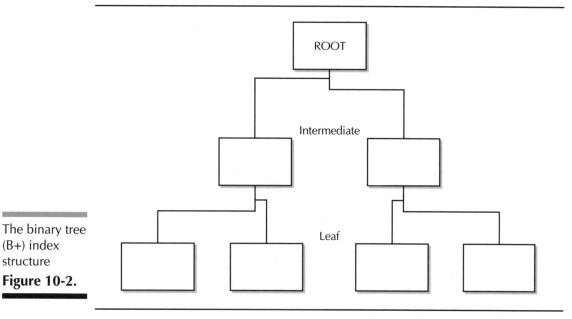

The binary tree
(B+) index
structure

Figure 10-2.

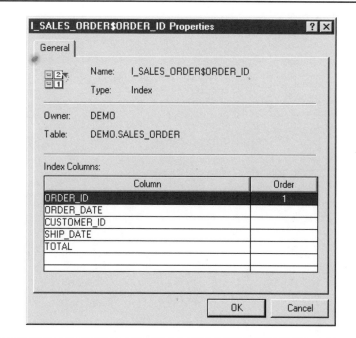

Index for
Sales_Order
table

Figure 10-3.

10

location based on the value in the cluster key column. Each time a row is inserted, its cluster key value is used to determine in which block it should be stored. This is called *hashing*. Hashing is used to improve the performance of equivalence queries. An *equivalence query* is one in which a column's value is compared to an exact value. Check your database documentation for instructions on hashing. It is complicated and best left to experts.

In addition to checking indexes, the query also checks the system (schema) tables to check privileges, to get table and column names, and to get information for the optimizer and other data.

Speed Up Your Queries!

This section is an assortment of suggestions to improve the processing speed of the query. For instance, two logical operators should be avoided in a query because it slows down the processing.

The first operator is OR. If you use IN instead, your processing time will increase. Here is a query as an example:

```
SELECT Name, City, State
FROM Customer
WHERE City = 'Atlanta'
    OR City = 'Boston'
    OR City = 'Chicago'
    OR City = 'Detroit'
    OR City = 'Englewood'
    OR City = 'Flushing'
ORDER BY City;
```

Here is the same query using IN:

```
SELECT Name, City, State
FROM Customer
WHERE City IN ('Atlanta', 'Boston', 'Chicago',
               'Detroit', 'Englewood', 'Flushing')
ORDER BY City;
```

Another logical operator that slows down your queries is BETWEEN:

```
SELECT Customer_ID, Order_ID, Ship_Date
FROM Sales_Order
WHERE customer_ID BETWEEN 100 and 200
```

You can use the operators <= and >=:

```
SELECT Customer_ID, Order_ID, Ship_Date
FROM Sales_Order
WHERE customer_ID >= 100 and customer_id <= 200;
```

Depending on the DBMS and the size of the tables, using the Greater Than and Less Than operators will be faster.

Because Oracle processes the query from the bottom to the top, it would make sense to put the part of your WHERE clause that has the least retrictive values on the top and build the more restrictive clauses on the bottom.

For example, if the Item_ID is the most restrictive part of your query, place this as your last section of your WHERE clause and have the least restrictive, say, Quantity, as the first.

Here is an example of optimizing your SQL statement to work with your database engine:

```
SELECT Customer.Name, Customer.City, Customer.State, Customer.Quantity,
       Sales_Order.Total, Sales_Order.Item_ID
FROM Customer, Sales_Order
WHERE Customer.Quantity > 10
       and Sales_Order.Total > 3000
       and Sales_Order.Item_ID >=245
       and Sales_Order.Item_ID <= 350
```

10

This way, the first part of the WHERE clause to be processed is Item_ID, which is in the 245-350 range (most restrictive), and then Total > 3000 (restricts less), and then Customer Quantity which is greater than 10 (least restrictive).

Now you can speed up your queries, but what about another relevant issue: understanding what you need to get from the database and the best way to write your query?

Neatness Counts

The readability of your SQL does not affect the performance of the database, but it does affect the ability of your fellow programmers to read your code. Most IT groups have a template for all programmers in their group to follow. The following is just a suggestion on the way to write your code:

```
SELECT C.Name, C.Customer_ID, C.City, C.State, SO_Total, SO_Order_ID
FROM Customer C,
     Sales_Order SO
WHERE C.Customer_ID = SO_Customer_ID
    AND C.Credit_Limit > 5000
    OR (C.Quanity >= 100);
```

This is a structured way to write a query, which is easier to read than the following:

```
SELECT C.Name, C.Customer_ID, C.City, C.State, SO_Total, SO_Order_ID
FROM Customer C, Sales_Order SO
WHERE C.Customer_ID = SO_Customer_ID AND C.Credit_Limit > 5000 OR
(C.Quanity >= 100);
```

The first example makes it easy for you to find your SELECT clause, your FROM clause, and your WHERE clause. Remember, aliases save you typing.

Understanding Your Data

Writing queries using SQL is probably the most straightforward structured process. What is not always so straightforward is the data you need to retrieve. Most of the time, it begins as a germ of an idea. A user needs to look at numbers for a report. So the user asks what seems like a simple question. You take the request back to your desk, you look at it, and it seems pretty easy. You open your database, you look at your tables, and then you look back at the question. If you understand the data and you understand the business processes of the user, chances are, it is a simple task. Panic may strike, however, if you don't understand what data is in the tables and how to pull the tables together.

When you get a question or a request for data, if anything is not clear to you, ask for more information from your user. After you have exhausted the user, then go to your database and look at what you have. Look at the tables and the data. Do you have a view available? Do you have another query similar to this request?

If you do, you are halfway there. If you don't, the first step is to find the tables you need. Write down the names of the tables and select the columns you need for the query. Will you need to group your data? Do you need a subquery?

Now you can define your WHERE clause. What are the search conditions? Remember, most databases work from the bottom to the top when reading SQL statements. Put the most restrictive columns first and the least restrictive last, in your WHERE clause. If you have a GROUP BY clause, then you need to use a HAVING clause in place of the WHERE clause for your search conditions.

Finally, do you want to have this query sorted in a specific way? If so, add your ORDER BY clause. Now, run your query. Is it giving you what you thought you requested? How is the processing time? Do you have many tables joined? If so, you may want to create a view to cut the number of columns you are dealing with in the query. If you have counts and sums, do they add up? Does the data make sense?

Check one more time and, if you are happy the data is correct, package it up and deliver it to your user. Be prepared to run the query again with minor changes from your user. This never fails. Once users see the query results, they always want to have one more thing.

You can practice with the following case study. Mr. Johnston wants to know how many customers ordered the Dunk Indoor Basketball. He also needs to know the name of the customers, where they are located, and what Sales Reps handles these customers. He also wants to see the orders they have and what quantity of the product they ordered.

10

First, you need to identify the tables in the database and the columns you need. Upon perusal of the tables, you find you need the Customer, Item, Sales Order, and Employee tables. From the Customer table, you get the Customer ID, Salesperson ID, Customer Name, and City. From the Item table, you need the Order_Id, Product_Id, Quantity, and Total. From the Sales Order table, you need the Order_Id and the Customer_Id. From the Employees table, you need the Emp_Id, First_Name, and Last_Name. You need the Employee table to get the salesperson's name.

With this information, you can build your SELECT clause and FROM clause.

```
SELECT C.Customer_Id, C.Name, C.City, C.Salesperson_ID, I.Order_ID,
        I.Product_ID, I.Quantity, I.Total, E.Emp_ID, E.First_Name,
E.Last_Name
FROM Customer C,
    Item I,
    Sales_Order SO
```

Now you can determine the WHERE clause. The first part of your WHERE clause should be the joins for these tables. Because these tables are small, you needn't worry about building a view. The Sales_Order table is the linking table between the Item and the Customer. Otherwise, there would be no common column to join the Item and the Customer table.

```
WHERE SO.Order_ID = I.Order_ID
    and SO_Customer_ID = C.Customer_ID
    and C.SalesRep_ID = E.Employee_ID
```

The joins are equi-joins because you want to see only those rows where these columns match.

Well, that looks like everything, right? No, it isn't quite right. You see, Mr. Johnston wants the total orders. You need to go back to your SELECT statement and add a SUM. Also, because this is an aggregate function, you must assign a GROUP BY.

```
SELECT C.Customer_Id, C.Name, C.City, C.Salesperson_ID, I.Order_ID,
        I.Product_ID, I.Quantity, Sum(I.Total), E.Emp_ID, E.First_Name,
        E.Last_Name
FROM Customer C,
    Item I,
    Sales_Order SO
WHERE SO.Order_ID = I.Order_ID
    and SO_Customer_ID = C.Customer_ID
    and C.SalesRep_ID = E.Employee_ID
GROUP BY C.Customer_Id, C.Name, C.City, C.Salesperson_ID, I.Order_ID,
            I.Product_ID, I.Quantity, E.Emp_ID, E.First_Name,
            E.Last_Name;
```

Is this everything?

No, not yet. You need one more thing. Mr. Johnston only wants this information on one product, Dunk Indoor Basketball. You looked up the code and it is Product_ID 104350. You also should have ORDER BY Customer Name. You also don't need all the fields you listed in the SELECT clause. This should be all.

```
SELECT C.Name, C.City, Sum(I.Total), I.Order_ID,Sum(I.Quantity),
    E.First_Name,E.Last_Name
FROM Customer C,
    Sales_Order SO,
    Item I,
    Employee E
WHERE SO.Order_ID = I.Order_ID
    and SO.Customer_ID = C.Customer_ID
    and C.Salesperson_ID = E.Employee_ID
    and I.Product_ID = 104350
GROUP BY C.Customer_ID, C.Name, C.City, I.Order_ID,
             I.Quantity,E.First_Name,E.Last_Name
ORDER BY C.Name
```

The results are listed in Figure 10-4.

Tuning a Database

When you tune a database, you are checking the following areas:

◆ Application design

◆ SQL

◆ Memory usage

◆ Data manipulation

◆ Physical storage

◆ Logical storage

◆ Network traffic

10

Tuning is part of the DBA responsibilities, but you will be affected if you design tables and write SQL statements that are processed by the database.

Different vendors have different ways of dealing with tuning their databases. You learn the tuning techniques for SQL in this chapter. This discussion focuses on the Oracle8 database.

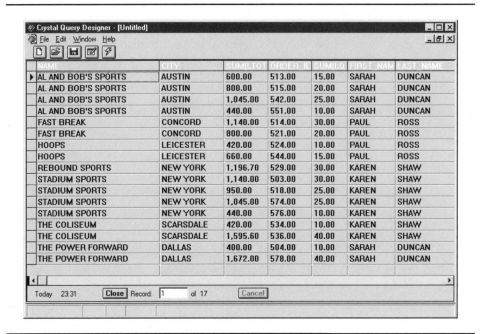

NAME	CITY	SUM(LTOT	ORDER_ID	SUM(LQ	FIRST_NAM	LAST_NAME
AL AND BOB'S SPORTS	AUSTIN	600.00	513.00	15.00	SARAH	DUNCAN
AL AND BOB'S SPORTS	AUSTIN	800.00	515.00	20.00	SARAH	DUNCAN
AL AND BOB'S SPORTS	AUSTIN	1,045.00	542.00	25.00	SARAH	DUNCAN
AL AND BOB'S SPORTS	AUSTIN	440.00	551.00	10.00	SARAH	DUNCAN
FAST BREAK	CONCORD	1,140.00	514.00	30.00	PAUL	ROSS
FAST BREAK	CONCORD	800.00	521.00	20.00	PAUL	ROSS
HOOPS	LEICESTER	420.00	524.00	10.00	PAUL	ROSS
HOOPS	LEICESTER	660.00	544.00	15.00	PAUL	ROSS
REBOUND SPORTS	NEW YORK	1,196.70	529.00	30.00	KAREN	SHAW
STADIUM SPORTS	NEW YORK	1,140.00	503.00	30.00	KAREN	SHAW
STADIUM SPORTS	NEW YORK	950.00	518.00	25.00	KAREN	SHAW
STADIUM SPORTS	NEW YORK	1,045.00	574.00	25.00	KAREN	SHAW
STADIUM SPORTS	NEW YORK	440.00	576.00	10.00	KAREN	SHAW
THE COLISEUM	SCARSDALE	420.00	534.00	10.00	KAREN	SHAW
THE COLISEUM	SCARSDALE	1,595.60	536.00	40.00	KAREN	SHAW
THE POWER FORWARD	DALLAS	400.00	504.00	10.00	SARAH	DUNCAN
THE POWER FORWARD	DALLAS	1,672.00	578.00	40.00	SARAH	DUNCAN

Query results

Figure 10-4.

Database Tuning the Oracle Way

Quite a few books are dedicated to tuning Oracle databases. This is not one of those books. In this section, you get an overview of what is involved in the tuning process.

Table Design   A poorly designed table drags down your database. You can expect poor performance if you have a badly designed table. The experts recommend you denormalize your tables and create smaller summary tables in place of larger 3NF tables. The reason is if users ask for the same data over and over again, and the data doesn't change, then it makes sense to put the data in a format the users need. Give users what they want and provide it to them in the most direct way possible.

In some cases, it might be prudent to create a reporting database for your users to query against. You can denormalize the tables and create an optimal environment for the users. Of course, extra maintenance is involved, such as refreshing the nonstatic tables on a time schedule, as well as the extra space needed. If your production database tables are not conducive to querying, however, you will notice a drop in performance when users query against it. In this case, the benefits may outweigh the costs of supporting a reporting database.

Oracle Application Guidelines First, the application should minimize the number of times it requests data from the database. You can denormalize the tables and implement the use of sequences and PL/SQL blocks. Use of snapshots can be helpful if it reduces the number of times a database is queried. A *snapshot* is a recent copy of a table or a subset of that table.

Second, similar users should query the database in similar ways. Sharing data includes tables and rows, as well as the queries used. If the queries already exist, then the parsed version is available in the Shared SQL Pool.

Third, the use of stored procedures (discussed in Chapter 16) can reduce the number of hits to the database. When stored procedures are used, the same code will likely be executed many times, thus taking advantage of the Shared SQL Pool. You can manually compile procedures, functions, and packages to avoid runtime compilation. To bypass the runtime compilation, you can use the ALTER PROCEDURE command.

NOTE: The SQL text for all procedures in a database can be seen through the TEXT column in the DBA_Source view. Figure 10-5 provides an example of the DBA Source view.

Tuning Tools

In this section, you get to peek into the Shared Pool. You learn about the tools Oracle provides to help you determine how your SQL statement will be processed. Figure 10-6 represents the v$sqlarea, a data dictionary view. This

10

	OWNER	NAME	TYPE	LINE	TEXT
1	SYS	AQ$_AGENT	TYPE	1	TYPE aq$_agent
2	SYS	AQ$_AGENT	TYPE	2	AS OBJECT
3	SYS	AQ$_AGENT	TYPE	3	(name||varchar2(30), -- M_IDEN, name of a message producer or
4	SYS	AQ$_AGENT	TYPE	4	address|varchar2(1024), -- address where message must b
5	SYS	AQ$_AGENT	TYPE	5	protocol|number)
6	SYS	AQ$_DEQUEUE_HISTORY	TYPE	1	TYPE aq$_dequeue_history
7	SYS	AQ$_DEQUEUE_HISTORY	TYPE	2	AS OBJECT
8	SYS	AQ$_DEQUEUE_HISTORY	TYPE	3	(consumer||varchar2(30),||| -- identifies dequeuer
9	SYS	AQ$_DEQUEUE_HISTORY	TYPE	4	transaction_id|varchar2(22)| -- M_LTID, transaction id of deque
10	SYS	AQ$_DEQUEUE_HISTORY	TYPE	5	deq_time||date,||| -- time of dequeue
11	SYS	AQ$_DEQUEUE_HISTORY	TYPE	6	deq_user||number,||-- user id of client performing dequeue
12	SYS	AQ$_DEQUEUE_HISTORY	TYPE	7	remote_apps||varchar2(4000), -- string repn. of remote agent
13	SYS	AQ$_DEQUEUE_HISTORY	TYPE	8	agent_naming||number,|| -- how was the message sent to agent
14	SYS	AQ$_DEQUEUE_HISTORY	TYPE	9	propagated_msgid|raw(16))

DBA_Source
view

Figure 10-5.

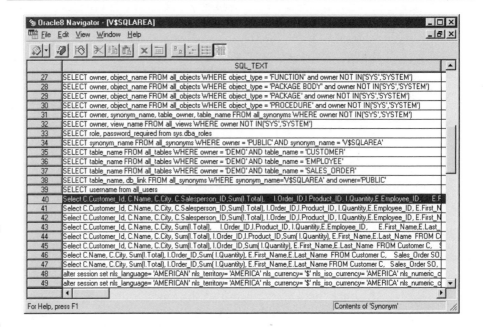

The v$sqlarea:
a peek into
Shared SQL
Pool

Figure 10-6.

shows you the current contents of the shared pool. As you can see, SELECT statements you used in this lesson are shown here. By looking at these statements, you can write your SQL statements so they are similar, thereby creating parsed SQL statements to share with your group. This allows faster processing of your queries.

The *explain plan* is a utility that inspects the indexes used during the execution of SELECT, UPDATE, INSERT, and DELETE statements. Before you can run explain plan, you need to have a table called plan_table available. You need access to a script called utlxplan.sql. This creates the table for you. Then, there are the SQL*Trace and tkprof, which measure the performance by time elapsed during each phase of the SQL statement processing. These are located in the RDBMS80 admin directory in Oracle8. You must run this script, otherwise, you will not have access to the plan_table. Of course, this option is only available with the Oracle8 edition and not the personal Oracle8 edition. To run the script, you need the Enterprise Service Manager.

Again, this is work for the DBA and they probably won't allow you to have access to these utilities. Ask the DBA to run them for you, so you can get an idea of what is involved in tuning the database.

You learned a few optimizing tips for your SQL statements. You also gained insight into how a database engine processes these SQL statements. You learned how to cosmetically enhance your query and also how to decipher user needs and transform them into working queries. You gain your experience in writing streamlined SQL statements through trial and error. If you gain access to your database tuning tools, however, you can use the processing information to guide you to building better SQL statements.

What's Next?

This ends the section on SQL basics. The next part covers creating a database for a fictional company. You provide a customer assessment, build the schema, create an entity-relationship diagram, and design the database using Access. Then you build forms, write queries, and design reports. You are introduced to reporting and how to choose the right report tool. This is the part where you put it all together and create a working database.

10

PART III

Putting It All Together— SQL in Action

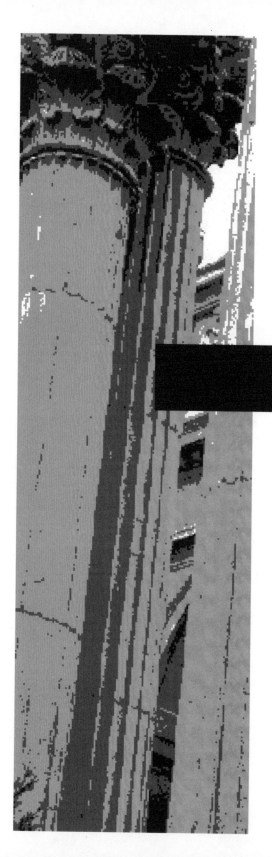

CHAPTER 11

Creating a Database

The first part of this book discussed how to use SQL. In this part, you apply what you have learned to solve a business problem. You learn how to conduct an analysis of the client's current system, interview the users, provide a business flow diagram, and design an entity relationship diagram.

You use Access for both front- and back-end development. What this means is Access is used to design the data entry forms. We also use Access for the back end, which means we use it as an RDBMS. You could just as well use Oracle, Sybase, Informix, Centura, and so forth as the RDBMS. Access was chosen because of the popularity of the tool and because it is widely accessible to most readers. Other development tools are discussed in the next chapter.

The business for which you create the database is purely fictional. However, the methods of analysis, modeling, and design are not. The business is a small business, but the techniques used to analyze, model, and design can be used to create larger, more sophisticated systems.

Business Needs Analysis

When you conduct a needs analysis, starting with the current system is best. Are you going to design a database to replace an older database system or will you build a new database from a paper system? In any event, whether it is a paper system or an older database system, you need to document the data flow of the system.

A data flow shows you how the data is handled within the company. You need to know who handles the data, where the data is stored, and what is done with the data. Data flows are usually represented in data flow diagrams. This is a people-oriented process and you need to conduct interviews of the people who handle the data, the people who store the data, and the people who manage the data.

After you complete your data flow diagram, you need to review it with your clients and make any necessary corrections. You must get your clients' feedback and approval that your data flow diagram is correct.

Next, you should review their business needs. Why do they need a new database? What does the new database need that was missing in the old one? What type of user interface do they prefer? How many users will there be? What types of reports will they need?

As you can see, there are many questions. You may have even more questions after you conduct your initial meeting with the client. You may also have more questions after you do an initial analysis of the current system. The best advice is to be a good listener and listen well to your client's needs. Then go to work and do your analysis. Establishing a good rapport with the client is paramount.

Some people like to hand out questionnaires to the client. The best approach, however, is a face-to-face meeting. You can write yourself a questionnaire to keep focused during your interview. The following sections walk you through the process. Once again, we use the Hush Detective Agency as our client. Mr. Snoop, the owner, is a main contact for the system. Mr. Templeton, a detective, has worked with a database system at his previous agency and he has some ideas. The current system is the old paper file system. The office manager is the keeper of the data.

Client: Hush Detective Agency, Interview Transcripts

The following are transcripts of the interviews with Mr. Alden Snoop, Mr. Simon Templeton, Ms. Adrian Diedrich, and Mr. George Rockford.

Mr. Alden Snoop, President

Could you take us through your process of handling a case?

"Of course, we'd be glad to. We have five detectives, including myself, who do case work. The detectives have notebooks where they make notes and, generally, they give a tape of their notes to the administrative assistant who types up their notes. Then the notes are put in the case brief (an oversized legal file)."

Who starts the paperwork on a client, say, when he or she first walks through the door?

"Well, not every person who comes in to see us is going to be a client. There's an initial interview where we talk and they talk. We see if we can handle the case and the client decides whether ours is the right firm for them. We have a form—an Initial Interview form—that has the name, address, referral, type of case, and our overall impressions of the potential client. We fill out an Initial Interview form for all the potential clients we interview.

"If we decide to take the case and the client decides to hire us, we have a standard contract that is filled out with the particulars of the case. We request a retainer from the client and then I assign the case to one of the detectives. This is when we open an official file and assign a case ID.

11

"Sometimes, the client comes in and wants a specific detective. These are referrals. We would like, at some point, to maintain a referral database, so we could track referrals for marketing purposes. Is this something we could track in this database without too much trouble?"

It might be possible. Now where else does the case brief go? Does the case brief include all information about the client? Can a client have more than one case going at the same time?

"Yes, we have several attorneys we work for, so they would have multiple cases open. Also, we have several corporate clients that tend to have multiple cases. We do background investigations on potential employees for a couple of corporations."

Do you have special codes for your types of investigations?

"We have special codes for typical cases. Of course, there are always the weird cases that fall in between categories. We usually label them miscellaneous. Currently, we have missing persons, unfaithful spouses, background investigation, murder investigation, and fraud."

What do you do with suspect lists?

"We don't have a list of suspects. We have suspects based on each case. We don't have a group of suspects on file like the police do, but that brings up another group I completely forgot. We do track informants. People we usually go to for information. How secure can we make this database? A lot of sensitive information exists that I would hate to have unauthorized people see."

We can make the database as secure as you need. What methods do you have now to secure your paper files?

"We lock them in a safe. Only my office manager and I have the combination. The detectives also keep their tapes and notebooks under lock and key. The guys are usually pretty closed-mouthed about their informants, but we all use some of them. Now, I suppose they could have access to their informants in the database if they wish, but we probably would have to keep others out of that information.

"Each detective would need to keep others out of his or her case files for privacy. I would be the only one who would have access to all files. The office manager would need to be secured from only the informant data. We don't have any laptops in the field and we don't plan to get any. Most of the guys are from the old school and feel comfortable with the pen and paper method.

"Our new guy, Templeton, is another matter. He's from a high-tech agency, New Scotland Yard. His group was into counterintelligence and it had the works, state-of-the-art, James Bond sort of stuff. He may want one of those Palm Pilots or something like that, so maybe he should be able to connect that to the database and transfer his notes into the computer. I hear that's possible. It's not top priority right now, though."

What forms do you have now that you would want to keep online? How do you want the data entry screens to look?

"I don't really have anything in mind. We have the Initial Interview form for potential clients. I can give you a copy of that. I would like that form online. I would like to keep it simple. The last thing we want is to have to learn a complicated system. Our administrative assistant probably would set up the file. Then it would be up to the detectives to fill in the rest. What they do is usually write notes to themselves, leads on people to interview, phone numbers, names of witnesses, and such. We can provide you with a transcript of one of our typical detective notes on a case."

That would be good. If you can provide us with any other forms or procedures, we would appreciate it. Thank you for your time.

Ms. Adrian Diedrich, Office Manager
Hi, Ms. Diedrich. Thanks for taking the time to help us. We're interested in how you keep all these cases organized. What is your system? If you could take us through the life cycle of a case, we would appreciate it.

"No problem. I figure this database will make my life easier and I'll have to worry less about losing paper. Let me give you the steps of a case brief life cycle:

1. I take the Initial Client form and give it to Mr. Snoop. If we don't take the client, we have a file of interview forms, alphabetical by month and year that we keep on file. We keep the interview forms for about six months. Sometimes we refer the client to another agency and, if we do this, we note the name of the agency on the form.

2. Mr. Snoop interviews the client and if we take on the client, I get the form back to begin the case brief.

3. Then I take the case brief and I make sure the contract has been signed. I send the contract to our Billing department so they can set up the billing. Our billing system is automated, but we do retain a copy of the contract in the case brief. Next, I put the case brief in the Active file cabinet. Oh, yes! I also make a copy of the Initial Interview form, place

11

it in a file, and give it to the detective. Usually Mr. Snoop sets up the next interview with the detective assigned.

4. The detective then starts his investigation and the notes and tapes are sent to the assistant for transcription and a copy of the transcription is kept in the case brief. Mr. Snoop asked me to provide you with a sample of a transcription from a case brief. The detectives keep their own notebooks and tapes in their file cabinets.

5. Each week, the detectives put in a timesheet on the hours worked on each case. This sheet is sent to Billing. A copy of the timesheet is kept in the case brief.

6. When the case is solved, the final notes are put into the brief. A closing timesheet and expense sheet is sent to Billing and a copy is kept in the case brief. The case brief is then moved from the Active file cabinet to the Case Closed file cabinet. There is also another file cabinet for Unsolved cases. If a client discontinues the case or if it cannot be solved, the case brief is put in this file cabinet. We keep files for three years in these file cabinets and then they are sent to a secured off-site storage facility. This is the end of the line for the case brief."

Thank you, Ms. Diedrich.

Mr. Simon Templeton, Sr. Investigator
Good afternoon, Mr. Templeton, we want to get your input on what you would like to see in the new system.

"Good afternoon, you can call me Simon. I know this is a smaller operation than my previous company, but I do have a few suggestions you might use for this new system.

"First of all, we had PDAs that we entered our notes in. Then it was a simple matter of downloading the information to our PCs when we returned from the field. We also had laptops with a printer, scanner, and digital camera to assist us in our field work and investigation. And we could dial into the lab database when necessary.

"I know this is not a high-tech office. Nonetheless, they do some fine detective work in spite of the primitive equipment. I would like to keep my PDA and be able to download my notes. Or a laptop would do in a pinch. I really don't have anything to add at this point. What I would like to do is maybe add something to your data entry screens once you have a sample of them. Would this be possible? I also will give you a model of the data entry screens I think would be helpful for us in the field."

Of course Simon, we'd love to see your ideas and we'd appreciate your feedback on our prototype design. Thank you for your time.

Mr. George Rockford, Lead Detective, Partner
As you know, Hush Detective Agency is undergoing a change in its business processes. Could you please give us an example of how you handle an investigation?

"You know, it's that new guy, Templeton, who got Alden all fired up about this computer system. I've worked with Alden since Day One. We opened this agency with just the two of us and a secretary. Heck, we're partners. We have a good system already. We don't need computers.

"Okay, my investigations usually begin with the interview of the client. We meet, the client tells me what he or she wants. I listen and jot down notes. I usually ask for people to speak to, like witnesses or someone to corroborate any information the client gives me. The client usually has a suspect in mind. I assure the client we will do our best and not to worry.

"After the interview, I do a background check on the client. I have a suspicious mind. I also check on the story I've been told. I may contact witnesses or other people who the client has given me to check out. If we are doing surveillance, I initiate the set-up of equipment. We have a few high-tech guys who handle this.

"If there is a police investigation, I find out who is the detective in charge and, if I don't know him or her, I check out the detective with the cops I do know. I let the police know I'm on the investigation. They usually don't like private investigators working on active cases. I feel like I keep them on their toes.

"I add to my notes as I progress through the case. If I have suspects, I list them along with any evidence; I check for priors, and so forth. If I need an informant on the case, I go to my usual informants and, if they give me good information, I pay them.

11

"When the case is finished, I submit the timesheet and expense report along with the final notes. These are all placed in the brief."

Thanks, Mr. Rockford, for your invaluable input. We hope to provide you with a system you can use.

As you can see, you have an appreciative group willing to help you. You are off to a good start. What you need to do next is take this information and design a data flow diagram. This diagram is a visual representation of what you have learned in your interviews. Once the diagram is finished, you should call a meeting and get buy-in from all your clients.

Finally, you need to present a needs assessment and your strategy for building the database to your client.

Many tools are available, which you can use to design your data flow diagram and your entity-relationship diagram, but a tool hasn't been invented yet that can design the database for you. This is still a cerebral function you must perform. The tools, however, do enable you to create a professional diagram, as opposed to your drawing circles with arrows on a piece of paper. You can begin with this, though, if you work best with pen and paper.

While you were at the client site, you got a copy of the Initial Interview form (Figure 11-1), the Investigator timesheet (Figure 11-2), and you looked at the investigator notes. Because the investigator notes are confidential, you perused a few of them to get a field list for the Investigator form.

Here is a list of the fields:

- Client ID
- Client Name
- Case Type
- Witness Name
- Witness Address
- Witness Telephone
- Suspect Name
- Suspect Address
- Suspect Telephone
- Suspect Priors
- Informant Name
- Informant Telephone
- Case Notes
- Electronic Surveillance?
- Evidence
- Police Investigation
- Police detective assigned to case

Once you analyze all the documentation and interview transcripts you prepare the data flow diagram. Figure 11-3 represents the data flow diagram for Hush Detective Agency. Figure 11-4 provides you with the description of the shapes used in this diagram. This diagram was designed using Visio 5.0.

At this point, you would call another meeting to review the data flow diagram. A revision of the diagram is then made. Now you need to discuss the business rules for the application and form design (data entry screens).

Name _____ Case ID _____ Date _____

Street Address _____

City _____ State _____ ZIP Code _____

Home Telephone _____ Work Telephone _____

Pager _____ Cell Phone _____

Can we contact you at home? _____ At work? _____ Pager? _____

Were you referred? Y N   If Yes, by whom _____

What services can we provide for you? Describe _____

_____

_____

_____

_____

_____

_____

_____

_____

_____

Take Case? Y N   Refer to _____ Assign to _____

Initial
Interview
form

Figure 11-1.

11

Hush Detective Agency

Hush Detective Agency   Phone: 213-555-4321
333 Danger Way   Fax: 213-555-1234
Los Angeles, CA 92001   E-mail: simont@hush.com

Weekly Time Record

Employee:
Manager:
Employee Phone:
Employee E-mail:
Tax ID:

Week ending: CASE ID:

Day	In	Out	In	Out	Regular Hours	Overtime Hours	Sick	Vacation	Total
Saturday									
Sunday									
Monday									
Tuesday									
Wednesday									
Thursday									
Friday									
				Total					
				Rate					
				Total					

Investigator Signature: Date:

Manager Signature: Date:

Investigator
timesheet

Figure 11-2.

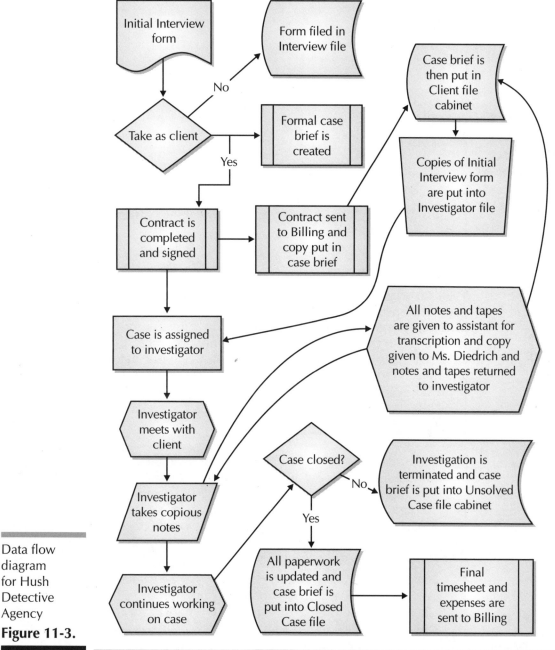

Data flow
diagram
for Hush
Detective
Agency

Figure 11-3.

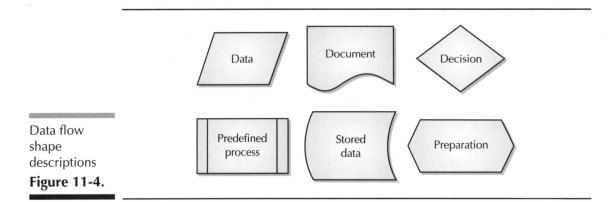

The business rules and form design help you design your tables for the database application.

Table Specification

The next step in the process is to design your tables. First, you need to do your table specifications. You have your data flow diagram, your Initial Interview form, and a list of fields for the Investigator form. You need to study these to create your table specifications. You need to create tables that are at least third normal form, you need to specify the data types you need, and from these tables, you create an entity-relationship diagram that shows the relationship between tables.

First, let's make some assumptions based on what we know from the interviews and the forms.

♦ You do not need to have a billing application because this is already automated. Copies of the document and timesheets are sent to Billing. No data is returned from Billing to the investigators. We called to verify this and Mr. Snoop said the only time this occurs is if there is a question about billing from the client or if the client is 90 days delinquent. Mr. Snoop also said there would be no added value to his database if we provide an electronic form for the timesheet.

♦ The Initial Interview form is either filed, if the firm does not take the case, or assigned a case ID number. At our business rule meeting, we asked if they would like the case ID automatically assigned. Mr. Snoop said yes. So, the first form—the Interview form—is entered into the system by the assistant (data entry operator). The operator is responsible for maintaining the Client form, which has all the demographic information on the client. We also auto assign the client ID number.

◆ The next step is to prepare an Investigator file and set up a first meeting between the client and the investigator. The investigator takes notes and starts the investigation process. At our business rule meeting, it was indicated that the investigators fill out their own forms. Under the advice of Mr. Templeton, the investigators will be assigned laptop computers and will be responsible for completing the forms. At this business meeting, it was also decided the Investigator form consist of a subform that enables the investigator to input information on witnesses, a subform for suspects, and a new form for informants. It was also advised that the investigators receive some basic PC training.

◆ It was requested during the interview process that a contact database be incorporated into this database. This module has been deferred, based on the decision that a separate contact referral database would be more efficient. We advised them that several good contact database products are available at their local software store, but we are storing referral names.

◆ If a client is new, the Client form must be completed before a Case form can be started. If this is an established client, the information and client ID will be in the database. Because the client list is relatively small, a drop-down menu can be provided on the Client form to fill in the client ID and name. They need to know the client ID to begin the Case form. This will be provided by printing an Initial Interview form from the system and placing it in the investigator's file.

◆ The investigator will be assigned to the case. The investigator's data must be stored in a table. The Investigator ID number will not be automatically assigned. Only five investigators and a numbering system—100 to 105—will be used.

11

After you analyze this information, you decide how many tables you need. You need to look for commonality among your fields and group them together. This provides the first cut of your tables. You can list all the fields needed from all the forms. When you create a table, you want to create a table free of redundant data. You need to analyze the table based on the normalization rules. You can refer to Chapter 2 for review. Then you need to set your primary key and any foreign keys you have for each table.

Review your tables and define the relationship among the tables. This is the basis of your entity-relationship diagram. Tables 11-1 through 11-7 show the tables with the field names and the data types we have created for the database.

Field Name	Data Type
CaseID	Autonumber
ClientID	Number
SuspectID	Number
InformantID	Number
DateCaseOpened	Date
DateCaseClosed	Date
PoliceInvestigation?	Yes/No
ElectronicSurveillance?	Yes/No

tblCase
Table 11-1.

Field Name	Data Type
ClientID	Autonumber
LNAME	Text
FNAME	Text
MI	Text
Address	Text
City	Text
State	Text
ZIP	Number
HomeTele	Text
WorkTele	Text
Pager	Text
CellPhone	Text
ServiceRequested?	Memo

tblClient
Table 11-2.

Field Name	Data Type
InvestigatorID	Number
Referred?	Yes/No
ReferredBy?	Text
Home	Text
Work	Text
Pagers	Text

tblClient
(continued)
Table 11-2.

Field Name	Data Type
InformantID	Number
InvestigatorID	Number
INFLNAME	Text
INFFNAME	Text
INFMI	Text
Codename	Text
TeleNo	Text
Paid	Yes/No
Amount	Currency
Notes	Memo

tblInformant
Table 11-3.

11

Field Name	Data Type
InvestigatorID	Number
ILNAME	Text
IFNAME	Text
IMI	Text

tblInvestigator
Table 11-4.

Field Name	Data Types
InvestigatorID	Number
CaseID	Number
Notes	Memo

tblInvestigator
Notes
Table 11-5.

Field Name	Data Type
SuspectID	Number
CaseID	Number
SLNAME	Text
SFNAME	Text
Evidence	Memo
Priors	Text

tblSuspect
Table 11-6.

Field Name	Data Type
WitnessID	Number
CaseID	Number
WLNAME	Text
WFNAME	Text
Address	Text
City	Text
State	Text
ZIP	Number
HomeTele	Text
WorkTele	Text
Witness or Other	Text
Notes	Memo

tblWitness-
OrOther
Table 11-7.

Now you are ready to create the entity-relationship diagram.

Entity-Relationship Diagram

An *entity* is a table. The *relationship* is an association between the two entities. The *diagram* is the graphical representation of these relationships. Your entities are represented by squares or rectangles, and the relationships are represented by diamonds. The cardinality of the relationships is shown inside the diagram.

A cardinality can be represented as:

◆   **1:1**   This is a one-to-one relationship

◆   **1:N**   This is a one-to-many relationship

◆   **N:1**   This is a many-to-one relationship

◆   **N:M**   This is a many-to-many relationship

Figure 11-5 represents the relationships of the entities in our database.

You are almost finished with your analysis. The last part of this process requires you to build the tables according to the specifications and to establish the relationships according to your ER diagram.

We assume you now have satisfied all the comments and questions your clients may have raised during this process. There may be more questions but, for now, you are reasonably satisfied you have the basic requirements. You begin your database by building your tables within the Access database.

There are two ways to do this. First, you may use the wizards for building a table. Second, you can go into the Design mode and start typing your field names and data types straight from the table specifications. You assign your primary keys according to the ER diagram. Primary keys are underlined in the diagram.

Next, the relationships need to be assigned. You can do this in the Relationships window. You can find Tools on the toolbar and click Tools | Relationships. You can then establish the relationships in this window. The relationships are based on the joins of these tables. So you may create an equi-join, a left outer join, or a right outer join. The type of entity relationship is described in the window you use for your Join tables window. Figure 11-6 illustrates the Relationships window for Hush database.

This finishes this chapter on database creation.

11

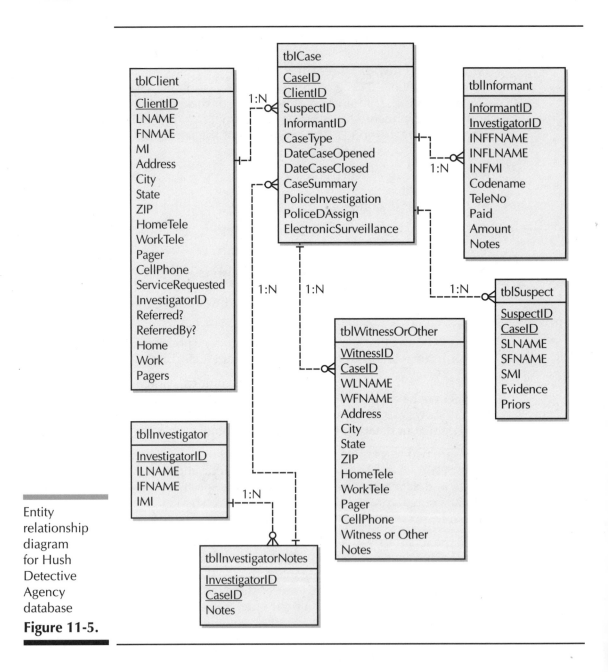

Entity
relationship
diagram
for Hush
Detective
Agency
database

Figure 11-5.

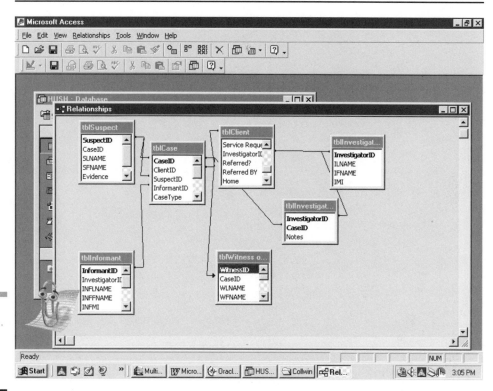

Access
Relationships
window
for Hush

Figure 11-6.

What's Next?

In the next chapter, you learn about creating a front end for the database. You learn about development tools, specifically Microsoft Access and some other tools the RDBMS vendors provide.

The final section in the next chapter discusses the creation of your front end. You learn some tips about creating and designing for the end user. Usability issues are also discussed.

Then you dive right into Chapter 13 and create your forms. If you have Access installed, please follow along with the book and learn how to create forms and write queries.

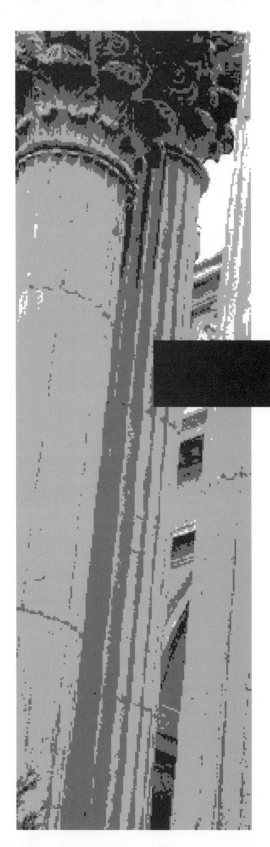

CHAPTER 12

Designing the Database Front End

Developers refer to designing the database front end as developing a graphical user interface (GUI). Usually, developers begin their applications by building the code and then the GUI. If you want to build an effective database application, however, you must start with the GUI first. The GUI is your end user's view of the database.

If you build the GUI first, you give your users an opportunity to give you feedback before you code. This saves you time. The more feedback you get, the less time you spend coding and recoding. This gives you an outline to follow, which enables you to code better and tighter, and also builds a good rapport between the designers and the users. Getting sign-off from the users is easier if they are actively involved in the processes. In the last chapter, you defined the user requirements. You gathered documentation, interviewed, and observed the users. This is stage one in the GUI process. The next stage is to plan the user interface. In this stage, you need to produce process plans, plan the user interface elements, and implement standards.

Planning the User Interface

In this stage, you plan and document how you plan to develop a user interface that meets you client's needs. If you are working in a development team, this is what is important:

◆ Develop a set of standards you and your team must follow. These standards include coding, design, syntax conventions, and testing. Setting standards for project management is also a good idea. Let your team know you plan to drive the project plan and keep it on schedule.

◆ Consider the platform-specific requirements and other restrictions you may have in the user environment.

◆ Map out each screen and decide which types of elements you need to include to meet your users' needs.

Creating Your Standards

Creating standards for layout, use, and behavior of GUI elements is a must. Everything should have a common look and feel, but this is easier to say than to do. Even the largest software developers find this hard to achieve.

Visual attributes, such as the font, color, and pattern properties are established for forms and menu objects. Your font properties include font name, font size, font style, font width, and font weight. Color and pattern properties include foreground color, background color, and fill pattern. Standards must be assigned for the visual attributes.

Create templates for your forms so graphics, toolbars, standard window layouts, menus, and other common objects are standardized in the template. This helps maintain a common look and feel.

IN DEPTH

Guidelines for Creating Portable Applications

If your application must run on more than one platform (UNIX, OS/2, WIN NT), then understanding how various GUI elements react on each platform is important. You should have answers to the following questions before you begin:

◆ Which platforms will you support? If you plan to have more than one platform, you need to consider the fonts, colors, layout, screen size, and screen resolution.

◆ Is character-mode support required? If so, your options sare limited.

◆ What diplays must you accommodate? Monitors can vary a great deal, even on the same platform.

◆ Do you want your GUI to look the same across all platforms or do you want your GUI to inherit the native look and feel of the platform environment?

The following are some guidelines to consider when developing portable applications:

◆ When considering the GUI, you need to create an object library for each platform you're supporting. This object library is a set of objects and standards you create; each object or standard can determine the appearance and layout of your entire frame, window, or region. A good idea is to create one library for each target platform.

◆ When you consider the monitors, if you have various sizes, try to develop for the smallest size monitor.

12

IN DEPTH

CONTINUED

◆ If you are using color, keep to three or four basic colors that work well together. Colors available on many platforms include blue, red, magenta, cyan, green, and yellow.

◆ Deciding on fonts is tricky. You need to decide how you want to handle boldface, italics, and underlining. Try to limit your choice to boldface and use it sparingly. To keep the fonts in line with the platform, you need to translate the fonts between platforms using one of these methods:

   ◆ Defining aliases for fonts on each deployment platform.

   ◆ Defining port-specific classes.

◆ Using icons that are platform-specific. The best advice is to create a separate icon directory for each platform. Use the same names for the icons on each platform and set the respective environment variable to point to the icon directory.

◆ When using buttons, make all buttons non-navigatable. Triggers are often dependent upon button navigation. This difference across platforms can create behavioral differences in the application.

◆ Finally, when building a form for multiple platforms, right-align all prompts. Text often expands when ported to other platforms and left-aligned prompts can cause fields to shift, creating a ragged margin.

In addition, check your development tool documentation for a chapter or appendix on designing portable applications.

Creating a Prototype

You know what they say, a picture is worth a thousand words. These are words to live by when developing a GUI. You begin with a storyboard and end with a fully functional application. A *storyboard* is a frame-by-frame drawing of screens showing transition and appearance. You should include a description of how

Client screen   Investigator screen

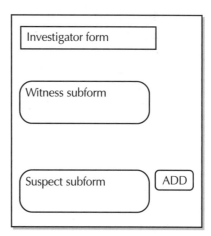

The administrator enters client information and then clicks the Add button. Client file must be added before investigator can assign client to Investigator form.

Storyboard of Hush database application

Figure 12-1.

The investigator makes notes for each client. He/she adds witnesses and suspects to the subforms. When finished, the investigator clicks the Add button.

the screens relate to the business needs of the end user. Figure 12-1 is an example of a storyboard for the Client and Investigation forms.

You need to show the storyboard to your users. Again, check to make sure these forms meet the way your users do business. Then follow the storyboard with a more detailed paper prototype. Now show this prototype to the users and get their approval. Based on the feedback, you can create your functional prototype by using your development tool and designing your GUI draft application.

Allow your users to experiment with the application. If possible, get a user who was not actively involved in the user meetings. You want to test the intuitiveness of the application.

You know you need to get user feedback, but how do you gather effective user feedback? To gather effective user feedback:

◆ Provide instructions for user tests using a task-based approach.

◆ Use at least six typical everyday users.

12

◆ Record user activity through notes. If you have access to sound and video monitoring, please use it.

◆ Question your users about the performance of the prototype.

◆ Get more than one of your team to interpret the results.

Get more feedback from the users and change the design where necessary. Once you have exhausted them and yourself with all the possible changes and refinements, then you are ready to design the GUI.

In the next chapter, you have an opportunity to develop your forms.

The following section presents the other development tools available from RDBMS vendors. This brief list is an overview of what is on the market.

Other Development Tools

In this section, we review Oracle Developer/2000, Centura Team Developer, Sybase Enterprise Application Studio, and Microsoft Visual Studio 6.

Oracle Developer/2000

Oracle Developer provides a set of integrated, productive builders that enable developers to build sophisticated and multilingual database forms, reports, and charts. It takes advantage of the ease and accessibility of the Web. Oracle Developer/2000 supports a three-tier architecture that delivers the benefits of both client/server and the Web in a single application.

Oracle Developer/2000 is a rapid application development environment for building enterprise-class database applications. It is a highly visual environment for building applications. Oracle Developer/2000 makes use of SQL and PL/SQL, its programming language. Figure 12-2 is the Oracle Developer/2000 Form Designer window.

Centura Team Developer 1.5

Centura (formerly Gupta) provides an integrated tool set for deploying Windows-based strategic business applications. This is the 32-bit descendent of SQLWindows. Centura gives the development team the tools for scaleable and robust business applications for the enterprise, workgroup, mobile, or Web-based deployment.

Centura uses Scaleable Application Language (SAL) as the main language for Team Developer and is built on an object-oriented foundation. SAL provides developers with complete control over run-time environment, including the

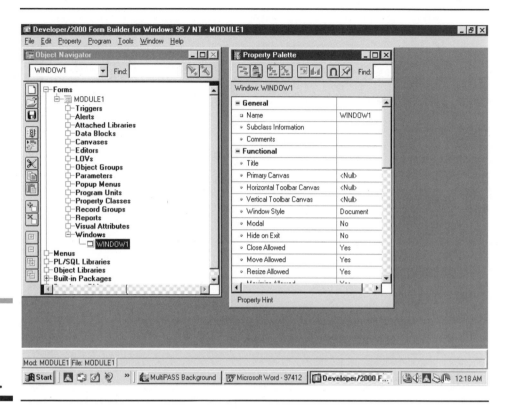

Oracle
Developer/
2000 Form
Designer
Figure 12-2.

capability to access the operating system, manipulate external data sources, and integrate with other applications and packages.

Centura Team Developer provides native database connectivity to Oracle, SQL Server, Sybase, Informix, SQLBase, DB2, and CA-OpenIngress, as well as ODBC.

Centura Team Developer offers Web deployment for Windows applications. Any Centura Team Developer application built with Web QuickObjects class library can be deployed to the Web with the Web App Manager.

Centura Team Developer is a fully scalable enterprise development tool. Figure 12-3 is the Centura Team Developer Sample App window.

12

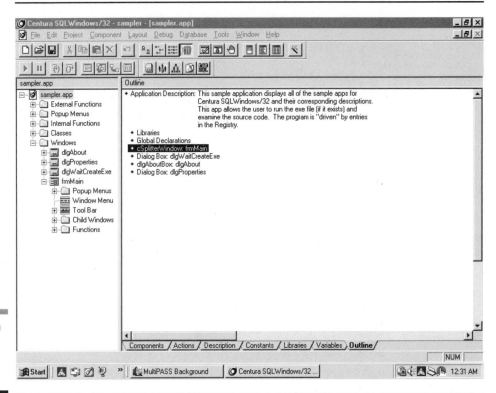

Sybase Enterprise Application Studio

Sybase's Enterprise Application Studio integrates the Rapid Application Development technology of PowerBuilder, PowerJ's environment for Java, and the high-performance deployment environment of Enterprise Application Server. This product also provides everything you need to build enterprise Web, distributed, and client/server applications.

In addition to PowerBuilder and PowerJ, the Enterprise App Studio makes accessing data easy. DataWindow is the point-and-click access to SQL data and powerful views through various presentation styles. Design Time Controls enable you to build Web applications using your DataWindow tool. The AppModeler enables you to develop simple data-entry applications that are ready to run without writing any code. A data-modeling tool enables you to lay the foundation for your application, either graphically or by reverse-engineering an existing database.

Flexible and extensible, Enterprise Apps Server's page engine enables you to build dynamic Web-based applications.

This suite of tools provide high-end enterprise services for business applications.

Microsoft Visual Studio 6

Visual Studio 6 provides a complete suite of tools for developing solutions based on the Windows DNA architecture. It covers all the bases for application development, such as integrated tools for multitier application design, user interface development, middle-tier component development and assembly, database programming and design, performance analysis, and team-based development support.

In addition, all the tools in the suite support the Component Object Model (COM), a component created in any language can be reused by any other tool in the suite. Please note, more and more software developers are following Microsoft's lead. COM is the acronym for the new century!

Universal Data Access enables all Visual Studio tools to access a wide variety of data sources on multiple platforms. VS 6 provides the ability to design and manipulate database structures directly within the development environment. Developers can integrate data quickly and design database structures rapidly—directly within the development environment.

Have you noticed a trend among these wonderful products? The trend is to develop Web-enabled applications that provide universal access to data and can reuse code components. We are moving toward a more Open environment.

It would be nice if SQL took the hint and moved toward a more universally acceptable standard. The vendors now recognize the differences between their SQL dialects and are providing for a common denominator—Universal Data Access with OLE DB. Figure 12-4 is the jdbcdemo.class window from Microsoft Visual Studio J++.

12

Access—A Developer's Tool!

Since its introduction in 1992, Microsoft Access continues to lead the desktop database category. The popularity of Access includes experienced database users, as well as first-time database users. Access is now fully integrated with the Office product and shares the same look and feel of Word, Excel, and Outlook.

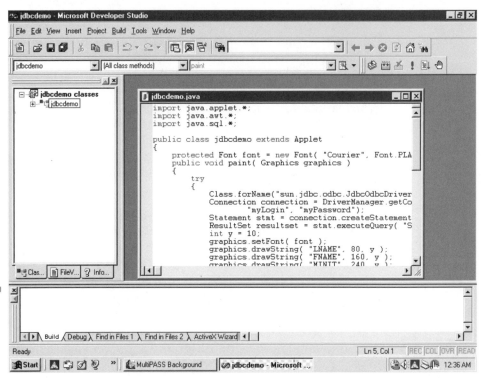

Microsoft
Visual Studio
jdbcdemo.class
example

Figure 12-4.

Access can act as a front-end client to a corporate-level, back-end database such as SQL Server or Oracle. You definitely need to know your SQL now. Access has closer conformity to ANSI SQL92 than before. Differences still exist between Access and other RDBMS, however.

This chapter presented a brief overview of form design and usability issues, and a brief synopsis of a few of the other development tools available. You also were provided with the new features of Access. In the next two chapters, you have the experience of developing your forms and queries using Access.

What's Next?

In Chapters 13 and 14, you learn form and query design using Access. You develop the forms and queries necessary for the Hush database. In Chapter 15, you conclude your database design with report development. We also review reporting tools and discuss how to choose the best tool for your database.

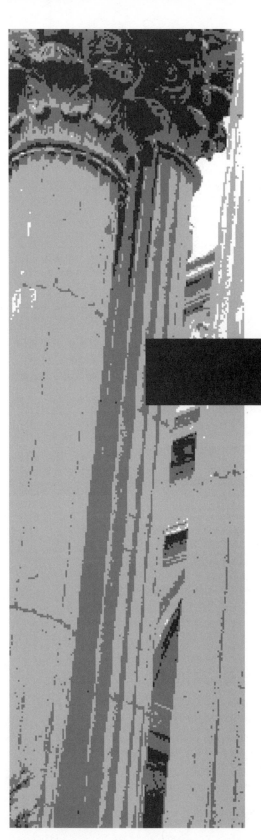

CHAPTER 13

Designing Forms in Access

In the last chapter, you learned about form design and how to create useable forms. You also created a storyboard for the application design. In this chapter, you finally get to design your forms for the Hush Detective Agency.

Now you have been through the user testing of your prototype and you are ready to design the real GUI. Let's begin.

Access Design Environment

Access is a nice environment for beginners to gain experience in designing a database application. If you are already proficient in Access, you may want to skip ahead to the design section of this chapter. This section provides you with basics for designing these forms in Access. You may want to take a class or purchase a book on Access to get complete training.

In Access, the forms provide you with a way for adding and editing the data in your database. The database in Access 97 may be downloaded from the Osborne Web site. You can open the database now as we discuss form design controls and properties. You can create the forms quickly by using the Microsoft Form Wizards. You can also design the forms manually by using the Form Design window.

The Form Design window is illustrated in Figure 13-1.

The form is expandable based on your needs. You can use the form to display graphics such as drawings, photos, or corporate logos. You can display data from your tables on forms. You can also use queries to display your data from multiple tables on one form.

You can view your form through the Design window, Form view, and Datasheet view. In the sample Northwind database, Figure 13-2 represents the Design view of the Customer Form, Figure 13-3 represents the Datasheet view of the Customer Form, and Figure 13-4 represents the View form. Data can be entered through the Datasheet and the Form views.

Here is a summary of these view types:

◆　Design view is used to make changes to the design of the form or to change the properties of the controls and other objects in the form.

◆　Form view is the view you use as you work with the data in the form. You can view, enter, and edit data in a one-record-at-a-time format.

◆　Datasheet view displays the data in the familiar row and column format, which is identical to a table's datasheet. You may notice this also resembles a spreadsheet format. In this view, you cannot use the list boxes or combination boxes, or see the contents of OLE Object fields.

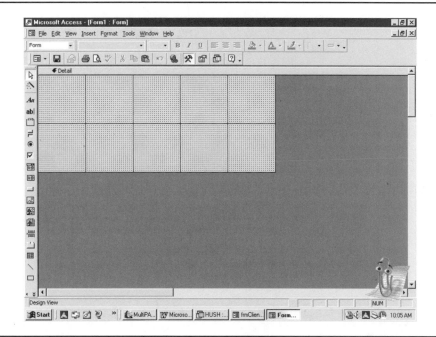

Access Form
Design
window
Figure 13-1.

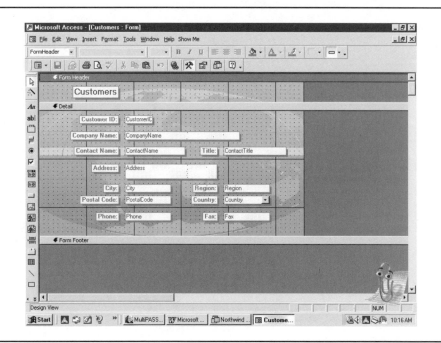

Customer
form—
Design view
Figure 13-2.

13

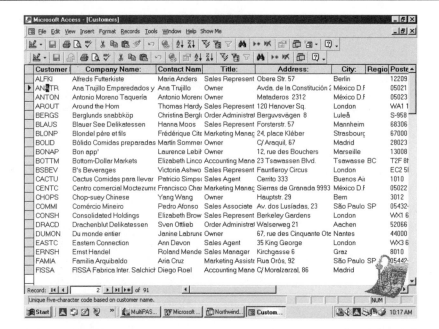

Customer
form—
Datasheet
view

Figure 13-3.

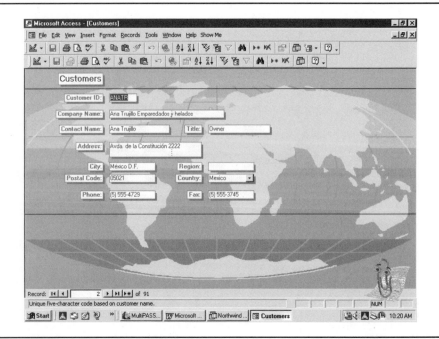

Customer
form—
Form view

Figure 13-4.

The Design View

To design a new form, under Objects, click Forms, and then click the Design Icon located on the toolbar (Figure 13-5). This brings up the New Form window (Figure 13-6). Choose the Design view and then Choose a table or query from the drop-down list. For our form, you need to choose qryClient. This query is explained in the next chapter. Figure 13-7 shows you the Design window and the data fields available for your form.

A form consists of several sections. Each form has a detail section that contains information displayed in the main section of the form. All objects placed within the form are *controls,* which can be used to display information from fields, give feedback to the viewer, or provide methods of interacting with Access.

In addition to the detail, forms can have form headers and form footers. If you have multiple pages of a form, you could use the form headers and footers. In the form, you can use grid dots, horizontal and vertical rulers, a Toolbox, and a Field List. These can all be turned on or off, depending on what you like to use.

Form Headers and Footers
These headers and footers contain any information that appears at the beginning and end of the form. Form headers are used for titles and form footers are used for any summary information you need.

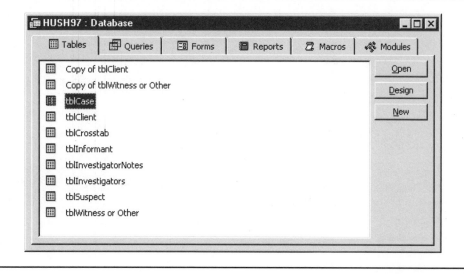

Hush Database
main window
Figure 13-5.

13

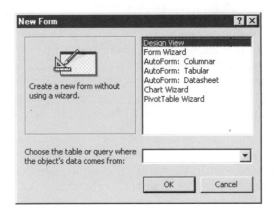

Page Headers and Footers

You can also add these to your form. These are usually reserved for reports, however, and are seldom used in forms.

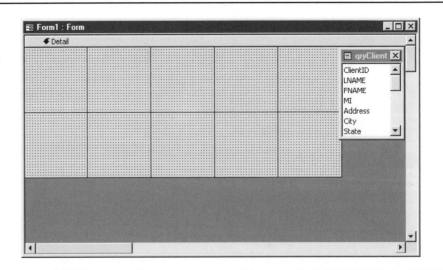

Adding Controls to Forms

Access calls on the objects you place on the form controls. Controls can display the contents of a field, calculations, text, list boxes, combination boxes, option group, option button, check box, image control, line, rectangle, ActiveX controls, and command buttons. Controls can run Access macros or call programs from the modules and you can imbed OLE objects, such as a movie clip, a Word document, or an Excel spreadsheet.

In Access, there are three types of controls to forms:

◆ Bound

◆ Unbound

◆ Calculated

A *bound control* is tied to a field in an underlying table or query. You can use bound controls to display, enter, and update values from fields in your database. A *calculated control* uses an expression as its source of data. An expression can use data from a field in an underlying table or a query of a form or report, or from another control on the form or report. An *unbound control* doesn't have a data source. You can use unbound controls to display information, lines, rectangles, and pictures.

Access also provides two tools you can use to add controls to your form easily: the Toolbox and the Field List. The Toolbox contains a set of controls. Table 13-1 lists the most used controls and what each control does.

Control	Description
Select Objects Pointer	Used to select, move, or size objects within the form.
Control Wizards	This button turns on/off the Control Wizards. These wizards are useful for building your controls.
Label	Used to add a label—descriptive text, titles, captions, or instructions. These are attached to text box controls to describe them or they can be unattached and provide additional information for your user.
Text Box	A text box displays the contents of the field or results of an expression. Text boxes are usually bound to a field in a table or dynaset.

Toolbox
Controls
Table 13-1.

13

Control	Description
Option Group	Used to add option groups. You can store two or more option buttons, toggle buttons, or check boxes. Only one of these options in an option group can be selected at a time.
Toggle Button	Toggle buttons are buttons that look like they have been pushed down when selected. They are used within option groups to select one choice from many or as a yes/no choice individually.
Option Button	Used to add an option button. These buttons are circles that darken when you select them.
Check Box	Check boxes are small squares that contain a small × when selected. You can use check boxes within an option group to choose one choice from many or to specify a yes/no choice individually.
Combo Box	Combination boxes serve as a combination of a list box and a text box. You can choose values from a pull-down list that appears in the box or you can type in a value. The choices in the list are generally taken from rows of a query, but they can either be based on SQL statements or from a list of predetermined values.
List Box	You use list boxes to choose values from a predetermined list. The choices in the list are generally taken from rows of a query, but they can also be based on SQL statements or from a list of predetermined values.
Graph	Use this tool to start the Graph Wizard.
Command Button	Command buttons carry out one or more commands and they are attached to macros or to routines. If you have the Control Wizards on, then a wizard helps you through the design.
Image	Used to add a frame you can use to display a static graphic image.
Unbound Object Frame	Used to add an OLE object. These frames are used to display graphic elements.

Toolbox
Controls
(continued)
Table 13-1.

Control	Description
Bound Object Frame	Used to display the contents of an OLE field from the underlying table or query in the form.
Page Break	Used to insert a page break into the form. These do not appear on the form, but are evident when the form is printed.
Subform	Used to add a subform to the form.
Line	Used to draw lines on the form. You can use the Palette to change the width and color of the line.
Rectangle	Used to add rectangles or squares to a form. You can use the Palette to change the width and color of the rectangle.

Toolbox
Controls
(continued)
Table 13-1.

Every control has its own properties that you can modify to affect the behavior of that control. Figure 13-8 is an example of a text box property.

If you want to see the properties for all the controls on your form, you can begin by clicking a control, opening the Property window, and moving it off to one side. If you click another control, you will notice the Property window moves to the property for this control. In addition to the control properties,

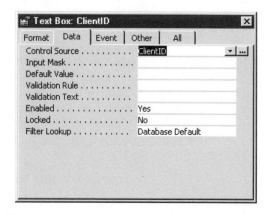

Text box
property
Figure 13-8.

13

the section of a form has properties. You can modify these to suit your specific needs.

Properties Defined

The most common types of control properties are outlined in the following list:

◆ **Control Source**   This property binds the control to a field in a table or query or names an expression that creates data displayed in the control.

◆ **Format**   This property specifies the desired format for displaying or printing the data.

◆ **Decimal Places**   This property is used with a number or currency field.

◆ **Input Mask**   This property controls how data displayed in the field appears. This is great when you want to have a phone number stored as 5055551234 but appear as (505) 555-1234 on your form.

◆ **Default Value**   This property enables you to specify a default value for the control. With forms used for routine data entry, a default value can be a time saving feature.

◆ **Validation Rule and Validation Text**   Use these properties to validate data entered into a form. The Validation Rule property contains an expression of your choosing that validates the data. The Validation Text property contains the text that appears as an error message if the data entered is not valid according to the validation rule.

◆ **Status Bar Text**   This property specifies the text that appears in the status bar when a control is selected. This can be useful for adding explanatory messages that help your users understand the purpose of the different fields on the form. You can enter a maximum of 255 characters for the Status Bar text.

◆ **Auto Tab and Enter Key Behavior**   Use these properties to determine the behavior of Access when you fill a field with allowable characters and the behavior of the Enter key. If the Auto Tab property is set to Yes, a tab is generated (the focus moves to the next field) when data fills the field. If Auto Tab is set to No, the focus does not move when the field fills with data and the user must press TAB to move to the next field.

◆ **Visible**   This property determines whether the control is visible.

◆ **Display When**   This property can apply to individual controls or to sections of the form. It determines whether the object or section is displayed or printed.

◆ **Enabled and Locked**   Use these properties to determine whether a control can have the focus and whether edits will be permitted to data through the control. If the Enabled property is set to Yes, a control can have the focus. If the Enabled property is set to No, the user cannot move the focus into or out of the control while in Form view. The Locked property, when set to Yes, prevents any changes to the data in the control. If the Locked property is set to No, data displayed within the control can be changed.

◆ **Tab Stop**   This property determines whether you can use the TAB key to move the focus to a control in Form view. When set to Yes—the default—you can tab into the control. When set to No, you can't tab into the control.

◆ **Tab Index**   This property determines the tab order for the controls within the form or which control successively gets the focus each time you press the TAB key. In the property, you enter a numeric value ranging from zero to one less than the total number of controls in the form.

◆ **Scroll Bars**   Use this property to add a vertical scroll bar to a control. The property provides the two options: vertical and none. Scroll bars can be useful if you have a control for a field with large amounts of text, such as a memo field, yet you do not want to size the control so large that it takes up too much room on your form.

◆ **Can Grow and Can Shrink**   These properties can apply to controls or to the sections of a form. Use them to determine whether a control or a section will be allowed to grow or shrink vertically to accommodate data of varying size. The default is No for both properties.

◆ **Setting the Default View and Views Allowed Properties** Two useful properties that affect how your users see the forms are the DefaultView and Views Allowed properties.

◆ **Changing the Form's Title Bar**   By default, a form's title bar contains the same name under which you saved the form. You can change the name by changing the Caption property for the form.

◆ **Making a Form Modal**   When a form is modal, you cannot click any other forms until you close the current form. To make a form modal, change the modal property to Yes. The changes take effect after you close the form, save the changes, and reopen the form.

13

Now that you are familiar with controls and their properties, you are ready to look at the first form, the Client form.

If you haven't already accessed the Osborne Web site to download the Hush database, do so now. This will enable you to analyze the design of the forms as we discuss them in the next section.

The Client Form

Figure 13-9 displays the Design window for our client form.

This form is of simple design. Most of the controls consist of text boxes. You can review the properties of the controls to get an idea of how these were built. You may want to open another design form and build your own using the 'qryClient' as a datasource. Let's see how creative you can be.

On this form, there is a Form Header, which is the Title. Then you begin to design the detail of the form. The data control source for this form is 'qryClient'. The following fields are all text boxes: ClientID, LNAME, FNAME, MI, Address, City, State, ZIP, HomeTele, WorkTele, Pager, and CellPhone. ServiceRequested, ILNAME, IFNAME, IMI, and ReferredBY. Figure 13-10 is an example of the Input Mask used for HomeTele field.

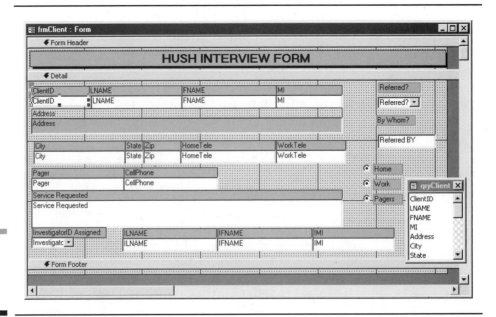

The Client
Form Design
window

Figure 13-9.

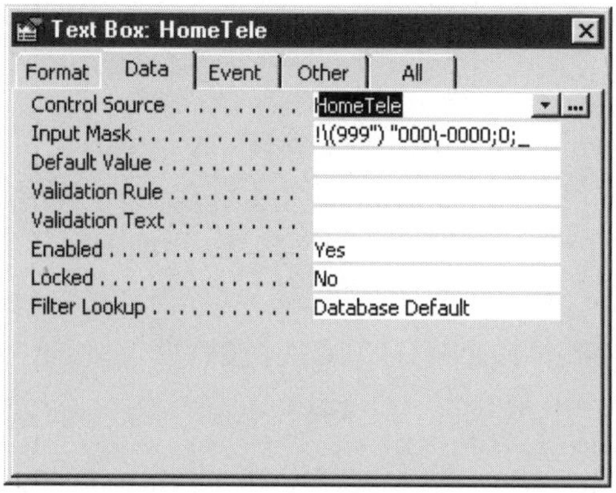

Text Box
property with
Input Mask

Figure 13-10.

The following fields are combo boxes: Referred? and InvestigatorID Assigned.
Figure 13-11 is an example of the Combo Box property for InvestigatorID
Assigned.

Notice under the Data tab that the control source is the InvestigatorID, the
row source type is Table/Query, and the row source is an SQL statement. The
statement is

```
SELECT InvestigatorID FROM tblInvestigators;
```

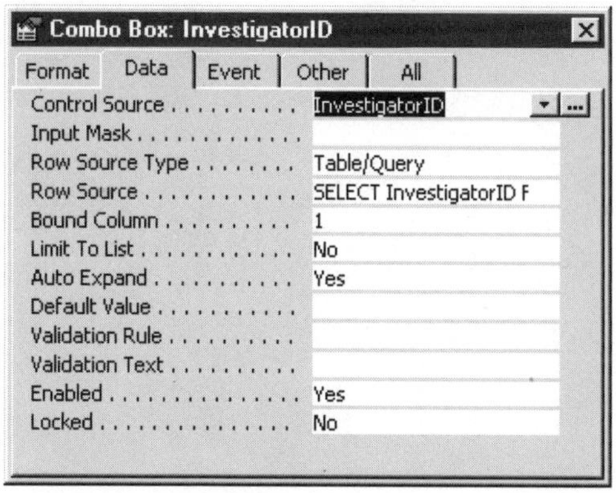

Combo Box
property for
InvestigatorID
Assigned

Figure 13-11.

13

The subsequent fields of ILNAME, IFNAME, IMI are from this row source. You use the drop-down list to assign an investigator based on the InvestigatorID. Then the name of the investigator appears in the three fields previously mentioned. Figure 13-12 is the Form view of frmClient. Notice the drop-down list for InvestigatorID Assigned.

Finally, the option buttons are Home, Work, and Pager. Figure 13-13 shows the property listing for option button.

The Investigator Form

Your next form is for the investigator. This form includes two subforms. Figure 13-14 is the Design view for the Investigator form.

On this form, there is a Form Header, which is the Title. Then you begin to design the detail of the form. The data control source for this form is 'qryCaseClient'. The following fields are all text boxes: CaseID, DateCaseOpened, DateCaseClosed, LNAME, FNAME, PoliceDAssign, and Notes. Combo boxes fields are: ClientID and CaseType. Figure 13-15 is the Property window for the ClientID combo box.

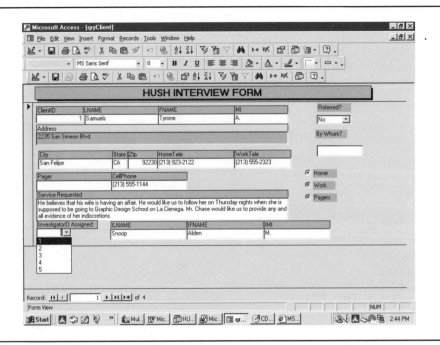

Form view of
frmClient

Figure 13-12.

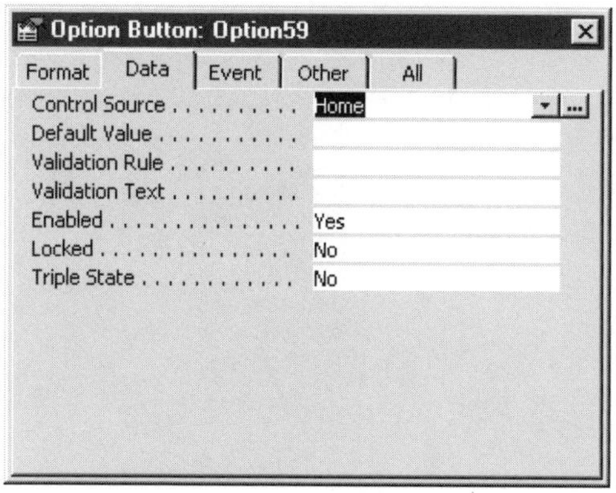

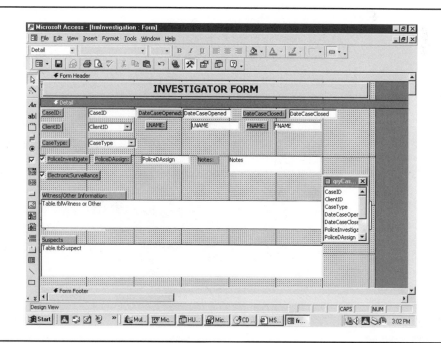

Option button
for Home
Figure 13-13.

Design view of
frmInvestigator
Figure 13-14.

13

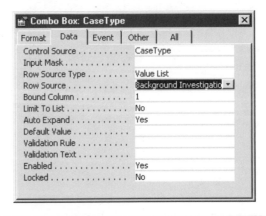

Property
window for
ClientID
combo box
Figure 13-15.

In this combo box, the control source is the ClientID, the row source type is
Table/Query, and the row source is an SQL statement. The statement is

```
SELECT ClientID FROM tblClient;
```

The next combo box, CaseType, is different from the other combo boxes.
Figure 13-16 is the Property window for this combo box.

Property
window for
CaseType
combo box
Figure 13-16.

Here the control source is CaseType, the row source Type is a Value List, and the row source is a list typed into this property as: Background Investigation; Murder Investigation; Missing Person.

This form also makes use of two subforms. The first subform is the Witness/ Other Information. This subform's data control source is the table: tblWitness or Other. Figure 13-17 shows the Property window for this subform.

The next subform is the Suspect subform. The Property window is similar to Figure 13-17 except the table assigned as data control source is tblSuspects. Figure 13-18 is the Form view of the Investigator form. In this view, you can see what the client will see. Notice the subreports are in a datasheet format. The vertical scroll is visible for both subforms. The Suspect form scroll is not visible in the figure, but on the property, it is set to visible. When a suspect is added to this subform, the vertical scroll appears.

A Short Discussion on Security

Both of these forms will be used within the Hush Detective Agency. They are treated as separate forms. One form is for the administrative staff to complete and the other is for the Investigator staff.

For security, we assign two user groups, Admin and Investigators. Each group receives a shortcut for their particular form. They need to sign in to the database to use the form. Mr. Snoop is the only one to have access to both forms. In the security wizard within Access, you can assign user groups or individuals access to Forms, Queries, Tables, Reports, Macros, and Modules.

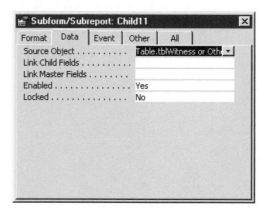

Property window for subform tblWitness or Other

Figure 13-17.

13

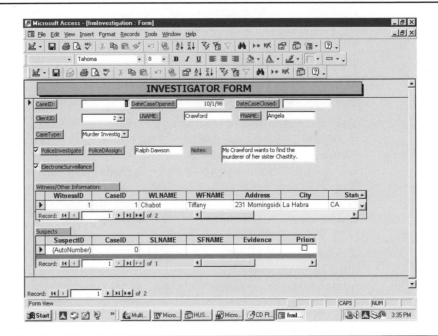

Form Design
window for
Investigator
form

Figure 13-18.

What's Next?

In Chapter 14, you write queries for the Hush database. The queries you write will be used for the forms. In addition, examples of more complicated queries will be written from the database to practice query building within Access. Your last development chapter, Chapter 15, is the reporting chapter. Now that data has been entered into this system, your users want the output, nicely designed reports.

CHAPTER 14

Querying the Database

Queries in Access are used to retrieve data from the database and as a data source for forms. In this chapter, you learn just how the query can be used in Access. The queries for the Hush database are used as the data source for your two forms. You can also use the query to retrieve data for reporting purposes.

In addition, you learn about the different types of queries available in Access. You also review how SQL is used in Access. Because Access uses the graphical query-by-example (QBE), you learn how Access takes the graphical representation and interprets it into SQL.

Access Queries

With Access QBE you can perform most of the query design by dragging and dropping the fields onto a query grid. In Access, you can create a query in either of two ways: manually or with the aid of the Query Wizards.

Many types of queries are in Access: select, crosstab, action, parameter, and SQL queries. They are powerful and enable you to manipulate your data in various ways. The following paragraphs describe the functions of these queries.

Select

A select query is the most common type of query. Two types of select queries exist: select and crosstab. A *select query* retrieves data from one or more tables and displays the results in a datasheet where you can update the records. You can also use a select query to group records and calculate sums, counts, averages, and other types of totals. The two queries for your Hush forms are both select queries. Figure 14-1 is the select query from the Hush database used as a data source for the client form.

Crosstab

A *crosstab query* displays summarized values (sums, counts, and averages) from one field in a table; it groups them by one set of facts listed down the left side of the datasheet and another set of facts listed across the top of the datasheet. You can use a query wizard to create a crosstab query. Figures 14-2 and 14-3 show the crosstab design and the results of the crosstab. In this crosstab, you want to see how many cases the investigators have been assigned. This crosstab provides a summary of the cases and the count for each investigator.

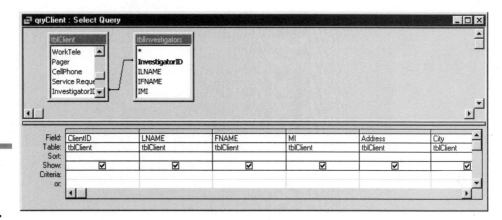

Select query from Hush database

Figure 14-1.

The SQL used for a crosstab is unique to Access's extension of SQL. Please note the use of TRANSFORM (used only in Access) in the code:

```
TRANSFORM Count(qryDataForXtab.InvestigatorID) AS CountOfInvestigatorID
SELECT qryDataForXtab.CaseID, qryDataForXtab.InvestigatorID,
qryDataForXtab.ILNAME
FROM qryDataForXtab
GROUP BY qryDataForXtab.CaseID, qryDataForXtab.InvestigatorID
PIVOT qryDataForXtab.ILNAME;
```

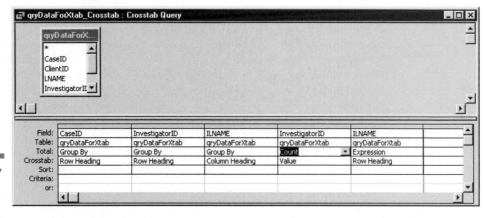

Crosstab query design

Figure 14-2.

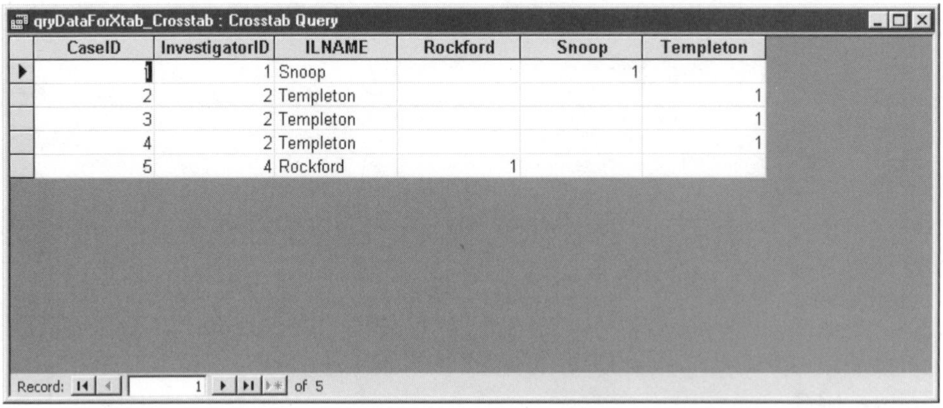

qryDataForXtab_Crosstab : Crosstab Query

CaseID	InvestigatorID	ILNAME	Rockford	Snoop	Templeton
1	1	Snoop		1	
2	2	Templeton			1
3	2	Templeton			1
4	2	Templeton			1
5	4	Rockford	1		

Record: 1 of 5

Crosstab query results

Figure 14-3.

Parameter Query

A *parameter query* is a query that when run, displays its own dialog box prompting you for information, such as criteria for retrieving records or a value you want to insert in a field. You can design the query to prompt you for more than one piece of information. For example, you can design it to prompt you for two dates. Microsoft Access can then retrieve all the records that fall in between those two dates.

Parameter queries are also handy when used as the basis for forms and reports. You can create a monthly report on all investigators and cases actively being worked. When you run the query or report, Microsoft Access displays a dialog box asking for the month you want the query or report to cover. This type of query would be handy for Mr. Snoop when he wants to see what his investigators have been doing. Figure 14-4 is the query design. In this query, the parameter field is the DateOpened. Mr. Snoop wants to see the active investigations for a one-month period. Figure 14-5 represents the results of running this type of query.

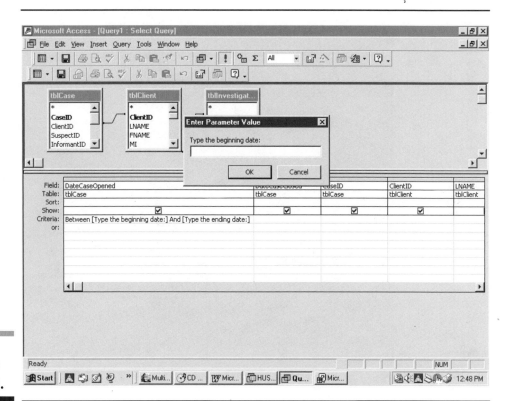

Parameter
query design
Figure 14-4.

Here is the SQL code Access translates from the graphical query:

```
SELECT tblCase.DateCaseOpened, tblCase.DateCaseClosed, tblCase.CaseID,
tblClient.ClientID, tblClient.LNAME, tblInvestigators.InvestigatorID,
tblInvestigators.ILNAME, tblInvestigators.IFNAME

FROM tblInvestigators INNER JOIN (tblClient INNER JOIN tblCase ON
tblClient.ClientID = tblCase.ClientID) ON tblInvestigators
InvestigatorID = tblClient.InvestigatorID

WHERE (((tblCase.DateCaseOpened) Between [Type the beginning date:]
And [Type the ending date:]));
```

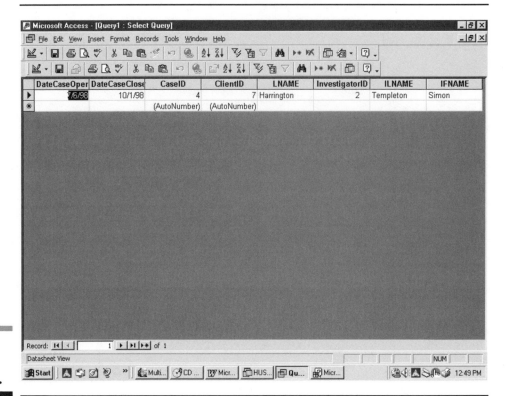

Parameter
query results
Figure 14-5.

Action Queries

An *action query* is a query that makes changes to many records in just one
operation. Four types of action queries exist: update, append, make-table,
and delete.

Update Query   An *update query* makes global changes to a group of records in
one or more tables. For example, if you want to raise the price of your product
by ten percent, you could create an update query that would update this record
in your group. Figure 14-6 shows you the query design for the update. What
you have updated is the Notes record from the copy of the tblWitness. You
have added Date to this table. Figure 14-7 shows you the results.

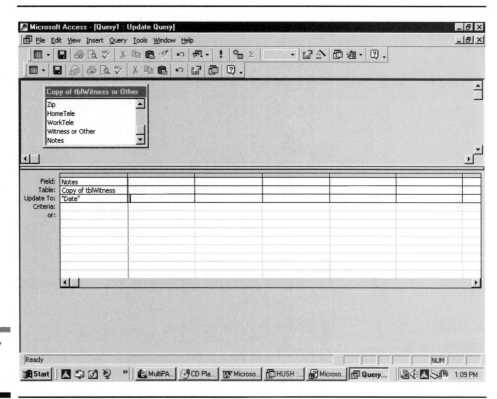

Update query
design view
Figure 14-6.

The SQL for this update query looks like this:

```
UPDATE [Copy of tblWitness or Other] SET [Copy of tblWitness or Other].
Notes = "Date";
```

Append Query   The *append query* adds a group of records from one or more tables to the end of one or more tables. For example, suppose we have some new clients and we want to add them. To avoid typing in all this information, you'd like to append it to your client table. Append queries are helpful for the following:

◆   Appending fields based on criteria.

14

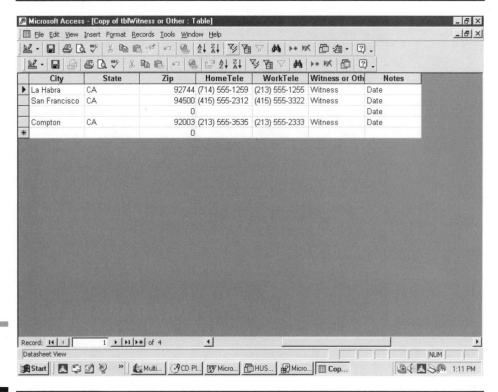

◆ Appending records when some of the fields in one table don't exist in
the other table.

Figure 14-8 shows the Design view of the append query. In this append
query, you append the tblClient to the copy of the tblClient, which is
currently empty. Figure 14-9 shows the results of the append. You now
have seven clients in the copy, as you do in the original table.

The SQL code for the append query is as follows:

```
INSERT INTO [Copy of tblClient] ( ClientID, LNAME, FNAME, MI,
Address, City, State, Zip, HomeTele, WorkTele, Pager, CellPhone,
[Service Requested], InvestigatorID, [Referred?], [Referred BY],
Home, [Work], Pagers )
```

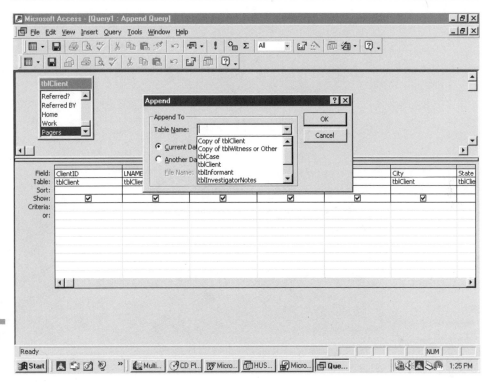

Append query
view

Figure 14-8.

```
SELECT tblClient.ClientID, tblClient.LNAME, tblClient.FNAME,
tblClient.MI, tblClient.Address, tblClient.City, tblClient
State, tblClient.Zip, tblClient.HomeTele, tblClient.WorkTele,
tblClient.Pager, tblClient.CellPhone, tblClient.[Service Requested],
tblClient.InvestigatorID, tblClient.[Referred?], tblClient
[Referred BY], tblClient.Home, tblClient.Work, tblClient.Pagers

FROM tblClient;
```

Make-Table Query   The *make-table query* creates a new table from all or part of the data in one or more tables. Make-tables are helpful for the following:

◆   Creating a table to export to other Microsoft Access databases.

◆   Making a backup copy of a table.

◆   Creating a history table that contains old records.

14

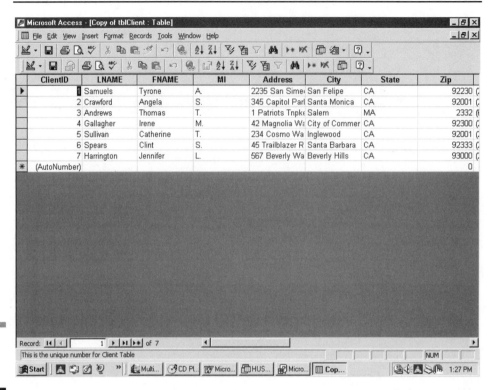

Append query
results

Figure 14-9.

◆ Improving performance of forms and reports based on multiple-table queries or SQL statements. However, the data in the table is frozen at the time you run the make-table query.

In Figure 14-10, you create a make-table query. You are creating a table from the crosstab query you ran earlier. Figure 14-11 shows the results of the make-table query.

The SQL code for the make-table query looks like this:

```
SELECT qryDataForXtab_Crosstab.CaseID, qryDataForXtab_Crosstab
InvestigatorID, qryDataForXtab_Crosstab.ILNAME,
qryDataForXtab_Crosstab.Snoop, qryDataForXtab_Crosstab.Templeton,
qryDataForXtab_Crosstab.Rockford INTO tblCrosstab
FROM qryDataForXtab_Crosstab;
```

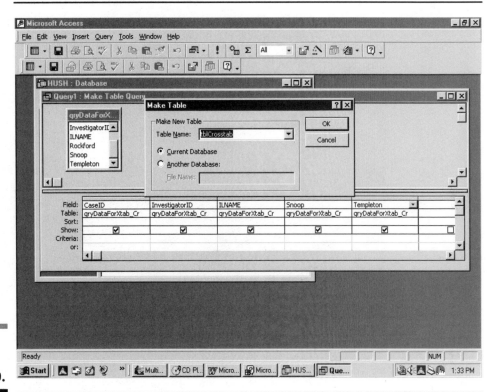

Delete Query   The *delete query* deletes a group of records from one or more tables. For example, you could use a delete query to remove records you no longer need. With delete queries, you always delete entire records, not just selected records.

CAUTION: Delete query is a destructive query; there is no way to recover what is deleted.

In Figure 14-12, you see the delete design view where you are going to delete the records from the copy of the tblClient. Figure 14-13 shows you the results of this query.

14

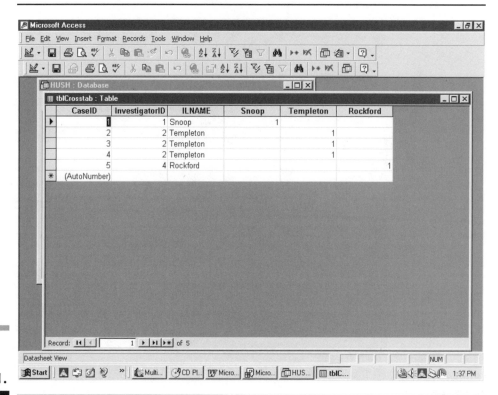

Here's the SQL code for the delete query:

```
DELETE [Copy of tblClient].ClientID, [Copy of tblClient].ClientID,
[Copy of tblClient].ClientID, [Copy of tblClient].LNAME, [Copy of
tblClient].FNAME, [Copy of tblClient].MI, [Copy of tblClient].
Address, [Copy of tblClient].City, [Copy of tblClient].State,
[Copy of tblClient].Zip, [Copy of tblClient].HomeTele, [Copy of
tblClient].WorkTele, [Copy of tblClient].Pager, [Copy of tblClient].
CellPhone, [Copy of tblClient].[Service Requested], [Copy of
tblClient].InvestigatorID, [Copy of tblClient].InvestigatorID,
[Copy of tblClient].[Referred?], [Copy of tblClient].[Referred BY],
[Copy of tblClient].Home, [Copy of tblClient].Work, [Copy of
tblClient].PagersFROM [Copy of tblClient];
```

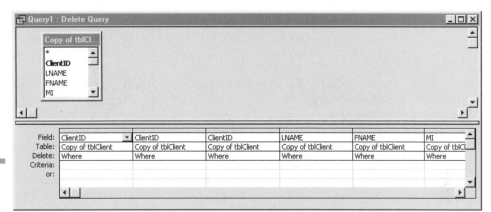

Delete query
design

Figure 14-12.

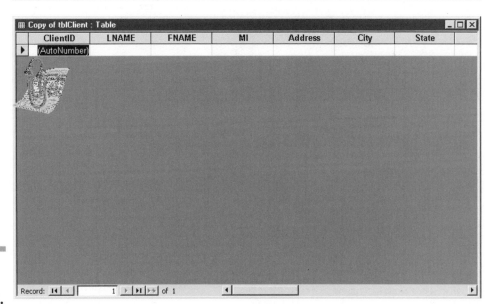

Delete query
results

Figure 14-13.

SQL Queries

An *SQL query* is a query you create using an SQL statement. Examples of these SQL-specific queries are the union query, pass-through-query, data-definition query, and subquery.

Union Query   The union query syntax in Access is the same as the SQL union query. The union query must be entered directly into Access as an SQL statement.

Pass-through-Query   The *pass-through-query* sends commands directly to ODBC databases, such as Oracle, using commands accepted by the server. The ODBC window prompts you to choose a data source. Then you need to log in to the database. Afterward, you must enter an SQL statement. The query design enables you to enter directly an SQL statement. You press the Design Icon and a drop-down list appears. You choose SQL view.

Data-Definition Query   The *data-definition query* creates, deletes, alters tables, or creates indexes in a database, such as Access or Foxpro. The SQL code for a data-definition query:

```
CREATE INDEX NewIndex
ON Friends ([LastName], [FirstName]);
```

This must be typed directly into Access as an SQL statement.

Subquery   You have already covered subqueries in another chapter; however, in the *subquery* in Access, the query consists of an SQL SELECT statement inside another select query or action query. You can enter these statements in the Field row of the query design grid to define a new field or in the Criteria row to define criteria for a field. In Figure 14-14, you have created a subquery by writing an SQL statement in the criteria field for InvestigatorID. Figure 14-15 shows the results.

The SQL code for the subquery is as follows:

```
SELECT qryDataForXtab.CaseID, qryDataForXtab.
InvestigatorID, qryDataForXtab.ILNAME
FROM qryDataForXtab
WHERE (((qryDataForXtab.InvestigatorID)=(SELECT[InvestigatorID] FROM
[tblInvestigators]WHERE[ILNAME]="Rockford")));
```

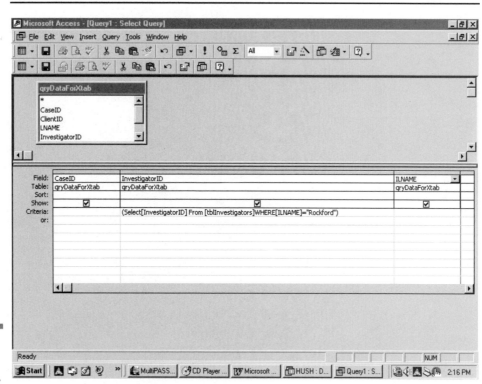

Subquery
design view

Figure 14-14.

As you can see, the queries in Access are indeed powerful and enable you to
manipulate your data, as well as help you create your database application.

The next section provides you with lessons on how to create your two select
queries that you use as data sources for your forms.

Creating Hush Select Queries

You create these queries manually, as opposed to using the Query Wizards.
If this is your first foray into Access, use the wizards to help you build
your queries.

14

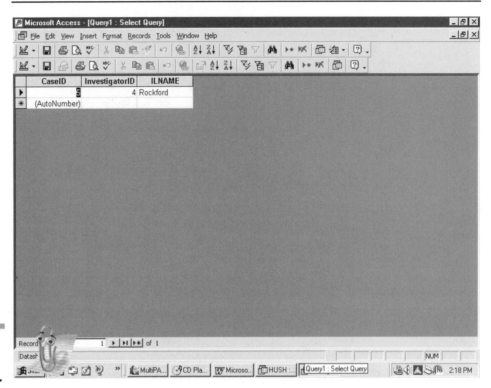

Subquery results

Figure 14-15.

Creating Client Query

You need to open the Hush database.

1. Select the Queries tab (see Figure 14-16).

2. Click the New button.

3. Select the Design query. A window opens, which contains the tables and queries in the database (see Figure 14-17).

4. Double-click the tables and/or queries you are going to use for the query. In this case, double-click tblClient and tblInvestigators (see Figure 14-18). You need to join these two tables. If primary or foreign keys exist for the table, Access will join the tables for you. Otherwise, you need to

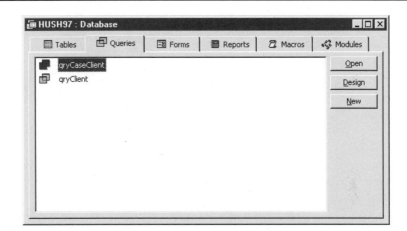

Figure 14-16.

join them. Because all the tables have keys, you won't need to join tables, but Steps 5 and 6 are included for your edification.

5. To join a table, click the field, keep your finger pressed on the mouse button, and drag the mouse over to the next table to the field on which you want to join. Let go of the mouse button; a line appears between the two tables.

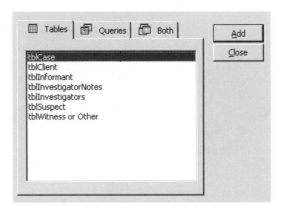

Table or query
selection
window
Figure 14-17.

14

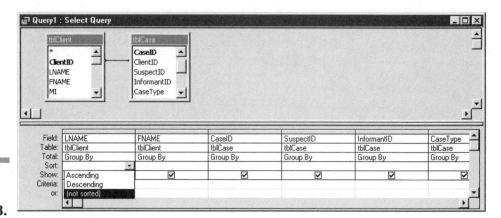

Select query
for qryClient
Figure 14-18.

6. Double-click the join line. This brings up the window that enables you to choose the type of relationship you need for your query, which looks like this:

7. Drag-and-drop the fields from each table you need for your query. The fields you need are all fields from both tables.

8. Save your query by clicking File icon on the toolbar. The best practice is to indicate it is a query by using qry at the beginning of the name.

9. Click the red exclamation point (!) to execute your query (see Figure 14-19).

You see the results of your query. To check if everything is correct, a query is already created, named qryClient.

ClientID	LNAME	FNAME	MI	Address	City	State
1 Samuels	Tyrone	A.	2235 San Simei	San Felipe	CA
2 Crawford	Angela	S.	345 Capitol Parl	Santa Monica	CA
3 Andrews	Thomas	T.	1 Patriots Tnpke	Salem	MA
4 Gallagher	Irene	M.	42 Magnolia Wა	City of Commer	CA
5 Jensen	Andrew	M.	1920 Flagstaff E	Brentwood	CA
(AutoNumber)						

Record: 1 of 5

qryClient
results

Figure 14-19.

CAUTION: Do not name your new query by the same name. The qryClient is already used as the data source for the Client form.

Creating CaseClient Query

The steps you follow to create the CaseClient query are similar to the previous query. The only difference is the tables you use. The *CaseClient query* is used as the data source for the Investigator form.

1. Select the Query tab.
2. Click the New button.
3. Select the Design query. A window opens that contains the tables and queries in the database.
4. Double-click the tables and/or queries you are going to use for the query. In this case, double-click tblCase, tblClient, and tblInvestigators (see Figure 14-20). You need to join these two tables. If there are primary or foreign keys for the table, Access will join the tables for you. Otherwise, you need to join them.

14

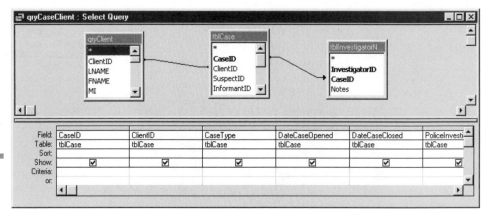

5. To join a table, click the field, hold down the mouse button, and drag the mouse pointer over to the next table to the field onto which you want to join.

6. Double-click the join line. This brings up the window that enables you to choose the type of relationship you need for your query.

7. Drag-and-drop the fields from each table you need for your query. The fields you need are all fields from both tables.

8. Save your query by clicking the File icon on the toolbar. It's a good idea to indicate this is a query by using qry at the beginning of the name.

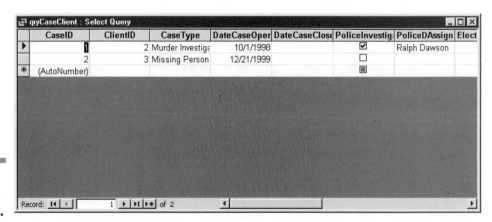

9. Click the red exclamation point (!) to execute your query (see Figure 14-21).

You see the results of your query. To check if everything is correct, a query is already created named qryCaseClient.

CAUTION: Do not name your new query by the same name. The qryCaseClient is already used as the data source for the Investigator form.

A nice feature added to Access is the ability to print the Relationships window, so you can keep track of your tables and the relationships. As you can see in Figure 14-22, this is useful when you create your queries and reports.

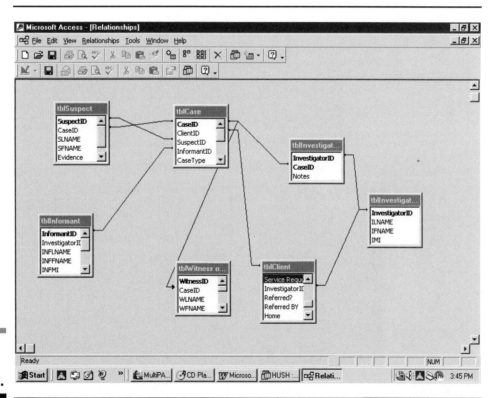

Relationships
window

Figure 14-22.

14

Access is truly a remarkable desktop database. You will enjoy developing your databases with this tool.

What's Next?

You have come to the end of the development section of this book. The next chapter wraps it all up by providing reports for the client, Mr. Snoop, and the employees at Hush Detective Agency. You run one report via Crystal Reports, Business Objects, and Access Reports.

You'll also learn how to choose the best reporting tool for your client.

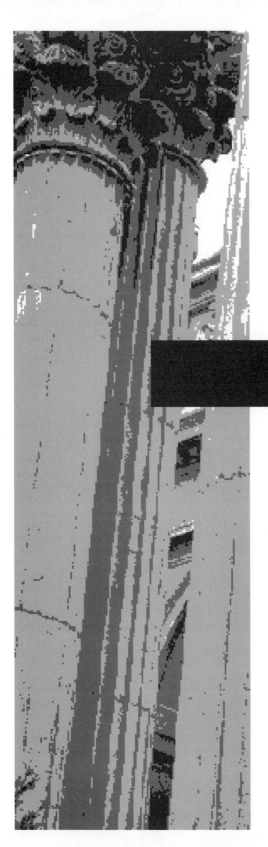

CHAPTER 15

Reporting

Many times developers are so enthralled with the creation process—developing the forms, designing the GUI, and ensuring the code is topnotch—by the time it comes to developing the reports, they don't want to think about it. A report is more administrative or clerical and not worth their time because they have created the database application. They are the artists. After all, would you ask Renoir to come home with you to hang his picture on your wall? Of course you wouldn't!

However, your users have gone through the interviews, attended many meetings, tested the application, entered the data, and learned a new application. The least they should get from all this work is a report or two. A report they can use, understand, and possibly create themselves.

You would be surprised by how many software vendors avoid designing reports for their database applications. Some provide a few canned reports. Most of the time these reports are not useful at all. Some recommend a report writer and leave it to you to write your own reports. While others leave you to your own devices. In fact, this might be the reason you are reading this book. You need to learn SQL to write reports.

This chapter is in this book because developing reports is important. Mostly everyone who uses a database either runs or requests a report from the database. The marketplace has a plethora of reporting tools, in fact, an increase of about 40 percent over what was available ten years ago. A market research group stated that at first only 10 percent of all software users used reporting tools. Now 100 percent of the software users use reporting tools 10 percent of the time.

Types of Reporting Tools

A *reporting tool* is a graphical interface design tool. With a reporting tool, you connect to a data source and retrieve records from tables and/or views. You drag-and-drop fields on your design sheet and you can format this information in a visually appealing manner. You may add OLE objects such as drawings, corporate logos, and even insert documents from Word or Excel, to name just a few objects. These reporting tools give you more flexibility than your typical datasheet design that we used in the Access queries.

Reporting tools can be divided into these groups: ad-hoc query/reporting tools, OLAP for multidimensional reporting, and Web reporting. A new buzz word for reporting even exists now: business intelligence. Today, most business intelligence vendors market all these products and they are sold separately and as suites.

The evolution of reporting is also influenced by the changing technology. Years ago, reporting was usually under the auspices of the Information Technology (IT) department. The IT department would receive requests throughout the corporation for reports. Programmers were the ones who developed the reports. Reports needed to be coded and were not end-user friendly. Most of the reporting was done from mainframe applications.

With the advent of the personal computer, the environment has changed. Nontechnical people have computers on their desktop. These nontechnical people, usually analysts, needed different types of reports. The analysts used spreadsheets to develop reports. Programmers were making dumps to ASCII files so these analysts could manipulate the data.

With the introduction of the client/server architecture and the arrival of desktop databases, the need for reports trickled down even further to the nonprogrammer population. The IT departments found they had to support requests from end users for both mainframe and PC-based databases. The industry has noticed a surge in demand for reporting. The non-IT analysts found they could develop their own reports with these databases (Paradox, Q&A, Access). So power users outside the IT departments were developing reports. These power users were creating reports and distributing them to those who needed the reports to make decisions.

The technology changes. The client/server systems, decision-support databases, and data warehousing have completely changed the way we distribute information. We have increased the amount of data available and proportionately increased the number of users who need to retrieve the data. Reporting is not just for IT programmers anymore. Chances are, no matter where you are in your corporation—stockroom clerk, business analyst, marketing representative or CEO—you must be able to create ad-hoc reports and use these reports to do your business.

Reporting tools have changed along with the needs of the end users. So how do you decide which tool is the best tool for you? This depends on many factors. Many reporting tools exist and not all are created equal. Each one focuses on a specific function or methodology to separate it from the pack. The next section discusses what questions you need to answer before you venture into the business intelligence jungle.

How to Choose Your Reporting Tool

The following is a set of questions you should ask yourself before you venture into the marketplace. Once you answer these questions, you can build a grid to compare the reporting tools you are reviewing. The one reporting tool with the most Yes answers is probably the best one for you.

◆ Have you analyzed your users? How many users need a report viewer? How many users need to write ad-hoc reports? Do you need to deliver reports to the Web? Do you need to schedule reports?

◆ Who will develop reports: IT staff, power users, end users?

◆ Do you have trained staff to implement a new business intelligence suite?

◆ What platforms are you running?

◆ What databases do you need to report against?

◆ Do you have a data mart or data warehouse? Do you plan to implement one?

◆ Do your current applications have reports?

◆ How many reports do your users need?

◆ Are you running SAP applications?

◆ Are you running Oracle applications?

◆ Are you running PeopleSoft applications?

◆ Do you need multidimensional analysis?

◆ Are the reporting needs for a single department or enterprise-wide?

◆ Are you keeping your present report tool?

◆ Do you have multiple reporting tools to support?

◆ Do you need to export the data? In what format do you need the data exported: ASCII, Lotus, Text, Word, Excel, HTML? Make sure to include the versions you are running of these applications.

◆ Do you need a scripting language for reports?

◆ Can your IT department support a metadata environment? This is information associated with stored data. You organize and prepare the data for your users by creating Info Views or Universes or Cubes (various vendor terms).

◆ How do you plan to train users?

◆ How much can you spend on purchasing the new software? How much can you spend to support it?

◆ How much can you afford for training?

Once you have answered these questions and any others you may have thought of during this process, then you should create a spreadsheet type grid. The grid should list the features and functions you need from the reporting tool.

Start researching the available tools via the Web, read the white papers, explore the demos, and speak with others who are now using the tools. Another good idea is to check out the technical support supplied by the vendor. Are they 24 hours a day, 7 days a week? Where are they located? Do they have offices near you? How long have they been in business? Will they be in business a few years from now? Check into the version support. How many versions back do they support?

Look at the technical support questions their users send in to them. This can be viewed via the Web. Some have knowledge bases or FAQ (frequently asked questions) sections to give you a fair idea of what types of problems users have with the product.

Whenever possible, talk to users who have similar needs. How does the product perform? If there are bugs, can you live with them and how soon will they be fixed? How do the users like the product and how easy was it to implement?

If you are prepared to do your homework, you should be able to get a product that serves your needs. In Appendix B, several report tool vendors are listed with URLs to their Web sites.

Report Development

In this section, you finish your work for Hush Detective Agency. Two reports must be designed. Because Hush Detective Agency has a small IT staff and, therefore, limited support, the best advice we can offer is to design the reports using Access. This way, support is easy and no need exists for them to learn another tool. At this point, they won't create their own reports until after the staff has completed its training.

After you create these reports in Access, you get to see how two other report designers work. We use Crystal Reports 6 and Business Objects 4.1.

Access Reports

Again, as with the Access forms, you may use either tables or queries as the data control source of your reports. The first report is for Mr. Snoop. He would like to get a monthly report of the cases his investigators are working on, along with the details and notes of the case. Because the information required involves a few tables, you need to base this report on a query. Use the qryCaseClientDatePrompted. This is a copy of the CaseClient query with a date parameter added to DateCaseOpened.

This is a basic report, so you can use the Report Wizard to build this report. We have already designed the report. It is listed under the Report tab as rptInvestigatorCases. Play around with this report; it is good practice and fun. When you feel comfortable with the report designer, you can create your own reports without using the wizards.

Figure 15-1 is the report Design view and Figure 15-2 is the report results. There are two date prompts for the report. The first requests the beginning

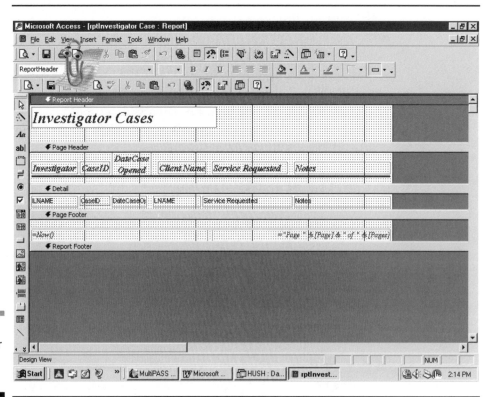

Design view
for Investigator
Cases report

Figure 15-1.

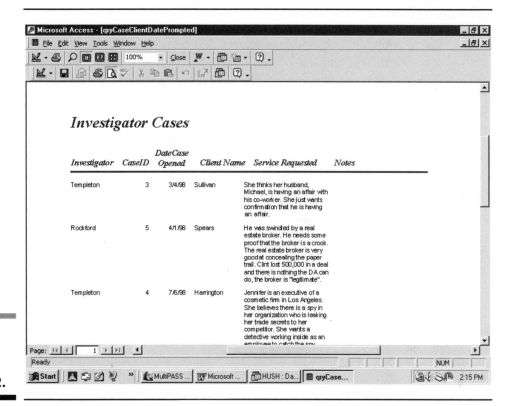

Results for
Investigator
Cases report

Figure 15-2.

date for the DateOpenedCase field. The second requests the ending date for
the DateOpenedCase field. In the report you have requested the date range:
January 1, 1998 through December 31, 1998.

The second report is to create a copy of the initial interview form. Remember,
a copy is to be placed in the case brief, as well as in the investigator's file. The
initial interview will be designed as a report.

Again, this is a fairly simple request. You just need to include all the fields
from the Client form. You can use the qryClient query for this report. Figure
15-3 is the report design for this report and Figure 15-4 is the report results.

Additional reports will be requested once the users become more familiar with
the application, so be prepared to develop additional reports. This is usually
the typical scenario. You design a set of standard reports the users must have.

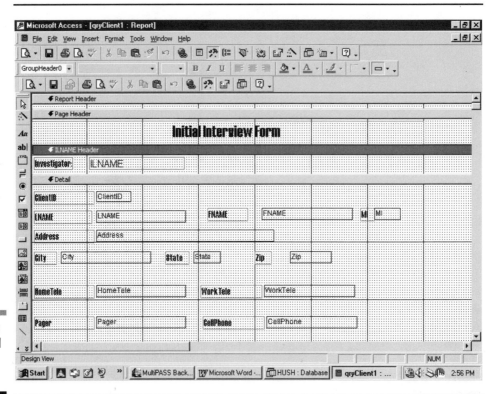

Report Design
view for Initial
Interview

Figure 15-3.

These reports generally are legacy reports based on the old system or, if this is a new system, the reports are probably based on Excel or Lotus spreadsheets.

The ideal is to train your users to write the ad-hoc reports. Don't forget to supply the new report writers with confidence in their ability to do the job.

You have just completed your first database design. Congratulations! Before we end this chapter, let's look at Seagate's Crystal Reports and Business Objects. These are two of the business intelligence tools on the market today.

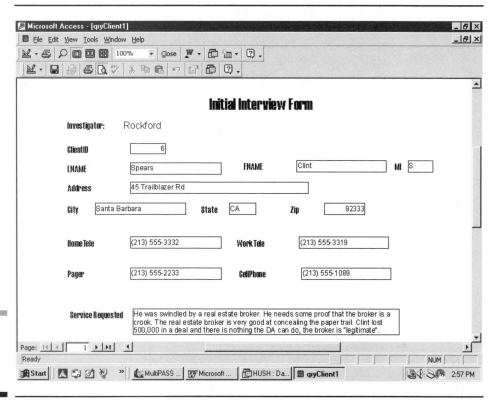

Report results
for Initial
Interview

Figure 15-4.

Seagate Info and Crystal Reports 6.0

In your examples today, you will use Crystal Reports 6.0. This is the query and reporting tool from Seagate's business intelligence suite. It can be purchased separately. In Seagate Info, the Crystal Reports and query designers are incorporated into the Seagate Info product. This product has enterprise reporting and analysis, OLAP capabilities, query capabilities, Web capabilities, distribution, scheduling, and enterprise-strength clustering technology. Well, that's the marketing evaluation of the product.

What you can do with this tool is design queries with the Query Designer. You can design reports with the Report Designer and you can perform multidimensional analysis with their OLAP cubes. Their scheduler schedules reports, queries, cubes, and window programs based on time, events, and custom business calendars.

You can distribute the reports to: Word, Excel, Exchange, Postscript, and Mail (MAPI), HTML, ODBC, Comma, Character, Tab and Text separated values, Data Interchange Format, Lotus 1-2-3, cc:mail (VIM) and Notes, Record Style and Rich Text (RTF), and Fax. The export capabilities to Word are weak, a lot of formatting is lost, and you end up tweaking the document more than you should. The Excel export is a little better, as is the RTF. HTML still needs improvement.

In Figure 15-5, you see the report designer for Crystal Reports 6.0. We have designed the Initial Interview report. Figure 15-6 represents the Visual Linking Expert. This is how you join the tables or queries you need for your report. Figure 15-7 is the final result, the Initial Interview report.

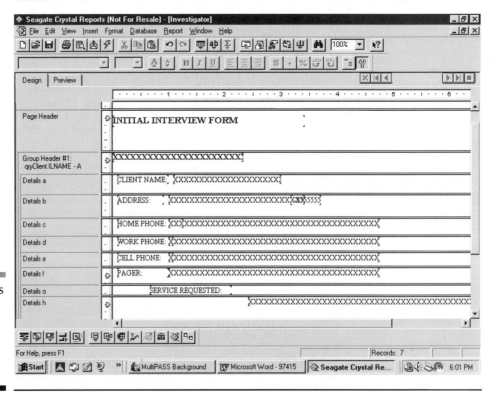

Crystal Reports designer for Initial Interview report

Figure 15-5.

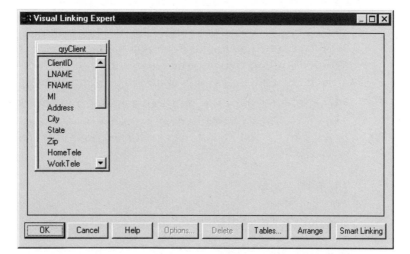

Crystal Reports
Visual Linking
Expert

Figure 15-6.

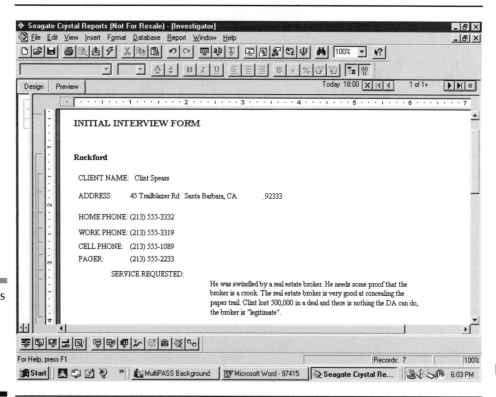

Crystal Reports
preview
of Initial
Interview
report

Figure 15-7.

Overall, the designer is somewhat easy to use. You can make changes to the design when you are in the Preview mode. It is easier to make changes to the Crystal Reports designer than to the Access report design view. In Access, you must leave preview to make changes to the design. In addition, in Crystal Reports, you can join your tables within the Report designer. In Access, you must build a query if you need to join multiple tables.

Crystal Reports designer has Smart Linking, which joins the primary and foreign keys automatically. This is similar to what Access does. The Smart Linking in Crystal Reports can be turned off if you prefer to join the tables yourself.

BusinessObjects

BusinessObjects is an integrated business intelligence suite, offering scalable solutions for the enterprise. It has the following products:

◆ **BusinessObjects Designer**   This provides the semantic layer setup (metadata).

◆ **BusinessObjects Supervisor**   This handles the administration and the security.

◆ **Document Agent Server**   This is for report scheduling and distribution.

◆ **BusinessQuery**   This provides Microsoft Excel access.

◆ **BusinessMiner**   This is a data mining tool.

◆ **BusinessObjects**   This is a query, reporting, and OLAP tool.

◆ **WebIntelligence**   This provides business intelligence via the Web.

These tools offer centralized control over operational databases, personal data files, business applications, OLAP servers, data warehouses, and data marts.

Figure 15-8 is the BusinessObjects Designer. This is where you set up your metadata layer or semantics layer. Figure 15-9 is the Report designer view and

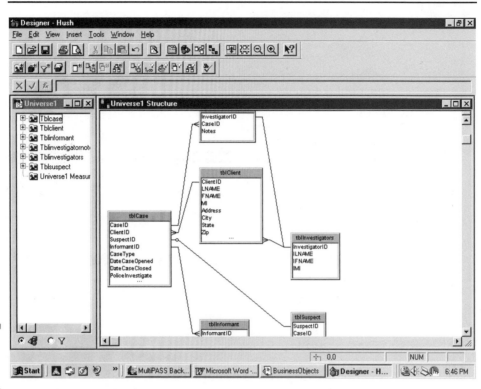

BusinessObjects
Designer
Figure 15-8.

Figure 15-10 is the preview mode for the Initial Interview report. This was the first time we used this tool. It took approximately 10 minutes to design the universe and another 15 minutes to design the report layout. Overall, we were up and running in no time.

As you can see, the tools vary in their methods but, overall, they strive to deliver the newest technology available for reporting.

15

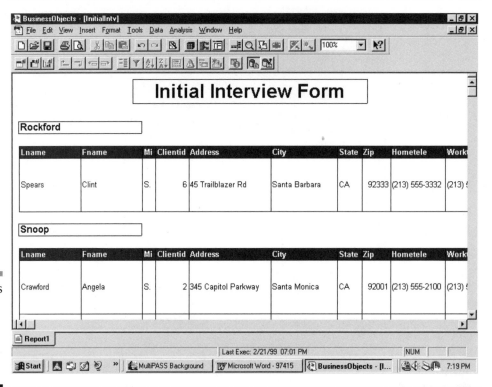

BusinessObjects
report design
for Initial
Interview
report

Figure 15-9.

What's Next?

In the next part, you delve into the more advanced subject matter. You cover advanced SQL, SQL and other programming languages, Oracle's SQL*Plus and PL/SQL, and Transact SQL, the accepted extension of SQL 92.

You also learn how to correct your errors and then get a sneak peek at what is promised in ANSI SQL 3, the next version of SQL.

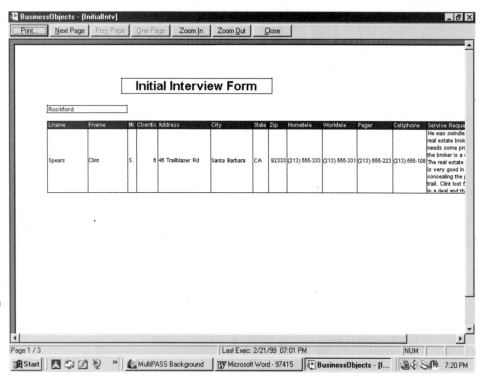

BusinessObjects
Initial Interview
report

Figure 15-10.

PART IV

SQL Today and Tomorrow

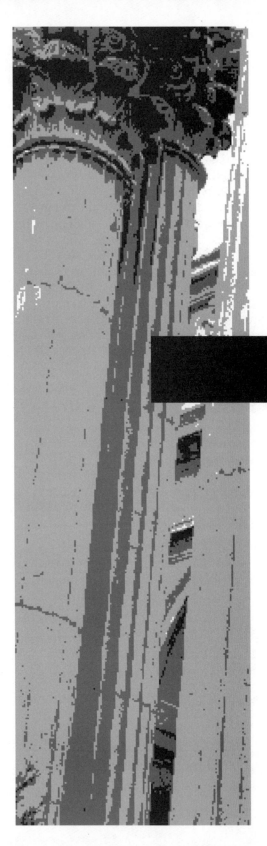

CHAPTER 16

T-SQL and Stored Procedures

In previous chapters, you've seen how to build SQL statements to retrieve data from the server. The variations of the SELECT statement you have already seen are adequate for retrieving the desired information from your database, but sometimes you need more than a SELECT statement. Some restrictions can't be expressed with a WHERE clause, no matter how complicated this clause can get. If the selection of a row depends on the field values of one or more previous rows, for instance, or you want to display running totals and format the output of the query, you need a small program to select and process the qualifying rows. Aren't there situations where the SQL statement that will process the rows is so complicated, you wish you could read the rows into an array (or equivalent structure) and process them yourself? Well, in addition to the SQL statements, statements exist that enable you to program SQL Server to process the selected rows and return one or more results. The result can be a single number or a special type of a result set, called *cursor*. The program that processes the rows is called *stored procedure* and it resides on the server (it's actually part of the database). Cursors and stored procedures are the two topics explored in this chapter.

Understanding Stored Procedures and Cursors

Let's start with a fairly complicated example, which demonstrates how you use both stored procedures and cursors. We return to this example later in this chapter and discuss its implementation in detail, so don't give up if you don't understand some of the statements used in the code. See how they work and try to understand the basic statements. A simpler example could have been used, but trivial examples don't always demonstrate the need for using advanced tools, like stored procedures and cursors.

Our example retrieves sales figures from the NorthWind database and calculates two running subtotals: the order totals and the customer totals. The order details are grouped according to customer, and each customer's total appears after the details.

NOTE: Certain columns, like the Discount column, were omitted, so that the table would fit on the printed page. If you enter the statements shown later in the Query Analyzer, you will see all the columns.

```
CompanyName          OrderID Product        UnitPrice   Qty   ExtPrice
Alfreds Futterkiste  10643   Rössle Sauer    45.6000     15   513.0000
Alfreds Futterkiste  10643   Chartreuse      18.0000     21   283.5000
Alfreds Futterkiste  10643   Spegesild       12.0000      2    18.0000
(3 row(s) affected)
```

```
sum
814.5000
(1 row(s) affected)
CompanyName            OrderID Product           UnitPrice   Qty  ExtPrice
Alfreds Futterkiste    10692   Vegie-spr         43.9000      20  878.0000
(1 row(s) affected)
sum
878.0000
(1 row(s) affected)
CompanyName            OrderID Product           UnitPrice   Qty  ExtPrice
Alfreds Futterkiste    10702   Aniseed           10.0000       6   60.0000
Alfreds Futterkiste    10702   Lakkali           18.0000      15  270.0000
(2 row(s) affected) sum
330.0000
sum
4273.0000
(1 row(s) affected)
```

As you can guess by looking at the invoice totals and the grand total at the end, the specific customer has more invoices than the ones shown here. SQL Analyzer reports all invoices, but only three are shown to conserve space. Here's the SQL statement that produced the previous output shown. You can enter this statement in the Query Analyzer's upper pane and then press CTRL-E or select Query | Execute to view the results in the lower pane of the same window.

NOTE: You will see more information in the Query Analyzer's window than is shown here, as explained earlier.

```
SELECT CompanyName, Orders.OrderID, ProductName,
       UnitPrice=ROUND([Order Details].UnitPrice, 2),
       Quantity, Discount=CONVERT(int, Discount * 100),
       ExtendedPrice=ROUND(CONVERT(money, Quantity * (1 - Discount) *
                     [Order Details].UnitPrice), 2)
    FROM Products, [Order Details], Customers, Orders
    WHERE [Order Details].ProductID = Products.ProductID AND
          [Order Details].OrderID = Orders.OrderID AND
          Orders.CustomerID=Customers.CustomerID
    ORDER BY Customers.CustomerID, Orders.OrderID
    COMPUTE SUM(ROUND(CONVERT(money, Quantity * (1 - Discount) *
            [Order Details].UnitPrice), 2))
            BY Customers.CustomerID, Orders.OrderID
    COMPUTE SUM(ROUND(CONVERT(money, Quantity * (1 - Discount) *
            [Order Details].UnitPrice), 2))
            BY Customers.CustomerID
```

The WHERE clause is straightforward: It connects the Order Details, Orders, Customers, and Products tables. The COMPUTE statement performs the specified calculations (sum the extended prices for each detail line of the invoices) over the rows with the same value in the column listed after the BY keyword. Both COMPUTE statements calculate the same sum, but the first one sums the extended prices (quantity times net price) for orders with the same ID, within the same customer. The second COMPUTE statement calculates the same sum over rows with the same customer ID—the total for each customer.

If this report is needed by many users, you can insert the SQL statements in the database itself as a stored procedure and call it by name. To add a stored procedure to a SQL Server database, use the following syntax:

```
DECLARE PROCEDURE procedure_name
AS
{SQL statements}
```

To add a stored procedure that retrieves all the invoices and displays them in the Query Analyzer's window, enter the procedure's declaration followed by the SQL statements in the upper pane of the Query Analyzer, as shown here:

```
CREATE PROCEDURE ShowAllSales
AS
SELECT CompanyName, Orders.OrderID, ProductName,
    UnitPrice=ROUND([Order Details].UnitPrice, 2),
    Quantity, Discount=CONVERT(int, Discount * 100),
    ExtendedPrice=ROUND(CONVERT(money, Quantity * (1 - Discount)*
                [Order Details].UnitPrice), 2)
    FROM Products, [Order Details], Customers, Orders
WHERE [Order Details].ProductID = Products.ProductID AND
        [Order Details].OrderID = Orders.OrderID AND
Orders.CustomerID=Customers.CustomerID
ORDER BY Customers.CustomerID, Orders.OrderID
    COMPUTE SUM(ROUND(CONVERT(money, Quantity * (1 - Discount) *
            Order Details].UnitPrice), 2))
BY Customers.CustomerID, Orders.OrderID
COMPUTE SUM(ROUND(CONVERT(money, Quantity * (1 - Discount) *
            Order Details].UnitPrice), 2))
        BY Customers.CustomerID
```

This statement attaches the specified procedure to the database. After that, all the users of the database can call it by name with the EXECUTE statement. The users of the database needn't be concerned with the details of the SQL statements that implement the stored procedure. The ShowAllSales procedure can be tested by a single developer and used by anyone who can access the NorthWind database. Moreover, because readers call a stored procedure and don't execute SQL statements against the database, the risk of ruining records is minimized. To execute the ShowAllSales procedure, clear the Query Analyzer's upper window, enter the following statement and then press CTRL-E to execute it:

```
EXECUTE ShowAllSales
```

(Don't forget to select the NorthWind database in the Query Analyzer's Database drop-down list. Alternatively, you can insert the USE statement followed by the name of the database on which the stored procedure should act: USE NorthWind).

The output generated by the stored procedure (shown earlier) appears in the lower pane. The raw information retrieved by the previous SQL statements may be needed by multiple applications. Some applications may just calculate customer totals, others may calculate invoice total, and another application may calculate totals over a specific product (or range of products). If the raw data are going to be used by multiple applications, you can create a cursor with the data and open it every time you need it.

The rows returned by the SQL Server and displayed in the lower pane of the Query Analyzer's window form a result set. These rows are returned to the Query Analyzer in response to an SQL statement and the Query Analyzer displays them in columns or on a grid. The actual rows sent by SQL Server to the application that requested them form the default result set. A cursor is a special result set, which actually resides either on the client or the server. The cursor can be scanned forward and backward. Moreover, the database can be updated through the cursor, something you can't do through the Query Analyzer, even when the rows are displayed on a grid.

The following T-SQL statements create a cursor with all the invoice details, grouped by customer and by order ID within the customer's section. The DECLARE statement tells SQL Server not to execute the SQL statement that follows the AS keyword, but to attach the cursor's definition to the database. Applications can then open the cursor and access its rows, as if they were tables. As you will see, different types of cursors exist and they can reside either on the server (the default cursor's location) or on the client.

```
DECLARE allSales CURSOR
FORWARD_ONLY
FOR
```

```
SELECT CompanyName, Orders.OrderID, ProductName,
    UnitPrice=ROUND([Order Details].UnitPrice, 2),
    Quantity, Discount=CONVERT(int, Discount * 100),
    ExtendedPrice=ROUND(CONVERT(money, Quantity * (1 - Discount)*
                [Order Details].UnitPrice), 2)
    FROM Products, [Order Details], Customers, Orders
    WHERE [Order Details].ProductID = Products.ProductID AND
          [Order Details].OrderID = Orders.OrderID AND
          Orders.CustomerID=Customers.CustomerID
    ORDER BY Customers.CustomerID, Orders.OrderID
```

Notice the last two COMPUTE statements that calculate the running totals were omitted from the cursor's definition. The cursor's rows must have the same fields, just like the rows of a table, or the result set of any other SQL statement. The lines with the totals have a single field and they don't match the structure of the other rows, so they were omitted. If you attempt to include the COMPUTE statements in the cursor's declaration, you get the following error message in the Query Analyzer's lower pane:

```
Server: Msg 16907, Level 16, State 1
[Microsoft][ODBC SQL Server Driver][SQL Server]'COMPUTE' is not
allowed in cursor statements.
```

The report shown at the beginning of this chapter is the best you can do with straight SQL. Notice the company names are repeated in every invoice line and the report could have a better structure. If you had access to the same rows through a programming language, you'd probably insert the name of the company once, above the invoices, and the invoice number once, above its details. The output shown next has a better structure:

```
COMPANY Alfreds Futterkiste
    ORDER   10643
        Rössle Sauerkraut               15 X 45.60 @ 25%      513.00
        Chartreuse verte                21 X 18.00 @ 25%      283.50
        Spegesild                        2 X 12.00 @ 25%       18.00
        **********TOTAL FOR ORDER 10643 *******************     814.50
    ORDER   10692
        Vegie-spread                    20 X 43.90 @ 0 %      878.00
        **********TOTAL FOR ORDER 10692 *******************     878.00
    ORDER   10702
        Aniseed Syrup                    6 X 10.00 @ 0 %       60.00
        Lakkalikööri                    15 X 18.00 @ 0 %      270.00
        **********TOTAL FOR ORDER 10702 *******************     330.00
```

```
ORDER    10835
         Raclette Courdavault              15 X 55.00 @ 0 %        825.00
         Original Frankfurter grüne Soß    2  X 13.00 @ 20%         20.80
         **********TOTAL FOR ORDER 10835 *******************       845.80
      ORDER    10952
         Grandma's Boysenberry Spread      16 X 25.00 @ 5 %        380.00
         Rössle Sauerkraut                 2  X 45.60 @ 0 %         91.20
         **********TOTAL FOR ORDER 10952 *******************       471.20
      ORDER    11011
         Escargots de Bourgogne            40 X 13.25 @ 5 %        503.50
         Flotemysost                       20 X 21.50 @ 0 %        430.00
         **********TOTAL FOR ORDER 11011 *******************       933.50
      ORDER    10308
      TOTAL for Alfreds Futterkiste                              4273.00
```

This report was generated with a small program, written in T-SQL (Transact-SQL). Every major Database Management System supports straight SQL (the statements you have learned so far in this book) and a set of statements that enable you to build small programs (like condition evaluation, looping statements, and so on). T-SQL is the programming language of SQL Server and it's similar to Visual Basic. Oracle's language is called PL-SQL and it's closer to Pascal (it's actually based on ADA, if you are familiar with this programming language). Because all these languages can't be discussed in a single chapter, I'll focus on T-SQL.

Here are the T-SQL statements that produced the previous report. Notice the AllSales cursor is opened and a small VB-like program scans the cursor's rows. Each row's fields are formatted and printed in the lower pane of the Query Analyzer window. The statements also keep track of the running totals (invoice and customer totals) in the variables *@CustomerTotal* and *@OrderTotal*. All T-SQL variables (which, by the way, must be declared) begin with the symbol @. In addition to the variables you declare in your T-SQL code, there are some built-in variables, whose names begin with the symbols @@. The *@@FETCH_STATUS* variable, for example, is non-zero if more rows are in the cursor to be fetched.

```
OPEN AllSales
/*** The following variables hold fields ***/
DECLARE @cCompany nchar(40)
DECLARE @prevCompany nchar(40)
DECLARE @cOrderID int
DECLARE @prevOrderID int
DECLARE @cProduct nvarchar(40)
DECLARE @cUnitPrice money
```

```
DECLARE @cQuantity smallint
DECLARE @cDiscount int
DECLARE @cExtPrice money
/*** The following two variables hold the running totals
     and are maintained by the stored procedure's code     ***/
DECLARE @CustomerTotal money
DECLARE @OrderTotal money
FETCH NEXT FROM allSales INTO
     @cCompany, @cOrderID, @cProduct,
     @cUnitPrice, @cQuantity, @cDiscount, @cExtPrice
SET @prevCompany = @cCompany
SET @prevOrderID = @cOrderID
PRINT "COMPANY " + @cCompany
PRINT "    ORDER   " + CONVERT(char(5), @cOrderID)
SET @CustomerTotal = 0
SET @OrderTotal = 0

WHILE @@FETCH_STATUS = 0
 BEGIN
    IF @prevCompany <> @cCompany
       BEGIN
          SET @CustomerTotal = @CustomerTotal + @OrderTotal
          PRINT "        *********TOTAL FOR ORDER " + CONVERT(char(5),
             @prevOrderID) + " ************************   " +
             CONVERT(char(8), @OrderTotal)
          PRINT "     TOTAL for " + @prevCompany + "               " +
             CONVERT(char(10), @CustomerTotal)
          SET @CustomerTotal = 0
          PRINT " "
          PRINT "COMPANY " + @cCompany
          PRINT "    ORDER   " + CONVERT(char(5), @cOrderID)
          SET @OrderTotal = 0
       END
    ELSE
       BEGIN
          IF @prevOrderID <> @cOrderID
             BEGIN
                PRINT "         *********TOTAL FOR ORDER " +
                   CONVERT(char(5), @prevOrderID) +
                   " ***********************   " +
                   CONVERT(char(8), @OrderTotal)
                PRINT "    ORDER   " + CONVERT(char(5), @cOrderID)
                SET @CustomerTotal = @CustomerTotal + @OrderTotal
                SET @OrderTotal = 0
             END
```

16

```
        PRINT "            " + CONVERT(char(30), @cProduct) + "      " +
            CONVERT(char(4), @cQuantity) + " X " +
            CONVERT(char(6), @cUnitPrice) + " @ " +
            CONVERT(char(2), @cDiscount) + "%       " +
            CONVERT(char(12), @cExtPrice)
        SET @OrderTotal = @OrderTotal + @cExtPrice
    END
    SET @prevOrderID = @cOrderID
    SET @prevCompany = @cCompany
    FETCH NEXT FROM allSales INTO
        @cCompany, @cOrderID, @cProduct,
        @cUnitPrice, @cQuantity, @cDiscount, @cExtPrice
 END
 PRINT "     TOTAL for " + @prevCompany + "             " +
    CONVERT(char(10), @CustomerTotal)
CLOSE AllSales
```

FETCH is a T-SQL statement that reads the columns of a row into a set of local variables. *FETCH NEXT* reads the next row in the cursor and is the only statement you can use to read rows from a FORWARD_ONLY cursor, like the one used here. Other variations of the FETCH statement are the FETCH NEXT, FETCH PREVIOUS, and FETCH LAST.

The procedure consists of a large loop, which scans all the rows of the *AllSales* cursor and keeps track of two running totals: the current customer and current invoice total. Every time the procedure runs into a new customer, it prints the total for the current invoice and current customer and resets both totals to zero. When it runs into a new order, it prints the order total and resets it to zero. The numerous calls to the CONVERT() function are required to convert numeric values to strings, before they can be concatenated to produce the desired output. You can ignore the calls to the CONVERT() function for now and focus on the variables printed by the PRINT statements. If T-SQL was as open-minded as Visual Basic, you wouldn't have to convert the various variable types—you wouldn't even have to declare them in the first place.

To summarize, the last procedure opens the AllSales cursor and processes the selected rows with programming statements (like the IF and WHILE statements). The procedure, however, is executed on the server, not on the client. And you don't need to use a programming language—T-SQL is built into the SQL Server. Of course, calling stored procedures, and reading and processing the rows of a cursor from within your favorite programming language are both possible.

The introductory examples were fairly complicated, but they should give you a good idea of what T-SQL can do for you and how cursors are used in producing complicated queries. Typically, things don't get much more complicated than that. In the following sections, you look at stored procedures, T-SQL statements, and cursors in more detail. Don't worry if you didn't understand every line in the examples presented in the previous pages or the syntax of the various statements. They're discussed shortly. The important thing to remember is you can predefine cursors and use them from within stored procedures, written in T-SQL. *T-SQL,* finally, is a programming language built into the SQL Server to address the needs of people who wish they could manipulate the selected rows with a more traditional programming language. Other DBMSs expose their own languages, but this book concentrates on SQL Server's language.

We begin our exploration of the advanced SQL topics with stored procedures and T-SQL. You learn the T-SQL flow control statements that enable you to write procedures to process the rows returned by a query, the built-in variables, and how to attach stored procedures to a database. Finally, you learn about cursors, and how to create and use them in your stored procedures. Later in this book, you learn how to access them through your other programming environments, like Visual Basic and Visual C++.

Stored Procedures

Any query you can execute against the database can also be stored into the database itself and be called by name. When an SQL statement, especially a complicated one, is stored in the database, the Database Management System can execute it efficiently. To execute an SQL statement, the query engine must analyze it and put together an execution plan. The *execution plan* is analogous to the compilation of a traditional application. The Database Management System translates the statements in the procedure to statements it can execute directly against the database. When the SQL statement is stored on the server as a procedure, its execution plan is designed once and is ready to be used. Moreover, stored procedures can be designed once, tested, and used by many users and/or applications. If the same stored procedure is used by more than one user, the Database Management System keeps only one copy of the procedure in memory and all users share the same instance of the procedure. This means more efficient memory utilization. Finally, you can limit user access to the database's tables and force users to access the database through stored procedures. This is a simple method of enforcing business rules.

Here are a few examples of stored procedures. Start the SQL Enterprise Manager and select the NorthWind sample database. Under the NorthWind folder, select Stored Procedures. You see the names of a few stored procedures that come with the database. The simplest one, is the Ten Most Expensive Products stored procedure, which retrieves the ten most expensive items in the Products table. To see the SQL statement that retrieves these products, double-click its name in the window and you see the definition of the stored procedure, as shown in Figure 16-1.

Here's the implementation of the Ten Most Expensive Products stored procedure:

```
CREATE PROCEDURE "Ten Most Expensive Products" AS
SET ROWCOUNT 10
SELECT Products.ProductName AS TenMostExpensiveProducts,
            Products.UnitPrice
FROM Products
ORDER BY Products.UnitPrice DESC
```

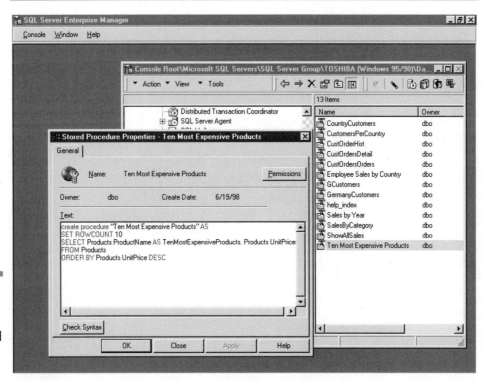

Browsing the stored procedures of the NorthWind database

Figure 16-1.

To execute this procedure, start the Query Analyzer, enter the following line in the window's upper pane, and click the Execute Query button or press CTRL-E:

```
EXECUTE [Ten Most Expensive Products]
```

The results appear in the lower pane of the window, as shown in Figure 16-2. These are the rows retrieved by the SQL statement of the stored procedure.

As you can see, apart from a declaration line, the stored procedure consists of an SQL statement. Typically, stored procedures accept arguments as well. You see later examples of stored procedures that accept arguments and how they are called. You can open a few more of the stored procedures that come with the database and examine them.

Of course, stored procedures are not limited to SQL Server. Microsoft Access supports stored procedures, in a way. Technically, Access enables you to enter queries and call them by name. They are not called stored procedures and they can't get as complicated as SQL Server stored procedures, but this is as close as Access comes to stored procedures.

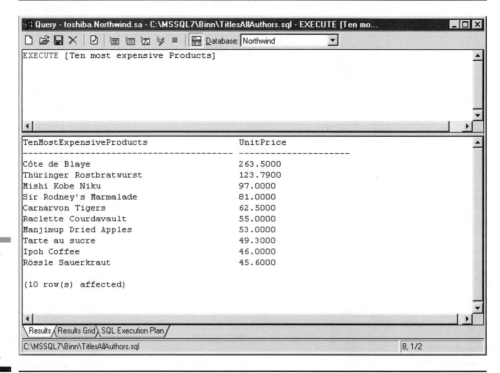

Executing the Ten Most Expensive Products stored procedure

Figure 16-2.

Start Access and open the NWIND database. This database contains the same data as the Northwind database that comes with SQL Server, but they are stored in different locations (same data, but different databases). The NWIND database is stored in a MDB file and is managed by the Jet Engine (the Access and Visual Basic's native Database Management System). Select Queries in the Database window and you see the queries stored in the database itself, which can be invoked by double-clicking their names. The Ten Most Expensive Products query is implemented with the following statement:

```
SELECT
    DISTINCTROW TOP 10 Products.ProductName AS
TenMostExpensiveProducts,
    Products.UnitPrice
FROM Products
ORDER BY Products.UnitPrice DESC;
```

The output of the Ten Most Expensive Products query is shown in Figure 16-3. As you can see, Access queries are straight SQL statements. There is no declaration section, but their name is stored in the database itself. Moreover, Access doesn't support a language (like the T-SQL language of SQL Server or PL/SQL of Oracle) that can be used to write small programs that can be executed on the server.

Access may not recognize T-SQL statements, but Access databases can be programmed in Access's own programming environment, which is closer to Visual Basic, rather than SQL. In the following section you learn the basics of T-SQL and you see how you can write queries in T-SQL to process and format the data retrieved from the database.

Transact-SQL

SQL is limited to statements for creating and managing databases, but it doesn't provide flow-control statements, which would allow developers to write procedures, just as they would with more traditional languages. Database Management System vendors, however, have added extensions to the SQL language, which extend SQL from a data manipulation and definition language to a real programming language. SQL Server's language is called Transact-SQL (T-SQL). *T-SQL* is a language you can use to create and manipulate database objects, and it's an enhanced version of the SQL-92 standard. Oracle uses a different language, which is similar to Pascal and ADA, and it's called PL/SQL. Like T-SQL, PL/SQL enables you to write small programs that are executed on the server, process rows locally, and return results to the caller. The caller can be another stored procedure or an external application written in Visual Basic or Visual C++.

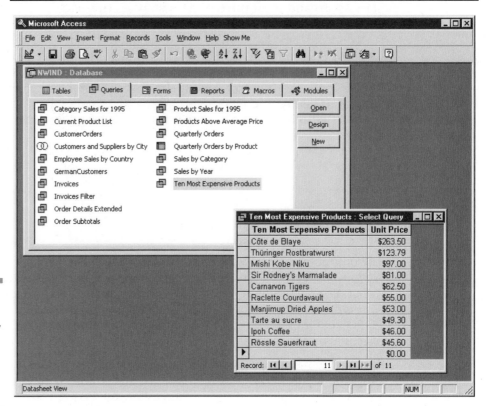

The Ten Most
Expensive
Products query
of the Access
NWIND
database

Figure 16-3.

This chapter is an introduction to T-SQL and the language is presented through examples. You can find a complete reference of T-SQL in the SQL Books Online (among other sources). I assume you have some programming experience and will not spend too many pages explaining what IF or WHILE statements do.

The basic elements of a programming language are variables, flow-control statements, and functions. *Variables* are used to store values during the execution of the procedure. By assigning different values to the same variables, the same procedure can act on different data. Variables are also used for storing intermediate results, as well as the values to be returned to the calling application. *Flow-control statements* are structures like IF ... ELSE, which enable you to write procedures that modify their behavior based on the values of the data they act upon. *Loop statements,* like the WHILE statement, execute a block of statement while a condition is true. For example, you can process invoice details as long as they belong to the same customer.

Finally, *functions* perform specific actions on data and return the results. The MIN() and MAX() functions return the minimum and maximum values of a column in the result set. The LEN() function returns the length of a string, passed to the function as an argument. There are more complex functions, which were designed specifically for manipulating database fields. The COALESCE() function, for example, accepts two or more column names as arguments and returns the value of the first column that's not NULL.

Variables

If you're spoiled by other languages, this may come as a shock, but T-SQL variables must be declared before they can be used. Variables are declared with the DECLARE statement and their names must begin with the character @. The following are valid variable names: *@Total, @Average_Price*. Before you can use a variable, you must declare it with the DECLARE statement, whose syntax is

```
DECLARE var_name type
```

where *type* is the name of a data type and it can be one of the following:

binary, varbinary   These variables store binary values. The two following statements declare two binary variables, a fixed length and a variable length:

```
DECLARE @bVar1 Binary(4), @bVar2 varBinary
```

Use binary variables to store the values of binary columns. To assign a value to a binary variable, use the hexadecimal notation:

```
SET @bVar1 = 0x000000F0
```

This statement assigns the value 255 to the *bVar1* variable.

The binary data types can store up to 8,000 bytes.

char, varchar   These variables store characters and their length can't exceed 8,000 characters. The following statements declare and assign values to char variables:

```
DECLARE @string1 char(20)
DECLARE @string2 varchar(20)
SET @string1 = 'STRING1'
SET @string2 = 'STRING2'
PRINT '[' + @string1 + ']'
PRINT '[' + @string2 + ']'
```

The last two statements print the following:

```
[STRING1              ]
[STRING2]
```

The char string is padded with spaces to the specified length, while the varchar is not. If the actual data exceed the specified length of the string, both types truncate the string (to 20 characters, in the case of the example).

The *nchar* and *nvarchar types* are equivalent to the char and varchar types, but they are used for storing Unicode strings.

int, smallint, tinyint   Use these types to store whole numbers (integers).

decimal, numeric   These two types store an integer to the left of the decimal point and a fractional value to the right of the decimal point:

```
DECLARE varDecimal DECIMAL(4, 3)
```

The first argument specifies the maximum total number of decimal digits that can be stored to the left and right of the decimal point. Valid values are in the range 1 through 28. The second argument specifies the maximum number of decimal digits that can be stored to the right of the decimal point and its value must be in the range 0 through the specified precision (in other words, the second argument can't be larger than the first argument).

datetime, smalldatetime   Use these two types to store date and time values. The datetime type uses 8 bytes: 4 bytes for the date and 4 bytes for the time. The time portion of the datetime type is the number of milliseconds after midnight and is updated every 3.33 milliseconds. The smalldatetime type uses 4 bytes: 2 bytes to store the number of days after January 1, 1900 and 2 bytes to store the number of minutes since midnight.

The following statements demonstrate how to add days, hours, and minutes to variables of datetime and smalldatetime variables:

```
DECLARE @DT datetime
DECLARE @SDT smalldatetime
PRINT "datetime type"
SET @DT = '8/12/1998 14:02.10'
PRINT @DT
/* Add a day to a datetime variable */
SET @DT = @DT + 1
```

16

```
PRINT @DT
/* Add an hour to a datetime variable */
SET @DT = @DT + 1.0/24.0
PRINT @DT
/* Add an hour to a datetime variable */
SET @DT = @DT + 1.0/(24.0 * 60.0)
PRINT @DT
PRINT "smalldatetime"
SET @SDT = '8/12/1998 01:10.50'
PRINT @SDT
/* Add a day to a smalldatetime variable */
SET @SDT = @SDT + 1
PRINT @SDT
/* Add an hour to a smalldatetime variable */
SET @SDT = @SDT + 1.0/24.0
PRINT @SDT
```

The output produced by these statements is shown in Figure 16-4.

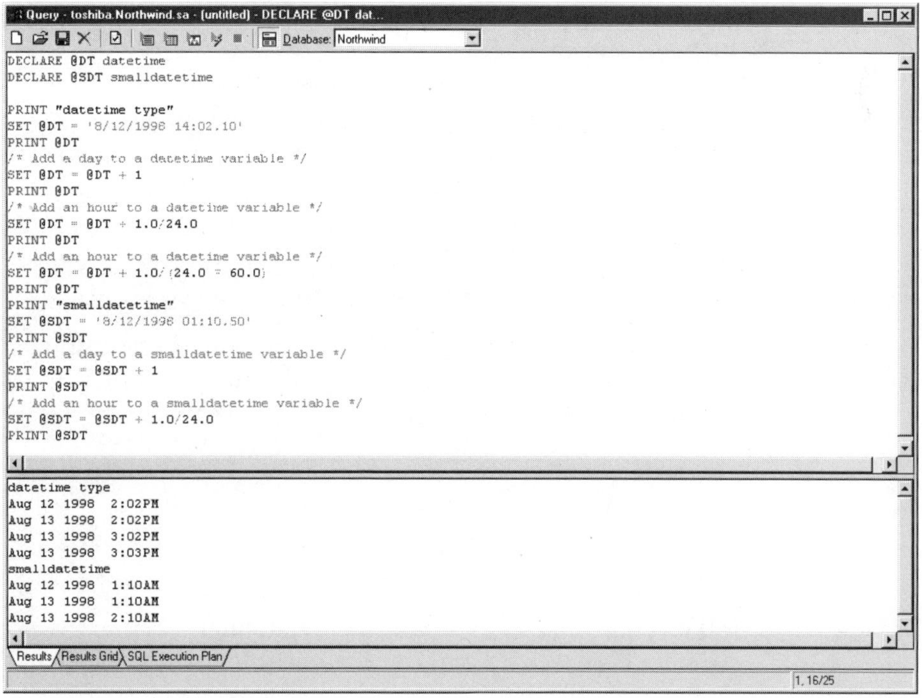

Manipulating
date and time
with T-SQL
statements

Figure 16-4.

float, real   The float and real types are known as approximate data types and are used for storing floating point numbers.

money, smallmoney   Use these two types to store dollar amounts. Both types use 4 fractional digits. The money type uses 8 bytes and it can represent amounts in the range -922,337,203,685,477.5807 to 922,337,203,685,377.5807. The smallmoney type uses 4 bytes and it can represent amounts in the range -214,748.3648 to 214,748.3647.

text   The text data type can store non-Unicode data with a maximum length of 2,147,483,647 characters.

image   Variable-length binary data up to 2,147,483,647 bytes in size.

Timestamp   Timestamp columns are commonly used to find out whether a row has been changed since it was read.

uniqueidentifier   A globally unique identifier, which is usually assigned to a column with the NEWID() function.

bit   Use the bit data type to represent integer values, which can be either 0 or 1.

Flow-Control Statements

The *flow-control statements* discussed in this section enable you to skip some of the statements in a procedure depending on the outcome of a comparison, branch to specific statements when certain conditions are met, and execute a block of statements repeatedly. T-SQL's flow-control statements are discussed briefly in the following paragraphs.

IF ... THEN   To execute a block of statements conditional (in other words, to execute them when certain conditions are met and skip them otherwise), use the IF ... THEN statement, whose syntax is

```
IF <condition>
    {statement}
ELSE
    {statement}
```

If the *<condition>* specified in the IF statement is True, then the following statement is executed and the statement following the ELSE clause is skipped.

Likewise, if the *<condition>* is False, then the following statement is skipped and the statement following the ELSE clause is executed.

If you want to execute more than a single statement in the IF or the ELSE clause, you must use the BEGIN and END keywords to enclose the block of statements:

```
IF <condition>
    BEGIN
    {multiple statements}
    END
ELSE
    BEGIN
    {multiple statements}
    END
```

Depending on the condition, one of the two blocks of statements between the BEGIN and END keywords are executed. Here's an example of the IF ... THEN statement with statement blocks:

```
IF (SELECT COUNT(*) FROM Orders WHERE CustID = '10204') > 0
    BEGIN
    {statements to process orders placed by customer with ID=10204}
    END
ELSE
    BEGIN
    PRINT "No orders were found for the specified customer"
    END
```

Notice the second pair of BEGIN/END keywords are optional because the ELSE clause is followed by a single statement.

CASE   The CASE statement is used to compare a variable (or field) value against several values and executes a block of statement, depending on which comparison returns a True result. Let's say you want to calculate insurance premiums based on the person's age and three age categories exist. Instead of multiple IF statements, you can use a CASE structure like the following:

```
SELECT
CASE @AgeCategory
    WHEN 'YOUTH' THEN 200
    WHEN 'ADULT' THEN 375
    WHEN 'AGED'  THEN 450
END
```

Notice this statement is similar to Visual Basic's SELECT CASE statement, but in T-SQL, it's called CASE. The SELECT keyword in the previous line simply tells SQL Server to display the outcome of the CASE statement. If the variable @AgeCategory is "ADULT," then the value 375 is printed in the Results pane of the Query Analyzer's window.

If the age is stored in a table, you can use the CASE statement to convert it to a description, as shown next:

```
SELECT CustomerName,
    CASE CustomerAge
        WHEN CustomerAge < 18 THEN 200
        WHEN CustomerAge >= 18 AND CustomerAge < 65 THEN 375
        WHEN CustomerAge >= 65 THEN 450
    END
```

WHILE   The WHILE statement repeatedly executes a block of T-SQL statements. If you want to repeat multiple lines, enclose them in a pair of BEGIN/END keywords, as explained in the description of the IF statement. The most common use of the WHILE statement is to scan the rows of a result set, as shown in the following example:

```
WHILE @@fetchstatus = 0
    BEGIN
    {statements to process the fields of the current row}
    FETCH NEXT INTO <variable_list>
    END
```

The FETCH NEXT statement reads the next row of the result set and stores its fields' values into the variables specified in the *<variable_list>*.

CONTINUE and BREAK   These two keywords are used in conjunction with the WHILE statement to alter the flow of execution. The CONTINUE keyword ends the current iteration and forces another one. In other words, the WHILE statement's condition is evaluated and the loop is re-entered. If the condition is False, then the WHILE loop is skipped and execution continues with the line following the END keyword that delimits the loop's body of statements.

The BREAK keyword terminates the loop immediately and branches to the line following the loop's END keyword. The following code segment shows how the two keywords are used in a WHILE loop:

```
WHILE <condition>
    BEGIN
        {read column values into variables}
```

16

```
        IF @balance < 0
            CONTINUE
        IF @balance > 999999
            BREAK
        {process @balance variable and/or other variables}
    END
```

This loop reads the rows of a table or cursor and processes only the ones with a positive balance, less than 1,000,000. If a row with a negative balance is found, the code doesn't process it and continues with the next row. If a row with a balance of 1,000,000 or more is found, the code stops processing the rows by breaking out of the loop.

GOTO and RETURN The last two flow-control statements enable you to alter the flow of execution by branching to another location in the procedure. The GOTO statement branches to a line identified by a label. Here's a simple example of the GOTO statement (in effect, it's a less elegant method of implementing a WHILE loop):

```
RepeatLoop:
        FETCH NEXT INTO <variable_list>
        IF @@FETCH_STATUS = 0
        BEGIN
            {process variables}
            GOTO RepeatLoop
        END
```

While more records are in the result set, the GOTO statement branches to the FETCH NEXT statement. The identifier *RepeatLoop* is a label (a name identifying the line to which you want to branch) and it must be followed by a colon. If there are no more records to be fetched and processed, the procedure continues with the statement following the END keyword.

The RETURN statement ends a procedure unconditionally and it, optionally, returns a result. To return a value from within a stored procedure, use a statement like the following:

```
RETURN @error_value
```

@error_value is a local variable, which can be set by the procedure's code. The calling application, which could be another stored procedure, should be aware of the possible values returned by the procedure.

PRINT output_list   Normally, all the output produced by the T-SQL statements forms the result set. This output is usually the data retrieved from the database. To include titles, or any other type of information in the result set, use the PRINT statement. When you use the PRINT statement with the Query Analyzer, its output appears in the lower pane of the window. You can't use the PRINT statement to insert additional lines into a cursor.

The *output_list* can be any combination of literals, variables, and functions. To display a message, use a statement like the following one:

```
PRINT "No rows matching your criteria were found in the table"
```

You can also display variable values along with literals:

```
PRINT "The average unit cost is " + @avgValue
```

The AllTitles Procedure   Let's put together all the information of the last few sections to build a stored procedure that retrieves all the titles from the Pubs sample database and prints them along with their authors. Notice, unlike the sample stored procedures that come with the database, the titles are not repeated for each author. This sample prints the title on its own line. The author name(s) are printed on the following lines and are indented from the left by ten spaces.

```
DECLARE TitleAuthors CURSOR
FORWARD_ONLY STATIC FOR
    SELECT Titles.title_id, Titles.title, Authors.au_lname,
    Authors.au_fname
        FROM Titles, TitleAuthor, Authors
            WHERE Titles.title_id=TitleAuthor.title_id AND
                Authors.au_id=TitleAuthor.au_id
OPEN TitleAuthors
DECLARE @currentTitleID AS varchar(6)
DECLARE @currentTitle As varchar(80)
DECLARE @currentAuthorLName AS varchar(40)
DECLARE @currentAuthorFName AS varchar(20)
DECLARE @prevTitleID AS varchar(6)
FETCH NEXT FROM TitleAuthors INTO
    @currentTitleID, @currentTitle, @currentAuthorLName,
    @currentAuthorFName
SET @prevTitleID = @currentTitleID
PRINT @currentTitle
WHILE @@FETCH_STATUS = 0
```

```
    BEGIN
       IF @prevTitleID = @currentTitleID
        PRINT SPACE(10) + @currentAuthorLName +", " +
        @currentAuthorFName
       ELSE
        BEGIN
           PRINT @currentTitle
           PRINT SPACE(10) + @currentAuthorLName + ", " +
           @currentAuthorFName
        END
      SET @prevTitleID = @currentTitleID
      FETCH NEXT FROM TitleAuthors INTO
           @currentTitleID, @currentTitle, @currentAuthorLName,
           @currentAuthorFName
   END
CLOSE TitleAuthors
```

You may find this code segment complicated to follow (it becomes simpler when we discuss cursors in Chapter 17). For now, you can ignore the statements that build the TitleAuthors cursor. Try to understand these lines now:

```
FETCH NEXT FROM TitleAuthors INTO
     @currentTitleID, @currentTitle, @currentAuthorLName,
     @currentAuthorFName
SET @prevTitleID = @currentTitleID
PRINT @currentTitle
WHILE @@FETCH_STATUS = 0
   BEGIN
      IF @prevTitleID = @currentTitleID
         PRINT SPACE(10) + @currentAuthorLName +", " +
         @currentAuthorFName
      ELSE
         BEGIN
            PRINT @currentTitle
            PRINT SPACE(10) + @currentAuthorLName + ", " +
            @currentAuthorFName
         END
       SET @prevTitleID = @currentTitleID
       FETCH NEXT FROM TitleAuthors INTO
           @currentTitleID, @currentTitle, @currentAuthorLName,
           @currentAuthorFName
   END
```

The FETCH statement at the top reads the fields of the cursor's next row into the local variables @currentTitleID, @currentTitle, @currentAuthorLName, and @currentAuthorLName. The current title's ID is stored in the @prevTitleID variable and you'll see shortly how this variable is used. Then the current title is printed and a WHILE loop starts. The @@FETCH_STATUS global variable is zero while the FETCH statement has successfully read another row. This variable assumes a non-zero value (1) when we hit the end of the result set. So, for each title in the cursor, the code prints the following:

◆ If the current title is the same as the previous title (@prevTitleID is the same as @currentTitleID) then only the name of the book's (second, third, and so on) author is printed.

◆ If the condition in the IF statement returns False, then the ELSE clause is executed. Here the program prints the title, followed by the name of its first author in the following line.

We then set the @prevTitleID variable to the current title's ID and we read the next line from the result set, with the FETCH statement. The last END keyword delimits the block of statement in the WHILE loop.

If you enter the previous T-SQL lines in the Query Analyzer and execute them, you see the output shown in Figure 16-5.

NOTE: In Figure 16-5, I have condensed a few lines to squeeze as much of the code into the upper window.

Global Variables

In addition to the local variables, you can declare in your procedures, T-SQL supports a number of global variables, whose names begin with the symbols @@. The @@FETCH_STATUS variable, for example, is zero if the FETCH statement successfully retrieved a row, non-zero otherwise. This variable is set after the execution of a FETCH statement and it's commonly used to terminate a WHILE loop that scans a cursor. The global variable @@FETCH_STATUS may also have the value –2, which indicates the row you attempted to retrieve has been deleted, since the cursor was created. This value applies to keyset-driven cursors only.

The @@CURSOR_ROWS global variable returns the number of rows in the most recently opened cursor and the @@ROWCOUNT variable returns the

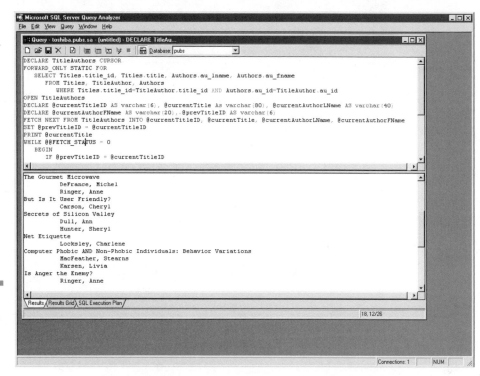

Retrieving all the titles along with their authors

Figure 16-5.

number of rows affected by the last statement. The @@ROWCOUNT variable is commonly used with UPDATE and DELETE statements to find out how many rows were affected by the SQL statement. The @@ERROR variable returns an error number for the last T-SQL statement that was executed. If this variable is zero, then the statement was executed successfully.

Many global variables relate to administrative tasks and they are listed in the following table. T-SQL exposes more global variables, but the ones listed in Table 16-1 shows the most commonly used ones.

T-SQL Functions

T-SQL supports a number of functions that simplify the processing of the various data types. You have already seen the CONVERT() function, which

Variable Name	Description
@@CONNECTIONS	The number of login attempts since SQL Server started for the last time.
@@CPU_BUSY	The number of ticks the CPU spent for the SQL Server since it was started for the last time.
@@IDENTITY	The most recently created IDENTITY value.
@@IDLE	The number of ticks SQL Server has been idle since it was last started.
@@IO_BUSY	The number of ticks SQL Server spent for input/output operations since it was last started.
@@LANGID	The current language ID.
@@LANGUAGE	The current language.
@@LOCK_TIMEOUT	The current lock-out setting in milliseconds.
@@MAX_CONNECTIONS	The maximum number of simultaneous connections that can be made to the SQL Server.
@@MAX_PRECISION	The current precision setting for decimal and numeric data types.
@@NESTLEVEL	The number of nested transactions for the current execution. Transactions can be nested up to 16 levels.
@@SERVERNAME	The name of the local SQL Server.
@@TOTAL_ERRORS	The number of total errors since SQL was started for the last time.
@@TOTAL_READ	The number of reads from the disk since SQL Server was started for the last time.
@@TOTAL_WRITE	The number of reads from the disk since SQL Server was started for the last time.
@@TRANCOUNT	The number of active transactions for the current user.

Some Commonly Used T-SQL Global Variables

Table 16-1.

converts variables from one type into another. The CONVERT() function's syntax is

```
new_variable = CONVERT(new_type, variable)
```

where *variable* is the name of the variable whose type you want to convert and *new_type* is the declaration of the type, to which you want to convert the variable. The result is a new value that must be stored to a properly declared variable (*new_variable*).

Let's say you have declared two variables with the following statements:

```
DECLARE @msg varchar(20)
DECLARE @val int
SET @msg="The value is"
SET @val=39
```

If you attempt to print their values with the statement:

```
PRINT @msg + @val
```

You get the following error message:

```
Syntax error converting the varchar value 'The value is'
to a column of data type int.
```

You must first convert the integer value to a string and then concatenate them, with a statement like the following one:

```
PRINT @msg + CONVERT(varchar(4), @val)
```

T-SQL supports a number of functions for the manipulation of strings, which are similar to the equivalent string functions of Visual Basic, but many of them have different names. The LEN() function returns the length of the string passed to the function as an argument. The UPPER() and LOWER() functions convert their argument to uppercase and lowercase, respectively.

The RIGHT() and LEFT() functions return a specified number of characters from a string. The function:

```
LEFT('February 21, 1999', 8)
```

returns the string "February" and the function:

```
RIGHT('February 21, 1999', 4)
```

returns the string "1999." This value is a string, even if all its characters are numeric digits.

The SUBSTRING() function extracts a substring from another string, similar to Visual Basic's MID() function. It accepts three arguments, which are a string, the substring's starting position, and its length. The function:

```
SUBSTRING('February 21, 1999', 10, 2)
```

returns the string 21 (the two characters at the 10th position in the specified string).

Other useful string functions are listed in Table 16-2.

T-SQL supports a number of functions for examining data types. The functions ISDATE(), ISNULL(), ISNUMERIC() return True if their argument is a datetime, NULL, or numeric type, respectively.

Another group of functions enables you to retrieve system information. The SUSER_ID() function accepts the user's login name as argument and returns the user's ID. The SUSER_NAME() function does the opposite. It accepts the user's ID and returns the user's login name. The USER_ID() and USER_NAME() functions are similar, only instead of the login name they work with the database user name and database ID. The USER function (this one accepts no arguments and must be called without the parentheses) returns the current user's database user name.

Finally, there's a group of administrative functions, which enable you to program administrative tasks. For more information on T-SQL functions, you can consult the Books Online. If you are familiar with a programming language, you can locate the function you need and use it easily.

Function Name	Description
CHARINDEX(str1, str2)	Returns the starting position of str2 in str1, where both arguments are strings.
REPLACE()	Replaces a few characters in a string with another string.
GETDATE()	Returns the current date and time on the machine that runs SQL Server.
DATEADD()	Increments a datetime argument by an interval, which can be days, hours, months, years, and so on.
DATEDIFF()	Returns the difference between two datetime arguments in a number of intervals, which can be days, hours, months, years, and so on.
DATEPART()	Returns an integer that represents the number of specified parts (days, weeks, and so on) of a given date.
DATENAME()	Returns the name of a part of a datetime argument. The function DATENAME(month, varDate) returns the name of the month in the *varDate* argument (January, February, and so on) and the DATENAME(weekday, varDate) returns the name of the weekday in the *varDate* argument (Monday, Tuesday, and so on).
DAY(), MONTH(), YEAR()	These functions return the weekday, month, and year part of the datetime argument passed to the function as argument.
COALESCE()	This function returns the first non-NULL expression in its argument list. The function COALESCE(CompanyName, Customer) returns the company's name, or the customer's name, should the CompanyName be NULL.

Some Useful
T-SQL
Functions
Table 16-2.

What's Next?

This concludes our discussion of stored procedures. A stored procedure contains mostly SQL statements, but it may also contain flow-control statements. Using flow-control statements, you can implement stored procedures that behave like small programs, similar to procedures you'd write with any traditional programming language. You have seen how to implement queries as stored procedures and call them by name. Stored procedures can accept arguments and return results, either in the form of cursors (result sets, made up of one or more rows) or in the form of single numbers.

In this chapter we focused on Microsoft's Transact-SQL, which is the language for programming the SQL Server. In Chapter 17, you learn more about T-SQL (specifically, how to create cursors and write stored procedure for administrative tasks).

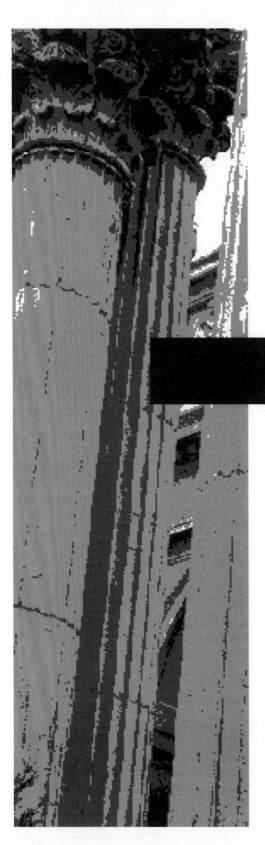

CHAPTER 17

Advanced T-SQL
Topics

In the last chapter, you learned the basics of T-SQL and stored procedures. Now we cover a few advanced T-SQL topics—namely, cursors, triggers, and jobs. *Cursors* are special result sets that you can pass between procedures. Cursors are essential in programming the SQL Server. Triggers and jobs are similar to stored procedures; they are used mostly by administrators. *Triggers* are procedures that are invoked automatically when certain tables are modified to protect the integrity of your database. *Jobs* are procedures that can be scheduled to run at predetermined intervals. Both triggers and jobs are developed by database administrators, so users need not be aware of them. We start our discussion of advanced SQL topics with cursors, which are essential in programming the SQL Server.

Using Cursors

The rows returned by a SELECT SQL statement you issue in the Query Analyzer are fetched from the database by the SQL engine and displayed in the Results pane of the Query Analyzer's window. This is the default result set and it contains all the qualifying rows. The data are displayed by the Query Analyzer, but you can't touch them. Moreover, you can't see any changes made to the data by other users. The default result set is quite static and it resides on the client computer. The default result set keeps the network busy while it is sent to the client (the computer running the Query Analyzer or whatever tool you're using to query the database), but after that, the server is free to process other requests. The result set simply consumes resources on the client computer.

When you access the SQL Server through a programming language, you must store these results somewhere and process them, or even update them, through your code. Or, you may have to create a different type of result set, which can be accessed again from within the same stored procedure. A fundamental concept in working with databases is that of the cursor.

A cursor is a representation of the rows retrieved by a query. It may consist of all the rows (the actual field values) or a series of pointers to the qualifying rows in the database. When the cursors contain pointers, the information is always up to date. Every time the application requests another row, it is read directly from the database and it will be "fresh" (it will reflect any changes made by other users since the cursor was first opened). When a dynamic cursor is created, SQL Server returns information about the qualifying rows so the application can quickly fetch the actual field values when it needs them.

To understand how cursors work, remember applications work with one row at a time. Even when an application displays a few rows, it must read and display one row at a time. This explains how some cursors can contain fresh data. If the row is fetched when needed, then the application sees the most recent data. This happens with a cursor that contains pointers to the rows that make up the result set. If the cursor contains the actual data, it returns the same data, no matter how frequently they are being updated by other users.

Cursor Types

17

Depending on how they store information, three types of cursors exist: static, keyset-driven, and dynamic.

Static Cursors

The *static cursor* provides an image of the data at the time the cursor was created. Changes made by other users after the cursor was created are not reflected in the cursor's contents, but it is possible for static cursors to update the database. SQL Server 7.0 static cursors can be used to update the database. Moreover, static cursors can be scrolled forward or backward.

Keyset-Driven Cursors

Keyset-driven cursors contain a pointer for each row in the result set. When this type of cursor is scanned, SQL Server fetches the key of the requested row and uses it to read the actual row from the database. The application fetches a fresh version of the row when it needs it. In other words, if another user has changed the row since the cursor was opened, the application sees the latest data.

Of course, if new qualifying rows are inserted after the creation of the cursor, these rows will not be seen by the application because there are no pointers for these rows in the keyset. If a row in a keyset-driven cursor is deleted after the creation of the cursor, when the application requests this row, it will see a "hole" in its place. The cursor will return an empty row, which the application must handle accordingly.

Dynamic Cursors

These are the most flexible, and the most expensive, cursors. *Dynamic cursors* keep track of inserted and deleted rows and are always up-to-date. Every time you fetch a row of a dynamic cursor, the cursor's rows may actually change. If a row has been deleted since the cursor was opened, then the next row will be returned. If a row was changed, the application sees the new row. Finally, if a row was inserted, it is added to the cursor automatically. For obvious reasons this is the most expensive type of cursor. The SQL Server must constantly compare the cursor to the database and update it every time another user changes the database.

As far as navigation goes, dynamic cursors can be scrolled in either direction and you can update the database through dynamic cursors.

Forward-Only Cursors

Many database management systems support another type of cursor, the forward-only cursor. As you can guess by its name, the *forward-only cursor* allows the application to move through the rows forward only. Other than this, the forward-only cursor is similar to the default result set.

The forward-only cursor is the least flexible one, but it's more efficient in terms of memory usage (rows that have already been visited need not reside in memory and SQL Server doesn't have to check the database to see if they have been deleted or altered). Whenever you want to open a cursor and iterate through its rows, use forward-only cursors.

Client-Side and Server-Side Cursors

In addition to the various types previously mentioned, cursors can also be classified according to the machine on which they reside. By default, the cursors created by the SQL Server reside on the server. Every time the user (or an application) needs a new row, a request is sent to the server, which in turn supplies the information. You can also create client-side cursors, which are downloaded to the client computer and are processed there by the application. Client cursors are supported by the interface you use to access the database, not the database management system.

Declaring and Opening Cursors

Before you can use a cursor, you must declare and open it. The declaration of the cursor is a SELECT statement that specifies which rows will be retrieved from the database and stored into the cursor. Then the cursor is opened with the OPEN statement and you can read its rows, one at a time. Cursors are declared with the DECLARE CURSOR statement, whose syntax is shown next:

```
DECLARE cursor_name CURSOR
[FORWARD_ONLY | SCROLL]
[STATIC | DYNAMIC | KEYSET]
[READ_ONLY | SCROLL_LOCKS | OPTIMISTIC]
FOR
SELECT <field_list>
FROM <table_list>
[FOR UPDATE OF <column_list>]
```

The FORWARD_ONLY keyword tells SQL Server the cursor can be scanned forward only. This type of cursor is less expensive in terms of resources than SCROLL cursors, which can be scanned forward and backward. If you don't specify one of the FORWARD_ONLY and SCROLL keywords, then the cursor is opened as FORWARD_ONLY.

The next keyword specifies the type of the cursor and must be STATIC (for static cursors), DYNAMIC (for dynamic cursors), or KEYSET (for keyset-driven cursors). If you omit the cursor type, a STATIC cursor is created by default.

17

Next, you can supply a keyword that determines the locking strategy. The READ_ONLY keyword excludes the use of the UPDATE and DELETE operations on the cursor and it overwrites the default capabilities of the cursor type. Use this option to make sure users can't change the database through the cursor, if they have no reason to do so. The SCROLL_LOCKS tells SQL Server to lock each row as it's read into the cursor, so the row can later be modified through the cursor. This keyword effectively locks all the rows in the cursor for as long as the cursor is open. You shouldn't use this option frequently. The OPTIMISTIC keyword does the opposite. The cursor's rows are not locked and when an attempt is made to update the database through the cursor, SQL Server examines the fields of the row. If they have not been modified since they were read, the UPDATE or DELETE operation succeeds. If the row has been modified, the operation fails.

Following the FOR keyword, you must specify the SELECT statement that reads the desired rows into the cursor. Finally, you can specify that only certain columns can be updated through the cursor with the FOR UPDATE clause. If the *<column_list>* is empty, then all columns can be updated (unless, of course, the cursor's type doesn't allow updates or the READ_ONLY keyword has been specified).

The following statement retrieves all the authors from the Pubs database and stores them into the AllAuthors cursor:

```
DECLARE AllAuthors CURSOR
    FOR SELECT * FROM Authors
```

Here's the declaration of a similar cursor. The TitleAuthors cursor contains all the titles along with their author(s). This cursor's rows contain a title, its ID, and an author. Titles with multiple authors are repeated as many times as necessary. The cursor is static (you can't update the database through the TitleAuthors cursor) and can be scanned forward only.

```
DECLARE TitleAuthors CURSOR
FORWARD_ONLY STATIC FOR
   SELECT Titles.title_id, Titles.title, Authors.au_lname,
    Authors.au_fname
      FROM Titles, TitleAuthor, Authors
      WHERE Titles.title_id=TitleAuthor.title_id AND
                      Authors.au_id=TitleAuthor.au_id
```

To use a cursor, you must first open it with the OPEN statement, whose syntax is shown next:

```
OPEN [GLOBAL|LOCAL] cursor_name
```

The GLOBAL or LOCAL keywords specify the scope of the cursor. If omitted, the cursor is open as local.

Finally, when you no longer need the cursor, you can close it with the CLOSE statement and release the resources allocated to the cursor with the DEALLOCATE statement:

```
CLOSE cursor_name
DEALLOCATE cursor_name
```

Fetching Rows from Cursors

After a cursor has been opened, you can examine the @@CURSOR_ROWS global variable to find out how many rows were returned into the cursor. You execute the following statements:

```
USE Pubs
--DEALLOCATE AllAuthors
DECLARE AllAuthors CURSOR
   KEYSET
   FOR SELECT * FROM Authors
OPEN AllAuthors
PRINT @@cursor_rows
```

If you have already declared the AllAuthors cursor, either un-comment the second line (which removes the cursor definition) or delete the cursor's DECLARE statement.

Notice the @@CURSOR_ROWS variable may return the value –1. This means the cursor has not been completely populated yet. Even if the @@CURSOR_ROWS variable returns a positive value, this value reflects the number of rows currently in the cursor. If the cursor contains too many rows,

SQL Server may return only a fraction of the qualifying rows. To read all the rows of a cursor, you should set up a WHILE loop, which keeps reading its rows with the FETCH NEXT statement until the @@CURSOR_ROWS variable returns –1.

To read a row from an open cursor, use the FETCH statement, which has the following variations:

FETCH FIRST	Reads the first row in the cursor
FETCH NEXT	Reads the next row in the cursor
FETCH PREVIOUS	Reads the previous row in the cursor
FETCH LAST	Reads the last row in the cursor

Of course, if the cursor was declared with the FORWARD_ONLY attribute, then only the FETCH NEXT and FETCH LAST statements can be used. The other two statements will result in an error.

In addition, you can use the ABSOLUTE and RELATIVE keywords to read a row by number or a row relative to the current one. The ABSOLUTE FETCH statement must be followed by a number, which is the row's number, and a FROM clause that specifies the cursor name. The statement:

```
ABSOLUTE FETCH 3 FROM Authors
```

will fetch the third row of the cursor. If you know the row's position with respect to the last row of the cursor, use a negative value. The statement:

```
ABSOLUTE FETCH -1 FROM Authors
```

will fetch the second to last row in the cursor.

If you use the FETCH statements previously listed, the fields of the row being fetched are displayed in the Query Analyzer's window. To process the field values of the current row further, you must store them into local variables. To do so, use the INTO keyword, which must be followed by a list of variables where the field values will be stored. The full syntax of the FETCH statement is

```
FETCH NEXT FROM cursor_name INTO <variable_list>
```

where *<variable_list>* is a comma delimited list with the names of the variables where the columns read by the FETCH statement end up. The variables must be declared with the same type as the table's column that will be stored in them. A column that stored integers should be stored into a variable declared as integer.

The following statements declare a number of variables, where the fields of the TitleAuthors table (in the Pubs database) will be stored. The FETCH NEXT statement reads all the fields of the next row in the table (or cursor) and stores them in the variables specified with the INTO keyword. Notice the fields are read in the order in which they appear in the table (or the order in which they were listed in the cursor's declaration) and the variables must match this order. After the execution of the FETCH NEXT statement, you can use these variables in your procedure.

```
DECLARE @currentTitleID varchar(6)
DECLARE @currentTitle varchar(80)
DECLARE @currentAuthorLName varchar(40)
DECLARE @currentAuthorFName varchar(20)
DECLARE @prevTitleID varchar(6)
FETCH NEXT FROM TitleAuthors INTO
     @currentTitleID, @currentTitle, @currentAuthorLName,
     @currentAuthorFName
```

For more information on scanning cursors and processing their rows, see the section "Understanding Stored Procedures and Cursors" in Chapter 16.

Updating Rows Through Cursors

As mentioned earlier, the default result set is not updateable. In other words, you can't edit the rows displayed in the Query Analyzer's Results or Results Grid pane. If you create a cursor, though, you can update its rows with a so-called *positioned UPDATE* statement. Normally, you'd issue an UPDATE WHERE statement to update a row, like the following one:

```
UPDATE Customers SET ContactName = 'Alfred and Sons'
    WHERE CustomerID = 'ALFKI'
```

SQL Server must locate the row with the specified ID and update it. If the rows of the Customers table belong to a cursor, you can use the WHERE CURRENT OF clause to update the current row:

```
UPDATE Customers SET ContactName = 'Alfred and Sons'
    WHERE CURRENT OF CustomersCursor
```

The WHERE CURRENT OF clause updates the column values of the current row in the cursor. To find out whether the changes took effect, issue a relative FETCH statement to read the row you just updated:

```
FETCH RELATIVE 0 FROM CustomersCursor
```

This technique works only if the cursor is updateable. If it was opened as READ_ONLY, none of the columns can be updated. Likewise, if a column holds totals or the result of some aggregate function, then it can't be updated.

Passing Arguments to Stored Procedures

Stored procedures are usually written as functions: they accept arguments and they return a value to the calling program. This value is usually a cursor, which the calling program can loop through and display its rows, process its columns, and so on. It is also possible for a stored procedure to return one or more single values, like the minimum and maximum values of a table column or a calculated value.

Stored procedures can be called from other applications, outside the SQL Engine. For example, a Visual Basic application can call a stored procedure through the Active Data Objects (ADO) and process the result set with VB statements. The examples in this chapter were designed with SQL Server 7.0, but the exact same procedures can be called from other programming environments as well.

Let's start with the structure of a stored procedure that accepts an argument and returns a numeric value. As you can guess, the argument and the procedure's return type must be defined along with the procedure. Let's write a procedure that counts the customers from Germany. Enter the following in the Query Analyzer's upper pane:

```
SELECT COUNT(*) FROM Customers
    WHERE Country='Germany'
```

If you execute this statement, the following appears in the window's lower pane:

```
11
(1 row(s) affected)
```

This is the number of German customers in the Customers table of the NorthWind database. To turn this simple T-SQL statement into a stored procedure, modify it as follows:

```
CREATE PROCEDURE GCustomers
AS
SELECT COUNT(*) FROM Customers
   WHERE Country='Germany'
```

These lines create a procedure, the GCustomers procedure, and attach it to the database. This procedure doesn't require any arguments and it doesn't return any values. Not a very useful one, but we revise it shortly. To execute the GCustomers procedure, clear the upper pane of the Query Analyzer window and enter the following statement:

```
EXECUTE GCustomers
```

The number of German customers in the Customers table are displayed. Now we'll revise the procedure, so it returns the number of customers in any single country, which is specified as argument when the procedure is called. Arguments must follow the name of the procedure and are declared like local variables, without the DECLARE keyword. To declare that the CountryCustomers procedure accepts one argument, the name of the country, use the following procedure declaration:

```
CREATE PROCEDURE CountryCustomers @WhichCountry nchar(20)
```

Then enter the AS keyword followed by the SQL statement that retrieves customers from a specific country. Use the name of the variable *@WhichCountry* in the place of the hard-coded country name:

```
CREATE PROCEDURE CountryCustomers @WhichCountry nchar(20)
AS
SELECT COUNT(*) FROM Customers
    WHERE Country = @WhichCountry
```

Execute the statement and the following message appears:

```
The command(s) completed successfully.
```

The stored procedure has been added to the database and you don't have to create it again. If you want to revise it further, change the T-SQL statements and replace the keyword CREATE with the keyword ALTER. Or, you can use the DROP statement to remove the stored procedure from the database:

```
DROP PROCEDURE CountryCustomers
```

You can save the procedure's declaration in a file with extension .SQL and then clear the upper pane of the Query Analyzer window. To test the CountryCustomers procedure, enter the following EXECUTE statement in the upper pane:

```
EXECUTE CountryCustomers @WhichCountry = 'Mexico'
```

When this statement is executed, the value 5 is displayed in the lower pane of the Query Analyzer window (the number of customers from Mexico).

Stored Procedures Returning Cursors

This is a more useful procedure, but most applications need more than a simple count. They need a cursor with the rows that correspond to the qualifying customers. Let's revise our stored procedure so it returns a cursor, which contains information about customers from a specific country.

This time we won't write a new stored procedure. Instead, we'll modify the CountryCustomers procedure with the ALTER PROCEDURE statement. If a stored procedure has already been declared (and attached to the database), you can redefine it by replacing the CREATE statement with the ALTER statement. You can drop the stored procedure with the DROP statement and then insert a new one, but you must set any permissions from scratch. The ALTER statement enables you to change the statements of the procedure, but its permissions remain the same.

To specify that the procedure must return a value, we must declare the name of the return value, its type, and the keyword OUTPUT (it indicates the direction of the parameter). If the procedure returns a cursor, then the output must be declared as CURSOR VARYING. Here's the modified procedure:

```
ALTER PROCEDURE CountryCustomers
@WhichCountry nchar(15),                    /* Argument (input) */
```

```
@CustomerCursor CURSOR VARYING OUTPUT    /* Result (output)   */
AS
SELECT CompanyName, ContactName, ContactTitle FROM Customers
    WHERE Country = @WhichCountry
```

The result set, which is also displayed in the lower pane of the Query Analyzer, is returned by the CountryCustomers procedure to the calling procedure (or external application). Notice the SQL statement that retrieves the desired rows from the database didn't change; only the declaration of the procedure changed. The name of the procedure is followed by a number of variables. Some of these variables are input variables (arguments). The output arguments are followed by the keyword OUTPUT. You can use the keyword INPUT to specify that a variable's value will be passed as argument to the procedure when it's called, but this is the default direction of the variable and you can omit the INPUT keyword.

To test the CountryCustomers procedure, declare a CURSOR variable, where the rows returned by the procedure will be stored. Then call the EXECUTE statement passing a value for the arguments and assign the local CURSOR variable to the procedure's OUTPUT variable. Here's how you can call the CountryCustomers procedure to retrieve a cursor with the customers in Mexico:

```
DECLARE @myCursor CURSOR
EXECUTE CountryCustomers @WhichCountry='Mexico',
                @CustomerCursor=@myCursor
```

Figure 17-1 shows the output created by the CountryCustomers stored procedure, when called with the 'Mexico' argument. The upper pane contains the cursor declaration and the EXECUTE statement that populates the cursor. The lower pane contains the rows returned by the stored procedure.

Notice how the result is assigned to the local cursor. We don't assign the name of the procedure's return argument (*@CustomerCursor*) to the local cursor variable (*@myCursor*), as one would probably expect. You must get used to this backward notation. If you switch the variable names in the assignment, SQL Server issues an error message, indicating the *@CustomerCursor* variable hasn't been declared.

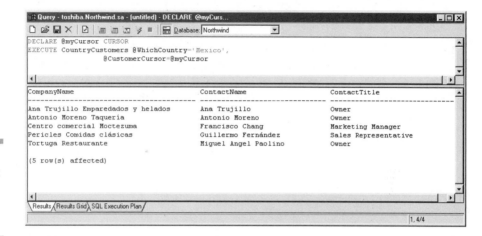

17

A stored
procedure that
returns a
cursor
Figure 17-1.

System Stored Procedures

SQL Server comes with a number of stored procedures, which you can use in your own procedures. Their names start with the sp_ and xp_ prefixes and there are too many to list in this book. Instead, you'll see how a few commonly used system procedures are used in custom stored procedures.

One of the simplest system procedures is the *xp_cmdshell procedure,* which executes an operating system command and returns the result as rows of text. A simple operating system command is the DIR command. To view the files and folders under the current folder, use the statement:

```
EXEC master..xp_cmdshell 'DIR'
```

Any argument you can pass to the DIR command, like DIR *.EXE, can also be used with the xp_cmdshell system procedure. For example, you can pass the argument 'DIR file_name' to find out whether a specific file (the one specified with the *file_name* argument) exists. Notice that the *xp_cmdshell* system procedure must be executed against the master database (most system procedures are executed against this database). Moreover, the name of the database is followed by two periods and the name of the system stored procedure.

Other system stored procedures perform common tasks, which you would have to code on your own. The xp_sscanf procedure, for example, parses a string and extracts its words into separate variables. The first parameter is the string to be parsed, the next argument is a string that specifies how the string is to be parsed, and it's followed by a number of output arguments, where the individual parts of the string will be stored. This procedure is similar to the sscanf() function of C, but only the %s formatting argument is supported (in other words, it can only extract words from the original string).

Let's say a variable holds a date in the *month day year* format and you want to retrieve the three parts of the date into separate variables. You could call the xp_sscanf procedure, as follows:

```
master..xp_sscanf @dateVar, '%s %s %s', @s1, @s2, @s3
```

where the @dateVar variable holds the date and the variables @s1, @s2, and @s3 will be assigned the month, day, and year parts of the date. To test the xp_sscanf system procedure, enter the following query in the Query Analyzer and execute it:

```
DECLARE @dateVar varchar(20)
DECLARE @s1 varchar(4), @s2 varchar(4), @s3 varchar(4)
SET @dateVar = 'May 12, 1999'
EXEC master..xp_sscanf @dateVar, '%s %s %s', @s1 OUTPUT,
                @s2 OUTPUT, @s3 OUTPUT
SELECT @s1 + '-' + @s2 + '-' + @s3
```

The sample code shown here produces the following output. Notice the comma after the day was interpreted as part of the second string. The xp_sscanf procedure parses strings and extracts string parts (while the sscanf() function of C can also extract numeric values).

```
May-12,-1999
```

Many stored procedures are used for administrative tasks, which are explored in the following section.

T-SQL for Administrators

T-SQL provides a number of statements for administrative purposes. As a database administrator, you may have to perform unusual tasks, which users are not allowed to perform through stored procedures or other means. Let's look at an operation that "violates" the integrity of the database. As you know, the customer's ID in the Customers table of the NorthWind database is used as a foreign key to the Orders table. Each order is related to a customer with the customer's ID. If you change the CustomerID field of a specific customer, then some orders will be left without a customer. For example, if you count all the orders and then total the orders for each customer, the two grand totals will not agree.

The NorthWind database contains a constraint that doesn't allow you to change a customer's ID. The following statement should change the ID of the customer Alfred's Futterkiste from ALFKI to ALFFI:

```
UPDATE Customers
    SET CustomerID='ALFFI'
    FROM Customers
    WHERE CustomerID='ALFKI'
```

If you execute it with the Query Analyzer, however, you get the following error message:

```
Server: Msg 547, Level 16, State 1
[Microsoft][ODBC SQL Server Driver][SQL Server]UPDATE statement
conflicted with COLUMN REFERENCE constraint 'FK_Orders_Customers'.
The conflict occurred in database 'Northwind', table 'Orders',
column 'CustomerID'.
```

To protect its integrity, the database itself won't let you change key columns. Let's say you have good reason to change a few customer IDs. After all, you're the administrator or owner of the database and you should be able to perform unusual tasks. The trick is to lift the *FK_Orders_Customers* constraint temporarily, change the ID, and then reinstate the constraint. Here's how you would bypass the *FK_Orders_Customers* constraint and modify the customer's ID:

```
ALTER TABLE Orders DROP CONSTRAINT FK_Orders_Customers
GO
UPDATE Customers
    SET CustomerID='ALFFI'
    FROM Customers
    WHERE CustomerID='ALFKI'
```

Of course, you must add the rule back to the database as soon as you are done with the changes. The following statement reinstates the *FK_Orders_Customers* constraint:

```
ALTER TABLE Orders ADD CONSTRAINT FK_Orders_Customers
FOREIGN KEY (CustomerID)
REFERENCES Customers (CustomerID)
```

Constraints are not simple to code in T-SQL but, fortunately, there's a simple method. You can have SQL Enterprise Manager write the T-SQL statements to build a primary or foreign key constraint. Because the constraint *FK_Orders_Customers* exists in the NorthWind database, you should write down its definition before dropping it from the database with the ALTER TABLE statement. Start the SQL Server Enterprise Manager, select the NorthWind database in the left pane, and select Database Diagrams. When the Relationships icon appears in the right pane, double-click it and you will see the Relationships diagram. Locate the Orders table in the diagram and right-click it. When the shortcut menu appears (see Figure 17-2) select Tasks | Generate SQL Scripts.

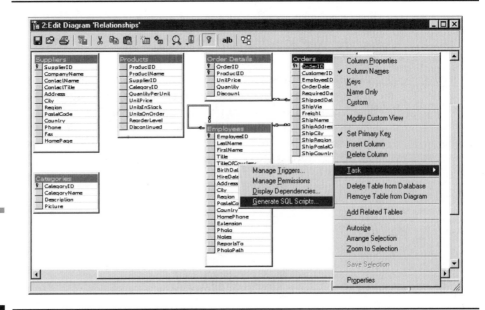

Viewing the scripts for the constraints on a database

Figure 17-2.

In the window that appears on your screen, select the Options tab and check the box Script PRIMARY and FOREIGN Keys. Then switch back to the General tab and click the Preview button. The Enterprise Manager generates the script for you and displays it in a separate window. This window shows the T-SQL code for generating the table and its constraints, as specified when the database was created. The following T-SQL code adds the *FK_Orders_Customers* constraint to the database:

```
CONSTRAINT [FK_Orders_Customers] FOREIGN KEY
(
    [CustomerID]
) REFERENCES [dbo].[Customers] (
    [CustomerID]
)
```

This is the code you must supply to the ALTER TABLE statement to add the *FK_Orders_Customers* constraint, which you dropped earlier from the database. The following T-SQL code drops the foreign key constraint *FK_Orders_Customers* from the Orders table, changes a value in a primary key column, and, finally, restores the dropped constraint:

```
ALTER TABLE Orders DROP CONSTRAINT FK_Orders_Customers
GO
UPDATE Customers
   SET CustomerID='ALFFI'
   FROM Customers
   WHERE CustomerID='ALFKI'
ALTER TABLE Orders ADD CONSTRAINT FK_Orders_Customers
FOREIGN KEY (CustomerID)
REFERENCES Customers (CustomerID)
```

Triggers

Being able to change the value of a column that's a foreign key to another table is of dubious value. By changing a customer's ID, you are going to leave a few "orphan" rows in the related table. In our case, the related table is the Orders table: some orders will reference to a nonexistent customer. This violates the integrity of the database and this is the very reason the *FK_Orders_Customers* constraint was introduced. If you must change a value in a primary or foreign key column, you must first change the matching values in the related table. Before you change the ID of a customer in the Customers table, you must change the same ID in the Orders table (it may appear in multiple rows) and then change the ID of the same customer in the Customers table. This way, the specific customer's orders will refer to the same customer.

You can write a procedure that changes the dependent rows in the Orders table and then change the ID of the corresponding customer in the Customer table. A better approach is to define a procedure that's invoked automatically every time the CustomerID column of the Customers table is modified. This way, you won't have to rely on database programmers to ensure the integrity of your database.

The trigger we are about to add to our database is a stored procedure, which is invoked automatically when the Customers table is modified. When the CustomerID is modified, either through the Query Analyzer or through a stored procedure, our trigger kicks in and changes this customer's orders automatically. To add a trigger to the database, use the following statements:

```
CREATE TRIGGER CascadeCustomerIDChange
    ON Customers
    FOR UPDATE
    AS
        IF UPDATE(CustomerID)
        BEGIN
            DECLARE @newID varchar(5)
            DECLARE @oldID varchar(5)
            SELECT @newID = CustomerID FROM inserted
            SELECT @oldID = CustomerID FROM deleted
            UPDATE Orders
                SET Orders.CustomerID = @newID
                WHERE Orders.CustomerID = @oldID
        END
```

The CascadeCustomerIDChange trigger is invoked automatically every time a customer's ID is changed. Let's test our trigger first and then examine its implementation. Clear the upper pane of the Query Analyzer's window and enter the following code to change a customer's ID:

```
ALTER TABLE Orders DROP CONSTRAINT FK_Orders_Customers
GO
UPDATE Customers SET CustomerID='ALFFI'
    WHERE CustomerID='ALFKI'
ALTER TABLE Orders ADD CONSTRAINT FK_Orders_Customers
FOREIGN KEY (CustomerID)
REFERENCES Customers (CustomerID)
```

and you see the following in the Results pane:

```
(6 row(s) affected)
(1 row(s) affected)
```

The first row was generated by the trigger and the second row by the statement. If you retrieve all orders by the customer ALFFI, there will be six lines:

17

```
SELECT * FROM ORDERS
    WHERE CustomerID='ALFFI'
```

If you specify the old ID (ALFKI), no rows are returned.

The CREATE TRIGGER statement is similar to the CREATE PROCEDURE statement. It is followed by the name of the trigger and the keyword ON, which specifies the table on which the trigger will act. The FOR keyword must be followed by the name of an action that invokes the trigger: UPDATE, INSERT, and DELETE. Obviously, if you write a trigger that's invoked every time a row of the Customers table is updated, you should also write a similar trigger that's invoked every time a customer is deleted. If you allow customers to be deleted, you should also remove the orders (and the corresponding details) placed by the specific customers. Following the AS keyword, you specify the T-SQL code to be executed every time the Customers table is updated.

Notice the items *inserted* and *deleted*. These are not variables, but temporary rows that hold the values of the columns. *inserted* contains the values you're about to insert into the table and *deleted* contains the original values. You can retrieve any column's value by specifying its name with the FROM keyword, as shown in the example.

Jobs

The last type of procedure you can attach to a database is a job. Many tasks, such as backups and restores, are repeated at regular intervals. A *job* is a special type of procedure that can contain one or more steps. The simplest method of specifying jobs is to use the Enterprise Manager. In the Job Properties window, you can specify new jobs (or alter existing ones), add steps to them, and schedule them for execution.

You can also do the same with T-SQL. The process of creating and scheduling jobs for your databases involves several steps, which are outlined here:

1. First add a job to the database.
2. Then add one or more steps to the job.
3. Next notify the SQL Server Agent about the job.
4. Finally, specify how often the job must be executed.

To add a job to a database, you must call the *sp_add_job* system procedure with the EXEC statement. You must always use the msdb database to add jobs to a database (or steps to a job). The *sp_add_job* procedure accepts a single parameter, the *@job_name* parameter, which is the name of the job.

Let's say you want to create a job that generates a report every week (or any other interval you specify). If the name of the job is Weekly Report, you can use the following statements to add it to the database:

```
USE msdb
GO
EXEC sp_add_job @job_name = 'Weekly Report'
```

To add a step to a job, call the *sp_add_jobstep* procedure. The *sp_add_jobstep* procedure recognizes several parameters, which are shown here:

Parameter	Description
@job_name	The name of the job to which the step is added
@step_name	The name of the step
@command	T-SQL statements to carry out the desired task
@database_name	The name of the database on which the T-SQL statements will act
@server	The name of the server on which the job will be executed
@output_file_name	The name of a disk file, to which any output of the T-SQL statements will be redirected

17

To add a step to the Weekly Report job, use the following statements:

```
USE msdb
GO
EXEC sp_add_jobstep
    @job_name = 'Weekly Report',
    @step_name = 'WeekSales',
    @command = 'SELECT * FROM Orders',
    @database_name='NorthWind',
    @output_file_name='WReport.dat',
    @server='EXPERTNEW'
```

The @command parameter is quite rudimentary for the purposes of this example. You can use a more complicated command, like the following one, which retrieves the orders placed in a specific week:

```
@command='SELECT CompanyName, Orders.OrderID, ProductName,
        UnitPrice=ROUND([Order Details].UnitPrice, 2),
        Quantity, Discount=CONVERT(int, Discount*100),
        ExtendedPrice=ROUND(CONVERT(money,
        Quantity*(1-Discount)*[Order Details].UnitPrice, 2)
        FROM Products, [Order Details], Customers, Orders
        WHERE [Order Details].ProductID=Products.ProductID and
        [Order Details].OrderID = Orders.OrderID and
        Orders.CustomerID=Customers.CustomerID and
        Orders.OrderDate <''01/01/95'' and
        Orders.OrderDate <''07/01/95''
        ORDER BY Customers.CustomerID, Orders.OrderID
        COMPUTE SUM(ROUND(CONVERT(money, Quantity * (1-Discount)
            * [Order Details].UnitPrice), 2))
            BY Customers.CustomerID, Orders.OrderID
        COMPUTE SUM(ROUND(CONVERT(money, Quantity * (1-Discount)
            * [Order Details].UnitPrice), 2))
            BY Customers.CustomerID'
```

NOTE: The preceding SQL statement is based on one of the examples in the previous chapter. You should use the time and date manipulation functions to specify the starting and ending date of the current week, so you won't have to modify the job's SQL statements every week.

Next, we must tell the SQL Server Agent about the new job and where it must execute it (the name of the server):

```
USE msdb
GO
EXEC sp_add_jobserver @job_name = 'Weekly Report',
                      @server_name = 'EXPERTNEW'
```

At this point, you can execute the job by calling the *sp_start_job* procedure, which starts the job immediately:

```
USE msdb
GO
EXEC sp_start_job @job_name = 'Weekly Report'
```

Job Scheduling

Jobs are rarely executed manually. We schedule them, so they are executed at regular intervals or on specific dates and time. To schedule a job, you must use the sp_add_jobschedule system procedure and set one or more of the following parameters to the appropriate value: @freq_type, @freq_interval, @freq_subday_type, @freq_subday_interval, and @freq_recurrence_factor. The @freq_type parameter specifies the interval used in measuring the frequency of the job and can have one of values shown here:

Value	Frequency Type
1	Once
4	Daily
8	Weekly
16	Monthly
32	Monthly (relative to the @freq_interval parameter)
64	When the SQL Server Agent is started

The @freq_subday_type parameter is quite similar, only it specifies smaller interval types, as listed here:

Value	Frequency Type
1	At specified time
2	Seconds
3	Minutes
4	Hours

The @freq_interval parameter specifies the day on which the job will be run. The values are as follows:

Value	Interval
1	Sunday
2	Monday
3	Tuesday
4	Wednesday
5	Thursday
6	Friday
7	Saturday
8	day
9	weekdays
10	weekends

Finally, the @freq_subday_interval parameter specifies the number of intervals (as specified by the @freq_subday_type parameter) to elapse between successive invocations of the job. The @freq_recurrence_factor parameter specifies the recurrence of the job. If you want a job to run every week, set the @freq_type parameter to 8 (weekly) and the @freq_recurrence_factor parameter to 1. If you want a job to run twice a month, set @freq_recurrence_factor to 2.

The following statements will schedule the Weekly Report job to be executed every Monday at midnight:

```
USE msdb
GO
EXEC sp_add_jobschedule @job_name='Weekly Report',
                        @name='WeekShedule,
                        @freq_type=8,
                        @freq_interval=2,
                        @freq_subday_type=1,
                        @freq_recurence_factor=1
```

To modify a job, step, or schedule, use the procedures sp_update_job, sp_update_step and sp_update_schedule, respectively, and specify the parameters you want to modify.

What's Next?

This chapter concludes our exploration of T-SQL, the language of Microsoft's SQL Server. You have seen the elements of T-SQL and how to use it to build stored procedures, triggers, and schedule maintenance jobs. You have also learned how to build cursors, which are at the heart of programming SQL Server. In the following chapters, you find out how to program the SQL Server from within other environments, such as Visual Basic and Visual C++, as well as the basics of other DBMS programming languages, such as Oracle's PL/SQL and Sybase's Interactive SQL.

CHAPTER 18

SQL*Plus

Are you aware that you are already using SQL*Plus? You see, you are using SQL*Plus to run the Oracle SQL code examples. SQL*Plus (pronounced *sequel plus*) is a program used in conjunction with the SQL database language and its procedural language extension, PL/SQL (Chapter 19).

With SQL*Plus, you can manipulate SQL commands and PL/SQL blocks, and you can perform the following tasks:

◆ Enter, edit, store, retrieve, and run SQL commands and PL/SQL blocks. A *block* is a group of SQL and PL/SQL commands related to one another through procedural logic.

◆ Format, perform calculations on, store, and print query results in the form of reports.

◆ List column definitions for tables.

◆ Access and copy data between SQL databases.

◆ Send messages to and accept responses from an end user.

You can accomplish these tasks by entering three kinds of commands at the command prompt:

◆ SQL commands, for working with information in the database.

◆ PL/SQL blocks, also for working with information in the database.

◆ SQL*Plus commands for formatting query results, setting options, and editing and storing SQL commands and PL/SQL blocks.

So let's begin by learning how to enter commands into SQL*Plus.

Getting Around in SQL*Plus

To enter a command into SQL*Plus, type the command you wish to enter. You separate the words in a command from each other by a space or a tab. You can use additional spaces or tabs between words to make the commands easier to read.

How you continue a command on additional lines, end a command, or execute a command differs depending on the type of command you enter and run. You have an opportunity to learn these different commands in the following section.

Log On

Figure 18-1 is the SQL*Plus Log On window. You enter your user name, password, and the host string that connects you to your Oracle database. Figure 18-2 is the Oracle SQL*Plus window where you enter and run your commands. The SQL> prompt means it is ready for you to enter your commands. After you enter the command and SQL*Plus processes the command, it then redisplays the command prompt, indicating you can enter another command.

18

Entering a SQL*Plus Command

In the following example, you enter a simple select statement. You process the command and the results are shown in Figure 18-3.

```
Select ENAME,JOB, HIREDATE
From Emp
Where Sal > 1000;
```

If you are still on the first line of the command, you can use BACKSPACE to erase it and re-enter. When you are finished, press RETURN to move to the next line. The semicolon (;) means this is the end of the command. Press

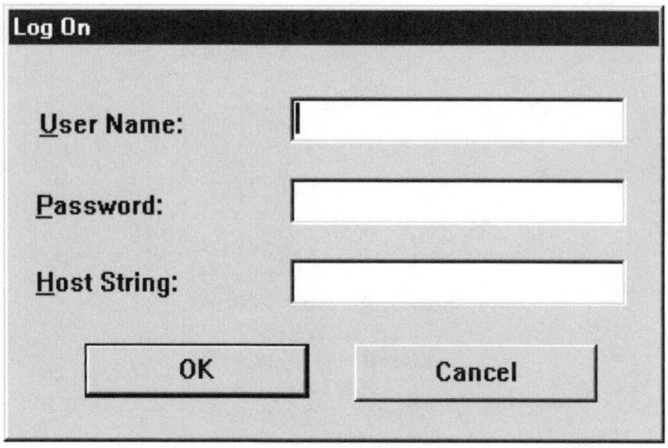

SQL*Plus
Log On
window

Figure 18-1.

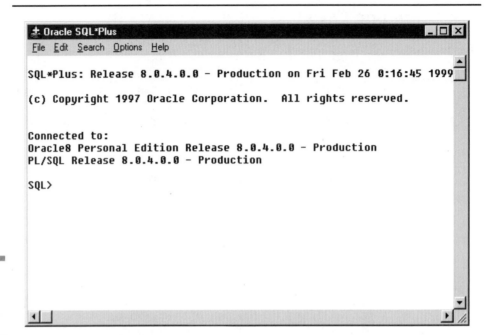

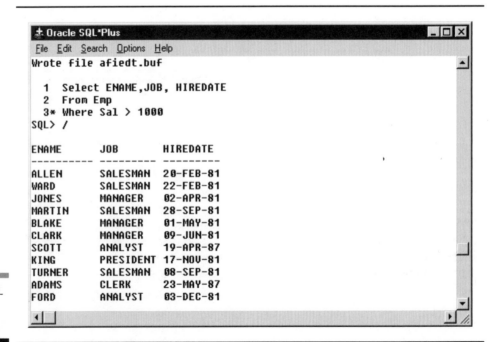

RETURN and SQL*Plus processes the command and displays the results. After the results are processed, the command prompt displays again.

You can divide your SQL command into separate lines at any point as long as you do not split a word between lines. As you know, most SQL commands are divided into clauses, one clause on each line.

Ending SQL Commands

18

You can end an SQL command in one of three ways:

◆ With a semicolon (;)
◆ With a slash (/) on a line by itself
◆ With a blank line

A semicolon (;) tells SQL*Plus you need to run the command. A slash (/) on a line by itself also tells SQL*Plus you want to run a command. A blank line indicates you are finished entering commands, but you don't want to run it. It does not execute the command, but stores it in the SQL buffer. If you enter another command, SQL*Plus will overwrite the previous command. You need to be careful when you use the "blank line."

Creating Stored Procedures

Stored procedures are PL/SQL functions, packages, or procedures. To create stored procedures, you use SQL CREATE commands. The following SQL CREATE commands are used to create stored procedures:

◆ Create Function
◆ Create Package
◆ Create Package Body
◆ Create Procedure
◆ Create Trigger

Entering any of these commands places you in PL/SQL mode where you can enter your PL/SQL subprogram. You learn more about PL/SQL in the next chapter.

When you finish typing your PL/SQL subprogram, enter a period (.) on a line by itself to terminate PL/SQL mode. To run the SQL command and create the stored procedure, you must enter RUN or slash (/). A semicolon will not execute these CREATE commands.

The SQL Buffer

The area where SQL*Plus stores your most recently entered SQL command or PL/SQL block is called the *SQL buffer.* The command or block remains there until you enter another. SQL*Plus does not store the semicolon or the slash you type to execute a command in the SQL buffer. In the next section, you learn about editing or rerunning commands or blocks stored in the buffer.

Table 18-1 shows the most common SQL*Plus commands you use to examine or change the command in the buffer without re-entering the command.

The following paragraphs discuss these editing commands in more detail. Any editing command, other than LIST and DEL, affects only a single line in the buffer. This line is the current line and is marked with an asterisk when you list the current command or block.

LIST   This command gives you one or more lines in the SQL buffer. The following is an example of LIST:

```
SQL> list
  1  select sal
  2* from emp
```

Notice the semicolon usually entered at the end of the SELECT command is not listed. This semicolon is necessary to mark the end of the command when you enter it, but SQL*Plus does not store it in the SQL buffer. This makes editing more convenient.

Command	Abbreviation	Purpose
APPEND text	A text	Adds text at the end of a line
CHANGE /old/new	C /old/new	Changes old to new in a line
CLEAR BUFFER	CL BUFF	Deletes all lines
DEL	(none)	Deletes the current line
INPUT	I	Adds one or more lines
LIST	L	Lists all lines in the SQL buffer

SQL*Plus
Editing
Commands

Table 18-1.

The last line listed becomes the new current line (marked by an asterisk). So line 2 is the current line.

CHANGE This command enables you to edit the current line. Various actions determine which line is the current line:

◆ LIST a given line to make it the current line.

◆ When you LIST or RUN the command in the buffer, the last line of the command becomes the current line.

◆ If you get an error message, the line containing the error automatically becomes the current line.

18

Here is an example of CHANGE:

```
SQL> select dptno, ename, sal
2  from emp
3  where deptno = 10;
select dptno, ename, sal
      *
ERROR at line 1:
ORA-00904: invalid column name
```

The deptno has been misspelled. Instead of retyping the entire command, you can correct the mistake by editing the command in the buffer. The line containing the error is now the current line. Use the CHANGE command to correct the mistake:

```
SQL> change /dptno/deptno
  1* select deptno, ename, sal
SQL> run
  1  select deptno, ename, sal
  2  from emp
  3* where deptno = 10

    DEPTNO  ENAME           SAL
---------- ---------- ----------
        10  CLARK          2450
        10  KING           5000
        10  MILLER         1300
```

CHANGE changes the first occurrence of the old text on the current line of the buffer to the new text. The current line is marked with an asterisk. You can also use CHANGE to modify a line in the buffer that has generated an Oracle error. SQL*Plus sets the buffer's current line to the line containing the error so you can make modifications.

INPUT   If you want to add another line to your SQL command, you would enter INPUT at the SQL prompt. SQL*Plus then prompts you for the new line:

```
SQL> input
  4  and deptno = 20
```

Press RETURN again to indicate you will not enter any more lines. Then use RUN to verify and rerun the query.

APPEND   When you want to add text to the end of a line in the buffer, use the APPEND command:

1. Use the LIST command (or just the line number) to list the line you want to change.
2. Enter APPEND followed by the text you want to add. If the text you want to add begins with a blank, separate the word APPEND from the first character of the text by two blanks. One blank to separate APPEND from the text and one blank to go into the buffer with the text.

```
SQL> append order by sal desc
  3* where deptno = 10 order by sal desc
SQL> run
  1  select deptno, ename, sal
  2  from emp
  3* where deptno = 10 order by sal desc

    DEPTNO ENAME           SAL
---------- ---------- ----------
        10 KING '        5000
        10 CLARK          2450
        10 MILLER         1300
```

DEL   To delete lines in the buffer, use the DEL command. Use the LIST command (or just the line numbers) to list the lines you want to delete. Then enter DEL with an optional clause. Let's delete the order by line you just added:

```
SQL> DEL * LAST
SQL> list
  1  select deptno, ename, sal
  2* from emp
```

Notice only lines 1 and 2 are still available. This is because line 3 had the
order by line appended to it and it was, indeed, the last line.

CLEAR Option   This command resets or erases the current value or setting
for the specified option. If you wish to clear the buffer, you would add
"buffer" as the option. The CLEAR command enables you to clear breaks,
buffers, columns, computes, screen, SQL, and timing.

18

```
SQL> clear buffer
buffer cleared
SQL> list
No lines in SQL buffer.
```

Another handy command is the EDIT command. You can run your host
operating system's default text editor without leaving SQL*Plus by entering
the EDIT command. EDIT loads the contents of the buffer into your system's
default text editor. You can then edit the text with the text editor's
commands. When you tell the text editor to save edited text and then exit,
the text is loaded back into the buffer. Figure 18-4 shows the text editor for
the Windows host.

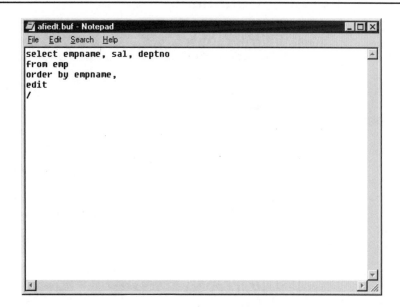

SQL*Plus
editor

Figure 18-4.

Saving Commands

You can store one or more commands in a file called a *command file*. Once you create this file, you can retrieve, edit, and run it. You can use this feature to save your complex commands and your PL/SQL blocks.

To save the current SQL command for later use, you must enter the SAVE command:

```
SQL> SAVE file_name
```

SQL*Plus adds the extension SQL to the file name to identify it as a SQL query file. If you wish to name a different extension, type a period after the file name and then your extension.

```
SQL> list
  1  select deptno, ename, sal
  2  from emp
  3  where deptno = 10
  4* order by sal desc
save deptinfo
Created file deptinfo
```

Running Command Files

The START command retrieves a command file and runs the command(s) it contains. Use START to run a command file containing SQL commands, PL/SQL blocks, and/or SQL*Plus commands. Follow the word START with the name of the file:

```
SQL> start deptinfo
    DEPTNO ENAME            SAL
---------- ---------- ----------
        10 KING            5000
        10 CLARK           2450
        10 MILLER          1300
```

You can also use the @ command to run a command file:

```
SQL> @ deptinfo
    DEPTNO ENAME            SAL
---------- ---------- ----------
        10 KING            5000
        10 CLARK           2450
        10 MILLER          1300
```

The @ command lists and runs the commands in the specified command file in the same manner as START.

Because commands and PL/SQL blocks can get complicated, being able to add comments is always nice. You can add comments in one of three ways:

◆   Using the SQL*Plus REMARK command

◆   Using the SQL comment delimiters, /*...*/

◆   Using ANSI/ISO comments, --

Use the REMARK command on a line by itself in the command file, followed by comments on the same line. If you need to have more than one comment line, enter another REMARK command on each line where you will input a comment.

```
REMARK Salary Report
REMARK Run this report weekly
Select empnno, empname, sal
From Emp
where deptno = 50;
```

Use the SQL comments delimiters, /*...*/, on separate lines in your command file, on the same line as the SQL command, or on a line in a PL/SQL block. The comments can span multiple lines, but cannot be nested within one another:

```
/* Salary  Report
to be run weekly */
Select empnno, empname, sal
From Emp
where deptno = 50;
```

Finally, use the ANSI/ISO "--" (two-dash characters) style comments within SQL statements, PL/SQL blocks, or SQL*Plus commands. No ending delimiter exists; the comment cannot span multiple lines.

```
--Salary Report to be run weekly
Select empno, empname, sal
From Emp
Where deptno = 50;
```

Retrieving Command Files

You can retrieve a command file from the buffer by using the SQL*Plus command GET:

```
SQL> GET deptinfo

  1  select deptno, ename, sal
  2  from emp
  3  where deptno = 10
  4* order by sal desc
```

This command only retrieves the query; it does not run it. You would use the START command to run it.

Writing Interactive Commands

An *interactive command* is one in which the end user is allowed to input:

◆ Defining user variables

◆ Substituting values in commands

◆ Using the START command to provide values

◆ Prompting for values

You can define user variables for repeated use in a single command file by using the SQL*Plus command DEFINE. For example,

```
SQL> define employee = Smith
SQL> define employee
DEFINE EMPLOYEE        = "Smith" (CHAR)
```

You may use DEFINE to define variables that have a CHAR value. To delete a user variable, use the command UNDEFINE followed by the variable name.

```
SQL> undefine employee
```

Substitution Variables

A *substitution variable* is a user variable name preceded by one or two ampersands (&). When SQL*Plus sees a substitution variable in a command, SQL*Plus executes the command as though it contained the value of the substitution variable, rather than the variable itself.

For example, here is a use for the substitution variable in a WHERE clause:

```
1  Select ename, sal
2  from emp
```

```
3* where deptno = &department
SQL> /
Enter value for department: 10
old    3: where deptno = &department
new    3: where deptno = 10
ENAME           SAL
---------- ----------
CLARK          2450
KING           5000
MILLER         1300
```

This variable required user input, a reason this is an interactive query.

You cannot use substitution variables in the buffer editing commands, APPEND, CHANGE, DEL, and INPUT, or in other commands where substitution would be meaningless, such as REMARK.

Three SQL*Plus commands—PROMPT, ACCEPT, and PAUSE—enable you to communicate with the end user.

Through PROMPT and ACCEPT, you can send messages to the end user and accept values as end-user input. PROMPT displays a message you specify onscreen; use it to give directions or information to the user. ACCEPT prompts the user for a value and stores it in the user variable you specify. Use PROMPT in conjunction with ACCEPT when your prompt for the value spans more than one line. Here is an example of PROMPT and ACCEPT:

```
SQL> input
1   prompt Enter a title up to 30 characters long.
2   Accept mytitle prompt 'title: '
3   ttitle left mytitle skip 2
4   select * from dept
5
SQL> save prompt1 replace
Wrote file prompt1
SQL> start prompt1
Enter a title up to 30 characters long.
title: My Report is Very Interesting

My Report is Very Interesting
    DEPTNO DNAME          LOC
---------- -------------- -------------
        10 ACCOUNTING     NEW YORK
        20 RESEARCH       DALLAS
        30 SALES          CHICAGO
        40 OPERATIONS     BOSTON
```

Before we venture into formatting your query results, you should know one more command. The DESCRIBE command is a handy command to use when you want to know about a specific table. The DESCRIBE command lists the column definitions for a table, view, or synonym or the specification for a function or procedure.

The description for tables, views, types, and synonyms contains information about each column's name, whether or not it accepts NULLs, the data type, and the precision and scale of columns. The description of functions and procedures contains information about the type of PL/SQL object, the name of the function or procedure, the type of value returned (for functions) and the argument names, types, whether they are input or output, and default values. Let's describe the Emp table:

```
00:51:39 SQL> desc emp
 Name                                      Null?    Type
 ---------------------------------------  --------  ----
 EMPNO                                    NOT NULL NUMBER(4)
 ENAME                                             VARCHAR2(10)
 JOB                                               VARCHAR2(9)
 MGR                                               NUMBER(4)
 HIREDATE                                          DATE
 SAL                                               NUMBER(7,2)
 COMM                                              NUMBER(7,2)
 DEPTNO                                            NUMBER(2)
```

One more command you always run into is SET. The *SET command* sets a system variable to alter the SQL*Plus environment for your current session, such as:

◆   The display width for NUMBER data

◆   The display width for LONG data

◆   Enabling or disabling the printing of column headings

◆   The number of lines per page

You see the SET command in action later in this chapter.

Formatting Queries

This section explains how you can format your queries in SQL*Plus and turn them into reports. The first place to start formatting is usually with the columns within the query. Of course, this is just a suggestion.

Columns

The COLUMN command enables you to change the column headings and reformat the column data in your query results. You can either use the default heading or you can change it using the COLUMN command. Default column names are usually short and nondescriptive. In your example, you create a report for the Emp table and provide new headings for Deptno, Ename, and Sal by entering the following commands:

```
SQL> column deptno heading department
SQL> column ename heading employee
SQL> column sal heading Salary
SQL> column comm heading Commission
SQL> Select Deptno, Ename, Sal, Comm
2   from Emp

My Report is Very Interesting

department employee      Salary Commission
---------- ---------- ---------- ----------
        20 SMITH            800
        30 ALLEN           1600        300
        30 WARD            1250        500
        20 JONES           2975
        30 MARTIN          1250       1400
        30 BLAKE           2850
        10 CLARK           2450
        20 SCOTT           3000
        10 KING            5000
My Report is Very Interesting

department employee      Salary Commission
---------- ---------- ---------- ----------
        30 TURNER          1500          0
        20 ADAMS           1100
        30 JAMES            950
        20 FORD            3000
        10 MILLER          1300

14 rows selected.
```

To display a NUMBER column, you can either accept the SQL*Plus default display width or you can change it using the COLUMN command. A NUMBER column's width equals the width of the heading or the width of the

FORMAT plus one space for the sign, whichever is greater. If you do not use FORMAT, then the column's width will be at least the value of SET NUMWIDTH (usually 10).

You can choose a different format for any NUMBER column by using a format model in a COLUMN command. A format model is a representation of the way you want the numbers in the column to appear, using 9s to represent digits.

For instance, you want to add a format to the Sal column in your query.

```
SQL> Column SAL format $99,990
SQL> /

My Report is Very Interesting

           Employee
department Name        Salary Commission
---------- ---------- -------- ----------
        20 SMITH          $800
        30 ALLEN        $1,600        300
        30 WARD         $1,250        500
        20 JONES        $2,975
        30 MARTIN       $1,250       1400
        30 BLAKE        $2,850
        10 CLARK        $2,450
        20 SCOTT        $3,000
```

Use a zero in your format model, as shown here, when you use other formats such as a dollar sign and wish to display a zero in place of a blank for zero values.

To set the width of a column, do the following:

```
Column ENAME format A4
           Empl
department Name Salary Commission
---------- ---- -------- ----------
        20 FORD $3,000
        10 MILL $1,300
           ER
```

The name column wraps around one line. If the Set Wrap On were set to Off, the name would truncate and not wrap. You can list the column display attributes for all columns in your query by entering the COLUMN command with no column names or clauses after it. Here is a segment of the results:

```
SQL> column
COLUMN    comm ON
HEADING   'Commission'

COLUMN    com ON
HEADING   'Commission'
COLUMN    SAL ON
HEADING   'Salary'
FORMAT    $99,990

COLUMN    ENAME ON
HEADING   'Employee|Name' headsep '|'
FORMAT    A4

COLUMN    deptno ON
HEADING   'department'
```

If you need to reset all columns, type CLEAR COLUMNS and all columns
will be cleared.

Detailing Your Report with BREAK and COMPUTE

When you use ORDER BY in your query, rows with the same value in the
ordered column are displayed together in your output. You can make this
output more attractive if you use BREAK and COMPUTE commands to create
subsets of records and add space and/or summary lines after each subset.

BREAK

The column you use in a BREAK command is called a *break column*. If you
include the break column in your Order By clause, you create meaningful
subsets of records in your output. You then may add formatting to the
subsets within the same BREAK command and add a summary line
(containing totals and averages) by specifying the break column in a
COMPUTE command.

For example, you can create a meaningful report by using BREAK:

```
SQL> break on deptno

SQL> select deptno, ename, sal
2   from emp
3   where sal < 3500
4   order by deptno;
```

```
            Employee
department  Name         Salary
----------  ----------   --------
        10  CLARK        $2,450
            MILLER       $1,300
        20  SMITH          $800
            SCOTT        $3,000
            FORD         $3,000
            ADAMS        $1,100
            JONES        $2,975
        30  ALLEN        $1,600
```

To place one blank line between departments, enter the following command:

```
BREAK ON DEPTNO SKIP 1
```

```
            Employee
department  Name         Salary
----------  ----------   --------
        10  CLARK        $2,450
            MILLER       $1,300

        20  SMITH          $800
            SCOTT        $3,000
            FORD         $3,000
            ADAMS        $1,100
            JONES        $2,975
```

You can clear breaks by the CLEAR BREAKS command.

COMPUTE

For the computations to occur, the following conditions must all be true:

◆ One or more of the expressions, columns, or column aliases you reference in the OF clause must also be in the SELECT command.

◆ The expression, column, or column alias you reference in the On clause must occur in the SELECT command and in the most recent BREAK command.

◆ If you reference either ROW or REPORT in the On clause, also reference ROW or REPORT in the most recent BREAK command.

For example, this report calculates the total of salaries less than $1,000 on a report:

```
SQL> COMPUTE SUM OF SAL ON REPORT
SQL> BREAK ON REPORT
```

```
SQL> COLUMN DUMMY HEADING ''
SQL> Select '      ' DUMMY, SAL, EMPNO
2   From Emp
3   Where Sal < 1000
4   Order By Sal;

My Report is Very Interesting

     Salary      EMPNO
---- -------- ----------
         $800       7369
         $950       7900
     --------
sum    $1,750
```

Remember, the COMPUTE command has no effect without a BREAK command. To remove COMPUTE definitions and the BREAK definition, enter the following commands: CLEAR BREAKS and CLEAR COMPUTES.

Page and Report Titles and Dimensions

The TTITLE command defines the top titles; the BTITLE command defines the bottom title. You can also set a header and a footer for each report. The REPHEADER command defines the header; the REPFOOTER command defines the footer. These commands consist of the command name followed by one or more clauses specifying a position or format and a CHAR value you wish to place in that position or give that format. Table 18-2 represents the most commonly used clauses for formatting titles and report headers and footers.

The following example illustrates how to place a top and bottom title on a page:

```
SQL> TTITLE CENTER -

>    'SALARY REPORT PERSONNEL'
SQL> BTITLE CENTER 'COMPANY CONFIDENTIAL'
SQL> /
                          SALARY REPORT PERSONNEL

     Salary      EMPNO
---- -------- ----------
         $800       7369
         $950       7900
     --------
sum    $1,750


                    COMPANY CONFIDENTIAL
```

18

Common
Clauses of
TTITLE,
BTITLE,
REPHEADER,
and
REPFOOTER
Table 18-2.

Clause	Example	Description
COL n	COL 72	Makes the next CHAR value appear in the specified column
SKIP n	SKIP 2	Skips to a new line *n* times
LEFT	LEFT	Left-align the following CHAR value
CENTER	CENTER	Centers the following CHAR value
RIGHT	RIGHT	Right-aligns the following CHAR value

You may want to create a report that displays two different managers' employee numbers, each at the top of a separate page, and the people reporting to the manager on the same page as the manager's employee number. First, create a variable, MGRVAR, to hold the value of the current manager's employee number:

```
SQL> COLUMN MGR New_Value MGRVAR NOPRINT
```

The NOPRINT clause tells SQL*Plus not to print the column MGR. Next, include a label and the value in your page title, and then enter the proper BREAK command.

```
SQL> COLUMN MGR NEW_VALUE MGRVAR NOPRINT
SQL> TTITLE LEFT 'Manager: ' MGRVAR SKIP 2
SQL> SELECT MGR, ENAME, SAL, DEPTNO
2   FROM EMP
3   WHERE MGR in (7698, 7839)
4   ORDER BY MGR;

Manager:        7698

Employee
Name        Salary department
---------- -------- ----------
ALLEN       $1,600          30
WARD        $1,250          30
TURNER      $1,500          30
MARTIN      $1,250          30
JAMES         $950          30
JONES       $2,975          20
BLAKE       $2,850          30
```

```
                         COMPANY CONFIDENTIAL

Manager:        7839

Employee
Name         Salary  department
----------  --------  ----------
CLARK         $2,450         10
            --------
            $14,825

                         COMPANY CONFIDENTIAL
```

18

This nearly covers the formatting part of this chapter. You may want to know about one final item: setting page dimensions.

Setting Page Dimensions

A page of a report contains the number of blank line(s) set in the NEWPAGE variable of the SET command, a top title, column headings, your query results, and a bottom title. What happens if your report is too long?

The default page dimensions are

◆ Number of lines before the top title: 1

◆ Number of lines per page, from the top title to the bottom of the page: 24

◆ Number of characters per line: 80

You can change these dimensions.

Let's change the settings of a page.

```
SQL> set pagesize 44
SQL> set newpage 0
SQL> set linesize 24
SQL> /
Manager:        7698

Employee
Name         Salary  department
----------  --------  ----------

ALLEN         $1,600        30
WARD          $1,250        30
```

```
TURNER        $1,500         30
MARTIN        $1,250         30
JAMES           $950         30
JONES         $2,975         20
BLAKE         $2,850         30
CLARK         $2,450         10
              --------
              $14,825
```

```
COMPANY CONFIDENTIAL
```

To list the current values of these variables, use the SHOW command:

```
SQL> SHOW Pagesize
pagesize 44
SQL> SHOW newpage
newpage 0
SQL> SHOW Linesize
linesize 24
```

Through the SQL*Plus command SPOOL, you can store your query results in a file or print them on your computer's default printer. To store the results of a query in a file, enter the SPOOL command in the following form:

```
SQL> SPOOL REPORT1
```

To get the report to print, you would issue the command: SPOOL OUT.

As you now know, quite a few commands are available in SQL*Plus. You have just learned the most common and the most useful commands.

What's Next?

In Chapter 19, you get an introduction to PL/SQL, Oracle's programming language for SQL. You are nearing the end of this book. Chapter 20 covers the use of SQL within other programming languages, such as Visual C, Visual Basic, and Java. Then you learn how to troubleshoot your errors in Chapter 21. The last chapter, Chapter 22, covers what promises to be a better SQL standard, SQL3.

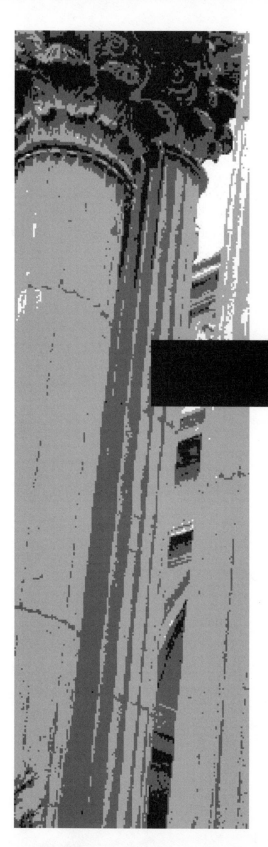

CHAPTER 19

PL/SQL Basics

PL/SQL is Oracle's procedural language. *PL/SQL* stands for Procedural Language/Structured Query Language. PL/SQL has so much richness, you cannot completely cover the language in just one chapter (see the appendix for books on PL/SQL). This is why this chapter covers only the basics of PL/SQL. In this chapter, you learn about the block structure, datatypes, writing PL/SQL functions, IF statements, and loops. Then you write packages and procedures. You conclude by learning how to write triggers and use cursors.

PL/SQL is integrated with SQL, however, it adds programming that is not part of the standard SQL.

Here is an example of code that uses PL/SQL construct IF:

```
Procedure watch_detective
    (dID_in in Number,
     daction_in in Varchar2,
     dname_in in Varchar2 := NULL)
IS
BEGIN
   IF daction_in = 'Update'
   THEN
      UPDATE FROM detective WHERE detective_ID = dID_In;
   ELSEIF daction_in = 'Insert'
   THEN
      INSERT INTO detective (detective_ID, dname)
      VALUES (dID_in, dname_in);
   ENDIF;
END;
```

PL/SQL is different but it is also powerful. This is what PL/SQL can do for you:

◆   Programs look like 3GL modules

◆   Manipulate data through cursors

◆   Supports packages that allow object-oriented design

◆   Trap and resolve errors

PL/SQL and SQL provide us with both declarative and procedural logic. PL/SQL is used in the database for stored procedures and database triggers, and it is in the application code. You can use this language for both client-side and server-side development. This next section describes the basics of the PL/SQL language.

What you learn in this chapter relates to the language rules of PL/SQL. You learn about the character set, identifiers, literals, the semicolon, the PRAGMA keyword, and all about the block structure. So, without further ado, let's get back to basics.

Character Set

Character sets vary according to languages. SQL-92 has set the standard for character sets. PL/SQL has its own character set, as follows:

19

Type	Characters
Letters	A-Z, a-z
Digits	0-9
Symbols	~ ! @ # $ % ^ & * () - + = I [] {} " '< > , . ? /
Whitespace	Tab, space, carriage return

PL/SQL is a case-insensitive language. You can use all these characters in various combinations. Table 19-1 shows the special symbols that combine these various characters in specified ways.

Symbol	Description
;	Semicolon is a statement terminator.
%	Percent sign is an attribute indicator (cursor attributes like %ISOPEN and indirect declaration attributes like %ROWTYPE). Used as a multibyte wildcard symbol in SQL.
_	Single underscore is a single-byte wildcard symbol as in SQL.
:	Colon is host variable indicator.
**	Double asterisk is an exponentiation operator.
<> and !=	"Not Equals".
I I	Double vertical bar is a concatenation operator.

PL/SQL Special Symbols
Table 19-1.

Symbol	Description
<< and >>	Label delimiters.
<= and >=	Relational operators.
:=	Assignment operator.
=>	Association operator for positional notation.
--	Double dash is a single-line comment indicator.
/* and */	Beginning and ending multiline comment block delimiters.

PL/SQL Special Symbols *(continued)*
Table 19-1.

Identifiers

An *identifier* is a name for a PL/SQL object, including any of the following:

◆ Constant

◆ Variable

◆ Exception

◆ Procedure

◆ Function

◆ Package

◆ Record

◆ PL/SQL table

◆ Cursor

◆ Reserved word

An identifier is up to 30 characters in length, must start with a letter, can include $, _, and #, and cannot contain spaces. Identifiers are the handles for objects in your program. Choose your names carefully and avoid ambiguity.

Reserved Words

PL/SQL has chosen to name many of the elements in the program. These are the reserved words. Oracle supplies you with all the reserved words for PL/SQL in the documentation for PL/SQL. The code from the previous example contains a few of the reserved words in PL/SQL: END, BEGIN, IF, ELSIF, ENDIF, THEN, and IS.

Literals

A *literal* is a value that is not represented by an identifier. A literal can be a number, a string, or a Boolean. A *string literal* is any sequence of characters enclosed by single quotes. String literals can be composed of zero or more characters from the PL/SQL character set. A literal of zero characters is ' ' and is defined as the NULL string. PL/SQL is case-sensitive when it comes to string literals.

19

The *numeric literals* are integers or real numbers. Boolean literal has the values of TRUE and FALSE and these are not strings. Never place single quotes around these values.

The Semicolon Delimiter

The *semicolon (;) delimiter* terminates a statement within the PL/SQL program. Do not get this confused with the physical end of a line. You can have one line covering multiple physical lines in a statement. For example, if you look at the portion of the previous code example:

```
INSERT INTO detective (detective_ID, dname)
      VALUES (dID_in, dname_in);
   ENDIF;
END;
```

There are three semicolons, but four physical lines. If you kept this code all on one physical line, it would be hard to read:

```
INSERT INTO detective (detective_ID, dname)VALUES (dID_in,
dname_in);ENDIF;END;
```

The former example is easier to read.

The Pragma Keyword

The PRAGMA keyword tells that the remainder of the PL/SQL statement is a *pragma,* a directive to the compiler. Pragmas are processed at compile time, not at runtime. PL/SQL has the following pragmas:

◆ **Exception_Init**   This tells the compiler to associate a particular error number with an identifier you have declared as an exception in your program.

◆ **Restrict_References**   This tells the compiler the purity level (freedom from side effects) of a packaged program.

◆ **Serially_Reusable**   This tells the PL/SQL runtime engine that package-level data should not persist between references to that data.

The syntax for using the PRAGMA keyword is as follows:

```
PRAGMA <instruction>;
```

Block Structure

PL/SQL is a programming language that uses the block structure. The block enables you to build your program in a logical unit. There are two key concepts and features at the heart of the block structure:

◆ **Modularization**   The *block* is the basic unit of work from which modules, procedures, and functions are built. This is the process where you break up large blocks of code into smaller pieces, called *modules,* that can be called by other modules.

◆ **Scope**   The block gives you scope for logically related objects.

Sections of the PL/SQL Block

A PL/SQL block can have up to four sections.

◆ **Header**   Relevant for named blocks only. The header determines the way the named block or program must be called.

◆ **Declaration section**   The part of the block that declares variables, cursors, and sub-blocks that are references in the execution and exception sections.

♦ **Execution section**   The part of the block that contains the executable statements, the code executed by the PL/SQL runtime engine.

♦ **Exception section**   The part that handles exceptions to normal processing (error conditions).

The syntax looks like this:

```
DECLARE
     variable declarations
BEGIN
     program code: such as cursor definitions, nested PL/SQL
     procedures,functions(can include SQL code)
END;
```

A block can have nested sub-blocks of code. The block code looks like this:

```
DECLARE
     variable declarations
BEGIN
     some program code
BEGIN
     code in a nested block
END;
more program code
END;
```

You cannot execute PL/SQL code except as part of a block.

A stored procedure contains one block and a database trigger contains one block.

The following code is an example of a simple PL/SQL block:

```
DECLARE
2  x       Integer;
3  BEGIN
4  x := 2;
5 END;
6  /

PL/SQL procedure successfully completed.
```

Notice there wasn't any screen output. The next example shows you how to get output from the block:

```
1   DECLARE
2   x       Integer;
3   BEGIN
4   x := 2;
5   dbms_output.put_line ('The variable X = ');
 6   dbms_output.put_line(x);
 7* END;
SQL> /
The variable X =2

PL/SQL procedure successfully completed.
```

CAUTION: Enter your code very carefully. If you miss a semicolon, you will get errors similar to this:

```
ERROR at line 5:
ORA-06550:  line 5, column 1:
PLS-00201:  identifier 'OUTPUT.PUT_LINE' must be declared
```

This occurred just because the semicolon was left off line 4.

Anonymous Blocks

An *anonymous block* is unnamed and does not form the body of a procedure, function, or trigger. This block can be used as part of a SQL*Plus script and can be nested inside procedure and function blocks. The syntax for an anonymous block is

```
[DECLARE
     variable declarations]
BEGIN
     program_code
[EXCEPTION
     error_handling_code]
END;
```

Here is an example of an anonymous block:

```
DECLARE
     my_date DATE := SYSDATE;
BEGIN
     birthdate := my_date;
END;
```

Anonymous blocks execute a series of statements and then terminate, similar to procedures.

19

Data Types

The data types in PL/SQL are also data types in SQL-92. Variations exist, as with all vendor implementations of SQL. Every constant and every variable element in your program has a datatype. PL/SQL has a set of predefined scalar and composite datatypes. A *scalar datatype* is atomic and is not made up of any other variable components. A *composite datatype* has internal structure or components. The two composite types are record and table.

Scalar datatypes fall into one of four categories: number, character, Boolean, and date-time. Because you have learned about datatypes throughout this book, only those datatypes particular to PL/SQL or that have not been covered before are discussed.

◆ RAW datatype is used to store binary data or other kinds of raw data, such as a picture or image.

◆ LONG RAW datatype stores raw data up to 32760 bytes and is just like the LONG datatype except data in LONG RAW is not interpreted by PL/SQL.

◆ ROWID datatype is a pseudocolumn that is part of every table you create. The *rowid* is an internally generated and maintained binary value that identifies a row of data in your table.

◆ BFILE declares variables that hold a file locator pointing to large binary objects in operating system files outside of the database.

Procedures, Functions, IF Statements, and Loops

Once you have learned the IF statements, loops, different control, conditional and cursor constructs, you will be ready to write programs. First you must learn to build and combine the PL/SQL modules.

Procedure

A *procedure* is a named PL/SQL block that performs one or more actions. It is called as an executable PL/SQL statement. You can pass information into and out of a procedure through its parameter list.

The syntax of a procedure:

```
PROCEDURE name [ (parameter [ ,parameter…]) ]
IS
     [declaration statements]
BEGIN
   executable-statements
[ EXCEPTION
    exception handler statements]
END [ name];
```

Here is a description of each component:

◆ **Name**   The name of the procedure comes directly after the keyword PROCEDURE.

◆ **Parameters**   An option list of parameters you define to put information into the procedure and send information out to the procedure back to the requesting program.

◆ **Declaration statements**   This statement contains the declarations of local identifiers for that procedure. If you don't have any declarations, then there is nothing between IS and BEGIN.

◆ **Executable statements**   The statements the procedure executes when called. You must have one executable statement after the BEGIN and before the END or EXCEPTION keywords.

◆ **Exception handler statements**   If you don't handle any exceptions, you can leave this out and terminate the procedure with END.

The following code is an example of a procedure block:

```
1  Create or Replace procedure replace1 (num_one in out number,
   num_two in out number, num_three in out number)
   IS
2  temp_num    Number;
3  BEGIN
4  temp_num := num_one;
5  num_one := num_two;
6  num_three := temp_num;
7* END;
8  /

Procedure created.
```

The following code executes the previous procedure block. It is an example of a nested procedure block. This syntax executes the block:

```
1  DECLARE
2      first_number NUMBER;
3      second_number NUMBER;
4      third_number  NUMBER;
5  PROCEDURE replace_no (num_one IN OUT number, num_two in out
   number, num_three in out number)
6  IS
7      temp_num    NUMBER;
8  BEGIN
9      temp_num := num_one;
10      num_one := num_two;
11      num_two := num_two;
12      num_three := temp_num;
13  END;
14  BEGIN
15    --set some initial value and display them
16      first_number := 30;
17      second_number := 35;
18      third_number := 125;
19      DBMS_OUTPUT.PUT_LINE ('first number = ' || to_char
        (first_number));
20      DBMS_OUTPUT.PUT_LINE ('second number = ' || to_char
        (second_number));
21      DBMS_OUTPUT.PUT_LINE ('third number = ' || to_char
        (third_number));
22  --swap the values
```

```
23          DBMS_OUTPUT.PUT_LINE ('Swapping the three values now.');
24          replace_no (first_number, second_number, third_number);
25   --display the results
26          DBMS_OUTPUT.PUT_LINE ('first number =' || to_char
             (first_number));
27          DBMS_OUTPUT.PUT_LINE ('second number =' || to_char
             (second_number));
28          DBMS_OUTPUT.PUT_LINE ('third number =' || to_char
             (third_number));
29* END;
20:32:46 SQL> /
first number = 30
second number = 35
third number = 125
Swapping the three values now.
first number =35
second number =35
third number =30

PL/SQL procedure successfully completed.
```

The procedure header is the part of the procedure that comes before the IS keyword. The header contains the procedure name and the parameter list.

The *procedure body* is the code to implement the procedure. It has the declaration, execution, and exception sections of the procedure. Everything after the IS keyword is the procedure body.

You can create the END label by appending the procedure name immediately after the END command and before the semicolon. This name links up the end of the program with the beginning. It makes sense to add an END label because, if you have a series of procedures and functions in your program, it will help identify the procedure.

Function

A *function* is a named PL/SQL block that returns a single value and is used just like a PL/SQL expression. You can pass information into a function through its parameter list. The structure of a function is the same as a procedure, except the function also has a RETURN clause. The syntax of a function:

```
FUNCTION name [ (parameter [, parameter...])]
     RETURN return_datatype
IS
```

```
     [declaration statements]
BEGIN
     executable statements
[EXCEPTION
     exception handler statements]
END [name];
```

Here is a description of the components:

◆ **Name**   Is the name of the procedure and located after the FUNCTION keyword.

◆ **Parameters**   An optional list of parameters you define to pass information into the function and send information out of the function, back to the requesting program.

◆ **Return datatype**   The datatype of the value returned by the function. This is required in the function header and is explained in more detail in the next section.

◆ **Declaration statements**   Consists of local identifiers for that function.

◆ **Executable statements**   The statements the function executes when it is called.

◆ **Exception handlers**   This is an optional exception handler for the function.

The Return Datatype
The return_datatype is the datatype of the value returned by the function. There are many datatypes:

◆ VARCHAR2

◆ NUMBER

◆ BINARY_INTEGER

◆ BOOLEAN

◆ PL/SQL table

◆ Nested table or variable array (VARRAY) (PL/SQL8)

◆ PL/SQL record

◆ Object type (PL/SQL8)

◆ Large objects (LOBs), such as CLOBs and BFILEs (PL/SQL8)

However, you cannot have these datatypes:

◆ **Named exception**   Once you declare an exception, you can reference that exception only in a RAISE statement and in the exception handler itself.

◆ **Cursor name**   You cannot return a cursor from a function unless you use a REF CURSOR TYPE declaration that enables you to return a cursor and declare a parameter as a cursor. This is in PL/SQL Release 2.2 and above.

An example of a function is provided in the following:

```
SQL> Create or Replace FUNCTION emptype (paytype in out char)
2   RETURN VARCHAR2 IS
3   Begin
4       If paytype = 'h' then
5           RETURN 'hourly';
6       ELSIF paytype = 's' then
7           RETURN 'salaried';
8       ELSIF paytype = 'e' then
9           RETURN 'executive';
10      ELSE
11          RETURN 'Invalid Type';
12  END IF;
13  EXCEPTION
14      WHEN OTHERS THEN
15          RETURN 'Error Encountered';
16  END emptype;
17  /
Function created.
```

To execute this function, use this code:

```
1   DECLARE
2   paytype    char;
3   Function emptype (paytype IN CHAR)
4       RETURN VARCHAR2 IS
5   Begin
6       If paytype = 'h' then
7           RETURN 'hourly';
8       ELSIF paytype = 's' then
9           RETURN 'salaried';
10      ELSIF paytype = 'e' then
11          RETURN 'executive';
```

```
12        ELSE
13            RETURN 'Invalid Type';
14  END IF;
15  EXCEPTION
16      WHEN OTHERS THEN
17            RETURN 'Error Encountered';
18  END emptype;
19  Begin
20      paytype := 'h';
21        DBMS_OUTPUT.PUT_LINE(emptype('h'));
22* END;
SQL> /

hourly

PL/SQL procedure successfully completed.
```

19

The function header is everything that comes before the keyword IS. The header gives you everything you need to call the function: function name, parameter list, and RETURN datatype.

The body is the code required to run the function. It has the declaration, execution, and exception sections of the function. This is everything after the keyword IS.

A function must have at least one RETURN statement in the execution section. The RETURN statement executed by the function determines the value returned by that function. The RETURN statement can accept any expression for evaluation and return. This expression can be composed of calls to other functions, complex calculations, and even data conversions. If none of the RETURN statements are executed, PL/SQL raises an error: ORA-6503: PL/SQL: Function returned without value.

The RETURN statement can also be used with procedures. The RETURN simply stops execution of the procedure and returns control to the calling code. It cannot pass a value back to the calling program. Do your best to avoid the RETURN statement in your procedures.

Parameters

A *parameter* is a value you can pass from a block of statements to a function. The syntax for defining a formal parameter is

```
Parameter_name [MODE] parameter_type [ := | DEFAULT value]
```

In the last example, we had the parameter (emptype char). To accept a parameter from a table, simply add a %TYPE after the parameter and the %TYPE will pick up the field type from the table. For example, suppose you had an Employee table and you want to have an empcom parameter:

```
Empcom employee.commission%TYPE)
```

This prevents having to hard code the parameter into the function because it may change.

The optional MODE statement gives control over the parameters coming in.

◆ **IN**   The parameter is read-only and protected.

◆ **OUT**   You are ignoring any parameters passed from the calling statement and assigning values to this parameter from within the function; it is write-only.

◆ **IN OUT**   This mode gives you full control over the parameter. You can read in the parameter and change the value of the parameter from within the function. You can return more than one value with this mode.

You can assign defaults to parameters. If no parameter is passed, then the default value is used. Here are two examples of how you can assign parameters:

```
Empcom NUMBER DEFAULT .10
empcom NUMBER := 100
```

IF Statement

As you probably know, the IF statement enables you to evaluate one or more conditions. The syntax for an IF statement is as follows:

```
IF <condition evaluates to true>
THEN
<perform statement>
END IF;
```

The condition is a Boolean condition. If it evaluates to true, the perform statement executes. The following is an example of an IF statement:

```
1   DECLARE
2   vacationhours Number := 35;
3   vacationhrstore Number:= 0;
```

```
4  BEGIN
5    If vacationhours < 40 THEN
6  vacationhrstore := vacationhours - 35;
7  DBMS_OUTPUT.PUT_LINE ('Vacation Hours Available =' ||
   vacationhrstore);
8  end if;
9* end;
SQL> /
Vacation Hours Available =0
PL/SQL procedure successfully completed.
```

You can nest IF statements. This lets you keep from executing inner IF statements unless the outer IF conditions apply. The syntax for a nested IF statement:

19

```
IF <condition2 evaluates to true>
THEN
     <perform statements>
ELSE <both conditions have been evaluated to false>
     IF <condition3 evaluates to true>
     THEN
        <perform statements>
     ELSE
        <perform statements>
     END IF;
   END IF;
END IF;
```

The following is an example of a nested IF statement:

```
1  DECLARE
2  vacationhours Number := 90;
3  vacationhrstore Number:= 0;
4  paytype char(1) := 'E';
5  BEGIN
6    If vacationhours > 40 THEN
7    If paytype = 'H' then
8          vacationhrstore := vacationhours - 40;
9  DBMS_OUTPUT.PUT_LINE ('Vacation Hours Available =' ||
   vacationhrstore);
10    ELSE
11     if paytype = 'S' then
12            DBMS_OUTPUT.PUT_LINE ('Employee is Salaried');
13    ELSE
```

```
14              DBMS_OUTPUT.PUT_LINE ('Employee is Executive
                Management');
15    END IF;
16    end if;
17  End If;
18* end;
SQL> /

Employee is Executive Management

PL/SQL procedure successfully completed.
```

T **IP:** Make sure every IF statement has a matching END. Place a space between END IF statement. Don't forget your punctuation; a semicolon after END IF and after each of the statements, but not after keyword THEN.

The next statement—IF...ELSIF—you use in an OR environment. Up to now, you have been dealing with IF...ELSE, which is an AND environment. The syntax for IF...ELSIF follows:

```
IF <condition1 evaluates to true>
THEN
     <perform statements>
ELSIF <condition2 evaluates to true>
THEN
     <perform statements>
ELSE <this is always optional as the default value>
     <perform statements>
END IF;
```

An example of how this works follows:

```
1   DECLARE
2   v_minorityid Number := 5;
3   v_minoritydesc Char(15);
4   BEGIN
5   If v_minorityid = 1 THEN
6        v_minoritydesc := 'Black';
7   ELSIF v_minorityid = 2 THEN
8        v_minoritydesc := 'Caucasian';
```

```
9   ELSIF v_minorityid = 3 THEN
10        v_minoritydesc := 'Asian';
11  ELSIF v_minorityid = 4 THEN
12        v_minoritydesc := 'Hispanic';
13  ELSIF v_minorityid = 5 THEN
14        v_minoritydesc := 'American Indian';
15  ELSE v_minoritydesc := 'Unknown';
16  END IF;
17      DBMS_OUTPUT.PUT_LINE ('Applicant Minority is:' ||
        v_minoritydesc);
18* END;
SQL> /

Applicant Minority is:American Indian

PL/SQL procedure successfully completed.
```

T IP: Remember to spell ELSIF not ELSEIF. Leave the E out of it!

Loops

Looping lets you execute a block of code repeatedly until some condition occurs. The syntax for loops follows

```
FOR loop_index IN [REVERSE] low_value…high_value LOOP
     Statements to execute
END LOOP;
```

An example of a loop follows

```
1   BEGIN
2   FOR v_loopdeloop in REVERSE 95..100 LOOP
3       DBMS_OUTPUT.PUT_LINE ('loopdeloop counting is fun ' ||
        v_loopdeloop);
4   END LOOP;
5* END;
SQL> /
loopdeloop counting is fun 100
loopdeloop counting is fun 99
```

```
loopdeloop counting is fun 98
loopdeloop counting is fun 97
loopdeloop counting is fun 96
loopdeloop counting is fun 95

PL/SQL procedure successfully completed.
```

You can even modify your loop increment:

```
1   BEGIN
2   FOR v_loopdeloop in REVERSE 95..100 LOOP
3      IF MOD(v_loopdeloop, 2) = 0 then
4        DBMS_OUTPUT.PUT_LINE ('loopdeloop counting is fun ' ||
           v_loopdeloop);
5      END IF;
6   END LOOP;
7*  END;
SQL> /
loopdeloop counting is fun 100
loopdeloop counting is fun 98
loopdeloop counting is fun 96

PL/SQL procedure successfully completed.
```

GO TO

The GO TO statement enables you to transfer control to another labeled PL/SQL block without the need for conditional checking. The syntax for the GO TO statement is

```
GO TO label_name;
```

The label_name is the matching label_name that must be contained within the same PL/SQL block of code. Many errors can be made when a GO TO statement is used. Please do not use this statement! In most cases, you can use another Oracle construct instead of a GO TO statement. In case you must use a GO TO statement, here is the syntax:

```
DECLARE
    v_wellbeing CHAR := 'OK';
BEGIN
    IF v_wellbeing = 'OK' THEN
        GOTO IAMOK;
    ELSE
```

```
        v_wellbeing := 'OK';
    END IF;
<<IAMOK>>
        NULL;
END;
```

WHILE Loops

The WHILE loop enables you to evaluate a condition before a sequence of statements would be executed. The syntax for the WHILE loop is

```
WHILE <condition is true> LOOP
    <statements>
END LOOP;
```

You must have the keywords LOOP and END LOOP to get the statements to execute.

Here is an example of the WHILE loop at work:

```
1   DECLARE
2       v_counter NUMBER := 0;
3   BEGIN
4      WHILE v_counter < 15 LOOP
5          v_counter := v_counter + 2;
6           DBMS_OUTPUT.PUT_LINE('The value of v_counter is  ' ||
            v_counter);
7      END LOOP;
8* END;
SQL> /
The value of v_counter is  2
The value of v_counter is  4
The value of v_counter is  6
The value of v_counter is  8
The value of v_counter is  10
The value of v_counter is  12
The value of v_counter is  14
The value of v_counter is  16

PL/SQL procedure successfully completed.
```

The logic is a little off in this example. To debug loops, you can run the DBMS_OUTPUT package to track the flow of the logic. Refer to your documentation for further information.

To escape out of loops, you may use the EXIT and EXIT WHEN statements. The syntax of these statements is

```
EXIT;
--Or you can use
EXIT WHEN <condition is true>;
```

Here is an example using the EXIT WHEN statement:

```
1    DECLARE
2         v_counter NUMBER := 0;
3    BEGIN
4        WHILE TRUE LOOP
5            DBMS_OUTPUT.PUT_LINE('The value of v_counter is  ' ||
             v_counter);
6            EXIT WHEN v_counter = 14;
7            v_counter := v_counter + 2;
8        END LOOP;
9* END;
SQL> /
The value of v_counter is  0
The value of v_counter is  2
The value of v_counter is  4
The value of v_counter is  6
The value of v_counter is  8
The value of v_counter is  10
The value of v_counter is  12
The value of v_counter is  14

PL/SQL procedure successfully completed.
```

The loop terminates after the counter has reached 14. In the last example, this same loop went up to 16. Always try to use the EXIT WHEN statement because it saves a lot of coding and is easier to read and use.

REPEAT...UNTIL Loop

Oracle doesn't have a built-in REPEAT...UNTIL loop statement. A workaround exists for this. This is the syntax for the simulated REPEAT...UNTIL loop:

```
LOOP
    <statement>
    IF <condition is true>
```

```
         EXIT;
      END IF;
END LOOP;
```

Here is an example of the simulated REPEAT...UNTIL loop:

```
1   DECLARE
2       v_cube Number := 3;
3   BEGIN
4       LOOP
5           DBMS_OUTPUT.PUT_LINE ('The Cube is  '|| v_cube*3);
6               v_cube := v_cube + 2;
7           EXIT WHEN v_cube > 15;
8       END LOOP;
9*  END;
SQL> /

The Cube is   9
The Cube is  15
The Cube is  21
The Cube is  27
The Cube is  33
The Cube is  39
The Cube is  45

PL/SQL procedure successfully completed.
```

There are guidelines on when to use the various loops you have learned. The FOR loop should be used when you want to know how many times the loop should execute. The WHILE loop is best used if you want to execute the loop one time. This is commonly used because of its flexibility. The LOOP loop is the simple loop and, if you want to create a REPEAT...UNTIL type of loop, this is the one for you.

Packages

A *package* is an encapsulated collection of related schema objects. These objects can include procedures, functions, variables, constants, cursors, and exceptions. The packages contain stored subprograms or standalone programs called *subprograms*. The package cannot be called, passed parameters, or nested. Packages enable you to organize your development more efficiently and to grant privileges easily.

You need to create the package specification. This specification publicly declares the schema objects continued in the body of the package. To create a specification, issue the CREATE PROCEDURE command:

```
CREATE OR REPLACE PACKAGE emp_type_spec as
FUNCTION emptyp (paytype varchar2(2))
RETURN VARCHAR2;

PROCEDURE vachours;
END emp_type_spec;
```

Let's create a package using some of the examples from this chapter:

```
1   CREATE OR REPLACE PACKAGE emp_type_spec as
2   FUNCTION emptype (paytype varchar2)
3   RETURN VARCHAR2;
4   PROCEDURE vachours;
5*  END emp_type_spec;6   /

Package created.
```

To recompile a package, use the ALTER PACKAGE command with the compile keyword. Recompiling a package recompiles all objects defined within the package. The following is an example of the ALTER PACKAGE command:

```
ALTER PACKAGE emp_type_spec compile body
```

Or

```
ALTER PACKAGE emp_type_spec compile package
```

Cursors

There are two kinds of cursors: implicit and explicit. PL/SQL implicitly declares a cursor for every SQL statement use. Implicit cursors are declared by Oracle for each UPDATE, DELETE, and INSERT SQL command. Explicit cursors are declared and used by the user to process multiple rows returned by a SELECT statement.

Explicit cursors are defined by the programmer to process a multiple-row active set, one record at a time. These are the steps to defining an explicit cursor:

1. Declare the cursor.
2. Open the cursor.
3. Fetch data from the cursor.
4. Close the cursor.

The following is the syntax for defining cursors:

```
DECLARE cursor_name
is
SELECT statement
```

19

An example of this step:

```
DECLARE c_Commission
is
    SELECT emp_commission from employee
      WHERE pay_type = 'S';
```

The second step is to open a cursor. The syntax for this is

```
OPEN cursor_name;
```

After the OPEN command, the cursor establishes its pointer at the very top of the active set. The pointer is before the first row because the FETCH command hasn't been issued yet.

The third step is to fetch the data. The syntax for the FETCH command is

```
FETCH cursor_name INTO record_list;
```

The record_list is a list of variables that receive the columns from the active set. After each fetch, the cursor pointer moves to the next row in the active set.

The fourth and final step is to close the cursor. This statement closes the previously opened cursor. After the cursor is closed, you can perform any operation on it.

The following example illustrates the use of the four steps for an explicit cursor:

```
1   DECLARE
2   v_emp_name    VARCHAR(32);
3   v_commission NUMBER(9,2);
4   v_pay_type    CHAR;
5   v_comm_total  NUMBER(9,2);
6   emp.comm NUMBER(9,2);
7   Cursor c_Commission is
8   SELECT emp.ename, emp.comm from emp
9   WHERE emp.deptno = 20;
10  BEGIN
11  OPEN c_Commission;
12  LOOP
13  FETCH c_commission INTO v_emp_name, v_commission;
14  EXIT when c_commission%notfound;
15  IF v_pay_type = 'S' then
16  v_comm_total := (v_commission * 1.10);
17  ELSE
18  v_comm_total := (v_commission * 50);
19  END IF;
20  INSERT INTO emp.comm values (v_comm_total);
21  END LOOP;
22* END;
```

The implicit cursor uses attributes. You cannot use the OPEN, CLOSE, and FETCH commands with the implicit cursor. The implicit cursor attributes are %isopen, %found, %notfound, and %rowcount.

After the execution of the SQL statement, the associate SQL cursor is always closed. The %isopen attribute evaluates to false.

The %found attribute equates to true if an INSERT, UPDATE, or DELETE affected one or more rows, or a SELECT INTO returns one or more rows. An example follows:

```
UPDATE detectives
set case_type = 'Murder Investigation'
WHERE LNAME = 'Templeton';

IF sql%found then
   COMMIT;

 ELSE
    detective_not_found_procedure;
END IF;
```

The %notfound attribute evaluates to true if the most recent SQL statement does not affect any rows. The following is an example of this implicit attribute:

```
UPDATE detectives
set case_type = 'Murder Investigation'
WHERE LNAME = 'Templeton';

If sql%notfound then
    detective_not_found_procedure;
ELSE
    COMMIT;
END IF;
```

Please be aware that you must have INSERT, UPDATE, or DELETE privileges to perform any of these attributes commands.

The %rowcount attribute tells you the total number of rows affected by the most recent SQL statement. Here is an example of the %rowcount attribute:

```
BEGIN
UPDATE detectives
set case_type = 'Murder Investigation'
WHERE Case_ID = 5;
message ('Total Cases Updated are: 'to_char(sql%rowcount));
END
```

Triggers

In Chapter 17, you were introduced to triggers. As PL/SQL is a different programming language than Transact SQL, they are handled in a slightly different way by PL/SQL. A trigger is a PL/SQL block that is associated with a table, stored in a database, and executed in response to a specific data manipulation event. A trigger is fired when responding to the following events:

◆ A row is inserted into a table.

◆ A row in a table is updated.

◆ A row in a table is deleted.

When you create a trigger it becomes part of the database. It is always executed when the event you defined occurs. An example of a PL/SQL trigger is listed in the following:

```
SQL> Create or Replace Trigger ename_insert_update
2     BEFORE INSERT OR UPDATE on EMP
```

```
3     FOR EACH ROW
4   DECLARE
5     dup_flag  integer;
6   BEGIN
7   :New.ENAME := LOWER(:NEW.ENAME);
8   END;
9   /
Trigger created.
```

To test the trigger, insert a few rows into the table. The trigger shows lowercase names for the inserts.

```
EMPNO ENAME
------- ----------
   7900 JAMES
   7902 FORD
   7934 MILLER
   8001 franklin
```

Triggers are classified according to when they fire. There are two choices for when a trigger fires: before or after. *Before triggers* are executed before the triggering SQL statement. *After triggers* are executed following the triggering SQL statement.

A trigger can be a row-level trigger or a statement-level trigger. A *row-level trigger* executes once for each row. A *statement-level trigger* is only fired once.

The syntax for defining a trigger is

```
CREATE OR REPLACE TRIGGER trigger_name
   {Before|After} verb_list ON table_name
   [[REFERENCING correlation_names] FOR EACH ROW [WHEN (condition)]]
DECLARE
   declarations
BEGIN
   pl/sql code
END;
```

The verb_list identifies the SQL verbs that fire the trigger. The verb list syntax follows

```
{INSERT|DELETE|UPDATE [OF column_list]} [OR verb_list]
```

The table_name is the table on which the trigger is defined.

The correlation_name enables you to specify correlation names other than the default of OLD|NEW. The referencing clause syntax is

```
{OLD as old_alias|NEW as new_alias [correlation_name]}
```

The condition is an optional condition placed on the execution of the trigger. It can be used only with row-level triggers.

The declaration consists of variable, record, or cursor declarations needed by this PL/SQL block.

19

The PL/SQL code is the PL/SQL code executed when the trigger fires.

You may be asking yourself, when would I use a trigger? The following is a list of common uses:

◆   Enforcing business rules

◆   Maintaining referential integrity

◆   Enforcing security

◆   Maintaining a historical log of changes

◆   Generating column values, including primary keys

◆   Replicating data

If you need to get a list of your triggers, just run a describe on USER_TRIGGERS:

```
DESCRIBE USER_TRIGGERS;
```

Here is a list of triggers:

```
Name                              Null?     Type
--------------------------------- --------- ----
TRIGGER_NAME                      NOT NULL  VARCHAR2(30)
TRIGGER_TYPE                                VARCHAR2(16)
TRIGGERING_EVENT                            VARCHAR2(26)
TABLE_OWNER                       NOT NULL  VARCHAR2(30)
TABLE_NAME                        NOT NULL  VARCHAR2(30)
REFERENCING_NAMES                           VARCHAR2(87)
WHEN_CLAUSE                                 VARCHAR2(4000)
```

```
STATUS                              VARCHAR2(8)
DESCRIPTION                         VARCHAR2(4000)
TRIGGER_BODY                        LONG
```

If you need to enable or disable a trigger, the code is

```
ALTER TRIGGER name {Enabled/Disabled};
```

A few limitations exist with triggers. For instance, you cannot query or modify a mutating table, execute data definition language (DDL) statements, or execute COMMIT, ROLLBACK, or SAVEPOINT statements.

A *mutating table* is one in the process of being changed while the trigger is executing.

You have now covered all the basics. This winds up the lesson on PL/SQL basics. Quite a lot wasn't covered and you may want to find out more about the PL/SQL language. You have choices. You may take a course, read another book, or just work with this material and read the documentation that comes with PL/SQL. If you plan to work with Oracle databases, you should learn this programming language. You can use this language to run procedures, functions, and triggers, and to manipulate the database.

What's Next?

In the next chapter, you discover how Visual C, Visual Basic, and Java incorporate SQL into their programming languages. Then you learn how to troubleshoot your code by learning about the top ten common errors in SQL. Finally, you get a glimpse of the new SQL3 in Chapter 22.

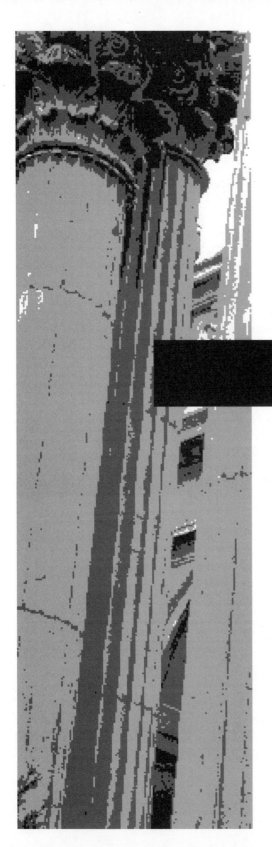

CHAPTER 20

Programming with SQL

In this chapter, you see how to apply SQL using three popular programming languages: C, Visual Basic, and Java. The same SQL query and fetch operations are used in each of the languages, demonstrating how to develop SQL-driven applications of your own in these languages.

In the years since SQL was first introduced, the programming world has been gradually moving away from procedural, job-oriented processing. This type of processing is where a program is seen as a long list of instructions to be executed from beginning to end. This view of programming was originally developed to conserve valuable computing time. Now that computing power is much cheaper, computers and their software are moving toward more and more interactive forms of computing. Specifically, languages and computing platforms have become event-driven, where interactive messages from the user, such as mouse clicks and keyboard input, define what happens next in the program. Operating systems such as Windows, MacOS, and X-Windows are all event-driven in nature, as are the programs developed for these environments.

Object-oriented programming has also grown in popularity as the average size of applications has grown from kilobytes to many megabytes. In object-oriented programming, data structures and the code that operates on those data structures are combined into a single entity called an *object*. This is known as *data encapsulation*. Data encapsulation protects portions of a large application from being damaged by bugs in other portions of the same program. This allows for larger groups of programmers to work together on a project without improperly accessing each other's data structures and thus causing bugs. It also eases code reuse if it is done carefully.

The three languages used in this chapter—C, Visual Basic, and Java—represent a range of approaches to programming. C is designed to be a procedural language, a language that basically consists of a simple list of instructions from beginning to end. Java, on the other hand, is an object-oriented, event-driven language. Visual Basic is somewhere in between. Although object-oriented in general structure, Visual Basic doesn't easily enable you to protect the properties of objects from other objects, a fundamental tenet of object-oriented philosophy.

Because these examples are so short as compared to a real object-oriented application, all these examples, except for the occasional object notation, may seem pretty procedural. For this reason, a C++ example isn't included. C++ is a superset of C and, in the absence of cross platform object-oriented standards for database access, our C++ example would be effectively identical to our C example: both would employ the ODBC API for database access.

Considering this drastic shift, SQL has so far weathered the years better than any other language in common use, primarily because of its very specific and natural conceptualization of the essence of relational databases. What presently seems certain is, as long as relational databases remain popular, SQL will always exist. In fact, in these days of increasing reliance on nonproprietary industry standards, SQL has only gained in popularity.

How Applications Employing SQL Are Built

Application programs that employ SQL are written in a programming language and connect to a database support package. The programming language is the actual environment in which you develop your SQL application. This can be a general-purpose language, such as C, or a language specifically designed for a particular type of database, such as Oracle's Developer product. The database support package provides all the software to connect your application to the database server, generally via a computer network. Database support packages can also be general-purpose, such as ODBC, which connects to any database, whether or not it is SQL-based, provided an ODBC driver exists for it. The database support package can also be specific to one type of database, such as Sybase's Open Client.

20

The interfaces that database support packages usually provide are known as *application programming interfaces* (APIs). They consist of a group of functions or procedures you can call from your programming language to manipulate databases from within your program. APIs are used by procedural languages like C.

Object-oriented packages generally consist of a list of objects or object templates you can manipulate from within your program to communicate with databases. These packages are generally referred to as *object libraries* or *class libraries*.

Many early database support packages employed embedded SQL, a process whereby you write SQL instructions into your source code and act on your source code with a preprocessing program before turning the resulting code over to your regular compiler and linker. This method has fallen out of favor as more general-purpose APIs, such as ODBC, arrived on the scene.

One advantage to general-purpose programming languages and database support packages is they enable you to migrate your data easily among all the leading database products. On the other hand, such solutions are generally not quite as high performance as those built with tools optimized for a specific type of database. Another possible advantage to database-specific tools is database vendors may offer features that address your particular application needs and, thus, speed your development. Working with a specific database vendor can be attractive, but consider carefully the probability and cost of migrating your data to another vendor before you decide to use tools designed for a particular type of database.

How ODBC Drivers and Databases Process SQL Commands

When your program sends an SQL command to your database server, the command is first passed to the API code linked with your program. This code may communicate directly with the database, but generally it calls a separately installed client driver layer that handles network communication.

In the case of ODBC, your SQL command is passed by the API code to the ODBC driver manager, which creates a link with the specific ODBC driver being requested. The ODBC driver then communicates with the database's client driver layer. Although generic, ODBC is generally slightly slower because of these extra steps.

Many non-SQL-based databases, such as DB2, have ODBC drivers. In this case, the SQL command never makes it to the database server. The ODBC driver translates the SQL statement into the native language of the database server before passing it to the client driver layer.

Next, the commands are processed by the client driver layer, which may do a little or a lot of preprocessing. Client driver layers generally use UNIX's streaming sockets protocol and TCP/IP to communicate over the network to the database server or mainframe. This stems from the fact that many database servers use some form of UNIX as their preferred operating system. This is a standard form of network communication today. The Internet and many local area networks use this protocol for most of their connections. If your network doesn't or can't use this protocol, make sure your database server and client can support your networking protocol.

The database server then processes the command. Unless this command is a query, the process basically ends here, except for a short confirmation message sent by the server back to the client. If the command is a query, the database creates and maintains a list of references to the members of the result set that was called for. Then it waits for the client to initiate retrieval of the data.

Rows are called for either in groups or one at a time by the client. Unless you have a special ODBC driver and set it up to return multiple rows at once, ODBC obtains result set data one row at a time from the database server. If static cursors are employed, these rows are cached to some degree on the client in case you want to fetch earlier rows more than once. If you know you will always be going through your result set once from beginning to end, you can save time and memory by specifying a forward-only cursor. Similar tradeoffs are often the case for database-specific tools as well.

Finally, the query data is returned to your application layer. This data is usually put into data structures you have passed to the API. In object-oriented interfaces, you would generally call a function to retrieve each piece of data.

How to Set Up an ODBC Data Source

Unfortunately, simply installing ODBC drivers for a particular database type is not enough. You need to set up a specific link to your data called an *ODBC data source*. This data source contains information about exactly what database server and data are being accessed.

20

Here are the steps for any version of 32-bit Windows:

1. Click the Start menu.
2. Choose Control Panel from the Settings menu.
3. Double-click the icon marked 32-bit ODBC. This launches the ODBC Data Source Administrator.
4. Click the Add button.
5. Choose the driver for your database type from the list. If your database type doesn't appear in the list, it hasn't been properly installed.
6. Click the Finish button.
7. You now enter a set of dialogs specific to the ODBC driver you are using. These dialogs generally ask for the name your data source should be called, your login and password information, which server to use, and other configuration data.

After completing these dialogs, you should see your newly created data source appear on the list of data source names.

Programming SQL with C

In this section, you examine a bare-bones example of a C program. This example uses direct calls to the ODBC application programming interface to execute an SQL query and to fetch the results.

As you may know, C programs generally consist of two sets of files: the first consists of one or more text files ending in .c and the second set, called include files, consists of one or more files, with names generally ending in .h. If an #include directive is present, C treats these include files as if everything contained in them is also part of the .c file in which they appear. The program consists of a single .c file named main.c. At the top of this file are some #include compiler directives that serve to include the .h files you will use:

```
#include <stdio.h>
#include <windows.h>
#include <sql.h>
#include <sqlext.h>
```

The include file stdio.h enables access to all the standard C input and printing functions such as printf(). The file windows.h describes variables specific to the Windows operating system and is required by the Microsoft ODBC interface. The files sql.h and sqlext.h contain the definitions for the ODBC interface itself.

Next, you define the global variables used in your program. Global variables can appear practically anywhere in a C program, but conventionally are listed at the top of the .c file in which they are used most:

```
HENV       hEnv  = SQL_NULL_HENV;
HDBC       hDBC  = SQL_NULL_HDBC;
HSTMT      hStmt = SQL_NULL_HSTMT;
```

The variable hEnv is called the *environment handle* and is used by ODBC to store and access its environment information. You need one environment for each type of database you connect to in your program. The type HENV and the other types are defined in the include file sql.h. The variable hEnv is given the initial constant value SQL_NULL_HENV, which is also defined in sql.h. This initial value, if passed to ODBC, allows it to determine that no environment has been allocated.

The variable hDBC is known as the *connection handle* and is used by ODBC to store and access information about a specific connection to a database that has been made. You need one connection handle for each database connection you make. The connection handle is initially set to SQL_NULL_HDBC so ODBC knows no connection handle has been allocated.

The variable hStmt is the statement handle and is used by ODBC to store and access information about a particular database query or other SQL statement. You need a statement handle to execute any SQL instruction, except COMMIT or ROLLBACK.

The SQL statements COMMIT and ROLLBACK are unique in ODBC in that they affect an entire connection instead of a single cursor or statement handle. If you need to commit or roll back several cursors separately, you must make a separate connection for each cursor.

Here are the function prototypes. Although prototypes are not required by C, they are highly recommended because they protect you from making mistakes in defining or calling these functions.

```
int main( void );
int check( RETCODE );
```

20

The function main() is where C programs begin execution. The operating system calls the function main() and main() returns control to the operating system when it is done executing. The function main() returns an integer value to the operating system, which can be used in batch files to determine whether the program executed successfully.

The function check() contains all the error checking and handling. It returns an integer value, which you use to determine the end of the data set you fetch. Because ODBC has defined standard function return values that are consistent across all ODBC function calls, you can use a single function to monitor the success of ODBC calls and handle any error conditions that arise from them.

```
int main( void )
{
```

At the top of the function are the variables used to store the row data you receive from your fetches. One variable is defined for each column. These are all arrays of ten characters, except for caBirthdate, which needs a little more room.

```
char    caLName[10];
char    caFName[10];
char    caMInit[10];
char    caStatus[10];
char    caGender[10];
char    caBirthdate[20];
```

These variables are used to store the sizes of each row of data returned. There is a size for each column.

```
SDWORD    sdLNameSize;
SDWORD    sdFNameSize;
SDWORD    sdMInitSize;
SDWORD    sdStatusSize;
SDWORD    sdGenderSize;
SDWORD    sdBirthdateSize;
```

Now to the actual code. The program begins by allocating its ODBC environment space:

```
check( SQLAllocEnv( &hEnv ) );
```

Remember, check() is the error handling function, which is defined later. Next you allocate the connection space:

```
check( SQLAllocConnect( hEnv, &hDBC ) );
```

This is the function call that creates a connection to a database:

```
check( SQLConnect( hDBC, "Company", SQL_NTS, NULL, 0, NULL, 0 ) );
```

The database name is "Company." This is the name of the ODBC data source as it appears in the ODBC setup dialog in your Windows 95, 98, or NT Control Panel. The constant SQL_NTS specifies the database name you supplied as a NULL terminated string, the standard type of C string. The two sets of NULL and 0 parameters are for login and password, respectively. This particular database has no security.

Now you allocate the statement handle:

```
check( SQLAllocStmt(hDBC, &hStmt) );
```

This completes all the initial setup you need to execute an SQL statement. You could, at this point, execute any kind of SQL command. The SQL statement is a straightforward query:

```
check( SQLExecDirect( hStmt, "SELECT * FROM Employee", SQL_NTS ) );
```

This call causes the query to execute. Depending on the SQL command, it could take quite some time to return from this call. SQL_NTS indicates your SQL command is in the form of a NULL terminated string.

After the query executes, it's time to bind data. *Binding data* is the process of giving ODBC access to memory you have previously reserved to store the results of the query.

```
check( SQLBindCol( hStmt, 1, SQL_C_CHAR, caLName, 10, &sdLNameSize ) );
check( SQLBindCol( hStmt, 2, SQL_C_CHAR, caFName, 10, &sdFNameSize ) );
check( SQLBindCol( hStmt, 3, SQL_C_CHAR, caMInit, 10, &sdMInitSize ) );
check( SQLBindCol( hStmt, 4, SQL_C_CHAR, caStatus, 10, &sdStatusSize ) );
check( SQLBindCol( hStmt, 5, SQL_C_CHAR, caGender, 10, &sdGenderSize ) );
check( SQLBindCol( hStmt, 6, SQL_C_CHAR, caBirthdate, 20, &sdBirthdateSize ) );
```

20

The preceding function calls allow ODBC to access the variable storage space you defined at the top of main(). The statement handle is passed in along with the column number of the data to be bound, the type that data should be converted to, the variable to be bound, the size of that data area in bytes, and a pointer to a location where the size of the data can be stored.

Now you fetch and print out the data from the database. First, print a title and column headings:

```
printf( "Employee\n" );
printf( "LNAME    FNAME    MINIT    STATUS    GENDER    BIRTHDATE\n" );
```

This is the beginning of the execution loop that fetches and prints out data:

```
while( check( SQLFetch( hStmt ) ) )
{
```

In this case, the loop continues to execute until the function check() returns a zero result. In the function check(), you determine what criteria to use to stop fetching data. The SQLFetch() call fetches data, provided any is available.

Inside the loop is a single call to printf() that prints the row of fetched data to the screen:

```
printf( "%-10s%-10s%-10s%-10s%-10s%-20s\n", caLName, caFName,
        caMInit,caStatus, caGender, caBirthdate );
}
```

Now that you're done fetching data, it's time to clean up and end your program. This call frees the statement handle and its associated data:

```
SQLFreeStmt( hStmt, SQL_DROP );
```

This call disconnects the database session:

```
SQLDisconnect( hDBC );
```

This call frees the connection handle and its associated data:

```
SQLFreeConnect( hDBC);
```

This call frees the environment handle and its associated data:

```
SQLFreeEnv( hEnv );
```

Here you return control to the operating system:

```
return( 0 );
}
```

That concludes execution. Next, consider the check() function, which handles all error checking and recovery:

```
int check( RETCODE wRetcode )
{
```

Again, the variables are defined at the top of the function call:

```
char caSQLState[10] = "";
SDWORD sdError = 0;
char caErrMsg[SQL_MAX_MESSAGE_LENGTH] = "";
SWORD swSize;
```

The variable caSQLState is used to store the ODBC error code. The variable sdError stores a specific numeric error returned by the specific database's

ODBC driver. The caErrMsg variable is used to store the long text description of the error returned by the ODBC driver. Finally, swSize stores the actual size of the error message returned.

```
if( (wRetcode == SQL_SUCCESS) || (wRetcode == SQL_SUCCESS_WITH_INFO) )
    return( 1 );
```

If an ODBC call returns either SQL_SUCCESS or SQL_SUCCESS_WITH_INFO, you can continue on your merry way. SQL_SUCCESS_WITH_INFO means additional information is available from the driver if you're interested. For example, the driver might want to tell you it connected using a certain method or some operation had to be retried. The integer value of 1 is returned to signal the fetch loop to keep fetching rows of data.

```
if( wRetcode == SQL_NO_DATA )
    return( 0 );
```

When you run out of data to fetch, SQLFetch() returns SQL_NO_DATA, therefore, check() returns zero to signal the fetch loop to stop trying to fetch more data.

At this point, you have exhausted regular operation of your program and are left with fatal errors. This reports the error code returned by the ODBC function:

```
printf( "Failed with return code %d\n", (int)wRetcode );
```

If this code is SQL_ERROR, which it is in most cases other than those already handled, you can call the function SQLError(), which gives more information about what's wrong:

```
if( wRetcode == SQL_ERROR )
{
    SQLError( hEnv, hDBC, hStmt, (unsigned char *)caSQLState, &sdError,
            (unsigned char *)caErrMsg, SQL_MAX_MESSAGE_LENGTH - 1, &swSize );
```

You must pass to SQLError() handles to all the relevant spaces. This is why carefully initializing these was important. The parameters SQLError() uses to

return information to you are also passed in. Upon the return of SQLError(),
you can print the information it returned:

```
        printf( "SQL state is %s\n", caSQLState );
        printf( "The native error number is %d\n", (int)sdError );
        printf( "Error message is %s\n", caErrMsg );
}
```

Next, handle cleanup of handles in case of an error. If you have allocated a
statement handle, you must free it or leak memory:

```
    if( hStmt != SQL_NULL_HSTMT )
        SQLFreeStmt( hStmt, SQL_DROP );
```

If you have allocated a connection handle, disconnect and free it:

```
    if( hDBC != SQL_NULL_HDBC )
    {
        SQLDisconnect( hDBC );
        SQLFreeConnect( hDBC );
    }
```

If you have allocated an environment, disconnect and free it:

```
    if( hEnv != SQL_NULL_HENV )
        SQLFreeEnv( hEnv );
```

Here you kill your program and return a value of –1 directly to the operating
system:

```
    exit( -1 );
```

This return statement never gets executed and is here to satisfy the compiler:

```
    return( -1 );
}
```

These two functions comprise a complete C program you can type in and
play with. If you are using Visual C/C++, choose the project type "Win32
Console Application" for best results. Other types of projects require you to
do some Windows-specific setup to use the printf() function call.

When you are done, your program's output should look like the output
shown in Figure 20-1.

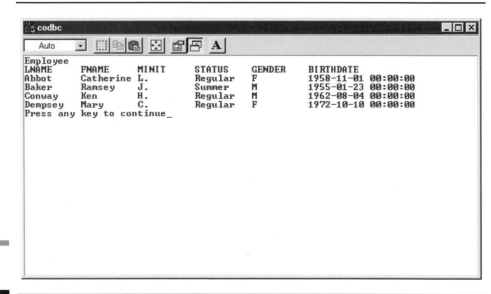

C output

Figure 20-1.

Here is the program again, without all the intervening comments:

```c
#include <stdio.h>
#include <windows.h>
#include <sql.h>
#include <sqlext.h>

HENV  hEnv = SQL_NULL_HENV;
HDBC  hDBC = SQL_NULL_HDBC;
HSTMT hStmt = SQL_NULL_HSTMT;

int main( void );
int check( RETCODE );

int main( void )
{
    char    caLName[10];
    char    caFName[10];
    char    caMInit[10];
    char    caStatus[10];
    char    caGender[10];
    char    caBirthdate[20];
    SDWORD  sdLNameSize;
    SDWORD  sdFNameSize;
    SDWORD  sdMInitSize;
    SDWORD  sdStatusSize;
```

```
SDWORD   sdGenderSize;
SDWORD   sdBirthdateSize;

check( SQLAllocEnv( &hEnv ) );
check( SQLAllocConnect( hEnv, &hDBC ) );
check( SQLConnect(hDBC, (unsigned char *)"Company", SQL_NTS, NULL,
        0, NULL, 0 ) );
check( SQLAllocStmt(hDBC, &hStmt) );
check( SQLExecDirect( hStmt,
        (unsigned char*)"SELECT * FROM Employee", SQL_NTS ) );
check( SQLBindCol( hStmt, 1, SQL_C_CHAR, caLName, 10,
        &sdLNameSize ) );
check( SQLBindCol( hStmt, 2, SQL_C_CHAR, caFName, 10,
        &sdFNameSize ) );
check( SQLBindCol( hStmt, 3, SQL_C_CHAR, caMInit, 10,
        &sdMInitSize ) );
check( SQLBindCol( hStmt, 4, SQL_C_CHAR, caStatus, 10,
        &sdStatusSize ) );
check( SQLBindCol( hStmt, 5, SQL_C_CHAR, caGender, 10,
        &sdGenderSize ) );
check( SQLBindCol( hStmt, 6, SQL_C_CHAR, caBirthdate, 20,
        &sdBirthdateSize ) );

printf( "Employee\n" );
printf( "LNAME     FNAME      MINIT     STATUS     GENDER\
BIRTHDATE\n" );
while( check( SQLFetch( hStmt ) ) )
{
    printf( "%-10s%-10s%-10s%-10s%-10s%-20s\n", caLName, caFName,
            caMInit, caStatus, caGender, caBirthdate );
}

SQLFreeStmt( hStmt, SQL_DROP );
SQLDisconnect( hDBC );
SQLFreeConnect( hDBC);
SQLFreeEnv( hEnv );
return( 0 );
}

int check( RETCODE wRetcode )
{
    char caSQLState[10] = "";
    SDWORD sdError = 0;
    char caErrMsg[SQL_MAX_MESSAGE_LENGTH] = "";
    SWORD swSize;
```

```
if( (wRetcode == SQL_SUCCESS) ||
        (wRetcode == SQL_SUCCESS_WITH_INFO) )
    return( 1 );
if( wRetcode == SQL_NO_DATA )
    return( 0 );
printf( "Failed with return code %d\n", (int)wRetcode );
if( wRetcode == SQL_ERROR )
{
    SQLError( hEnv, hDBC, hStmt, (unsigned char *)caSQLState,
            &sdError, (unsigned char *)caErrMsg,
            SQL_MAX_MESSAGE_LENGTH - 1, &swSize );
    printf( "SQL state is %s\n", caSQLState );
    printf( "The native error number is %d\n", (int)sdError );
    printf( "Error message is %s\n", caErrMsg );
}
if( hStmt != SQL_NULL_HSTMT )
    SQLFreeStmt( hStmt, SQL_DROP );
if( hDBC != SQL_NULL_HDBC )
{
    SQLDisconnect( hDBC );
    SQLFreeConnect( hDBC );
}
if( hEnv != SQL_NULL_HENV )
    SQLFreeEnv( hEnv );
exit( -1 );
return( -1 );
}
```

20

Programming Dynamic SQL with Visual Basic

In this section, you work through a simple example of a Visual Basic program. It uses calls through the Microsoft Jet Engine to execute an SQL query and fetch the results. Part of building this application is graphical and part is code.

Visual Basic programs generally consist of one or more graphical objects called *forms*. These forms appear as dialog boxes when you run your Visual Basic Program. These forms in turn contain *controls*. You put the controls, such as buttons and list boxes, on the form by dragging them from a palette of controls and dropping them onto the form. You can move or resize the controls from there. The Visual Basic code is attached to these forms and controls.

The application you see in this section consists of a single form with two standard controls on it: a button and a list box. All the Visual Basic code will be associated with the button's click event, which is the code that runs if the user clicks the button. This code fills the list box with the results of the query.

Any database with an ODBC driver can be accessed via the Microsoft Jet Engine. To access the database in question, you must import its tables into a Jet database. You can import the tables either permanently or temporarily. The best solution is to build a Jet database that permanently contains these links so your program doesn't have to waste time rebuilding these links every time it executes. You can distribute this database along with your Visual Basic program. Note, the database doesn't contain actual data, only links to where the data can be found via ODBC.

The easiest way to create Jet databases with permanent links is by using either Microsoft Access or the Data Manager add-in in Visual Basic. These two methods are provided as step-by-step procedures in the following paragraphs.

Here's how to create a Jet database containing permanent links using Microsoft Access:

1. Create a blank database.
2. Go to the File menu and select Get External Data | Link Tables.
3. From this dialog, select files of type ODBC Databases.
4. A dialog containing data sources pops up. Select the Machine Data Sources tab to see your ODBC data sources.
5. Select your data source. Supply login information if asked.
6. Finally, you can select the tables to link from another dialog.

Here's how to create a Jet database containing permanent links using Visual Basic's Data Manager add-in:

1. From the Add-Ins menu in Visual Basic, select Data Manager.
2. Inside the Data Manager application select New Database from the File menu.
3. Click the Attached Tables button. An empty list pops up.
4. Click the New button. This brings up the New Attached Table dialog.
5. In the Connect String combo box select ODBC.
6. Click the Table to Attach combo box. A dialog containing data sources pops up.
7. Select the Machine Data Sources tab to see your ODBC data sources.
8. Select your data source. Supply login information, if appropriate.
9. Finally, you can return to the New Attached Table dialog to select a table.

Now that you have your Jet database filled with permanent links, you can proceed to creating your Visual Basic program.

The first critical thing to do as you create a new Visual Basic application that employs databases is to select the references you need. In Visual Basic parlance, *references* are external libraries of objects you can add to your program to extend its abilities. From the Tools menu, select References. Make sure the latest version of the Microsoft DAO Compatibility Library appearing in the list is checked. Unless this box is checked, none of the database related object types, such as Workspace or Database, will be recognized by Visual Basic.

Drag a ListBox control and a CommandButton control to the blank form of your new project. Change the font in the list box to Courier New or some other fixed pitch font. When you are done, your form should look something like the one in Figure 20-2.

20

Next, right-click the Command1 button and select View Code from the popup menu. The combo box labeled *proc* should already have Click selected and you will see an empty program body that looks like this:

```
Private Sub Command1_Click()

End Sub
```

This is the subroutine you put your code in.

First, define your variables:

```
Dim MyDatabase As Database
Dim MyRecordset As Recordset
Dim MyString As String
```

The *Database object* is used to make the connection with the Jet database. The *Recordset object* stores one row at a time of the query. The *String object* stores a

What your
form should
look like

Figure 20-2.

list of characters. You use the String object to form the output string to display in the list box.

Now you are ready to open your Jet database:

```
On Error GoTo DBError
    Set MyDatabase =
            DBEngine.Workspaces(0).OpenDatabase(
            "c:\vbasic\customer.mdb")
```

The DBError branch and other error handling branches appear at the bottom of the subroutine. *DBEngine* is the overall object used in Visual Basic to create and maintain database connections. DBEngine can contain several workspaces, each of which can reference several databases. *Workspaces(0)* is the default workspace that is always present. The OpenDatabase() call connects to the Jet database you created. This Jet database contains the ODBC links to other database tables you want to access and takes as its parameter the file name of your Jet database (including path information, if necessary).

Next, perform your SQL query:

```
On Error GoTo TableError
Set MyTable = MyDatabase.OpenRecordset("SELECT * FROM Employee")
On Error GoTo 0
```

The rest of the code fetches data from the record set created by this call. Error traps are disabled after the query returns successfully.

The fetch loop comes next:

```
Do Until MyTable.EOF
        MyString = Format(MyTable![LNAME], "!@@@@@@@@@@")
        MyString = MyString & Format(MyTable![FNAME], "!@@@@@@@@@@")
        MyString = MyString & Format(MyTable![MINIT], "!@@@@@@@@@@")
        MyString = MyString & Format(MyTable![STATUS], "!@@@@@@@@@@")
        MyString = MyString & Format(MyTable![GENDER], "!@@@@@@@@@@")
        MyString = MyString & Format(MyTable![BIRTHDATE], "MM/DD/YY")
        List1.AddItem MyString, 0
        MyTable.MoveNext
    Loop
    List1.AddItem
"LNAME     FNAME     MINIT     STATUS     GENDER     BIRTHDATE", 0
```

The record set is traversed much like a file. The loop looks for the EOF condition. Here a left-justified string of data in ten-character columns is built by concatenating each column of data onto the end of the string contained in MyString. This string is then inserted into the top line of the list box. At the bottom of the loop, the record set is moved to the next row. Finally, column headers are added last so they appear at the top of the list. Note, the fetches will be shown in reverse order, so if you are using ORDER BY logic, you must reverse it to achieve an accurate list.

Finally, the ending and error handling code:

```
    MyTable.Close
    MyDatabase.Close
    Exit Sub
DBError:
    MsgBox "Can't open the Customer database", vbExclamation
    Exit Sub
TableError:
    MsgBox "Can't query the Employee table", vbExclamation
    MyDatabase.Close
    Exit Sub
End Sub
```

Here you handle all the error conditions you're interested in noting separately. Make sure to close the record set and database when you finish.

When you run your program and click the button, it should look something like Figure 20-3.

Here's the code again as a whole:

```
Private Sub Command1_Click()
  Dim MyDatabase As Database
  Dim MyTable As Recordset
  Dim MyString As String
  On Error GoTo DBError
  Set MyDatabase =
```

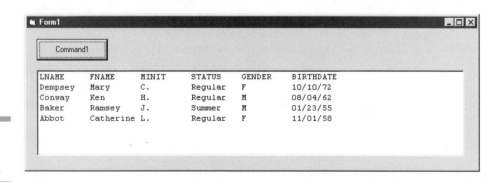

Visual Basic output
Figure 20-3.

20

```
        DBEngine.Workspaces(0).OpenDatabase("customer.mdb")
    On Error GoTo TableError
    Set MyTable = MyDatabase.OpenRecordset("SELECT * FROM Employee")
    On Error GoTo 0
    Do Until MyTable.EOF
      MyString = Format(MyTable![LNAME], "!@@@@@@@@@@")
      MyString = MyString & Format(MyTable![FNAME], "!@@@@@@@@@@")
      MyString = MyString & Format(MyTable![MINIT], "!@@@@@@@@@@")
      MyString = MyString & Format(MyTable![STATUS], "!@@@@@@@@@@")
      MyString = MyString & Format(MyTable![GENDER], "!@@@@@@@@@@")
      MyString = MyString & Format(MyTable![BIRTHDATE], "MM/DD/YY")
      List1.AddItem MyString, 0
      MyTable.MoveNext
    Loop
    List1.AddItem
  "LNAME      FNAME      MINIT     STATUS     GENDER     BIRTHDATE", 0
    MyTable.Close
    MyDatabase.Close
    Exit Sub
  DBError:
    MsgBox "Can't open the Customer database", vbExclamation
    Exit Sub
  TableError:
    MsgBox "Can't query the Employee table", vbExclamation
    MyDatabase.Close
    Exit Sub
  End Sub
```

Programming with SQL in Java

In this section, you use Java and JDBC to perform the same query and fetch operation as in the other sections. As Java programs go, this is a simple one. Still, it demonstrates the minimum code required to use SQL with Java. Java has many constructions similar to C and C++ so, if you're familiar with these languages, you'll feel somewhat at home with Java.

Java executables can take many forms. This example program is a Java applet, which can be executed by Web browsers. You will also learn how to write a small Web page that will execute your Java applet.

At the top of the program, we define what packages we will use. *Packages* add functionality to the Java program, just as include files and libraries add functionality to C programs and references add functionality to Visual Basic programs.

```
import java.applet.*;
import java.awt.*;
import java.sql.*;
```

First, you need to define your own object that customizes the functions and data already contained in applet objects so the object does what you want. In this case, you are reading data out of a database using JDBC. An applet object supplies all the code and data we need to run inside a Web browser. All you need to describe in your Java program is how it differs from the basic applet template.

```
public class jdbcdemo extends Applet
{
```

20

You replace the applet object's default paint() function (which does nothing) with your own. Your paint function accesses the database and prints the results in the applet window. You get a Graphics object passed to you as a parameter of paint(). You can manipulate this Graphics object to draw or write things in the applet window.

```
    public void paint( Graphics graphics )
    {
```

This next bit demonstrates how errors are handled in Java. The main body of the program (or, optionally, only parts of it) are put inside a try{} block. If an error is encountered in the execution of this code, the code immediately jumps to the appropriate catch{} block at the bottom of the program, depending on the data type of object passed back as a result of the error.

```
        try
        {
```

This line of code loads the driver that enables us to talk to ODBC data sources via JDBC. Note, the example uses the same ODBC data source used in the previous C example.

```
            Class.forName("sun.jdbc.odbc.JdbcOdbcDriver");
```

Once the driver is loaded, you can connect to the ODBC data source. The login and password must be the login and password required to access your particular data source.

```
Connection connection = DriverManager.getConnection(
    "jdbc:odbc:Company",
        "myLogin", "myPassword");
```

Here we create the Statement object. The purpose of this object is exactly the same as the data stored in the statement handle in the C example. The Statement object stores information about the position of the cursor and other data about this particular query.

```
Statement stmt = connection.createStatement();
```

Here comes the SQL. The familiar query is sent using the executeQuery() function call. Note this function is a member of the Statement object we defined. Note, too, a Resultset object is also created here. You use it later to get to the column data.

```
ResultSet resultset = stmt.executeQuery(
        "SELECT * FROM Employee" );
```

This code prints the column titles in the applet window:

```
int y = 10;
graphics.drawString( "LNAME", 80, y );
graphics.drawString( "FNAME", 160, y );
graphics.drawString( "MINIT", 240, y );
graphics.drawString( "STATUS", 320, y );
graphics.drawString( "GENDER", 400, y );
graphics.drawString( "BIRTHDATE", 480, y );
```

Here is the loop that fetches the results of the query one row at a time. The next() function owned by the Resultset object we defined is used to get the data. You have to call next() once to get the first row.

```
while( resultset.next() )
{
```

Here we add ten to the *y* position of the text we draw on the screen. This causes each successive row of result set data to be printed lower in the applet window.

```
y += 10;
```

These five pairs of function calls get the data out of the row (converting it to a string, if needed) and print it in the applet window. The function getString() gets row data and is owned by the Resultset object. The function drawString() prints the string to the applet window and is owned by the Graphics object.

```
String string = resultset.getString("LNAME");
graphics.drawString( string, 80, y );
string = resultset.getString("FNAME");
graphics.drawString( string, 160, y );
string = resultset.getString("MINIT");
graphics.drawString( string, 240, y );
string = resultset.getString("STATUS");
graphics.drawString( string, 320, y );
string = resultset.getString("GENDER");
graphics.drawString( string, 400, y );
string = resultset.getString("BIRTHDATE");
graphics.drawString( string, 480, y );
```

This completes the fetch loop and the main body of the program.

```
    }
  }
```

Next comes the code that handles error conditions, known in Java and C++ as *exceptions*. The first exception handles the situation where the JDBC/ODBC driver can't be found. The second exception handles any SQL error. In a real JDBC application, you would examine this exception object to determine the exact nature of the failure and either recover from the error or at least accurately report it. For the purposes of simplicity, these example catch{} blocks are simple.

```
catch( ClassNotFoundException exception )
{
  graphics.drawString( "The jdbc/odbc driver was not found",
        10, 100 );
```

```
        }
        catch( SQLException exception )
        {
          graphics.drawString( "An SQL error happened", 10, 100 );
        }
    }
}
```

This concludes the Java applet code. You need to compile this example with Java 2, available free of charge from the Java Web site at http://www.java.sun.com/. You also need a Web page from which to launch your Java applet from a browser:

```
<applet
    code=jdbcdemo
    width=800
    height=200>
</applet>
```

This HTML code just specifies that a Java applet named jdbcdemo should be given an 800 × 200 pixel area in the browser window.

Put your compiled jdbcdemo.class file in the same directory as this HTML file and then load the HTML file into your Web browser. The Java applet appears, as shown in Figure 20-4.

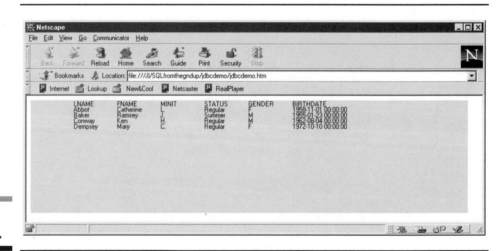

Java output

Figure 20-4.

Here's the entire jdbcdemo.java source file so you can read through the
example without interruption:

```java
import java.applet.*;
import java.awt.*;
import java.sql.*;

public class jdbcdemo extends Applet
{
  protected Font font = new Font( "Courier", Font.PLAIN, 12 );
  public void paint( Graphics graphics )
  {
    try
    {
      Class.forName("sun.jdbc.odbc.JdbcOdbcDriver");
      Connection connection = DriverManager.getConnection(
          "jdbc:odbc:Company", "myLogin", "myPassword");
      Statement stmt = connection.createStatement();
      ResultSet resultset = stmt.executeQuery(
          "SELECT * FROM Employee" );
      int y = 10;
      graphics.setFont( font );
      graphics.drawString( "LNAME", 80, y );
      graphics.drawString( "FNAME", 160, y );
      graphics.drawString( "MINIT", 240, y );
      graphics.drawString( "STATUS", 320, y );
      graphics.drawString( "GENDER", 400, y );
      graphics.drawString( "BIRTHDATE", 480, y );
      while( resultset.next() )
      {
        y += 10;
        String string = resultset.getString("LNAME");
        graphics.drawString( string, 80, y );
        string = resultset.getString("FNAME");
        graphics.drawString( string, 160, y );
        string = resultset.getString("MINIT");
        graphics.drawString( string, 240, y );
        string = resultset.getString("STATUS");
        graphics.drawString( string, 320, y );
        string = resultset.getString("GENDER");
        graphics.drawString( string, 400, y );
        string = resultset.getString("BIRTHDATE");
        graphics.drawString( string, 480, y );
      }
    }
    catch( ClassNotFoundException exception )
```

```
    {
      graphics.drawString( "The jdbc/odbc driver was not found",
          10, 100 );
    }
    catch( SQLException exception )
    {
      graphics.drawString( "An SQL error happened", 10, 100 );
    }
  }
}
```

What's Next?

In this chapter, you examined three popular methods for accessing SQL databases from custom computer applications: a C console application using ODBC, Visual Basic application using the Microsoft Jet engine and ODBC, and a Java applet using JDBC and ODBC.

Other methods also create applications that access SQL databases. Many of these methods are specific to one database vendor. General-purpose interfaces, such as ODBC, are slower, but they provide an easy migration path to any major database type.

Your choice of development tools ultimately depends on what tools you are familiar with and whether you may have a future need to migrate your data.

In the next chapter, you'll learn about common mistakes people make when writing SQL statements.

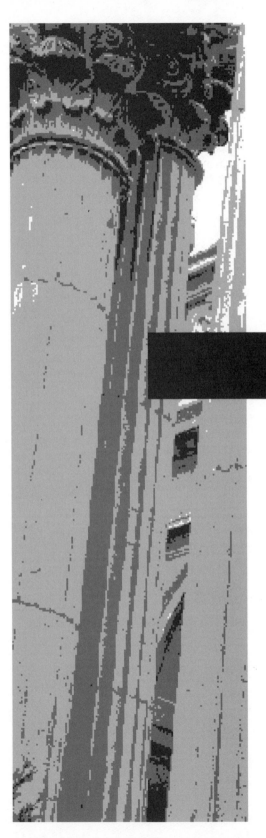

CHAPTER 21

Everyone Makes Mistakes

People make mistakes—this is why erasers exist. In this chapter, you learn what the most common SQL errors are and how to correct them.

It doesn't matter how long you have been writing SQL statements, you can still make mistakes. Some are made from simple typos, while others take a little more time to identify. Any of these errors can keep your SQL statements from processing, however, and you do want to avoid this problem.

Let's examine some of the most common mistakes you can make when writing SQL statements.

Top Ten Common Mistakes

David Letterman is not the only one with a top ten list. Have you made these mistakes lately?

One: Invalid Username or Password

In this error, you either entered the wrong username, the wrong password, or you have the wrong database. For example:

```
SQL*Plus: Release 8.0.4.0.0 - Production on Mon Mar 1 4:5:14 1999
(c) Copyright 1997 Oracle Corporation.  All rights reserved.
ERROR:

ORA-01017: invalid username/password; logon denied
```

Check your username and password and try again. If you attempt to log in more than the allotted number of times, you will need to have your password reset. If you cannot get past this error, you never get the chance to make the other nine errors!

Two: Table or View Does Not Exist

The second most common error is the table or view does not exist, as in the following example:

```
04:05:27 SQL> select * from employee;
select * from employee
              *
ERROR at line 1:
ORA-00942: table or view does not exist
```

Check your spelling of the table. If you have Oracle Navigator or a similar product, you can bring up the tables for your database and check to see if the table exists. If you cannot see the table in the list of tables, check with your DBA. Is the table still available and do you have security to access the table or view?

Three: Invalid Column Name

The third most common mistake is an invalid column name. Here's an example:

```
SQL> select empname, sal
2   from emp
3   /
select empname, sal
        *
ERROR at line 1:

ORA-00904: invalid column name
```

21

This is a common mistake. If you mistype a column name, you definitely get this error. In Chapter 18, you learned the DESCRIBE command. If you run this command for your tables and views, it reduces the chance of this error occurring.

Four: Keyword Not Where Expected

Here's an example of the fourth most common mistake:

```
SQL> select *
2   where ename = 'Smith'
3   /
where ename = 'Smith'
*

ERROR at line 2:

ORA-00923: FROM keyword not found where expected
```

Again, if you forget your clauses or incorrectly type a line of code, you get this error. If a keyword is not where you expected it and you can see the keyword is, indeed, in the statement, then look around for a misplaced comma or an omission of some kind.

Five: SQL Command Not Properly Ended

Here's an example of not properly ending the SQL command:

```
SQL> select * from emp
2   order by ename
3   where ename='smith'
4   /
where ename='smith'
*
ERROR at line 3:

ORA-00933: SQL command not properly ended
```

You may think this statement is properly ended because it ends with the slash (/). You are right, but if you look closer, you will also see you have clauses out of sequence. For instance, the WHERE clause should precede the ORDER BY clause.

Six: Missing Expression

The sixth most common error is leaving out an expression. Here's an example:

```
SQL> select * from emp
2   group by *
3   /
group by *
            *

ERROR at line 2:

ORA-00936: missing expression
```

You cannot group by an asterisk. You need to group by a field name. If you receive this error, look closely at your SQL statement. Are you following the proper sequence of clauses?

Seven: Missing Comma

Here's an example of a missing comma:

```
SQL> insert into emp values
2   ('SMITH' 800, 300)
```

```
3  /
('SMITH' 800, 300)
          *
ERROR at line 2:
ORA-00917: missing comma
```

A comma needs to be inserted between the Ename and the 800 number.

Eight: TNS—Could Not Resolve Server Name

This error usually occurs when you cannot connect to your database. Make sure your database is up and running and you have the proper connection string.

Nine: Insufficient Privileges During Grants

The ninth most common mistake is not having sufficient privileges for grants. Here's an example:

```
SQL> grant select on demo.employee to david;
grant select on demo.employee to david
                     *

ERROR at line 1:

ORA-01031: insufficient privileges
```

This error occurred because you were trying to grant select on a database on which you don't have grant privileges. You must own the table to grant privileges on the table to other users or you must have been granted the privilege to grant privileges on another owner's tables. Remember the GRANT command covered in Chapter 6 on security.

Ten: Column Name Ambiguity

And last, but not least—the tenth most common mistake is column name ambiguity, as in the following example:

```
SQL> select ename,sal,deptno,dname
2  from emp, dept
3 where e.deptno = d.deptno;
3  /
```

21

```
select ename,sal,deptno,dname

                        *

ERROR at line 1:

ORA-00918: column ambiguously defined
```

This error occurred because you have two tables and the deptno is in both tables. You have not indicated which table the deptno is from, but this can be corrected by including the table name with each column name or you can create a table alias:

```
Select e.ename,e.sal, d.deptno, d.dname
from emp e, dept d
where e.deptno = d.deptno;
```

You may have your own list of common errors after you begin writing SQL statements. The vendor usually supplies documentation on errors and error handling. You may encounter these errors the most, though. The next section is about errors that don't produce an SQL error statement. Even if no errors are reported, you know something doesn't look right.

Something Doesn't Look Right!

This is the potpourri of errors. These errors are errors in logic and judgement. With these errors, you have nonsequitur thinking or your brain has gone out to lunch.

Forget to Grant Privileges

This occurs when you create a table or a view and you forget to grant privileges to your users. When they try to access the table or view, they get the message:

```
ORA-00942: table or view does not exist
```

The solution is simply to grant them the privileges needed. This error is both embarrassing for you and an annoyance for your users.

Dropping the Wrong Table or View

When you develop, you are always creating tables or views. Once you finish the development process, you then go back and delete the views and tables you do not need. Sometimes in this process, you delete a table or view by mistake. This can again cause havoc for both you and your users. Check your views and tables before you drop them.

Dropping an Unqualified Table

Always use the schema of the table when you drop a table. This way, if duplicate table names are in the database, you won't drop the wrong table. Use the following code to drop the table:

```
Drop table david.emp;
```

The Cartesian Product

21

Do you remember the Cartesian product introduced to you in Chapter 8? The following is an example of this faulty logic:

```
Select ename, sal, deptno,dname
from emp,dept
```

ENAME	SAL	DEPTNO	DNAME
SMITH	800	10	ACCOUNTING
ALLEN	1600	10	ACCOUNTING
WARD	1250	10	ACCOUNTING
JONES	2975	10	ACCOUNTING
MARTIN	1250	10	ACCOUNTING
BLAKE	2850	10	ACCOUNTING
CLARK	2450	10	ACCOUNTING
SCOTT	3000	10	ACCOUNTING
KING	5000	10	ACCOUNTING
TURNER	1500	10	ACCOUNTING
ADAMS	1100	10	ACCOUNTING

ENAME	SAL	DEPTNO	DNAME
JAMES	950	10	ACCOUNTING

```
FORD               3000         10 ACCOUNTING
MILLER             1300         10 ACCOUNTING
SMITH               800         20 RESEARCH
ALLEN              1600         20 RESEARCH
WARD               1250         20 RESEARCH
JONES              2975         20 RESEARCH
MARTIN             1250         20 RESEARCH
BLAKE              2850         20 RESEARCH
CLARK              2450         20 RESEARCH
SCOTT              3000         20 RESEARCH

ENAME               SAL      DEPTNO DNAME
---------- ----------- ----------- ---------------
KING               5000         20 RESEARCH
TURNER             1500         20 RESEARCH
ADAMS              1100         20 RESEARCH
JAMES               950         20 RESEARCH
FORD               3000         20 RESEARCH
MILLER             1300         20 RESEARCH
SMITH               800         30 SALES
ALLEN              1600         30 SALES
WARD               1250         30 SALES
JONES              2975         30 SALES
MARTIN             1250         30 SALES

ENAME               SAL      DEPTNO DNAME
---------- ----------- ----------- ---------------
BLAKE              2850         30 SALES
CLARK              2450         30 SALES
SCOTT              3000         30 SALES
KING               5000         30 SALES
TURNER             1500         30 SALES
ADAMS              1100         30 SALES
JAMES               950         30 SALES
FORD               3000         30 SALES
MILLER             1300         30 SALES
SMITH               800         40 OPERATIONS
ALLEN              1600         40 OPERATIONS

ENAME               SAL      DEPTNO DNAME
---------- ----------- ----------- ---------------
WARD               1250         40 OPERATIONS
JONES              2975         40 OPERATIONS
MARTIN             1250         40 OPERATIONS
BLAKE              2850         40 OPERATIONS
CLARK              2450         40 OPERATIONS
```

```
SCOTT          3000          40 OPERATIONS
KING           5000          40 OPERATIONS
TURNER         1500          40 OPERATIONS
ADAMS          1100          40 OPERATIONS
JAMES           950          40 OPERATIONS
FORD           3000          40 OPERATIONS

ENAME           SAL     DEPTNO DNAME
---------- ---------- ---------- --------------
MILLER         1300          40 OPERATIONS
```

56 rows selected.

As you know, this error occurs when you leave out a WHERE clause. If you add a WHERE clause, the results are

```
1  select e.ename,e.sal,d.deptno,d.dname
  2  from emp e, dept d
  3* where e.deptno = d.deptno
 SQL> /

ENAME           SAL     DEPTNO DNAME
---------- ---------- ---------- -------------
SMITH           800          20 RESEARCH
ALLEN          1600          30 SALES
WARD           1250          30 SALES
JONES          2975          20 RESEARCH
MARTIN         1250          30 SALES
BLAKE          2850          30 SALES
CLARK          2450          10 ACCOUNTING
SCOTT          3000          20 RESEARCH
KING           5000          10 ACCOUNTING
TURNER         1500          30 SALES
ADAMS          1100          20 RESEARCH

ENAME           SAL     DEPTNO DNAME
---------- ---------- ---------- -------------
JAMES           950          30 SALES
FORD           3000          20 RESEARCH
MILLER         1300          10 ACCOUNTING
```

14 rows selected.

You see quite a difference in your result set.

21

Users Entering Bad Data

These mistakes can run the gamut from entering field names inconsistently to correcting errors online without the proper error-handling on the back-end of the database. For example, you can have users delete data online and enter new data that is not updated on the database tables. Safeguards should exist for this, but sometimes application vendors do not place constraints on the fields of a screen. You would be surprised at how many database application vendors leave out CHECK clauses from the DDL.

What happens in this scenario is users are expecting data just like the data online when the queries and reports are run. You may get into quite a discussion trying to re-write SQL statements based on the end user input. Always check the online data before you troubleshoot your SQL statements.

You Do Not Retrieve Correct Data

If you do have data integrity and you still have problems, chances are you may not be joining the tables correctly. Check your joins and see if you are requesting the data properly. Do you really want a left outer join? Are you joining on too many fields? Examine your SQL statement carefully. Most often your error is in the join type you have requested.

Error Prevention

An ounce of prevention in SQL can prevent many problems. Most of these errors can be prevented if you periodically run quality assurance (QA) queries. With QA queries, you can verify your data and correct data integrity problems. Run a report to verify if you have duplicate data. If you are running many queries and reports for an application, assign a heavy power user the task of verifying the data against your queries and reports. This way, if any user errors are on the online application, the power user should be able to find it.

What's Next?

You have come to the end of your learning journey. Chapter 22 discusses the plans for the next release of SQL: ANSI SQL3. Do not expect full compliance by vendors immediately. As you have seen throughout this book, the compliance from vendor to vendor varies greatly. Some interesting things are planned, however.

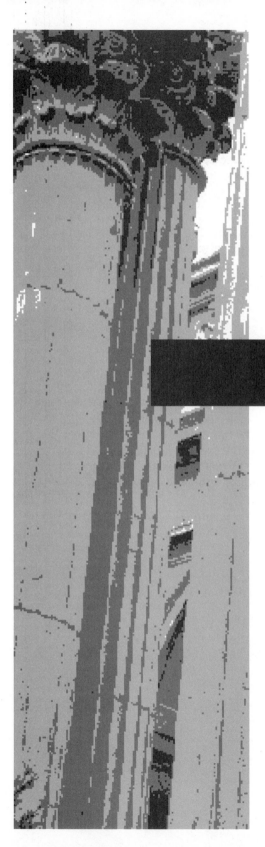

CHAPTER 22

The Future—SQL3

There's a saying: If you need something done immediately, do it yourself; if you need it done tomorrow, delegate it; and if you have all the time in the world, form a committee. Evidently, SQL3 is in the latter category because it has been discussed in the standards committee for over five years. The committee has plans to release SQL3 sometime in 1999.

This chapter reveals the latest developments with SQL3. Thousands of pages of material are devoted to SQL3, a culmination of five years' work by the standards committee. Of course, this material is a moving target and no guarantee exists that all this material will be approved.

However, the following are the main themes for SQL3.

◆   Enhanced relational capabilities

◆   Support for the object paradigm—closely aligned to the Java model

SQL3

The goal for SQL3 was to turn SQL-92 into a complete language for the definition and management of persistent, complex objects. Since the release of SQL-92, the computer industry has changed. The Internet now plays a large part in the computer industry. Java has exploded onto the scene. In addition, data marts and data warehousing have changed the way we use databases. Our needs are changing and our databases are becoming larger and more complex. As a result, development is underway to change SQL as we know it. The developments include

◆   Generalization and specialization hierarchies

◆   Multiple inheritance

◆   User-defined data types

◆   Triggers

◆   Assertions

◆   Support for knowledge-based systems

◆   Recursive query expressions

◆   Additional data administration tools

◆   Specification of abstract data types (ADTs)

◆   Object identifiers

◆   Methods

◆   Inheritance

- Polymorphism
- Encapsulation
- Other facilities associated with object data management

This is quite an undertaking. Are these too many features to load into one version? The answer depends on whom you ask. If you ask end users, the answer would probably be No. However, if you ask vendors who have to comply in some part to these additions, the answer would be Yes.

Because many features are in development for SQL3, it has been divided into the following sections:

- **Framework (SQL/Framework)**   The framework provides a description of the SQL environment and a brief description of the concepts used in the International Standards Organization (ISO) 9075 document.

- **Foundation (SQL/Foundation)**   The foundation provides information on data types and tables. In addition, it discusses classes of SQL statements: SQL schema statements, SQL data statements, SQL transaction statements, SQL control statement (RETURN), SQL connection statements, SQL session statements, and SQL diagnostic statements.

22

- **Call-Level Interface (SQL/CLI)**   This specifies a method of binding between an application program in one of a number of standard programming languages and an SQL implementation. Procedures are specified that can be used to allocate and free resources, initiate, control, and terminate SQL connections between SQL clients and SQL servers, and cause the execution of SQL statements, including the preparation of statements for subsequent execution.

- **Persistent Stored Modules (SQL/PSM)**   This makes SQL computationally complete by specifying the syntax and semantics of additional SQL statements. This includes facilities for the specification of statements to direct the flow of control, the assignment of the result of expressions to variables and parameters, the specification of statements to signal and resignal conditions, and the declaration of local cursors and variables.

- **Host Language Bindings (SQL/Bindings)**   This specifies three methods of binding an SQL agent to an SQL implementation and certain facilities for the management of SQL sessions. These are Dynamic SQL, Embedded SQL, and Direct Invocation of SQL.

◆ **XA Specialization (SQL/Transaction)** This specification would standardize an application programming interface (API) between a global Transaction Manager and an SQL Resource Manager. It would standardize the function calls, based upon the semantics of ISO/IEC 10026, "Distributed Transaction Processing," which an SQL Resource Manager would have to support for two-phase commit.

◆ **Temporal (SQL/Temporal)** This deals with time-related data. This concept is useful to query data to discover what it looked like at a particular point-in-time.

◆ **Management of External Data (SQL/MED)** This defines extensions of database language SQL to support management of external data through the use of abstract tables, abstract large objects (LOBs), and datalink data types.

◆ **Object Language Bindings (SQL/OLB)** This is fondly called SQLJ, which consists of a set of programmatic extensions that define an interaction between the SQL database language and the Java programming language.

At this time, no further information is available on the eighth section (Object Language Bindings). The following discussion covers some of the exciting additions.

New Data Types

A new structure now exists for SQL data types. Every data type is predefined, constructed, or user-defined. The name of a predefined or constructed data type is a reserved word specified by the standard. The name of the user-defined type is provided in its definition.

A *predefined data type* is a data type specified by the standard and is, therefore, provided by the SQL-implementation. An *SQL-implementation* is a processor that processes SQL-statements. A data type is predefined even though the user is required (or allowed) to provide certain parameters when specifying it (for example, the precision of a number). This data type is atomic. An *atomic type* is a data type whose values are not composed of values of other data types. The existence of an operation (Substring, Extract) capable of selecting part of a string or datetime value does not imply that a string or datetime is not atomic.

A *constructed type* is either atomic or composite. A *composite type* is a data type whose values are composed of zero or more values, each of a declared data type.

Reference Types

A *reference type* is a predefined data type, a value of which references (or points to) some site holding a value of the referenced type. The only sites that may be so referenced are the rows of the base tables and have the *with REF value* property. Because this property is permitted only on base tables of a named row type, it follows that every referenced type is a named row.

User-Defined Types

Let's discuss the user-defined types because they are new to SQL. A *structured-type* is a named, user-defined data type. A value of a structured type comprises a number of attribute values. Each attribute of a structured type has a data type, specified by an attribute type that is included in the descriptor of the structured type. You use the statement CREATE TYPE to create both structured and distinct types.

Attribute values are said to be encapsulated; that is, they are not directly accessible to the user. An *attribute* is a named component of a structured type. It has a data type and a default value. An attribute value is accessible only by invoking a function known as an observer function, which returns the value. An instance of a structured type can also be accessed by a locator.

A *locator* for UDTs identifies a value of the UDT specified by the locator specification. In general, a locator is an SQL-session object, rather than an SQL data object that can be used to reference an SQL data instance. A locator is a large object locator, a user-defined type locator, or an array locator.

A structured type may be defined to be a subtype of another structured type, known as its *direct supertype*. A subtype inherits every attribute of its direct supertype and may have additional attributes of its own. A value of a subtype may appear anywhere a value of any of its supertypes is allowed (this concept is known as *substitutability*). Here is an example of how to create a structured type:

```
Create type Model
(     A numeric,
      B numeric
)
```

If the Model object retrieved has an A value of 10 and a B value of 2, the structured type object Model will contain the values 10 and 2.

To complicate the description further, one or more base tables can be created based on a structured type. A base table based on a structured type (ST) can be a subtable of a base table based on a supertype of ST.

22

For example, let's use type Noun and type Word. You can say type Noun is a subtype of type Word. Also you can say Word is a supertype of Noun. Every Noun is a Word, but not every Word is a Noun. Therefore, every operator that applies to Word in general applies to Noun.

The type Noun inherits the operators and constraints from type Word. But the type Noun also has operators and constraints of its own that don't apply to type Word.

Now why is this important for SQL? Adding this type to SQL enables you to make the assumption that if the software application works for Word, then the application can work for Nouns also. You can reuse the code you write. Please note, this type of inheritance and typing is one of the segments still under discussion with the standards committee.

A *distinct type* is a user-defined data type based on some data type other than a distinct type. The values of a distinct type are represented by the values of its base type. An argument of a distinct type can be passed only to a parameter of the same distinct type. This allows precise control of what routines can be invoked on arguments of that data type. This distinct type is similar to *typedef* in C or C++ in that it is a new type based on an existing type. Let's look at how to create a distinct type:

```
Create type Dollars as Numeric (10,2);
```

This creates a new data type, Dollars, which is numeric and has a base 10 with two digits after the decimal point. Dollars is now a datatype in the schema in which it was defined and you can store instances of Dollars in a table that has a column of type Dollars.

There are a few more new data types: Boolean and the string types of BLOB, CLOB, and ARRAY. A Boolean data type is either true or false. The true value of unknown is sometimes represented by the NULL values. For example, if you were to create a new table, the code would be something like this:

```
Create Table Detective (
    LNAME Character varying (30),
    Former_Police Boolean)
```

A value of a character type is a string (sequence) of characters drawn from some character repertoire. A character string type is either of fixed length or of variable length up to some implementation-defined maximum.

A value of a *character large object* (CLOB) type is a string of characters from some character repertoire and is always associated with exactly one character set. A CLOB is of variable length, up to some implementation-defined maximum, which is probably greater than that of other character strings.

A value of binary string type (known as *binary large object* or BLOB) is a variable-length sequence of octets, up to an implementation-defined maximum.

The ARRAY data type is like C and Pascal. It enables you to define a domain whose values are restricted to a small set of values. For example, in the Hush database, a field was called Case_Type. The case type was a choice of: Missing Persons, Murder, Investigate, Fraud, and so on. If you were to create an ARRAY data type for this field, you would define the following:

```
Create Domain case_type (missing persons, murder investigation,
fraud)
```

You can then take this data type and use it to define a column:

```
. . . .
Case_Type case_type,
```

Then when you wanted to insert a row into that table, you could code:

```
Insert into Case
    values (case_type:murder investigation);
```

An important feature about BLOB, CLOB, and ARRAY objects is you can manipulate them without having to bring all the data from the database server to your client machine. An instance of any of these types is actually a logical pointer to the object in the database the instance represents. Because an SQL BLOB, CLOB, or ARRAY object may be very large, this feature can improve performance dramatically.

Triggers

A *trigger*, though not defined to be a component of a base table, is an object associated with a single base table. A trigger specifies a *trigger event,* a *trigger action time,* and one or more *triggered actions*. A trigger event specifies what action on the base table shall cause the triggered actions. A trigger event is INSERT, DELETE, or UPDATE. A trigger action time specifies whether the triggered action is to be taken BEFORE or AFTER the trigger event. A triggered action is either an SQL procedure statement or BEGIN ATOMIC, followed by one or more SQL procedure statements terminated with semicolons, and followed by END.

For instance, if you want to create a trigger on the Detective table, you would use the following code:

```
Create Trigger trigger-name time event
    ON table-name [referencing] action
```

Trigger-name is the name given to the trigger. The time is either BEFORE or AFTER, which tells us if the trigger is fired before or after the event occurs. The event is INSERT, DELETE, or UPDATE.

The table-name shows the table that the DBMS must watch for a triggering event. A trigger specifies referencing only when the event is UPDATE. Referencing specifies a correlation name that can identify the values of columns in the row being updated before the update occurs and after the update occurs. The format of referencing:

```
Referencing OLD [AS] old-correlation-name
    [NEW [AS] new-correlation-name]
```

Finally, action specifies the actions the DBMS is required to take whenever the trigger fires. The format action:

```
[When (search-condition)] (statement [ , statement]…) [granularity]
```

The search-condition enables the database developer to identify certain conditions that will cause the trigger to fire. The granularity is either For Each Row or For Each Statement. For Each Statement is the default. If you specify For Each Row, the trigger's action is executed for every row that is inserted, deleted, or updated by the event. Otherwise, it is executed only once.

Recursive Queries

The *Recursive Union operation* is a feature of SQL3 and it effectively moves through a tree of rows in the database. The format of Recursive Union is

```
( initial Recursive Union correlation-names
    [ (columns)] iteration
        [search] [cycle] [limit] )
```

Initial is a query expression that determines the starting point for your search. For instance, suppose you are gathering the cases for a particular detective. You would provide a query expression to locate the primary row for the detective. The format is

```
Correlation-name [, correlation-name] ...
```

You indicate one or more correlation-names that can be used in the iteration to identify the parents of any row being accumulated into the result. If each accumulated row has only one parent, then there is only one correlation-name and the Recursive Union is said to be *linear*. If the accumulated row has more than one parent, there will be one correlation-name for each parent and the Recursive Union is said to be *nonlinear*. The column is

```
Column-name [ , column-name]...
```

This can be used to name the columns that result from the Recursive Union. The number of column-names must be exactly equal to the degree of the initial query expression.

The iteration is another query expression that specifies how child rows of any parent row are to be found. If a search is required, then it is

```
Search order Set column-name
```

22

The order is either Preorder or Depth First by sort-spec, or Breadth First by sort-spec. Preorder says "to do the acquiring in whatever order is convenient for the implementation." Depth First means "move along the tree structure depth first." Breadth First means "move along the breadth first." The column identified by column-name must be an integer column and is set to a value that indicates when the accumulated row was found.

The *cycle* helps the DBMS decide whether a row, if encountered again, has already been accumulated into the result. *Limit* is used to control how long you want the search to go on. If the limits are reached, the limit clause controls whether the Recursive Union returns or gives you an error.

This summarizes the pertinent information regarding SQL3. This information was gathered from the set of ISO/IEC 9075 documents from meetings held in September and December 1998. In addition to new data types, triggers, and object-oriented functions in SQL3, there is also a new compliance level.

In Chapter 1, we discussed the ANSI/ISO standard and the levels of compliance: Entry, Intermediate, and Full. What is being attempted in SQL3 is a simplification of the compliance requirements. The new compliance, Core SQL, is discussed here.

An SQL implementation shall support Core SQL and at least one of the following:

◆ The SQL-client module binding as specified in the foundation document, for at least one host language.

◆ Embedded SQL for at least one host language

The SQL-implementation shall provide an Object Identifier that states the parts of the standard for which conformance is claimed. An SQL-implementation may additionally support the requirements of one or more packages of features. For each package conformance claimed, the SQL-implementation shall comply with all conformance requirements specified for that package.

An SQL-implementation shall process every SQL statement according to the applicable rules. It shall also provide and maintain an Information Schema for each catalog.

An SQL-implementation can also provide features additional to those specified by Core SQL and it may add to the list of reserved words. If the SQL-implementation provides additional facilities, then it shall provide a SQL flagger. As you recall, a flagger identifies SQL language extensions or other SQL processing alternatives.

A SQL flagger provides one or more of the following "level of flagging" options:

◆ Core SQL Flagging
◆ Part SQL Flagging
◆ Package SQL Flagging

Finally, a claim of conformance to one or more parts shall include a list of those parts to which conformance is claimed and the definition of every element and action that the standard specifies to be implementation defined.

The following is a list of SQL packages referred to in the Core SQL requirements.

♦ **Enhanced datetime facilities**   This package consists of intervals, datetime arithmetic, and time zone specifications.

♦ **Active database**   This package consists of the basic trigger capability.

♦ **Enhanced integrity management**   This package consists of the following features of the SQL language:

  ♦ Referential delete actions

  ♦ Assertions

  ♦ Referential update actions

  ♦ Constraint Management

  ♦ Subqueries in Check constraints

  ♦ Basic trigger capability

  ♦ Enhanced trigger capability

  ♦ Referential action RESTRICT

♦ **OLAP facilities**   This package consists of CUBE and ROLLUP, INTERSECT table operator, row and table constructors, and full outer join.

♦ **PSM**   This package consists of overloading of SQL-invoked functions and SQL-invoked procedures, stored modules, computational completeness, and Information Schema views.

♦ **CLI**   This package features the SQL/CLI.

♦ **SQL/MM support**   This package consists of basic structured types, enhanced structured types, basic array support, arrays of UDTs, user-defined cast functions, and overloading of SQL-invoked functions and procedures.

♦ **Basic object support**   This package consists of the basic structured types, basic reference types, create table of type, and type predicate.

♦ **Enhanced object support**   This package consists of ALTER TYPE statement, enhanced structure types, enhanced reference types, SQL-paths in function and type name resolution, subtables, only in query expressions, subtype treatment, user-defined cast functions, structured type locators, and transform functions.

22

The Early Bird Catches the Worm?

One of the vendors to jump on the SQL3 object wagon is Oracle. Oracle8 makes use of many of the new features proposed for SQL3. You may have noticed some of the datatypes represented in Chapter 19 on PL/SQL. Oracle8 uses REFs (reference pointers), which enables you to retrieve attributes from related "virtual objects" using dot notation rather than via explicit joins. This is accomplished through "object views."

Object views enable the programmer to enjoy the benefits of objects: efficient access, convenient navigation alternatives, and consistency with new object-based applications. Object views can have their own triggers. These INSTEAD OF triggers enable you to write PL/SQL code to support insert, update, or delete through almost any view you can write.

The basic syntax for creating an object view is

```
CREATE [ or replace] View <view name>
OF <object type name>
[WITH OBJECT OID DEFAULT| (<attribute list>)]
AS <query>
[WITH {READ ONLY|CHECK OPTON ]];
```

◆   **WITH OBJECT OID**   Indicates only the OID (object identifier) specification follows.

◆   **DEFAULT**   If the object view is defined on an underlying object table or object view, you can tell Oracle to use the OID of the underlying project.

◆   **Attribute list**   Comma-separated list of type attributes, which comprise an identifier.

◆   **Query**   The query must retrieve columns or expressions that match one for one, in order, the individual attributes of the object type.

IN DEPTH

CONTINUED

◆ **WITH CHECK OPTION**   This option will prevent inserts or updates of data that cannot be selected because of a WHERE clause restriction.

◆ **WITH READ ONLY**   Prevents any DML operation from being executed.

In addition, the following features are also from the proposed SQL3:

◆ The external procedures feature enables you to call anything you can compile into the native "shared library" format of the operating system. In Oracle8, C will be the most common language for external procedures because all the support libraries are written in C.

◆ PL/SQL8 supports several variations of LOB or large object datatypes. LOBs can store large amounts (up to four gigabytes) of raw data, binary data, or character text data.

Oracle8 has positioned itself in the lead again. If any of the features are not approved by the standards committee, however, Oracle8 may be out of compliance. I don't think this will happen. They probably have members on the committee to ensure Oracle's interests are upheld.

What's Next?

We have come full circle. In Chapter 1, you were introduced to the ANSI/ISO SQL-92 standards, our standard for the past five years. Ironically, not all vendors have achieved Full SQL conformance, but they are already introducing some of the new SQL3 standards before full approval by the ANSI/ISO committees.

We are in the midst of change. We began the book discussing relational databases and these databases are getting larger, in fact, Very Large Databases (VLDB) are on the horizon. In addition, SQL-92 is a structured query language and in SQL3, efforts by Java enthusiasts are being made to push the

Object model. There is already an object query language used by those with Object Data Management Group (ODMG) bindings. For now, the two query languages are separate. Still, discussions are taking place to include as a subset, a read-only form of OQL into SQL3, and, subsequently, a read-only subset of SQL3 in OQL.

SQL3 is trying to make everyone happy. What we have is SQL3 retaining complete compatibility with SQL-92 while offering object extensions. SQL-92 represents data in a tabular format. Even with the object extensions, SQL3 may be difficult to manage because of its relational roots. The models, SQL and Object, seem to be juxtaposed. The paradigm debate continues.

This chapter covered the most relevant topics, at least the themes that have persisted over the last five years. Seeing what falls out and what gets added will be interesting. Will SQL3 be released? Or will the paradigms of relational versus object converge, explode and, out of the ashes, a new phoenix (paradigm) arise? Will this phoenix revolutionize the computer world? Well, that, my friends, is material for another book. The saga of SQL will continue.

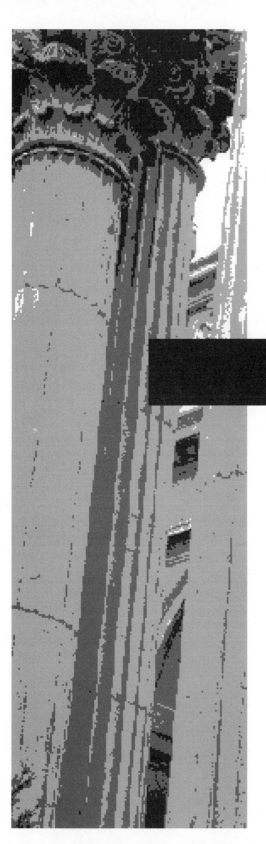

APPENDIX A

Terms

Term	Description
ActiveX control	A reusable software component you can add to an application, which saves you time. This is a Microsoft product and can be used only with Windows systems.
Alias	A shorter name for a table name.
Anomaly	An unwanted result of a data modification that primarily occurs in the normalization of tables.
ANSI character set	This is a set of predefined characters that computers use. This set includes letters and numbers plus special symbols, funny symbols, and lines and boxes.
Applet	A small application stored on a Web server, which is downloaded to and executed oon the Web client that connects to the server.
Application programming interfaces (APIs)	Define a standard way programs work with pull-down menus, dialog boxes, and windows. Microsoft Windows and DOS are examples of APIs.
Array	A collection of similar data stored under the same name. Data is assigned a different number in the array.
ASCII file	A list containing ASCII characters; a text file.
Attribute	A column or a field of a table.
Back end	The part of the DBMS that communicates directly with the database.
Base	The number of digits used in a counting system. Base ten uses ten digits, base two (binary) uses two digits, and base sixteen (hexadecimal) uses sixteen digits.
Batch file	A special file that contains lists of operating system commands. Entering the name of the batch file tells the computer to follow the instructions.
Binary digit (bit)	Can be 0 or 1. Bits are used to measure the capability of a microprocessor to process data, such as 16-bit or 32-bit.
Binding	Regarding data, the process of giving ODBC access to memory you have previously reserved to store the result of a query.
Boyce-Codd normal form	A relation in third normal form where every determinant is a primary or foreign key.

Term	Description
Buffer	A storage area for the temporary holding of data.
Byte	The amount of memory needed to store one character. Four bits are a nibble and eight bits make up a byte.
Cache	A place in memory where the computer can temporarily store data to avoid accessing the slow hard drive or the floppy disk drive over and over again.
Call	A programming term that describes the temporary transfer of control from the main program to a subprogram.
Cardinality	In a binary relationship, the maximum or minimum number of elements allowed on each side of a relationship. The maximum cardinality can be 1:1, 1:N, N:1, or N:M. The minimal can be optional-optional, optional-mandatory, mandatory-optional, or mandatory-mandatory.
Cartesian product	This type of product or cross join gives you all possible pairs of rows from two tables. This occurs when you do not provide a WHERE clause in your SELECT statement.
Case-sensitive	The distinction made between uppercase and lowercase letters.
CASE statement	Used to compare a variable or field value against several values and to execute a block of statement, depending on which comparison returns a True result.
Catalog	A named collection of schemas.
Cluster	A named collection of catalogs.
Column	A multiset of values that may vary over time. All values of the same column are of the same data type or domain and are values in the same table. A value of a column is the smallest unit of data that can be selected from a table and the smallest unit of data that can be updated.
Compiler	A special program that converts programs written in a programming language (C, C++) into a language the computer can understand (machine code).
Computer-aided software engineering (CASE) tool	Software to support the designb and development of information systems and application software.

A

Term	Description
Concatenate	To join two character strings into one character string, such as joining ABC and DEF into ABCDEF.
Correlated subquery	When SQL performs a subquery and produces the same results for every row or row group. A subquery contains an outer reference.
Crack	To modify a program illegally.
Cursor	An SQL feature that specifies a set of rows, an ordering of rows, and a current row within that ordering.
Database	A nonredundant, self-defining collection of interrelated files designed according to the user's business requirements.
Database management system (DMS)	A software application that controls data in a database.
Database server	In a local area network with a client/server architecture, the computer that runs the DBMS and processes actions against the database on behalf of the client computers.
Data Control Language (DCL)	The part of SQL that protects the database from intruders or harm.
Data Definition Language (DDL)	The part of SQL that defines, modifies, and eradicates database structures.
Data dictionary	A user-accessible catalog of both database and application metadata. The dictionary can either be updated automatically by the DBMS or manually when changes are made.
Data flow diagram	The graphical display by developers that illustrates business processes and the data interfaces. This shows the flow of the system from the perspective of the data.
Data Manipulation Language (DML)	The part of SQL that operates on database data.
Data type	A set of representable values. The logical representation of a value is a literal (non-NULL) value.
DBMS engine	A DBMS subsystem that processes logical I/O requests from other DBMS subsystems and submits physical I/O requests to the operating system.

Term	Description
Deadlock	A condition that can occur during concurrent processing in which each of two or more transactions is waiting to access data the other transaction has locked.
Deadly embrace	See *deadlock*.
Determinant	One or more attributes that functionally determine another attribute or attributes.
Diagnostic area	A data structure managed by the DBMS that contains detailed information about the last SQL statement executed and any of its errors.
DISTINCT	This keyword eliminates duplicate rows from query results.
Domain	The set of all possible values an attribute can have. This is also a description of the format (data type, length) and the semantics of an attribute.
Encapsulated data	Data contained in a program or object not visible or accessible to other programs or objects.
Equi-join	A join based on matching identical values.
Firewall	Software or hardware and software that isolates an intranet from the Internet. It only lets secure traffic to travel back and forth.
First normal form (1NF)	Must have data stored in a two-dimensional table with no repeating group, which means a column with more than one value in each row.
Flow-control statements	Structures like IF...ELSE, which enable you to write procedures that modify their behavior based on the values of the data they act upon.
Foreign key	An attribute that is a key of one or more relations other than the one in which it appears.
Form	A display on a computer screen used to present, enter, and modify data.
Front end	The part of the DBMS that communicates directly with the user.
Function	A computer language subprogram that performs some calculations and returns a single value to the main program.

A

Term	Description
Graphical User Interface (GUI)	Provides people with a way to communicate with the computer through icons and pull-down menus.
Grouping query	A query that groups rows of data based on common values in one or more columns. Also can compute summary values from each group. You use the GROUP BY clause in your SELECT statement to create a grouping query.
HAVING	This clause is a search condition, similar to the WHERE clause. The groups are formed first and the search condition is applied to the group.
Hierarchical database	A database in which some records are subordinate to others in a structure resembling a tree. This resembles an organizational chart.
Host	This computer is the one that controls the network and stores the program and data the other computers on the network have.
Host language	A programming language in which SQL statements are embedded.
Index	A table of pointers used to locate rows quickly in a data table.
Indexed sequential access method (ISAM)	A technique for storing and retrieving data efficiently using tables and indexes. This is often used by database programs.
Information schema	The system tables that hold the database metadata.
Inheritance	When one object copies the features of another object. It enables programmers to re-use code.
Inner join	Where the rows of the tables are combined with each other and produce new rows equal to the product of the number of rows in each table.
Input/Output (I/O)	The process in the operating system that reads and writes data from and to peripheral storage devices.
Interactive SQL	Individual SQL statements entered from the keyboard and processed immediately.
INTERSECT	This operator returns only the rows found by both SELECT statements.

Term	Description
Isolation level	In transaction management, specifies the degree of access a transaction has to read data modified by another, uncommitted transaction.
Java	A platform-dependent, compiled language designed specifically for Web application development.
JavaBeans	A component model that enables application developers to develop applications and package them as components.
Java database connectivity (JDBC)	A standard interface between a Java applet or application and database. This is modeled after ODBC.
Join	A relational algebra operation on two relations (A and B) that produces the third relation (C).
Loop	A set of standards in a program running repeatedly.
Loop statements	Statements like the WHILE statement, which execute a block of statements while a condition is true.
Metadata	Data concerning the structure of data in a database stored in the data dictionary. Metadata describes tables, columns, constraints, indexes, and so on.
Mnemonic	A way of naming something that helps you remember its purpose.
Murphy's law	A universal law that states: Whatever can go wrong, will go wrong.
Nested subquery	A subquery inside a main query.
Network database	A database in which records can be subordinate to more than one record child and a child record may have more than one parent. These records form a one-to-many and a many-to-many relationship.
Normalization	The capability to create a database with relational tables that have no redundant data and can be consistently and correctly modified.
Normal form	The theoretical rules that a relation (table) must follow to be normal. The higher the normal form, the better the design of the database.

A

Term	Description
NULL	A database value of unknown. NULL is not an empty column. IS NULL is an operator that can be used to select NULL fields from your query.
Object	A structure in an object-oriented program that contains an encapsulated data structure and data methods. These objects are arranged in a hierarchy, so objects can inherit methods from their parents.
Object-oriented	A style of programming where you bundle sets of instructions into packages known as objects. Object-oriented programming loads all the instructions into self-efficient modules. You can use these modules and put them into a program other than the one for which they were originally written. Again, you can reuse code.
ORDER BY	This clause enables you to sort your data in either ascending or descending order.
Outer join	Preserves unmatched rows from one or both tables. This returns the rows that are matched and unmatched from one or both tables.
Outer reference	A column name that does not refer to any of the values of the tables named in the FROM clause of the main query.
Parameter	A value you enter into an equation or statement.
Polymorphism	In object-oriented programming, this means using the same name to specify different procedures within different contexts.
Precision	The maximum number of digits allowed in a numeric data item.
Procedural language	A computer language that solves a problem by executing a procedure in a sequence of steps.
Query optimizer	The portion of a DBMS that selects the most efficient strategy for processing a query.
Read-committed isolation	This level means the transaction can read the same data more than once, but the read returns the same row.
Read-uncommitted isolation	This level means the transaction can read the same data more than once and can read updates made to the data by other uncommitted transactions.

Term	Description
Referential integrity	1) A state in which all the tables in a database are consistent with each other; 2) When tables have achieved nirvana.
Relational database	Organizes data in a table format consisting of related rows and columns. SQL is based on the relational database model.
Repeatable read level	This isolation level is when a transaction can read the same data more than once, retrieving rows that satisfy a WHERE clause.
Report	An extraction of data from a database that can be displayed, printed, or saved to a file.
Role	A privilege or set of privileges granted to users in a database.
Scale	The number of digits in the fractional part of a numeric data item.
Schema	A collection of tables and views from a single database. A schema has a name, an authorization identifier of the owner of the schema, a character set, and a descriptor of every component in the schema.
Scope	Describes the area within a program in which a variable can be used.
Second normal form (2NF)	Includes only tables that do not have composite primary keys. This means the table and all the non-key columns are functionally dependent on the entire primary key.
SELECT statement	Used to query the database and to create views from your tables.
Serializable isolation level	This level is fully isolated from other transactions. Here, Transaction A is completed before Transaction B has begun and vice versa.
STARTING WITH	This clause works in conjunction with the WHERE clause and is similar to the LIKE expression. You are requesting data that starts with what you indicate as the condition, for example, LNAME STARTING WITH "L".
Stored procedures	A program that processes the rows and returns one or more results. This program resides on the server.
Subquery	A query within a query.

A

Term	Description
Table	A relation. This is a multiset of rows and a two-dimensional array of rows and columns. A table is usually independent of other tables in the database and has a primary key and, sometimes, a foreign key.
Tablespace	A collection of one or more datafiles. All database objects are stored in tablespaces.
TCP/IP	Transmission control protocol/Internet protocol is the network protocol used by the Internet and intranets.
Third normal form (3NF)	This table requires the table is already a 2NF table and every non-key column is nontransitively dependent upon its primary key. You cannot have two keys that are determiners of the non-key columns.
Transaction	A sequence of SQL statements that must be run sequentially and will only be successful if all statements are successful.
Transact-SQL	A language you can use to create and manipulate database objects; an enhanced version of the SQL-92 standard.
Trigger	A small piece of code that tells the DBMS what to do after specific SQL statements have been executed.
Tuple	Same as a row in a table.
Union	This operator returns the results of two or more queries minus the duplicate rows.
Variable	A symbol that represents a numerical value or a string of text used in the program. Using variables gives the programmer the flexibility of changing the value at any point in the program.
View	A subset of a database that can be processed by an application. A virtual table.
WHERE	This clause searches for a condition and narrows your selection of data from your query.

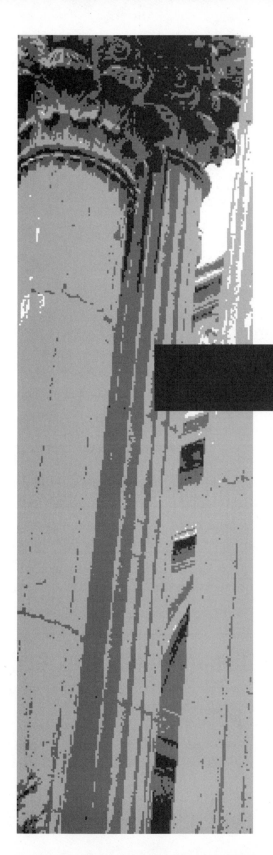

APPENDIX B

Read More About It

The following is a collection of reading material and Web sites that may interest you. In addition, a few of the major database and business intelligence tool vendors are listed.

Books

The following books are provided for additional reading on some of the topics.

Database Design

◆ *Database Design for Mere Mortals: A Hands-On Guide to Relational Database Design,* by Michael J. Hernandez (Addison-Wesley Publishing Co., 1996, ISBN 0201694719).

◆ *Relational Database Design Clearly Explained,* by Jan L. Harrington (AP Professional, 1998, ISBN 0123264251).

◆ *Handbook of Relational Database Design,* by Candace C. Fleming et al (Addison-Wesley Publishing Co., 1998, ISBN 0201114348).

◆ *Database Modeling and Design (Morgan Kaufmann Series in Data Management Systems),* by Toby J. Teorey (Morgan Kaufman Publishers, 1998, ISBN 1558605002).

◆ *Database Design for Smarties: Using UML for Data Modeling,* by Robert J. Muller (AP Professional, 1999, ISBN 1558605150).

◆ *Oracle8 Design Using UML Object Modeling,* by Dr. Paul Dorsey, Joseph R. Hudicka, and Martin Fowler (Osborne/McGraw-Hill, 1998, ISBN 0078824745).

Oracle 8

◆ *Oracle8 PL/SQL Programming,* by Scott Urman (Osborne/McGraw-Hill, 1998, ISBN 0078823056).

◆ *Oracle8 Advanced Tuning & Administration,* by Eyal Aronoff et al (Osborne/McGraw-Hill, 1998, ISBN 0078825342).

◆ *Oracle8: The Complete Reference,* by George Koch and Kevin Loney (Osborne/McGraw-Hill, 1997, ISBN 007882396X).

◆ *Oracle Security,* by Marlene Theriault, William Heney, and Debby Russell (O'Reilly & Associates, 1998, ISBN 1565924509).

Database Tuning

◆ *Client/Server Database Design with Sybase: A High-Performance and Fine-Tuning Guide,* by George W. Anderson (McGraw-Hill, 1996, ISBN 0070016976).

◆ *Informix Performance Tuning,* by Elizabeth Suto (Prentice Hall, 1996, ISBN 0132392372).

◆ *Optimizing Microsoft SQL Server 7,* by Robert Schneider and Jeffrey R. Garbus (Prentice Hall, 1998, ISBN 0130122564).

SQL

◆ *Understanding SQL's Stored Procedures: A Complete Guide to SQL/PSM,* by James Melton (Morgan Kaufmann Publishers, 1998, ISBN1558604618).

◆ *Teach Yourself Transact-SQL in 21 Days,* by Bennett William McEwan and David Solomon (SAMS Publishing, 1997, ISBN 780672310454).

◆ *Teach Yourself Microsoft SQL Server in 21 Days,* by Richard Waymire and Rick Sawtell (SAMS Publishing, 1999, ISBN 0672312905).

Magazines, Journals, and Organizations

This next section provides a hodgepodge of interesting items for those of you with inquiring minds and a thirst for more database knowledge.

◆ **Intelligent Enterprise (formerly DBMS magazine)**   This free magazine covers pertinent subject matter regarding databases and SQL. You can subscribe at the following Web address: www.intelligententerprise.com.

◆ **Academy of Computer Machinery (ACM)**   This is the world's oldest and largest educational and scientific computing society. Since 1947, ACM has provided a vital forum for the exchange of information, ideas, and discoveries. Today, ACM serves a membership of more than 80,000 computing professionals in more than 100 countries in all areas of industry, academia, and government. A wide array of journals are available both online and on hard copy. The Web address is: www.acm.org.

◆ **Compuserve Forum**   Compuserve is an online service similar to AOL. For years it has provided computer professionals and enthusiasts a place to chat via their forums, which have a broad range of interests—from Access to Xenix and beyond. A monthly fee is charged for this service.

B

◆ **Microsoft Developer's Network (MSDN)**   MSDN provides developers with a journal, white papers, tech tips, and much more. You may sign up free by going to the Microsoft Home Web page.

◆ **American National Standards Institute (ANSI)**   This organization is responsible for the SQL-92 Standard. It also has an online store where you may purchase ANSI standards. The address is

American National Standards Institute
11 West 42nd Street
13th floor
New York, N.Y. 10036
Phone: (212) 642-4900
Fax: (212) 398-0023
E-mail: info@ansi.org
Web: www.ansi.org

◆ **SQL3 Meeting Notes**   This Web site has the most recent working documents of ISO/IEC meetings:
ftp://jerry.ece.umassd.edu/isowg3/dbl/BASEdocs/public/.

Business Intelligence Vendors

The following companies, in alphabetical order, represent my top five choices for business intelligence tools in the industry today. Please remember, more tools are available, but I have researched and/or used these for various clients. This list will start you on your own search for the ideal business intelligence tool.

Actuate Software Corporation

999 Baker Way
San Mateo, CA 94404
Phone: Sales (800) 914-2259; Headquarters (650) 638-2000
Fax: (650) 638-2020

Brio Technology

3460 W. Bayshore Road
Palo Alto, CA 94303
Phone: (877) 289-2746 (toll free) or (650) 856-8000
Fax: (650) 856-8020
E-mail: sales@brio.com

Business Objects Americas

2870 Zanker Road
San Jose, CA 95134
Phone: (800) 527-0580 (toll free) or (408) 953-6000
Fax: (408) 953-6001
Web: www.businessobjects.com

Cognos Corporation

67 South Bedford Street
Burlington, MA 01803-5164
Phone: (800) 426-4667 (toll free) or (781) 229-6600
Fax: (781) 229-9844
Web: www.cognos.com

Seagate Software

Crystal Reports
840 Cambie Street
Vancouver, BC, CANADA V68 4J2
Phone: (604) 681-3435
Fax: (604) 681-2934
Web: www.seagatesoftware.com

B

Database Vendors

Again, you may choose from many database vendors. This list encompasses the databases mentioned in this book and is by no means exhaustive.

Centura Software Corporation

975 Island Drive
Redwood Shores, CA 94065
Phone: (800) 444-8782 (toll free) or (650) 596-3400
Fax: (800) 596-4787
Web: www.centurasoft.com

IBM/DB2

IBM Corporation
New Orchard Road
Armonk, NY 10504
Phone: (914) 499-7777
Web: www.software.ibm.com/data/db2

Informix Software, Inc.

(Corporate and North America Sales Headquarters)
4100 Bohannon Drive
Menlo Park, CA 94025
Phone: (650) 926-6300
Web: www.informix.com

Microsoft Corporation

(Corporate Headquarters)
One Microsoft Way
Redmond, WA 98052-6399
Phone: (425) 882-8080
Web: www.microsoft.com

Oracle Corporation

(World Headquarters)
500 Oracle Parkway
Redwood Shores, CA 94065
Phone: (650) 506-7000 or (650) 506-7200
Web: www.oracle.com

Sybase, Inc.

6475 Christie Avenue
Emeryville, CA 94608
Phone: (510) 922-3500
Fax: (510) 922-3210
Web: www.sybase.com

Index